"This new edition of Tilly's excellent book is much more than a simple update. Castañeda very helpfully combines the historical and theoretical complexity of Tilly's original monograph with the accessibility of an undergraduate textbook to produce in one small space almost everything a course on social movements needs. The addition of new contemporary case studies—thoughtfully chosen and analyzed here and written collaboratively with Castañeda's students—brings to life Tilly's conceptual framework and provides a ready-made lesson plan to teach this framework for social movement analysis to graduate and undergraduate students. The cases are international in scope and include a focus on the role of social media and the internet where these new technologies have played important roles in movement mobilization. This new edition has also expanded the original chapter discussion questions and added a whole new set of research questions for the case studies that are guaranteed to generate good classroom discussions and interesting essays. Highly recommended!"

Rebecca Overmyer-Velázquez, Whittier College

"Charles Tilly (1929–2008) was one of our most insightful and imaginative analysts of social movements and related forms of political contention. His remarkable knowledge of contentious politics spanned centuries and continents. This accessible volume introduces readers to Tilly's ideas about the historical invention and global spread of social movements. And in this edition Tilly's students (and their students) bring the story right up to the present, drawing on Tilly's concepts to make sense of collective protest in the twenty-first century, including the immigrant rights movement, the Indignados and Occupy movement, and the Black Lives Matter movement. This volume will interest readers new to social movements as well as practiced scholars."

Jeff Goodwin, New York University

"This new edition of *Social Movements* builds on Charles Tilly and Lesley J. Wood's now-classic work. Tilly's position on what social movements are, how they operate, and why—and crucially, how they relate to other kinds of political action and what social movements are *not*—as ever provides needed clarity in an otherwise often-muddy field. Through a case-study approach, Ernesto Castañeda now builds a new story onto the already-impressive edifice: a guide for contemporary students to how Tilly's approach can help us to make sense of what's going on in contemporary movements, and also to see what might be changing in the landscape of contentious politics."

John Krinsky, City University of New York

SOCIAL MOVEMENTS, 1768–2018

Social Movements, 1768–2018 provides the most comprehensive historical account of the birth and spread of social movements. Renowned social scientist Charles Tilly applies his synthetic theoretical skills to explain the evolution of social movements across time and space in an accessible manner full of historical vignettes and examples. Tilly explains why social movements are but a type of contentious politics to decrease categorical inequalities. Questions addressed include what are the implications of globalization and new technologies for social movements, and what are the prospects for social movements? The overall argument includes data from mobilizations in England, Switzerland, Czechoslovakia, Russia, China, India, Argentina, Chile, Cuba, Mexico, Egypt, Tunisia, Iran, Iraq, and Kazakhstan.

This new edition has been fully updated and revised with young researchers and students in mind. New case studies focus on social movements in Mexico, Spain, and the United States including Black Lives Matter, immigrants' rights struggles, The Indignados, the Catalan movement for independence, #YoSoy132, Ayotzinapa43, mass incarceration and prisoner rights, and more. Timelines are included to familiarise the reader with the events discussed and discussion questions are framed to increase understanding of the implications, limits, and importance of historical and ongoing social movements.

Charles Tilly was Joseph L. Buttenwieser Professor of Social Science at Columbia University. He is the author of more than fifty books, including *The Vendée: A Sociological Analysis of the Counter-Revolution of 1793* (Harvard University Press 1964).

Ernesto Castañeda is Assistant Professor at American University in Washington, DC. He is the author of *A Place to Call Home: Immigrant Exclusion and Urban Belonging in New York, Paris, and Barcelona* (Stanford University Press 2018).

Lesley J. Wood is Associate Professor and Chair of Sociology at York University in Toronto. She is the author of *Crisis and Control: The Militarization of Protest Policing* (Pluto Press 2014).

SOCIAL MOVEMENTS, 1768–2018

Fourth Edition

Charles Tilly, Ernesto Castañeda, and Lesley J. Wood

Routledge
Taylor & Francis Group
NEW YORK AND LONDON

Fourth edition published 2020
by Routledge
52 Vanderbilt Avenue, New York, NY 10017

and by Routledge
2 Park Square, Milton Park, Abingdon, Oxon, OX14 4RN

Routledge is an imprint of the Taylor & Francis Group, an informa business

[First edition published by Paradigm 2004]
[Second edition published by Paradigm 2008]
[Third edition published by Paradigm 2013]

Library of Congress Cataloging-in-Publication Data
A catalog record has been requested for this book

ISBN: 978-0-367-07607-8 (hbk)
ISBN: 978-0-367-07608-5 (pbk)
ISBN: 978-0-429-29763-2 (ebk)

Typeset in Garamond
by Swales & Willis Ltd, Exeter, Devon, UK

MIX
Paper from responsible sources
FSC™ C013985

Printed in the United Kingdom
by Henry Ling Limited

This book is dedicated to:

Charles Tilly, whose contagious smile left us ten years ago. His work remains with us, helping us to understand collective actions against categorical inequalities and threats to democracy.

And to all the activists and social movement participants who have put work, time, dedication, and energy to advance social justice and decrease categorical inequalities.

CONTENTS

PREFACE TO FIRST EDITION

In June 2003, when the good people at New York Presbyterian Hospital began what an optimistic view projected as four or five months of chemotherapy and related treatments for lymphoma, they faced me with an interesting choice: mope as an invalid or invent a special project that would lend coherence to a difficult interlude. With vivid inspiration from friends who have borne hardship resolutely, the second course looked more attractive. Having long thought that someone else should write the book you see before you, I started writing it to calm my nerves during my first chemotherapy session, with the fantasy of finishing it precisely as the last drop of chemicals entered my veins on the final day of treatment. Like most fantasies, this one did not quite work out. But it did discipline my efforts during months of chemo, and it did lead to the book's completion during what we all hope will be the treatment's final, successful phase.

Although I did not speak much of "contenders" before the 1970s, did not explicitly define my subject as "contention" until the 1980s, and did not start theorizing about "contentious politics" until the 1990s, for half a century a major stream of my work has concerned how, when, where, and why ordinary people make collective claims on public authorities, other holders of power, competitors, enemies, and objects of popular disapproval. For many years I generally avoided the term "social movement" because it sponged up so many different meanings and therefore obscured more than it clarified. Preparing detailed catalogs of contentious events for periods from the seventeenth to twentieth centuries in Western Europe and North America changed my mind. The catalogs made clear that major shifts in the array of means by which ordinary people made collective claims on others—their contentious repertoires—occurred in those regions between 1750 and 1850; that despite considerable differences in timing from regime to regime, in each regime the shifts clustered together; and that within the cluster emerged a distinctive combination of campaigns, performances, and displays. Participants and observers alike eventually began calling that new form of politics a "movement." Why not pin down that change?

Despite the current tendency to call everything from fads to established interest groups "movements," the emergence, transformation, and survival of that new, distinctive political form deserved historical attention. With some trembling about likely turf wars and definitional disputes, I decided to use the standard term "social movement" instead of inventing some substitute such as "full-fledged social movement" or "the type of social movement that first emerged in Western Europe and North America at the end of the eighteenth century." It certainly simplified the text.

Fortunately for friendship and future collaboration, in the book that most resembles this one with respect to argument and content, my friend and collaborator Sidney Tarrow explicitly disavows undertaking the social movement's history (Tarrow 1998: 3). This book therefore picks up where Tarrow's splendid survey of social movements leaves off. *Social Movements, 1768–2004* provides a historical survey of social movements from their eighteenth-century origins into the twenty-first century, ending with speculations about possible futures for social movements.

In order to avoid encumbering the text with references to my own previous publications, I have borrowed evidence freely from my earlier work, mostly without citing it. I have adapted a few passages from *Stories, Identities, and Political Change* (Rowman & Littlefield, 2002), *The Politics of Collective Violence* (Cambridge University Press, 2003), and *Contention and Democracy in Europe, 1650–2000* (Cambridge University Press, 2004), but at least 95 percent of the text is quite new.

For information, citations, criticism, and editorial advice, I am grateful to Lance Bennett, Vince Boudreau, Pamela Burke, Dana Fisher, Elisabeth Jay Friedman, William Ivey, Vina Lanzona, Daniel Menchik, Vicente Rafael, Sidney Tarrow, Cecelia Walsh-Russo, Lesley Wood, and Viviana Zelizer. I hope they will be pleasantly surprised by what they helped create.

Charles Tilly, New York, 2003

PREFACE TO SECOND AND THIRD EDITIONS

Charles Tilly passed away just before I finished the second edition of this book. Since his death, there has been a flood of Chuck stories—stories of his mentorship, stories of his kindness, and stories of his rigorous and prodigious scholarship. Legions of his past students marveled at his ability to clarify their ideas through asking a few incisive questions. Until his death he didn't stop asking those questions.

As he explained in the preface to the first edition, this book is a short answer to a recurring set of questions. Why do social movements look so similar around the world, and how and why have such movements become a major form of political action globally?

Since the first edition, Tilly wrote incisively and extensively on protest, social organization, and political relationships. The books of the past four years are *Contention and Democracy in Europe, 1650–2000* (2004), *Trust and Rule* (2005), *Identities, Boundaries, and Social Ties* (2005), *Regimes and Repertoires* (2006), *Why?* (2006), *Democracy* (2007), *Credit and Blame* (2008), and *Contentious Performances* (2008). Working with Sid Tarrow, he also wrote *Contentious Politics* (2006). I won't begin to list the numerous journal articles, book chapters, and edited volumes. I have tried to incorporate the ideas from these new works into this text where appropriate.

A great deal has happened in the world since the first edition in 2004 and the second edition in 2008. First and foremost, the economic crisis has rocked the globe—especially Europe and the United States. Economic convulsions and the inability to contain them have led to unemployment, hunger, and state attempts to solve the problems partly through austerity budgets, leading to further mobilizations. In this context, prodemocracy social movements have emerged in North Africa and the Middle East—overturning authoritarian regimes in Tunisia and Egypt and challenging others across the region. Only time will tell how many of them will be successful. This new edition pays attention to these movements and the context within which they are operating. Partly because of the obvious importance of economic dynamics in the current cycle of struggle, I've returned to some of Chuck's work on capitalism and reemphasized these dimensions in the text, without altering the shape of the overall argument. I've also used his earlier work on state formation to highlight the way that colonialism is part of the story of both state formation and the emergence of the social movement.

Chuck asked me to work on *Social Movements* in 2006, perhaps knowing that he wouldn't be able to finish it before his death. We talked about what revisions would be useful and appropriate, and I've tried to incorporate them here in ways that will offer students of social movements and contentious politics insight into the emergence and development of the social movement. Except in Chapter 5, where I've added the most material, I've kept the text in the first person, because obviously, this is Chuck's book.

Finally, I must thank Sid Tarrow and Chris Tilly for their help in ensuring that I didn't mess too much with the tone and message of the text.

Lesley J. Wood, Toronto 2012

Post-script for the fourth edition, seven years later.
The world keeps changing, and with it, popular struggle. I am deeply grateful to Ernesto Castañeda for his committed work on this expanded fourth edition. I thank him (and his students) for bringing Chuck's analysis to a new generation of readers and activists.

Lesley J. Wood, Toronto 2019

PREFACE TO FOURTH EDITION

Social Movements is only one of the many influential works written by distinguished American sociologist Charles Tilly (Walsh-Russo and Castañeda 2018). In this book, Tilly focuses on the social movement, which is only one type of contentious politics; and ties it to state formation, democratization, the widening of citizenship and the erasure of categorical inequalities, processes that Tilly studies elsewhere (see Castañeda and Schneider 2017). This new edition includes Tilly's original historical context and theoretical arguments about the birth and growth of social movements. A brand-new Part II adds a set of recent social movements that the reader may be partially familiar with and briefly discusses them within the context of Tilly's Social Movement's framework. We leave it to readers to see continuities and contradictions and invite them to apply these tools and examples to study other social movements.

Part II of this book discusses contemporary social movements that began in the twentieth and twenty-first centuries. To be very clear, while most of the discussion and analysis of these chapters follows what was done in Part I, neither Tilly nor Wood wrote these cases. I followed Tilly's methodology and criteria for determining social movements, but the work is still separate from what he produced. The topics and various cases covered in Part II include Black Lives Matter, Catalonia's movement for independence, and immigrants' rights movements in the United States. Basic background and key events will be provided but because many of these movements are ongoing, readers will likely have some previous understanding of these cases. Only time will tell whether these recent events will be considered as social movements or only campaigns.

Although Charles Tilly passed away in 2008, his work is very much alive and with us as we try to make sense about contemporary social movements. Lesley Wood and Chris Tilly provided feedback on all the new chapters. I thank Lesley, as well as Chris, Louise, Kit, and Sarah Tilly for entrusting this new edition to me and allowing me to bring my own vision and approach to it—all errors are my own. At Routledge, I want to thank Dean Birkenkamp and Tyler Bay for their professionalism and efficiency. Mirjam Kuenkler, Adrienne LeBas, Aliza Luft, Cathy L. Schneider, Randa Serhan, Cecelia Walsh-Russo, Viviana Zelizer, Jorge Cadena Roa, Craig Calhoun, Marco Estrada Saavedra, Gil Eyal, George Steinmetz, Saïd Arjomand, Marie Kennedy, Mauricio Font, Jeff Goodwin, Bill Roy, Sidney Tarrow, Chares Demetriou, Gustavo Urbina, Nuria Vilanova, as well as many other researchers, and former students and colleagues of Tilly have been important interlocutors as I try to reassess Tilly's oeuvre. Conclusions and all remaining errors are my responsibility.

Students at American University provided feedback as readers, researchers, and observers of contemporary movements. Maura Fennelly provided valuable editorial assistance in all chapters. Erica Lesto helped locate typos in Part II. Lucy Weiler helped with the timeline for Part I. Many students helped with writing, copy-editing, and research assistance, some of them are listed as co-authors, but all students in these classes contributed their opinions and suggestions; so, I am listing all their names here. From my combined graduate and advanced undergraduate seminar Social Movements and Social Change in the Fall of: Jasmin Ceron, Aras Coskuntuncel, Maria Duplat, Aleshia Faust, Kenya Goods, Taylor Heath, Emily Johnson, Barbara Martinez, Hannah McNamara, Carly Miller, Max Miller-Golub, Moira Nolan, Meghan Ott, Liza Sweitzer, Monica Villacorta, Madeline White. From two sections of Contemporary Social Theory Spring 2017: Josiah Adams, Diego Aleman, Riham Amin, Kabira Barlow, Jordan Burns, Cynthia Cristobal, Maria Duplat, Abby Ferdinando, Lizzy Gallagher, Amanda Gardner, Madison Guare, Catherine Harlos, Genae Hatcher, Amelia Haymes, Rachel Koller, Elana Lipkin, Alexander Miller, Abigail Mitchell, Laura Oliver, Daniel Oshiro, Colby Parkinson, Alaina Rudncik, Marta Rybczynski, Emma Walker, Kathryn Whelan, as well as Helen Abraha, Sarah Anderson, Christina Brown, Catherine Lu Clougherty, David Curtiss, Grace Flad, Amaya Gomez, Rachael Gordon, Elizabeth Guillen, Swati Guin, Jeffrey Guzman, Claire Ison, Jojo Leung, Jeta Luboteni, Gianna Manzella, Aurora McLellan, Maura Mendes, Carly Miller, Anisa Shafiq, Margaret Shircliff, Ashlee Smith, Lindsey Smith, Iashai Stephens, Liza Sweitzer, and Davis Taske. The Rise of Critical Social Thought Fall 2017: Samir Adechoubou, Hailey Crowell, Justin Ezra, Arthur Flower, Natzinet Ghebrenegus, Emily Glover, Zaria Guignard, Amelia Haymes, Dillon Johnson, Liliana King, Takahiro Kinoshita, Valeria Kottke, Araseli Lara, Jennifer Linsenmeyer, Sebastian Megens Sedor, Samantha Miller, Zainab Mirza, Maxwell Nitto, Daniel Oshiro, Kayla Owens, Rafaela Peralta, Ammarah Rehman, Marco Rojas-Machazek, Neil Ross, Benjamin Ryan, Bethlehem Sisay, Amanda Sky, Lilli Specter, Angelina Torres, Katharine Turner, Michael Valenti, Daniel Wachsberg, Lucy Weiler, and Zerong Zhao. Thank you, everyone!

Ernesto Castañeda, Washington, DC, 2018

A BRIEF HISTORY OF SOCIAL MOVEMENTS IN THE 18TH CENTURY

1500
First wave of globalization begins

May 17, 1756–February 15, 1763
Seven Years War

1757
John Wilkes enters Parliament

1762
John Wilkes begins publishing ***The North Briton***, an opposition newspaper

1763
John Wilkes charged with seditious libel, flees to France to avoid arrest after publishing ***Essay on Woman***

March 22, 1765
Stamp Act passed by Parliament

March 18, 1766
Stamp Act repealed

1767
Townshend Act imposes new taxes on colonies

1768
John Wilkes returns to England, wins Parliament seat, is imprisoned and denied seat

January 1768
Massachusetts legislature unsuccessfully petitions King for tax reprieve

May 1768
British officials seize John Hancock's ship, triggering wide-scale protest, the arrival of Irish and Canadian forces, and assembly of Massachusetts militia men.

1770
John Wilkes freed from Tower of London

1771
John Wilkes becomes London's sheriff

1774
John Wilkes elected as Lord Mayor, returns to Parliament

1775–1783
Revolutionary War

1777
Vermont constitution bans slavery

1780
Pennsylvania and Massachusetts constitutions abolish slavery

1780–1784
Fourth Anglo-Dutch War regarding Dutch trade with British enemies during wartime

1783
English Quakers petition Parliament for abolition of slave trade

1784
Rhode Island and Connecticut constitutions abolish slavery

1784–1787
Netherland's Patriot Revolution

1789
French Revolution

A BRIEF HISTORY OF SOCIAL MOVEMENTS IN THE 19TH CENTURY

1793
Genevan Revolution

January 1795
French invading forces move into Netherlands

1798
Basel, Vaud, Zurich revolutions

May 1798
Switzerland conquered by France

1800
London is second-biggest city in the world (second to Beijing), and Europe's greatest port

1802
French troops withdraw from Switzerland, leaving instability in their absence

1803
Napoleon imposes new constitution

April 30, 1803
Thomas Jefferson arranges the Louisiana Purchase with France

1806
Kingdom of Holland established

1810–1813
Holland annexed into France

June 18, 1812–February 18, 1815
The War of 1812 between the United States and Britain

March 20, 1815
Treaty of Paris declares Swiss neutrality

1817
Parliament passes Seditious Meetings Act, making it illegal to hold a meeting of over 50 people

October 1818
Stockport Union for the Promotion of Human Happiness formed

August 16, 1819
Manchester and Salford yeomanry attack reform meeting sponsored by Stockport union

1824
Parliament repeals Combination Laws, legalizing public activity of trade unions

1833
Parliament passes emancipation act

May 1838
Publication of ***The People's Charter*** begins the Chartist movement in England

1839–1842
Opium War of England and China

November 3, 1847–November 29, 1847
Sonderbund War in Switzerland spurs negotiation for democratic constitution

1848
Chartism disintegrates

February 1848
Karl Marx and Friedrich Engels publish the ***Communist Manifesto***

February 24, 1848
French Revolution begins in Paris—Second Republic

March 4, 1848
Karl Marx expelled from Belgium

A BRIEF HISTORY OF SOCIAL MOVEMENTS IN THE 19TH CENTURY

1850
German sociologist Lorenz von Stein introduces term "social movement" into academia

1850–1914
Second wave of globalization

1851–1864
Taiping Revolution (otherwise known as Taiping Civil War) in China

December 1851
Louis Napoleon stages coup d'état

1864
Napoleon's Second Empire permits limited right to strike

1868
France (under Napoleon) grants workers the right to hold public meetings without prior authorization from government

1885
Indian National Congress founded

1895–1898
Cuban rebellion against Spain

1896
Argentine Socialist Party founded

1897
Chilean Socialist Party founded

1899–1900
Boxer Rebellion in China

July 28, 1914–November 11, 1918
World War One

A BRIEF HISTORY OF SOCIAL MOVEMENTS IN THE 20TH CENTURY

March 8, 1917–November 7, 1917
Bolshevik Revolution in Russia ushers in rise of the Soviet Union

1926
Charles Edward Coughlin starts radio show

1931
CBS drops Coughlin's radio show in response to Coughlin attacking the government and capitalists such as Ford

1934
Charles Edward Coughlin founds National Union for Social Justice to oppose Roosevelt's New Deal

1936
Coughlin changes organization to the Christian Front, ushering in legacy of conservative talk radio

September 1, 1939–September 2, 1945
World War Two

August 15, 1947
Indian independence from Britain

January 30, 1948
Mahatma Gandhi assassinated by Hindu nationalist

1952
Fulgencio Batista leads coup in Cuba

1954
British military forces leave Egypt

1959
Fidel Castro leads revolution in Cuba

1962
Soviet Communist Party publish two volumes surveying social movement

A BRIEF HISTORY OF SOCIAL MOVEMENTS IN THE 20TH CENTURY

April 4, 1968
Martin Luther King, Jr. assassinated in Memphis, Tennessee

May 1968
French students and workers act against Charles de Gaulle and Georges Pompidou

October 2, 1968
Mexican military and police kill demonstrators and arrest thousands assembled to demand civil liberties

1981
President Anwar Sadat (Egypt) assassinated, succeeded by Hosni Mubarak

May 17, 1989
Millions march through Beijing to occupy Tiananmen Square

June 3, 1989
Troops assault Tiananmen Square, breaking up movement and killing nearly 250

December 3, 1989
Czechoslovakian Prime Minister Ladislav Adamec resigns

December 30, 1989
Václav Havel nominated president, marking the end of the Communist Party in Czechoslovakia

August 2 1990–February 28 1991
Gulf War

November 30, 1999
Protests against World Trade Organization in Seattle

March 19, 2003
United States invades Iraq

November 2004
Arizona passes Prop 200, restricting public benefits to those without documentation

A BRIEF HISTORY OF SOCIAL MOVEMENTS IN THE 21ST CENTURY

June 1, 2007
Xiamen residents march to protest chemical factory being built in province

January 2008
Gov. Napolitano (Arizona) signs the State Employer Sanctions Law, levying penalties against businesses which hire undocumented immigrants.

March 2008
Guangzhou protest of chemical factory

June 6, 2010
Death of Khaled Said in police custody helps fuel revolution in Egypt

July 2010
Gov. Brewer (Arizona) signs SB1070, a bill which requires police to question people about status if suspected to be undocumented

2011
Arab Spring

January 28, 2011
Egyptian authorities suspend internet access; President Hosni Mubarak resigns 18 days later

February 2011
EuroAnarkismo conference

October 2011
Occupy Wall Street movement gains widespread acclaim

April 8, 2011
Police Day protests in Egypt

April 17, 2011
Farmers in 29 countries protest simultaneously in “International Day of Peasant Struggles”

August 11, 2011
San Francisco Transit Authority suspends cellphone service in 4 stations to disrupt protests against racist police brutality

PART I

A Theory and History of Social Movements

1

SOCIAL MOVEMENTS AS POLITICS

Charles Tilly and Lesley Wood[1]

"The 'March of Millions' in Cairo marks the spectacular emergence of a new political society in Egypt," Paul Amar explained in the online ezine *Jadaliyya* on February 1, 2011. He continues,

> This uprising brings together a new coalition of forces, uniting reconfigured elements of the security state with prominent business people, internationalist leaders, and relatively new (or newly reconfigured) mass movements of youth, labor, women's and religious groups. President Hosni Mubarak lost his political power on Friday, 28 January. On that night the Egyptian military let Mubarak's ruling party headquarters burn down and ordered the police brigades attacking protesters to return to their barracks. When the evening call to prayer rang out and no one heeded Mubarak's curfew order, it was clear that the old president been reduced to a phantom authority.
>
> (Amar 2011a)

The protests developed within a context of rising frustrations and economic inequality. In recent years, human rights violations and police brutality had created a climate of fear in the country. The wave of protest started with strikes over working conditions and low wages and morphed into marches against police brutality. Groups such as the Kefiya Movement and the April 6 Movement used both flyers and electronic media to mobilize for a large protest on January 25 "Police Day" (a national holiday) as expectations increased following a successful uprising in nearby Tunisia, where another decades-long dictator had suddenly been brought down by popular protests. By the end of January 25, 2011 hundreds of thousands of people were in Cairo's Tahrir Square and in other cities throughout Egypt demanding the ouster of the longtime president.

The protests were successful in many ways. Former president Hosni Mubarak and his two sons were arrested and interrogated and put on trial.

Some political prisoners were released, the dominant political party was abolished, various politicians were fired, the State Security Investigations Service was dismantled, and shop owners who had losses during the curfew were told they would be reimbursed. A referendum was held about the timing of the next election. The fragile relationships among police, military, the wealthy, and Mubarak were destabilized (Amar 2011a).

Six months later, mobilization and frustration were ongoing. Despite attempts by the transitional Supreme Council of the Armed Forces to limit protest through longstanding emergency laws, multiple strikes and sit-ins continued. Sections of the labor movement demanded the renationalization of privatized companies. Activists met in tent cities in the public squares throughout the country to demand the end to military trials for thousands of imprisoned civilians. They also sought justice for families of those killed during the revolution, an increase to the minimum wage, and quick trials for former government officials. Other groups formed and new issues were raised; for example, one thousand women marched in Cairo on International Women's Day in March 2011 to demand representation in the new constitution. In September, after a rally demanding the end to security laws, about one thousand people marched on the Embassy of Israel, where some entered, destroying documents, and others clashed with security personnel. Salafists, a strain of fundamentalist Sunni Muslims, protested the ongoing detention of affiliated activists, demanded the release of the World Trade Center bomber Sheikh Omar Abdel Rahman, and protested in support of the prodemocracy movements in Yemen and Syria (Hisham and Halim 2011). Environmentalists protested dependence on fossil fuel (Eriksen 2011), university students demanded the dismissal of university leaders and the election of university deans without any interference from state security (*Al Masrya al Youm* 2011), and doctors from the Ministry of Health went on strike to demand better working conditions, higher wages, and increased government spending on health care (Carr 2011). Then, tragically, Coptic Christians who rallied and marched against the burning of a church in Southern Egypt were attacked by security forces in early October 2011. Violence spread across the contentious landscape, as frustrations with military rule increased.

Divisions existed between those who highlighted the importance of constitutional reforms and those who prioritized the protection of civil liberties. Some thought that a proposed timeline for reforms was appropriate, while others wanted faster changes. Nonetheless, it was clear that across Egypt, people were willing to meet, march, and rally in order to make the changes they wanted to see.

Neoliberal Designs

As people in Egypt and around the world sought to solve political and economic problems by calling for a social movement, global leaders had a different agenda.

In 2011, the Group of Twenty (G20) Finance Ministers and Central Bank Governors proposed to resolve ongoing economic problems by announcing austerity budgets, with cuts to education, health care, public spending, and infrastructure. In response, many people called for a global movement for "real democracy" that would challenge these plans. A motion passed by the EuroAnarkismo conference, which met in London (UK) in February 2011, explained:

> A response on the European scale is more than ever necessary if the street is to reclaim the political sovereignty which is being more and more totally taken away from us, to question the iniquitous decisions of the EU, later presented as insurmountable and inevitable, and to fight the transnational power of financial markets. We need a social movement on the European scale.
>
> (EuroAnarkismo 2011)

Latin America and Asia chimed in as well: in September 2011, Camila Vallejo, a leader in the Chilean student movement, argued that the movement should build a coalition with other sectors unhappy with the regime (Abramovich 2011). In April 2011, speakers at a discussion during Anti-Corruption Week in Bangladesh underscored the need to forge a social movement against corruption to build a poverty-free country (*Daily Sun* 2011).

The hopeful appeal to social movements also rang out in North America. Along with calls for movements for healthy eating, First Nations sovereignty, and gun control, as well as against the Keystone XL tar sands pipeline, one of the fastest growing social movements in the United States in recent years had been the conservative Tea Party movement. One website defines it as "an American grassroots movement which . . . is advocating reductions in taxes and government spending" (teaparty.org). Its various local manifestations mobilized against publicly funded health care and bank bailouts, and some of its offshoots have been involved in protests against immigrant rights (United Press International [UPI] 2010).

Social Movements

By the twenty-first century, people all over the world recognized the term "social movement" as a clarion call, as a counterweight to oppressive power, as a summons to popular action against a wide range of injustices.

It was not always so. Although popular risings of one kind or another have occurred across the world for thousands of years, what observers described in Egypt were organizations—with leadership, members, and resources—that held meetings and developed a strategy by learning from past movements. In the early twenty-first century, activists built their movement by using Facebook groups and Twitter feeds, adding these to longstanding routines of handing out flyers outside of mosques and in neighborhoods, calling for massive public rallies against police brutality and for democratic reform (Al Jazeera 2011).

Even without social media, such a form of politics existed nowhere in the world three centuries ago. Popular politics then looked very different. Then, during the later eighteenth century, people in Western Europe and North America began the fateful creation of a new political phenomenon. They began to create social movements. This book traces the history of this invented political form. This book treats social movements as a distinctive form of contentious politics—*contentious* in the sense that social movements involve collective making of claims that, if realized, would conflict with someone else's interests; *politics* in the sense that governments of one sort or another figure somehow in the claim making, whether as claimants, objects of claims, allies of the objects, or monitors of the contention (McAdam, Tarrow, and Tilly 2001; Tilly and Tarrow 2015).

Social Movements 1768–2018 shows that this particular version of contentious politics requires historical understanding. History helps explain why social movements incorporated some crucial features (for example, the disciplined street march) that separated the social movement from other sorts of politics. History also helps identify significant *changes* in the operation of social movements (for example, the emergence of professional staffs and organizations specializing in the pursuit of social movement programs) and thus alerts us to the possibility of new changes in the future. History helps, finally, because it calls attention to the shifting political conditions that made social movements possible. If social movements begin to disappear, their disappearance will tell us that a major vehicle for ordinary people's participation in public politics is waning. The rise and fall of social movements mark the expansion and contraction of democratic opportunities.

As it developed in the West after 1750, the social movement emerged from an innovative, consequential synthesis of three elements:

1. *social movement campaign*: a sustained, organized public effort making collective claims on target authorities;
2. *social movement repertoire*: combinations from among the following forms of political action: creation of special-purpose associations and coalitions, public meetings, solemn processions, vigils, rallies, demonstrations, petition drives, statements to and in public media, and pamphleteering; and
3. *WUNC displays*: participants' concerted public representations of WUNC: worthiness, unity, numbers, and commitment on the part of themselves and/or their constituencies.

Unlike a onetime petition, declaration, or mass meeting, a *campaign* extends beyond any single event—although social movements often include petitions, declarations, and mass meetings. A campaign always links at least three parties: a group of self-designated claimants, some object(s) of claims, and a public of some kind. The claims may target governmental officials, owners of property, religious functionaries, and others whose actions (or failures to act) significantly affect the welfare of many people. Not the solo actions, but interactions among the claimants, objects, and public, constitute a social movement. A few zealots may commit themselves to the movement night and day, but the bulk of participants move back and forth between public claim making and other activities.

The social movement *repertoire* overlaps with the repertoires of other political phenomena such as trade union activity and electoral campaigns. During the twentieth century, special-purpose associations and crosscutting coalitions in particular began to do an enormous variety of political work across the world. But the integration of most of these performances into sustained campaigns differentiates social movements from other varieties of politics.

The term "WUNC" sounds odd, but it represents something quite familiar. WUNC displays can take the form of statements, slogans, or labels that imply worthiness, unity, numbers and commitment: Citizens United for Justice, Mothers for Peace, the 99%, and so on. Collective self-representations often act them out in idioms that local audiences will recognize, for example:

- *worthiness*: sober demeanor; neat clothing; presence of clergy, dignitaries, and mothers with children;
- *unity*: matching badges, headbands, banners, or costumes; marching in ranks; singing and chanting;
- *numbers*: headcounts, signatures on petitions, messages from constituents, filling streets, retweets, repostings, and numbers of *likes*;
- *commitment*: braving bad weather; visible participation by the old and disabled; resistance to repression; ostentatious sacrifice, subscription, and/or benefaction.

Particular idioms vary enormously from one setting to another. These elements had historical precedents. Well before 1750, Europe's Protestants had repeatedly mounted sustained public campaigns against Catholic authorities on behalf of the right to practice their "heretical faith." Europeans engaged in two centuries of civil wars and rebellions in which Protestant/Catholic divisions figured centrally (te Brake 1998). As for the repertoires, versions of special-purpose associations, public meetings, marches, and other forms of political action existed individually long before their combination within social movements. We will soon see how social movement pioneers adapted, extended, and connected these forms of action. Displays of WUNC had long occurred in religious martyrdom, civic sacrifice, and resistance to conquest; only their regularization and their integration with the standard repertoire marked off social movement displays from their predecessors. No single element, but the *combination* of repertoire and WUNC displays within campaigns, created the social movement's distinctiveness.

Some overlapping political phenomena also emerged in the time of social movements. As later chapters will show in detail, political campaigns, with their parties and electoral contests, interacted extensively with social movements at times, yet developed their own bodies of rights, obligations, personnel, and practices. At various times in the nineteenth century, workers in capitalist countries generally acquired rights to organize, assemble, strike, and speak collectively, sometimes winning those rights by means of social movement campaigns, performances, and WUNC displays. Organized interest groups such as manufacturers and medical professionals similarly achieved special political rights to speak and act collectively, although rarely by social movement means. Mostly, groups that already commanded substantial resources, connections, and prestige acquired rights through direct negotiation with governments.

During the nineteenth and twentieth centuries, most states that had established churches conceded to new religious sects the rights to assemble and speak—if not always giving them the right to enforce their doctrines or practices on members. Separatist communities—religious, political, or lifestyle—have sometimes emerged from social movements, although most regimes have either repressed or contained such communities energetically. Organizations participating in social movements, furthermore, sometimes moved into these other political spheres: conducting political campaigns, establishing labor unions, creating durable interest groups, becoming religious sects, or forming separatist communities. These overlaps should not keep us from recognizing that after 1750 a distinctive body of law and practice grew up around social movements as such.

Interpretations of Social Movements

In a book titled *History of the French Social Movement from 1789 to the Present* (1850), German sociologist Lorenz von Stein introduced the term "social movement" into scholarly discussions of popular political striving (von Stein 1959). At first, it conveyed the idea of a continuous, unitary process by which the whole working class gained self-consciousness and power. When von Stein wrote, Marx and Engels's *Communist Manifesto* (1848) had recently adopted just such a meaning in its declaration that "all previous historical movements were movements of minorities, or in the interest of minorities. The proletarian movement is the self-conscious, independent movement of the immense majority, in the interests of the immense majority" (Marx and Engels 1958: I, 44).

Nevertheless, political analysts also spoke of social movements in the plural; in 1848, the German journal *Die Gegenwart* [The Present] declared that "social movements are in general nothing other than a first search for a valid historical outcome" (Wirtz 1981: 20). Most nineteenth-century analysts of social movements differentiated them by program, organization, and setting. Engels himself adopted the plural in his preface to the *Manifesto*'s English edition of 1888, remarking that "wherever independent proletarian movements continued to show signs of life, they were ruthlessly hunted down" (Marx and Engels 1958: I, 26). From the later nineteenth century, political analysts not only regularly pluralized social movements but also extended them beyond organized proletarians to farmers, women, and a wide variety of other claimants (Heberle 1951: 2–11).

Names for political episodes gain weight when they carry widely recognized evaluations and when clear consequences follow from an episode's naming. To call an event a riot, a brawl, or a case of genocide stigmatizes its participants. To tag an event as a landslide election, a military victory, or a peace settlement generally polishes the reputations of its organizers. When either happens widely, critics or supporters of disputed actions regularly try to make the labels stick: to label an enemy's encounter with police a riot, to interpret a stalemate as a military victory, and so on. As our short case studies show (see book's timeline and Part II), the term "social movement" has acquired attractive overtones across the world. Consequently, participants, observers, and analysts who approve of an episode of popular collective action these days frequently call it a social movement, whether or not it involves the combination of campaign, repertoire, and WUNC displays.

Furthermore, in the case of episodes that meet the standards, three confusions often arise.

1. Analysts and activists often extend the term "social movement" loosely to all protest activity or at least all relevant popular protest of which they approve. Feminists, for example, retroactively incorporate heroic women of the centuries before 1750 into the women's movement, while for environmental activists any popular initiative anywhere on behalf of the environment becomes part of the worldwide environmental movement.
2. Analysts often confuse a movement's collective action with the organizations and networks that support the action, or even consider the organizations and networks to *constitute* the movement, for example by identifying the environmental movement with the people, interpersonal networks, and advocacy organizations that favor environmental protection rather than the campaigns in which they engage.
3. Analysts often treat "the movement" as a single unitary actor, thus obscuring both (a) the incessant jockeying and realignment that always go on within social movements and (b) the interaction among activists, constituents, targets, authorities, allies, rivals, enemies, and audiences that makes up the changing texture of social movements.

Inflation of the term to include all sorts of protest past and present; conflation of the movement with its supporting population, networks, or organizations; and treatment of movements as unitary actors do little harm in casual political discussion. In fact, within social movements they often aid recruitment, mobilization, and morale. But they badly handicap any effort to describe and explain how social movements actually work—especially when the point is to place social movements in history. That is the task at hand.

Let us make our own claims clear. No one owns the term "social movement"; analysts, activists, and critics remain free to use the phrase as they want. But a distinctive way of pursuing public politics began to take shape in Western countries during the later eighteenth century, acquired widespread recognition in Western Europe and North America by the early nineteenth century, consolidated into a durable ensemble of elements by the middle of the same century, altered more slowly and incrementally after that point, spread widely through the Western world, and came to be called a social movement. That political complex combined three elements: (1) campaigns of collective claims on target authorities; (2) an array of claim-making performances including special-purpose associations, public meetings, media statements, and demonstrations; and (3) public representations of the cause's worthiness, unity, numbers, and commitment. We call that historically specific complex a social movement. This book traces the history of that complex.

Despite incessant small-scale innovation and variation from one political setting to another, the social movement's elements evolved and diffused as a connected whole. In that sense, the social movement has a history. The social movement's history distinguishes it from the history of other political forms, such as electoral campaigns, patriotic celebrations, displays of military force, investitures of public officials, and collective mourning. When this book refers to social movements, then, it does not mean all popular action, all the actions people ever take on behalf of a cause, all the people and organizations that back the same causes, or heroic actors that stand astride history. Instead, it means a particular, connected, evolving, historical set of political interactions and practices. It means the distinctive combination of campaign, repertoire, and WUNC displays.

By these exacting standards, do the Egyptian, European, Chilean, Bangladeshi, and U.S. mobilizations with which we began qualify as social movements? Yes, mostly. Egypt's citizens have been using procedures of social movement claim-making, such as demonstrations, meetings, and flyers, in the face of a regime that treated any such claims as subversive. The Bangladeshi campaign against corruption has involved meetings, coalition-building with international organizations and political parties, rallies, and large-scale conferences. Confronted with an increasingly powerful European Union and an internationalized economic crisis, European youth, students, workers, and unemployed people began to occupy public squares, march, and rally, linking up their national social movement routines and building protest on an international scale. In the United States, activists—on both the left and on the right—could look back on almost two hundred years of associating, demonstrating, meeting, and making WUNC-style claims. Across a great deal of the world, the social movement has become a familiar, generally reliable vehicle of popular politics (Edelman 2001; Ellis and van Kessel 2009; Fallon 2008; Ibarra and Tejerina 1998; Johnston and Almeida 2006; Mamdani and Wamba-dia-Wamba 1995; Ngoma Leslie 2006; Ray and Fainsod Katzenstein 2005; Ray and Korteweg 1999; Tarrow 1998; Wignaraja 1993).

Partly because of the social movement's unquestioned contemporary prevalence, students of particular social movements have shown little interest in the locations of those movements within the larger history of the social movement as a form of politics. On the whole, analysts of social movements treat them as expressions of current attitudes, interests, or social conditions rather than as elements of longer-run histories. True, students of nineteenth-century movements such as antislavery, temperance, and suffrage have had to place them in their historical contexts and follow their historical developments (see, for example, d'Anjou 1996; Buechler 1990; Drescher 1986, 1994, 2009; Eltis 1993; Gusfield 1966; McCammon and Campbell 2002; Newman and Mueller 2011; Young 2006). Self-styled histories of regional, national, or international labor movements often reach back well before the nineteenth century's glory days for precedents and frequently sweep in a wider range of social movements than those focusing specifically on workers' welfare (see Bogolyubov, R'izhkova, Popov, and Dubinskii 1962; Dolléans and Crozier 1950; Kuczynski 1967a, 1967b; Zaleski 1956).

Broad surveys of protest, violence, and political conflict likewise regularly transect the zone of social movement activity (see Ackerman and DuVall 2000; Botz 1976, 1987; Brown 1975; Gilje 1987, 1996; Grimsted 1998; Lindenberger 1995; McKivigan and Harrold 1999; Mikkelsen 1986; Olzak 2006; Tilly, Tilly, and Tilly 1975; R. Tilly 1980; Walton and Seddon 1994; Williams 2003). Nearby, the reflecting mirrors of an abundant historical literature on policing, surveillance, and repression often capture social movements at unusual angles (see Balbus 1973; Broeker 1970; Bruneteaux 1993; Carey 2009; Cunningham 2005; Earl, Soule, and McCarthy 2003; Emsley 1983; Emsley and Weinberger 1991; Fillieule 1997b; Goldstein 1983, 2000, 2001; Gurr 2000; Huggins 1985, 1998; Husung 1983; Jessen 1994; Liang 1992; Lüdtke 1989, 1992; Monjardet 1996; Munger 1979, 1981; Palmer 1988; Storch 1976; Wilson 1969).

Some particular social movement performances—notably French and Irish marches and demonstrations—have attracted first-rate histories (Blackstock 2000; Farrell 2000; Favre 1990; Fillieule 1997a; Jarman 1997; Mirala 2000; Pigenet and Tartakowsky 2003; Robert 1996; Tartakowsky 1997). Broader social and political histories, furthermore, commonly pay attention to social movements as they trace their overall historical trends (e.g., Anderson and Anderson 1967; Cronin and Schneer 1982; González Calleja 1998, 1999; Hobsbawm 1975, 1988, 1994; Montgomery 1993). All these kinds of historical study will serve us well in later chapters. Even taken together, however, they do not provide a coherent global history of the social movement as a political phenomenon parallel to, say, the histories of legislative elections, political parties, revolutions, or coups d'état as this book does.

For particular countries and periods, some general historical surveys of social movements as such do exist (see, for example, Ash 1972; Bright and Harding 1984; Burke 1988; Castells 1983; Clark 1959; Clark, Grayson, and Grayson 1975; Duyvendak, van der Heijden, Koopmans, and Wijmans 1992; Fredrickson 1997; Gamson 1990; Kaplan 1992; Klausen and Mikkelsen 1988; Kriesi, Koopmans, Duyvendak, and Giugni 1995; Lundqvist 1977; Nicolas 1985; O'Brian 2008; Poulson 2006; Tarrow 1996; Wirtz 1981). In one of the sharpest available statements on the subject, John Markoff sets the explanatory problem deftly:

> Social movements as we know them today were beginning to flourish in England by the late eighteenth century and during the nineteenth century took root in Europe, North America, and elsewhere. To understand why, we need to consider many linked changes: a strengthened government but a weakened king; a people organizing themselves to assert claims on that government; a political elite prone to claim that it ruled in the name of the people; transportation improvements and commercial relations linking distant people; the beginnings of widespread literacy and new communication media leading people separated in space to feel themselves moving to a common rhythm.
>
> (Markoff 1996b: 45)

In general, however, such surveys subordinate the history to some other line of analysis, such as S. D. Clark's demonstration of divergence in the paths of Canadian and U.S. movements after the 1830s and William Gamson's investigation of whether American political opportunities narrowed during the twentieth century. Markoff himself subordinates his analysis of the formation and transformation of social movements to the spread of democracy. We draw on these surveys repeatedly, as well as on historical studies of particular movements. We give special attention to chronologies and catalogs such as Gamson's because they provide material for comparison and systematic evidence of change (Tilly 2002b). Still, the following historical analysis has required a good deal of interpolating, synthesizing, and borrowing from Tilly's own historical research.

Social movement history poses an acute version of a characteristic problem in political analysis. Social movements unquestionably have a distinctive, connected history. This book pursues just that history. The pursuit brings on two strong—and quite opposite—temptations. From one side beckons the temptation to treat the social movement as a phenomenon sui generis, and to search for general laws of its operation. Similar temptations beset students of revolutions, strike waves, and election campaigns. The search for grand laws in human affairs comparable to the laws of Newtonian mechanics has, however, utterly failed. Some such laws might conceivably exist (in the form, let us say, of evolutionary and/or genetic universal laws), but they surely do not operate at the levels of particular structures or processes such as churches, corporations, revolutions, or social movements. Anyone who wants to explain political structures and processes in the present state of knowledge does much better sorting out the more limited causal mechanisms that produce change, variation, and salient features of those structures and processes. The effort necessarily depends on turning away from "laws" of social movements toward causal analogies and connections between distinctive aspects of social movements and other varieties of politics (Goldstone 2003; Tilly 2001a, 2001b; Tilly and Tarrow 2006; Tilly 2008a). Explanations of social movements and their history must mesh with explanations of other sorts of contentious politics.

That effort, however, calls up the opposite temptation: having noticed smaller-scale regularities in social movements, one may see social movements everywhere. Considered separately, campaigns, performances (such as public meetings or petitions), and WUNC displays (such as badge wearing and ostentatious sacrifice) often occur outside of social movements: within churches, schools, corporations, intellectual communities, and elsewhere (Binder 2002; Davis and Thompson 1994; Davis, McAdam, Scott, and Zald 2005). Sometimes, by analogy, they even attract the label "movement." Take the so-called militia movement in the United States of the 1990s. Across the United States, hundreds of small, loosely connected groups wore military garb, conducted war games, distributed apocalyptic texts, declared their independence from U.S. jurisdiction including the obligation to pay taxes, and prepared for the Armageddon their leaders predicted for the year 2000. The Southern Poverty Law Center (SPLC), which keeps tabs on such groups, counted 370 militias across the country in 1996, a number that shrank to forty-three by 2007, and rebounded to 273 in 2017 (*Economist* 2003: 22; Southern Poverty Law Center 2011, 2018).

If such groups took up the full combination of campaigns, social movement performances, and WUNC displays, then they would enter the terrain of social movements properly speaking. If, on the other hand, some of them organized as the Militia Party began running candidates in local or state elections, and started buying time on local television stations, they would have opted for yet another available form of public politics: the electoral campaign. In the absence of such unlikely shifts in strategy, instead of declaring that the activities of militias "really are" social movements, we may define them as constituting another form of contentious politics. That recognition allows us to study their similarities to social movements but also to see what distinctive theoretical and explanatory problems they pose.

The worlds of science and medicine sometimes generate analogies to social movements, but mostly without forming full-fledged social movements. Take just one example: recent disputes over water in the Klamath River Basin, near the California–Oregon border. The headwaters of the Klamath, including the desert-surrounded Upper Klamath Lake, supply irrigation for many dry-earth farmers in the uplands. But they also drain into the lowland region where salmon breed and where the Klamath Tribes insist on treaty rights to fishing established by an 1864 settlement with the United States. In 2002, a report of the National Academy of Sciences concluded that there was "no sound scientific basis" for terminating irrigation flows in favor of sending more water to downstream fisheries. The scientists' statement satisfied neither side, including the biologists lined up with one group of water users or the other. "The report's conclusion," remarked *Science* magazine's reporter from Klamath Falls, Oregon,

> sparked an outcry in this small farming community that federal agencies are supporting "junk science," and it bolstered calls for reforming or scrapping the Endangered Species Act (ESA). But over the past year, it has also sparked another, more muted outcry, this one among fisheries biologists. They contend that the report's analyses were simplistic, its conclusions overdrawn, and—perhaps worst of all—that the report has undermined the credibility of much of the science being done in the region if not fueled an outright antiscience sentiment.
>
> (Service 2003: 36)

Opposing groups of advocates are clearly conducting campaigns and occasionally employing such performances as press conferences to publicize their claims. If the farmers, the biologists, or members of the Klamath Tribes started to combine public campaigns, social movement performances, and WUNC displays in sustained claims on federal authorities or the National Academy of Sciences, they would move their struggles onto the terrain of full-fledged social movements. They, too, could conceivably take up the public politics of electoral campaigns—or, for that matter, move in the direction of regularly constituted interest groups by creating lobbyists, Washington offices, and newsletters broadcasting their causes. In the meantime, however, we will understand their actions better if we recognize analogies and differences without simply treating the Klamath Basin controversy as one more variety of social movement. The same goes for analogous struggles within corporations, churches, schools, intellectual disciplines, art worlds, and neighborhoods (Davis, McAdam, Scott, and Zald 2005). In exactly that sense, the historical project of tracing the social movement's distinctive politics forms part of the larger program of explaining contentious politics at large.

Toward Historical Explanations

This project, therefore, has four interdependent aspects. First, we must trace the origins and transformations of the social movement's major elements: campaigns, repertoires, and WUNC displays. How, for example, did the now-familiar street demonstration take shape and even acquire an uneasy legal standing in most democratic countries? Second, we must uncover the social processes that encourage or inhibit proliferation of social movements. What causal connections explain that correspondence between democratization and social movements? Third, we must examine how the elements of social movements interacted with other forms of politics. To what extent and how, for example, did industrial strikes, electoral campaigns, and social movements intersect and influence each other? Finally, we must show what causes important aspects of change and variation in social movements. Does the emergence of professional political brokers, for instance, help explain the formation of a specialized, connected sector of social movement organizations in leading capitalist democracies (Ibarra 2003; Meyer and Tarrow 1998)? Close historical analysis helps answer all four sorts of questions.

Following that line of inquiry, here are the book's main arguments:

From their eighteenth-century origins onward, social movements have proceeded not as solo performances, but as interactive campaigns. Like electoral campaigns, popular uprisings, and religious mobilizations, they consist of interactions between temporarily connected (and often shifting) groups of claimants and the objects of their claims, with third parties such as constituents, allies, rival claimants, enemies, authorities, and various publics often playing significant parts in the campaigns' unfolding. We will never explain social movements' variation and change without paying close attention to political actors other than the central claimants, for example the police with whom demonstrators struggled, collaborated, and co-developed their strategies.

Social movements combine three kinds of claims: program, identity, and standing. Program claims involve stated support for or opposition to actual or proposed actions by the objects of movement claims. Identity claims consist of assertions that "we"—the claimants—constitute a unified force to be reckoned with. WUNC (worthiness, unity, numbers, and commitment) performances back up identity claims. Standing claims assert ties and similarities to other political actors, for example, excluded minorities, properly constituted citizens' groups, allies or loyal supporters of the regime. They sometimes concern the standing of *other* political actors, for example in calls for expulsion of immigrants or their exclusion from citizenship. Program, identity, and standing claims conform to partly separate codes built up from a regime's particular political history; Egyptians and Americans do not—and cannot—signal collective worthiness in exactly the same way.

The relative salience of program, identity, and standing claims varies significantly among social movements, among claimants within movements, and among phases of movements. A good deal of negotiation within social movements centers on the relative prominence the different claims will receive: do we, for example, present ourselves as a durable alliance of rights-deprived people who are currently lining up against this governmental program (but tomorrow might line up in support of another), or as a diverse cross section of the general population whose main connection consists of the harm that all of us will receive from this particular program and who therefore may never again join in making claims?

Democratization promotes the formation of social movements. By democratization, let us mean development of regimes featuring relatively broad and equal citizenship; binding consultation of citizens with respect to governmental policy, personnel, and resources; and at least some protection of citizens from arbitrary actions by governmental agents (Tilly 2004, 2007). This means that through contestation, a particular kind of state emerges. The emergence of such a state is more likely in particular economic contexts (Tilly 1992). Democratization actually limits the range of feasible and effective popular collective action. Democratic institutions, for example, generally inhibit violent popular rebellions (Tilly 2006). But empowerment of citizens through contested elections and other forms of consultation combines with protections of civil liberties such as association and assembly to channel popular claim making into social movement forms.

Social movements assert popular sovereignty. Although particular movements differ fiercely over who counts as "the people," the whole apparatus of campaign, repertoire, and WUNC displays embodies the more general claim that public affairs depend, and should depend, on the consent of the governed. The claim is not necessarily democratic, since ethnic, religious, and nationalist movements sometimes invest their powers in charismatic leaders rather than democratic deliberation, yet still insist that those leaders embody the will of the people at large. Such movements, furthermore, often reject whole races, classes, ethnicities, or genders of the local population as unworthy of belonging to "the people." But the stress on popular consent fundamentally challenges divine right to kingship, traditional inheritance of rule, warlord control, and aristocratic predominance. Even in systems of representative government, as we will soon see, social movements pose a crucial question: do sovereignty and its accumulated wisdom lie in the legislature or in the people it claims to represent?

As compared with locally grounded forms of popular politics, social movements depend heavily on political entrepreneurs for their scale, durability, and effectiveness. The local routines of retaliation, rebellion, and resistance that prevailed across most of the world before the era of social movements drew on widely available local knowledge and existing interpersonal networks. The social movement combination of campaigns, WUNC displays, and coordinated performances, in contrast, always results at least in part from prior planning, coalition building, and muting of local differences. As we will soon see, smart political entrepreneurs figured in campaigns, social movement performances, and WUNC displays from the very birth of social movements. During the twentieth and twenty-first centuries, however, professional political organizers, brokers, and partly autonomous nongovernmental organizations took on increasingly prominent parts in promotion of social movements—to the dismay of populist critics. Ironically, a good deal of twentieth- and twenty-first-century social movement work therefore went into disguising the entrepreneurial effort in favor of images portraying the spontaneous emergence of WUNC.

Once social movements establish themselves in one political setting, modeling, communication, and collaboration facilitate their adoption in other settings. Transfers often occur within the same regime from the initial foci of social movements—more often than not, claims on national governments—to other objects of demand or support, such as local leaders, landlords, capitalists, or religious figures. Social movement strategies also transfer *among* regimes as political organizers, exiles, and members of international religious groups collaborate across national boundaries and as rulers of authoritarian regimes (especially those that claim to rule on behalf of a coherent, united people) find themselves under pressure from other countries to concede something to their critics. Colonies of countries that already have established social movements provide inviting environments for infusion of social movement activity.

The forms, personnel, and claims of social movements vary and evolve historically. Three distinguishable but interacting sources of change and variation in social movements produce variation in time and space. First, overall political environments (including democratization and de-democratization) alter in partial independence of social movement activity and affect its character. Second, within the interactions that occur in the course of social movements (for example, interactions between demonstrators and police), change occurs incrementally as a consequence of constant innovation, negotiation, and conflict. Third, participants in social movements—including not only activists but also authorities and other objects of claims—communicate with each other, borrowing and adapting each other's ideas, personnel, assistance, rhetoric, and models of action. They also borrow, adapt, and innovate as they compete with each other for advantages or constituencies. Sometimes the borrowing and adaptation take place over great distances and between quite disparate social movements (Chabot 2000; Chabot and Duyvendak 2002; Scalmer 2002b). Changes in political and economic environments, incremental changes within the social movement sphere, and transfers among movements interact to produce substantial change and variation in the character of social movements.

The social movement, as an invented institution, could disappear or mutate into some quite different form of politics. Many forms of popular justice and rebellion that once prevailed have quite vanished; we have no guarantee that the social movement as it has prevailed for two centuries will continue forever. Since the social movement spread with the growth of centralized, relatively democratic states, for example, either governmental decentralization, extensive privatization of governmental activities, or weakening of government capacity, the eclipse of the state by transnational powers, or widespread de-democratization could all put the social movement as we know it out of business. Indeed, with the set of changes occurring that people loosely call "globalization", citizens who count on social movements to make their voices heard must look very hard at the future.

This book follows these arguments through a straightforward historical analysis. Chapter 2 looks at the eighteenth-century invention of the social movement, concentrating on North America and England but looking briefly at other parts of Western Europe as well. Chapter 3 surveys the nineteenth century, during which extensive national and international movements grew up in the West and some also formed in European colonies. Chapter 4 moves up to the twentieth century, a time of worldwide proliferation in social movement activity. Chapter 5 follows up with the twenty-first century, focusing on the expansion of international communication and coordination among social movement activists. Chapter 6 analyzes what the previous chapters tell us about mutual influences of democratization and social movements: when, how, and why democratization promotes social movements, but also under what conditions and how social movements advance democratization or de-democratization. Chapter 7 draws together conclusions in the form of possible futures for the social movement. Between here and there we will see that social movements have a dramatic history, one that today's participants will gain from recognizing. We provide a timeline of the movements discussed in these chapters. In Part II, we then provide recent case studies to test whether they meet the social movement threshold and characteristics discussed in Part I.

Note

1 Ernesto Castañeda edited the text, updated the language, added a few references, lightly restructured some sections, and added an image to the text.

2

INVENTIONS OF THE SOCIAL MOVEMENT

Charles Tilly[1]

Imagine an eighteenth-century voyage investigating variations in political contention and protest. You sail from London to Boston to Charleston during the turbulent year of 1768. Instead of using a tourist guide—the great guide-making pioneer Karl Baedeker, after all, was not born until 1801!—you carry an atlas of contentious gatherings (CGs). In a contentious gathering, a number of people (let us say ten or more) gather in a publicly accessible place and collectively make claims on others outside their group, claims that if realized would affect those others' interests (Tilly 1995: chap. 2 and appendix). The claims can run from physical attacks to pleas for mercy to expressions of political support.

As of the 1760s, most CGs in London, Boston, and Charleston do not resemble the marches, meetings, and delegations of social movements. Much more often, they involve direct applications of force or threat to parties who have offended group standards or interests. Yet the 1760s also bring important signs of change in popular contention. An inventory of CGs for London during April 1768 includes these events:

2 April: Near suburban Brentford, England a crowd stops a passing carriage and forces the occupants to shout, "Wilkes and Liberty!" on behalf of parliamentary candidate John Wilkes.

14 April: In the house of a master weaver behind the Shoreditch church, journeymen (fully trained, but not yet masters) weavers cut cloth from six looms.

14 April: At the houses and shops of journeymen weavers in Spitalfields, other journeymen cut cloth from another six looms belonging to blacklisted masters.

15 April: During a battle between striking and non-striking coal heavers in Wapping, participants sack nearby houses.

15 April: On the Brentford road, Wilkes's supporters stop a carriage and demand that the passengers declare their support for Wilkes and liberty.

16 April: Coal heavers of Shadwell attack a coal merchant whose servant tore down a poster advertising their strike.

18 April: At Sutton Common, part of the audience at an execution seizes the corpses of the victims and buries them, shouting against the surgeons whom they accuse (plausibly) of planning to carry off the bodies for dissection.

20 April: In the Roundabout Tavern of Shadwell, coal heavers attack a publican–a coal merchant who also serves as a hiring agent.

21 April: In Goodman's Fields, brothel workers attack a man who is trying to retrieve his daughter from prostitution, as a result of which a crowd sacks the brothel.

21 April: Spitalfields journeymen weavers cut cloth from looms.

26 April: Coal heavers board coal boats in Wapping and rough up their captains.

27 April: Supporters of Wilkes accompany him up the Strand and across Westminster Bridge on his way to prison, then free him from his captors, but Wilkes escapes and commits himself to prison.

28 April: Around the King's Bench Prison (Southwark) where Wilkes has incarcerated himself, Wilkes's supporters call for candles to be placed in the windows of houses as well as ritually burning a boot and a bonnet.

The vivid chronology identifies abundant, colorful contention in the London of April 1768.

Three main conflicts dominate the month's CGs. First, coal handlers in Shadwell and Wapping (near London's major port) are backing their demands for higher piece rates by blocking the sale and shipment of coal. Second, silk weavers of London's East End (especially Spitalfields) are putting pressure on wage-cutting masters and the journeymen who persist in producing for them at the lower wage by cutting cloth from the incriminated parties' working looms. Third, a political hurricane roars around the controversial figure of John Wilkes. In the first two conflicts, we see routines of pressure and vengeance that English workers have been employing for centuries. But in the third we witness an innovation that foreshadows the social movement repertoire: conversion of a parliamentary election campaign into an occasion for displays of popular solidarity and determination. In a time of limited voting rights, disciplined mass participation of nonvoters breaks with customary electoral decorum.

John Wilkes (1727–1797) was an agitator, but certainly not a commoner. Using his own money and his position as a member of the lesser aristocracy, he had entered Parliament in 1757. While in Parliament, in 1762 he started to edit an opposition newspaper, *The North Briton*. Wilkes named his polemical paper in response to *The Briton*, a proadministration paper that Scots-born novelist and pamphleteer Tobias Smollett had started earlier the same year, in part to defend the regime against Wilkes's attacks. Wilkes's title referred slightingly to Scots in the royal administration, especially the king's favorite, Lord Bute. (The boot and Scots bonnet burned on April 28, 1768 punned on the name and Scottish origins of Minister Bute.)

The North Briton's issue number 45 (1763) criticized a royal speech, written by the minister, in which the king praised the Treaty of Paris that had just ended the Seven Years War:

> The *Minister's speech* of last Tuesday is not to be paralleled in the annals of this country. I am in doubt whether the imposition is greater on the Sovereign, or on the nation. Every friend of this country must lament that a prince of so many great and admirable qualities, whom England truly reveres, can be brought to give the sanction of his sacred name to the most odious measures and the most unjustifiable public declarations from a throne ever renowned for truth, honour, and unsullied virtue.
>
> (Rudé 1962: 22)

For this statement, the Crown's attorneys charged Wilkes with seditious libel. In the legal environment of the time, not even a Member of Parliament could publicly imply that the king had lied. For that offense, Wilkes spent time in the Tower of London. In his subsequent court appearances, Wilkes challenged the general warrant on which the king's officers had arrested him and seized his papers. He also explicitly identified his personal wrong with a general cause. In the Court of Common Pleas (May 1763), Wilkes declared that

> the LIBERTY of all peers and gentlemen, and, what touches me more sensibly, of all the middling and inferior class of the people, which stands most in need of protection, is in my case this day to be finally decided upon: a question of such importance as to determine at once, whether ENGLISH LIBERTY be a reality or a shadow.
>
> (Brewer 1976: 168)

He eventually won his case, receiving compensation from the government for his illegal arrest and for seizure of his papers. He also appealed to freedom of speech, which won him cheers in the courtroom and the streets. His courtroom speeches launched the cry "Wilkes and Liberty!" as a fateful slogan for resistance to arbitrary power.

Wilkes's victory did not convert him to smug conformity. Later in 1763, he not only reprinted issue number 45 but also produced a scandalous pamphlet called *Essay on Woman*. When government agents seized the proofs, began new proceedings against Wilkes, and assigned the London sheriff and the hangman to burn number 45 publicly in Cheapside, an assembled crowd assaulted the sheriff and hangman, rescuing the sacred text from their hands. Wilkes himself soon fled across the Channel into France to escape prosecution. Parliament expelled him, and the courts declared him an outlaw.

In 1768, however, Wilkes secretly returned to England, stood again for Parliament, won the poll, entered jail to be tried for his earlier offenses, and saw Parliament refuse to seat him. The Wilkite events of April 1768 listed earlier sprang from Wilkes's parliamentary campaign. During 1769, Parliament formally expelled Wilkes again, then rejected three elections that he won from his prison cell. While Wilkes served his term as a popular hero, he received ample press attention, distinguished visitors, and gifts from all over the country; supporters in the town of Stockton, for example, sent him forty-five hams, forty-five tongues, and forty-five dozen bottles of ale (Brewer 1976: 177). By that time, the number forty-five was becoming a popular icon not only for Wilkes but also for liberty in general.

Wilkes went on to a distinguished career as public official and dissenting voice. In 1769, he managed election as a London alderman while still serving his prison term. He only went free (to great popular acclaim, fireworks, illuminations, and salvos of forty-five artillery shells) in 1770. He became London's sheriff in 1771 and soon began campaigning for the supreme municipal post of Lord Mayor. He actually won the City of London poll for the office in 1772, but the aldermen chose his less tainted competitor, James Townsend. At that point, 3,000 people entered the yard of Guildhall (the Lord Mayor's residence), shouting "Damn my Lord Mayor for a scoundrel, he has got Wilkes's right, and we will have him out" (Rudé 1971: 125).

After one more failed attempt, Wilkes gained election as Lord Mayor in 1774 and finally reentered the House of Commons that same year. He became a major speaker for the American cause during the bitter years of the Revolutionary War. Despite his time in prison, his court cases definitively established the legal rights of British periodicals to report and criticize governmental actions, including those of the Crown. He not only commanded widespread popular support (including bands of activists from among the Spitalfields silk weavers) but also found allies among London merchants and officials who sought a counterweight to arbitrary royal power. An elite association that began as Friends of Mr. Wilkes and the Constitution soon became the Society of Supporters of the Bill of Rights, an important force for parliamentary reform. Although no one then used the term "social movement," the association laid some of the foundations for the social movement as a new form of public politics in Great Britain.

In the very process of supporting Wilkes for Parliament, Wilkes's plebeian backers innovated. Almost no workers could vote in parliamentary elections of the 1760s, but workers came out in droves to accompany Wilkes to the polls. After Wilkes won the first round at Brentford on March 28, 1768, his followers began the attacks on opponents and the demands for cheers that continued through the election. The conservative *Annual Register* (founded by Edmund Burke in 1758, and still going strong in the twenty-first century) tut-tutted:

> The mob behaved in a very outrageous manner at Hyde Park corner, where they pelted Mr. Cooke, son of the city marshal, and knocked him from his horse, took off the wheels of one of the carriages, cut the harness, and broke the glasses to pieces; several other carriages were greatly damaged. The reason assigned for their proceedings is, that a flag was carried before the procession of Mr. Wilkes' antagonists, on which was painted, "No Blasphemer."
>
> (Annual Register 1768: 86).

Over the long run, Wilkites pushed out the boundaries of previously permissible public assemblies. They not only expanded electoral processions and public meetings into mass declarations of support for their hero but also converted delegations and petition marches into opportunities to fill the streets instead of simply sending a few dignified representatives to speak humbly on behalf of their constituents. They pioneered the synthesis of crowd action with formal appeals to supporters and authorities. Although Wilkites remained stronger on Unity, Numbers, and Commitment than on public displays of Worthiness, they helped fashion the connection between the social movement repertoire and displays of WUNC.

Long before the 1760s, ordinary English and American people had made public claims of one kind or another. Authorized public assemblies such as holidays, funerals, and parish assemblies had, for example, long provided opportunities for people to voice complaints and to express support for popular leaders. Within limits, organized artisans and militia companies exercised the right to parade on their own holidays, and they sometimes used that right to state their opposition to powerful figures or oppressive programs. With proper shows of respect, they could also send humble delegations to petition for redress of collective wrongs. Within their own communities, workers, consumers, and householders repeatedly mounted resistance or vengeance against offenders of local rights or morality (Tilly 1983). The custom of Rough Music, for instance, involved an assembly outside the house of a moral offender, such as a widower who proposed to marry a young woman; a racket made by the striking of pots and pans, calling of insults, and/or singing of obscene songs; reparations, such as payment for the avengers to go off for drinks; and dispersal of the crowd (Thompson 1972, 1991). Retaliatory rituals of this sort varied dramatically in detail from place to place. They had nothing like the transferability across settings—the modularity—of later social movement performances such as the demonstration and the formation of special-purpose associations.

Seen from the authorities' perspective, the implicit British theory of popular public politics during the earlier eighteenth century ran something like this,

- British subjects group into legally recognized bodies, such as guilds, communities, and religious sects, which exercise some specifiable collective rights, for example the right to meet regularly in designated places of assembly.
- The law protects such collective rights.
- Local authorities have an obligation to enforce and respect the law.
- Chosen representatives of such recognized bodies have the right—indeed, the obligation—to make public presentations of collective demands and grievances.
- Authorities have an obligation to consider those demands and grievances, and to act on them when they are just.
- Outside this framework, no one who has not been brought together by established authorities has a clear right to assemble, to state demands or grievances, or to act collectively.
- Anyone who presumes to speak for the people at large outside these limits infringes illegally on the prerogatives of Parliament; in fact, even electors have no right to instruct their parliamentary representatives once those representatives have been elected.

Local and national authorities often looked the other way when local people violated these principles by activating customary routines of vengeance, approbation, and control. But authorities commonly invoked the principles—as represented, for example, in the Riot Act—when popular action threatened ruling-class property, targeted influential members of the ruling classes, or banded together across local boundaries. During major episodes of rebellion and civil war like those that beset the British Isles between 1640 and 1692, to be sure, ordinary people frequently voiced radical claims in the names of religion and political tradition. They even violated the final principle in the list above by staging meetings without governmental authorization or even in straightforward competition with Parliament (see, e.g., Mendle 2001). But before the later eighteenth century, postrebellion repression always shut down those forms of popular expression that threatened authorities.

On both sides of the Atlantic, members of the ruling classes had less risky ways of making claims. Authorities tolerated their clubs, dinners, pamphlets, and sometimes boisterous legislative assemblies. Elections to assemblies, especially to Parliament, provided splendid opportunities for license, as candidates treated electors, paid them off, and made extravagant public shows of their patronage. Despite a highly restricted franchise, Wilkes's 1757 election to Parliament cost him 7,000 pounds, at a time when a farm laborer in London's hinterland was lucky to earn 30 pounds in a year (Armstrong 1989: 693–98; Rudé 1962: 19). Social movements innovated not by inventing any one of these elements but by converting, expanding, standardizing, and combining them into disciplined vehicles for expression of popular demands. Equally important, social movement efforts created a contested but genuine legal space within which their combination of campaigns, claim-making performances, and WUNC displays acquired political standing.

War and the Elements of Social Movements

The Seven Years War (1756–1763) gave this sort of political innovation a major impetus. For half a century before the 1750s, France and Great Britain had fought each other intermittently in Europe, on the high seas, and over colonies in Asia and across the Americas. France, which had earlier conquered Louisiana and what eventually became eastern Canada, found itself under attack in North America from both British colonists and British armies. Since colonists and armies alike were pushing back Native American settlements, the French recruited ready allies within the major Amerindian federations. For residents of North American colonies, the Seven Years War therefore became the French and Indian War.

Although the British side won dramatically—seizing Canada from the French, for example—momentous military efforts in Europe, India, and the Americas left the British treasury depleted and the government heavily in debt. In the North American colonies, British authorities tried to recoup some of their financial losses and to spread the cost of their greatly expanded military establishment by tightening customs surveillance and imposing expensive duty stamps on a wide range of commercial and legal transactions. Resistance against customs and the Stamp Act united colonists against Britain as never before. Resistance stimulated boycotts of British imports and the formation of extensive communication among cities of the thirteen colonies as well as some of their Canadian counterparts. Chapters of the Sons of Liberty organized and enforced boycotts throughout the colonies. The Stamp Act's repeal (1766) came only after merchants, artisans, and other city dwellers had created an elaborate resistance network.

Boston and Massachusetts led the early resistance effort, but other colonies soon joined them. Boston merchants had formed a Society for the Encouragement of Trade during the early 1760s; that society became a nucleus of dignified opposition to excessive taxation and regulation. This society coordinated elite resistance to the Stamp Act, for example, in 1765 and 1766. At the same time, a group of smaller businessmen with substantial ties to workers began speaking out as Boston's Sons of Liberty, thus linking the mercantile community with the street activists who burned effigies, sacked houses, and assailed tax collectors. Radical members of the mercantile elite, such as Samuel Adams (1722–1803), served as brokers between the two groups.

In December 1766, Adams wrote to Christopher Gadsden, leader of the Charleston, South Carolina, Sons of Liberty, proposing regular communication among patriotic merchants from all the colonies (Alexander 2002: 45). In response to the 1767 Townshend Acts, which imposed a wide range of levies on the colonies, Adams drafted a circular letter of protest in hopes of collecting endorsements from Massachusetts and the other colonies. Late that year, a meeting of Boston inhabitants organized by the expanding web of patriotic associations resolved to encourage American manufacturing and reduce reliance on British imports. In January 1768, the Massachusetts legislature itself submitted a humble petition to the king stating provincial objections to taxation in muted, respectful terms. After initial rejection, in February the same legislature endorsed a strong version of the Adams-initiated circular letter to the other colonies. By this time, Massachusetts patriots were insisting that Parliament had no right to pass bills solely for the purpose of raising revenue from the colonies.

"These resolutions," reported the *Annual Register*, distancing itself prudently from the American claims,

> were adopted, or similar ones entered into, by all the old Colonies on the continent. In some time after, a circular letter was sent by the Assembly of Massachusett's Bay, signed by the Speaker, to all the other Assemblies in North America. The design of this letter was to shew the evil tendency of the late Acts of Parliament, to represent them as unconstitutional, and to propose a common union between the Colonies, in the pursuit of all legal measures to prevent their effect, and a harmony in their applications to Government for a repeal of them. It also expatiated largely on their natural rights as men, and their constitutional ones as English subjects; all of which, it was pretended, were infringed by these laws.
>
> (*Annual Register* 1768: 68)

Despite an explicit demand from King George, the Massachusetts legislature voted 92 to 17 not to rescind its assent to the circular letter. To rescind would, the majority declared, "have left us but a vain Semblance of Liberty" (Alexander 2002: 55).

While leading merchants pursued their program by means of deliberate legal action, Boston sailors and artisans frequently took the law into their own hands. They forcefully resisted being forced into military service, blocked the government's attempt to quarter soldiers in neighborhoods, attacked customs agents, and hung effigies of British officials or their collaborators on the so-called Liberty Tree near the common that had been a flashpoint of action during the Stamp Act crisis of 1765–1766. They often doubled mercantile and official resistance with direct action.

When negotiations with the governor (representative of the Crown in Massachusetts) and the British government grew rancorous, for example, the populace of Boston joined in. In May 1768, British customs officers seized Boston merchant (and smuggler) John Hancock's ship *Liberty* for its failure to pay duties, whereupon Bostonians manned another ship, cut loose the sequestered vessel, and took it away.

> The populace having assembled in great crowds upon this occasion, they pelted the Commissioners of the Customs with stones, broke one of their swords, and treated them in every respect with the greatest outrage; after which, they attacked their houses, broke the windows, and hauled the Collector's boat to the common, where they burnt it to ashes.
>
> (*Annual Register* 1768: 71; for details, see Hoerder 1977: 166–68)

The customs officers fled first to a royal warship and then to Castle William in Boston Harbor. Town meetings of protest convened without official authorization throughout the Boston area. When word reached Boston (September 12) that two regiments were coming from Ireland and another body of military was assembling in Halifax (Nova Scotia) to restore order in Boston, members of the Massachusetts Bay assembly began organizing resistance committees throughout the colony.

Massachusetts patriots quickly gathered allies throughout the other colonies. Mostly, alliances were formed by using the established forms of elite public politics: resolutions, petitions, and solemn meetings. Innovative forms of contentious gatherings elsewhere in America regularly adapted the forms of previously tolerated assemblies. Consider this account of the king's birthday celebration of Charleston (Charles Town), South Carolina, in June 1768.

> The same was celebrated here, with every demonstration of joy, affection and gratitude, that the most loyal subjects could give. The morning was ushered in with ringing of bells: At sunrise, the forts and shipping displayed all their colours. Before noon, the detachment of his Majesty's troops posted here, under the command of Capt. Lewis Valentine Fyser; the Artillery company

> in a new and very genteel uniform, commanded by Capt. Owen Roberts; the Light-Infantry company, in their uniform; and the other companies of the Charles Town regiment of Militia, commanded by the honourable Colonel Bexie, were drawn up in different places, and marched to the Parade, where they made a handsome appearance, and were reviewed by his honour the Lieutenant-Governor, attended by his Council, the public Officers, &c. At noon, the cannon, &c. were fired as usual, and his Honour gave a most elegant entertainment at Mr. Dillon's, to a very numerous company, consisting of the Members of his Majesty's Council, and of the Assembly, the public officers, civil and military, the Clergy, &c., &c. The afternoon was spent in drinking the usual, with many other loyal and patriotic toasts, and the evening concluded with illuminations, &c.
>
> (*South Carolina Gazette* 6 June 1768: 3; for toasting as political claim making, see Epstein 1994: chap. 3)

Note the parallels with the fall's elections to the colonial assembly, when "mechanicks and other inhabitants of Charles Town" met at Liberty Point to choose candidates:

> This matter being settled, without the least animosity or irregularity, the company partook of a plain and hearty entertainment, that had been provided by some on which this assembly will reflect lasting honour. About 5 o'clock, they all removed to a most noble LIVE-OAK tree, in Mr. Mazyck's pasture, which they formally dedicated to LIBERTY, where many loyal, patriotic, and constitutional toasts were drank, beginning with the glorious *NINETY-TWO Anti-Rescinders of Massachusetts Bay*, and ending with, *Unanimity among the Members of our ensuing Assembly not to rescind from the said resolutions*, each succeeded by three huzzas. In the evening, the tree was decorated with 45 lights, and 45 sky-rockets were fired. About 8 o'clock, the whole company, preceded by 45 of their number, carrying as many lights, marched in regular procession to town, down King Street and Broad Street, to Mr. Robert Dillon's tavern; where the 45 lights being placed upon the table, with 45 bowls of punch, 45 bottles of wine, and 92 glasses, they spent a few hours in a new round of toasts, among which, scarce a celebrated Patriot of Britain or America was omitted; and preserving the same good order and regularity as had been observed throughout the day, at 10 they retired.
>
> (*South Carolina Gazette* 3 October 1768: 2)

In addition to its impressive capacity for alcohol, the Charleston electoral assembly's blend of political ingredients boggles the mind. In general form, it resembles the king's birthday, except for the notable absence of military and royal officials. But Charleston's Liberty Tree directly emulated its Boston model. The toast to ninety-two antirescinders (those members of the Massachusetts assembly who voted against withdrawing Samuel Adams's circular letter) identified the South Carolinians with Massachusetts patriots. The number forty-five, obviously, signaled the relevance of John Wilkes. Lighting up candles (in this case the procession rather than the city's windows) likewise enacted a public declaration of allegiance and solidarity.

As of 1768, opponents of arbitrary rule in London, Boston, and Charleston had not yet invented social movements. Nevertheless, their innovations moved popular public politics toward social movement forms. They enlisted ordinary citizens such as artisans and sailors in campaigns of sustained opposition to royal policies (in contrast to Boston's small merchants, Charleston's Sons of Liberty expanded from a volunteer fire company composed largely of artisans [Maier 1972: 85]). They combined special-purpose associations, public meetings, marches, petitions, pamphleteering, and statements widely reported in the public media. To some extent, they even adopted displays of WUNC. The *South Carolina Gazette* remarked on "the same good order and regularity as had been observed throughout the day."

Although the "mechanicks and other inhabitants" of Charleston remained quite capable of attacking royal officials, resisting customs agents, and sacking the houses of their designated enemies, at least on ceremonial occasions they abandoned direct action in favor of program, identity, and standing claims: we are upright people, we deserve a voice, and we oppose arbitrary rule with determination. In fact, Charleston's artisans "spearheaded" the city's anti-importation agreements in alliance with merchant-patriot Christopher Gadsden (Maier 1972: 116). Integration of popular forces into elite opposition campaigns split the ruling classes but took an important step toward the creation of the social movement as a distinct form of public politics.

Political and Economic Contexts

The social movement emerged in England and America against the background of profound political and economic changes. Four catchwords tag the essential changes: war, parliamentarization, capitalization, and proletarianization. As the influence of the Seven Years War has already suggested, war did not simply mobilize national populations; it also expanded state structures, inflated governmental expenditures, increased extraction of resources from the government's subject population, created new debt, and at least temporarily fortified the state's repressive apparatus. All of these factors were to influence the ways that both the emerging state and popular contention would emerge.

In North America, the aftermath of the Seven Years War weighed heavily, as the British stationed a peacetime army of 10,000 men, tightened control over customs, and imposed a series of revenue measures such as the Stamp Act of 1765. The Revolutionary War (as the struggle of 1775 onward came to be known across the thirteen rebellious colonies) cost the Americans incomparably more in personal services, money, and debt than had British impositions after the Seven Years War. The war effort created the thin national state structure that prevailed for decades. During the European wars of the French Revolution and Napoleon, the new United States first evaded, then abrogated, its treaty obligations to France, which had provided crucial aid to the American cause during the American Revolution.

The next major American involvement in Europe's war came with the Jefferson administration's 80-million-franc purchase of Louisiana from Napoleon's France (1803), which doubled the territory of the United States. With minor exceptions, the United States then kept its distance from the European war until 1812, spending its military strength pushing First Nations people, Native Americans, to the south and west. But in 1812 the Americans ended five years of uneasy negotiation by declaring war on Great Britain, invading Canada, battling Mohawks and other First Nations people allied with Britain, and conducting a series of maritime battles in the Great Lakes, the Atlantic, and the Gulf of Mexico. They also suffered the torching of Washington and the invasion of Maine before the European war ground to a halt in 1814.

Parliamentarization occurred more subtly than making war, but with no less effect on public politics. It had two related components: a general expansion of Parliament's power and a shift of national political struggles from the king and his clients toward a Parliament that was slightly more accountable to a narrow strata of men (Tilly 1997; Tilly and Wood 2003). War-driven taxation and debt increased parliamentary power; each governmental request for new funds initiated a struggle in which Parliament extracted new concessions. The extraction of wealth from distant colonies became increasingly attractive. As parliamentary power increased locally, Parliament intervened more broadly in public affairs, and the stakes of parliamentary actions for national constituencies (whether enfranchised or not) greatly increased. Consent of the population became more important—at least within the ruling region.

Capitalization occurred on both sides of the Atlantic, as agrarian, commercial, and industrial capital all greatly increased in scope. Great Britain was becoming the world's greatest center of manufacturing and trade, while its agricultural production increased dramatically in scale. Much of this wealth was rooted in slavery and the extraction of wealth from labor, land, and colonized peoples more generally. The older American colonies and their successor, the United States served chiefly as tributaries to the British economy, but they too experienced momentous agrarian, commercial, and industrial expansions after 1750, also tied to slavery. Although landlords certainly did well and manufacturers were beginning to make their marks, merchant capitalists in particular gained heft within the growing British and American economies (Drescher 2009).

By "proletarianization," let us understand not just the growth of routinized factory labor (although that did occur to an unprecedented extent) but more generally an increase in the proportion of the population depending on wage labor for survival (Marx 1847; Tilly 1984). In British agriculture, the concentration of landholding and leaseholding in few hands greatly increased the share of wage laborers among all cultivators. Proletarianization occurred even more rapidly in manufacturing, where self-employed artisans lost ground to wage-dependent workers in shops, factories, and their own households. The picture differed significantly in North America, where slaves performed an increasing proportion of all labor in southern agriculture; proletarianization resembling its British counterpart occurred in the coastal zones of commerce and manufacturing, but the expanding frontier provided abundant opportunities for smallholders and petty traders. Of course, this process was not a single one, but one complicated by gender, religious, racial, and ethnic categories (Castañeda 2018).

What connects war, parliamentarization, capitalization, and proletarianization, on one side, with the growth of social movements, on the other? To put complex matters very schematically:

- Mobilization and payment for war simultaneously increased the influence of governmental activity on ordinary people's welfare and engaged governmental agents in negotiation over the terms under which landlords, merchants, workers, soldiers, sailors, and others would contribute to the collective effort.
- Despite the fact that only a narrow set of people could vote, the shift of power toward Parliament meant that the impact of legislative actions on everyone's welfare greatly increased and that, because of parliamentary representation's geographic organization, everyone in Great Britain and the colonies acquired a more direct connection to the male elected legislators, who were taking consequential political actions.
- Although big landlords continued to dominate national politics, capitalization expanded the independent influence of merchants and financiers in London and elsewhere who increasingly became the government's creditors and managers of capital.
- These merchants and financiers built their increasing power and wealth partly through the exploitation of land and peoples in colonies outside of the arena of political bargaining.
- As many a social commentator feared, where proletarianization occurred, workers (especially male, Protestant workers in the British context) were less dependent on particular landlords, masters, and other patrons, and were thereby freer to enter political life on their own.
- In combination, these changes promoted contingent alliances between dissident aristocrats and bourgeois (who lacked the numbers for independent action against the bulk of ruling classes) and dissatisfied workers (who lacked the legal and social protection supplied by patrons).
- Such alliances, in their turn, facilitated appropriation and expansion of special-purpose associations, public meetings, petition campaigns, disciplined marches, and related forms of claim making by working-class and petit bourgeois activists while making it more difficult for authorities to maintain legal prohibitions of those activities when poor people engaged in them.
- Such alliances turned the same working-class and petit bourgeois activists away from direct action as a means of making claims.
- Joint actions of dissident aristocrats, radical bourgeois, indignant petit bourgeois, and workers thus created precedents and legal spaces for social movement actions, even when current campaigns and alliances ended.

Of course, these changes did not occur in an instant. Between the turbulent events of 1768 and the clear availability of social movement politics to a wide variety of actors on either side of the Atlantic, another half century of struggle and evolution elapsed.

On the British side, London provided the first major setting for social movement innovation. Growing from about 675,000 to 865,000 inhabitants between 1750 and 1800, London competed with Istanbul for the rank of largest European city and, thus, of earth's second-biggest metropolis (after Beijing). By that time, London had become Europe's greatest port, a vastly influential center of trade, and the world center of banking, housing the preeminent Bank of England. As Adam Smith put it in 1776:

> The stability of the Bank of England is equal to that of the British government. All that it has advanced to the public must be lost before its creditors can sustain any loss. No other banking company in England can be established by act of parliament, or can consist of more than six members. It acts, not only as an ordinary bank, but as a great engine of state. It receives and pays the greater part of the annuities which are due to the creditors of the public, it circulates exchequer bills, and it advances to government the annual amount of the land and malt taxes, which are frequently not paid up till some years thereafter.
>
> (Smith 1910: I, 284–85)

London's financiers had their fingers on the pulse (or their hands on the throat) of the entire British Empire.

Within London, however, financiers did not become radicals. On the contrary: the bourgeois who supported Wilkes and his radical successors were concentrated disproportionately among middling tradesmen (Rudé 1971: 172–77). These folks aligned themselves against both the court and great capitalists, whom they portrayed as coconspirators against the public good. Their popular backers, in turn, came especially from workers in London's better organized trades: the sailors, coal heavers, and silk weavers we have already seen in action, but also a host of other artisans and clerks.

Not that all London workers supported radical causes; the thousands mobilized by Lord George Gordon's anti-Catholic Protestant Association in 1780, for example, also seem to have come chiefly from the London working classes. Members of the Protestant Association first marched with Lord Gordon to Parliament for presentation of a petition for repeal of a 1778 act that had made minor concessions to Catholic rights, then (on parliamentary refusal to negotiate under pressure) broke into groups, some of which went on to sack Catholic chapels, houses of prominent Catholics, and houses of officials reputed to be protecting Catholics. Of those apprehended and prosecuted for participating in attacks on Catholic properties, "two in every three of those tried were wage-earners, journeymen, apprentices, waiters, domestic servants and labourers; a smaller number were petty employers, craftsmen and tradesmen" (Rudé 1971: 226). Broadly speaking, nevertheless, London's major mobilizations of the later eighteenth century pitted worker–bourgeois alliances against coalitions of finance and court, with a dissident segment of Parliament typically aligned against the court.

As the Protestant Association's temporary prominence suggests, mass-membership associations figured ever more centrally in British popular mobilizations. The eighteenth century's greatest surge of associational activity occurred during the early years of the French Revolution. During those years, elite demands for parliamentary reform that had been active for two decades coupled with popular demands for democratization in the French style, both based in clubs, societies, and popular associations as well as religious congregations. Revolutionary societies, constitutional societies, and corresponding societies took the French Revolution, the American Revolution, and Britain's own Glorious Revolution of 1689 as their points of reference. Defenders of church and king likewise mobilized against secular democrats by means of specialized associations. From 1794 to the end of the Napoleonic Wars, governmental repression damped down associational activity, especially on the part of workers. Associations returned in a great burst after war's end. By that time, with the prominent exception of still-illegal workers' "combinations," associations and their public meetings had become standard means of popular expression.

Crystallization of the British Social Movement

At what point, then, can we reasonably say that the social movement had become a distinctive, connected, recognized, and widely available form of public politics? We are looking for times and places in which people making collective claims on authorities frequently form special-purpose associations or named coalitions; hold public meetings; communicate their programs to available media; stage processions, rallies, or demonstrations; and through all these activities make concerted public displays of worthiness, unity, numbers, and commitment. If the complex occurs together regularly outside of electoral campaigns and management–labor struggles, we will be more confident that the social movement has arrived on its own terms. We recognize all the individual elements in British public politics of the later eighteenth century. But by these standards British politics did not institutionalize social movements until late in the Napoleonic Wars.

In Britain, those late war years proved crucial. From about 1812 onward, nationwide campaigns arose for parliamentary reform: broadened franchise, more equal representation of electors, annual meetings of Parliament, and often further refinements, such as secret ballots and MP stipends that would make officeholding possible for poorer men. At the same time, and in overlapping efforts, unprecedented energy went into organizing workers to demand parliamentary action on their behalf. They coupled with demands for peace after a long, costly, disruptive war. In a Bristol by-election of 1812, radical Henry Hunt lost badly because most of his support came from disfranchised workers who marched in huge crowds to the cry "Hunt and Peace" behind a loaf of bread on a pole and Cap of Liberty, cheered his stentorian harangues, assailed anyone wearing blue with a volley of mud, stones and dead cats, and attacked the White Lion (headquarters of the Loyal and Constitutional Club) and Council House. Troops were called to restore order.

(Prothero 1979: 82)

Figure 2.1 Discrediting Cartoon of Wilkes by William Hogarth 1763

By 1812 the Liberty Cap, derived from the headgear that Romans placed on the head of an emancipated slave, had a long iconic history in Great Britain. Borrowed from the Dutch as William of Orange became the English king in the Glorious Revolution of 1688–1689, it had represented Dutch liberation from Spain. In Britain, it came to signify liberty in the Wilkite sense of free speech and religious freedom (Epstein 1994: 78–80). In fact, during the Wilkite agitation of the 1760s, William Hogarth produced a famous drawing of the "mad and ugly" Wilkes with a crossed-eyed look holding a pole topped by a Liberty Cap.

In the nineteenth century's early decades, marches with Liberty Caps did not get radicals elected. But they did dramatize popular support for radical programs. Since officials often refused authorization for popular reformers to meet in public buildings, assemblies repeatedly took place on the streets or in open fields. They thus became half meetings, half demonstrations. What is more, delegations frequently marched to the place of assembly, thus linking the twinned forms of the demonstration: the street march and the disciplined assembly in a public space. Although London continued to play a significant role, greater innovations occurred in England's northern industrial districts, where workers organized and acted energetically during the postwar years.

In the cotton manufacturing center of Stockport, the formation of the Stockport Union for the Promotion of Human Happiness in October 1818 helped mobilize people of the industrial North on behalf of relief for political prisoners as well as on behalf of parliamentary reform. The Seditious Meetings Act of 1817 had forbidden closed meetings that planned direct efforts to influence the government. But it tolerated open public meetings to express support for parliamentary reform. The Stockport Union pioneered popular political organizers' response to the new repressive context, becoming the model for political unions all over the country, including London.

The Stockport Union sponsored repeated reform meetings, organized petitions for political prisoners, issued remonstrances, and staged demonstrations. The union sent a delegation of some 1,400 men and 40 women marching in ranks with banners to the famous reform meeting of August 16, 1819 at St. Peter's Fields, Manchester, a meeting attacked by the Manchester and Salford Yeomanry (the incident was thenceforth infamous as Peterloo). Of the delegation's march, Manchester merchant Francis Philips reported:

> On the 16th August I went on the Stockport Road about eleven or a little after, and I met a great number of persons advancing toward Manchester with all the regularity of a regiment, only they had no uniform. They were all marching in file, principally three abreast. They had two banners with them. There were persons by the side, acting as officers and regulating the files. The order was beautiful indeed.
>
> (Glen 1984: 245)

Particular organizations such as the Stockport Union rose and fell with the times and continued to face governmental surveillance or outright repression.

Threatened governments tried repeatedly to squelch organizational activity through such acts as the Coercion and Seditious Meetings Acts of 1817, the broadly repressive Six Acts of 1819, and the Malicious Trespass Act of 1820. But dissident organizations and their parliamentary allies fought back. Sometimes they actually won. In 1824, for example, Parliament conceded ground by repealing the Combination Laws that it had enacted in 1799 to suppress workers' associations; it thereby partially legalized public activity by trade unions. The relaxation of repression promoted social movement activity. By the later 1820s, all the essential elements of social movements—campaigns, repertoires, and public WUNC displays—had cohered and become widely available to organized interests in Great Britain.

Vast, effective mobilizations of the 1820s and 1830s for workers' rights, Catholic emancipation, and parliamentary reform locked those elements in place (Belchem 1990: 73–144; Tilly 1995: 240–339). In the process, the social movement repertoire separated increasingly from older forms of signaling support or opposition such as forced illuminations, Rough Music, serenades, and the sacking of houses. By the 1830s, furthermore, social movement strategies had become available not only to reformers and radicals but also to conservative activists. Conservative users of social movement tactics included the widely influential, if ultimately unsuccessful, English opponents of Catholic emancipation (Hinde 1992; O'Ferrall 1985; Tilly 2004: 149–56).

Social Movements Nevertheless?

In 1925, leading American historian J. Franklin Jameson devoted an influential lecture series to "The American Revolution Considered as a Social Movement." As celebrations of the 150th anniversary of the revolution were beginning, Jameson called for students of the American Revolution to emulate specialists in the French Revolution by expanding from political and military history to social history. He argued that

> The stream of revolution could not be confined within narrow banks, but spread abroad upon the land. Many economic desires, many social aspirations were set free by the political struggle, many aspects of colonial society profoundly altered by the forces thus let loose. The relations of social classes to each other, the institution of slavery, the system of land-holding, the course of business, the forms and spirit of the intellectual and religious life, all felt the transforming hand of revolution, all emerged from under it in shapes advanced many degrees nearer to those we know.
>
> (Jameson 1956: 9)

He closed his lectures with his major claim: "that all the varied activities of men in the same country and period have intimate relations with each other, and that one cannot obtain a satisfactory view of any one of them by considering it apart from the others" (Jameson 1956: 100). For Jameson, it turns out, "social movement" equaled large-scale social transformation rather than a specific form of politics. As our earlier looks at Boston and Charleston might lead us to expect, Jameson drew attention away from the heroic leaders and dramatic moments of revolutionary action to the broad participation of colonists in the struggles of 1765 to 1783. But he did not make the case for the revolution as a social movement in the narrower historical meaning of the term.

Might we nevertheless claim the American Revolution as a social movement or a series of social movements? Considering the same period, we have examined in London and Boston, Sidney Tarrow points to innovations in political actions: amid the burning of effigies and sacking of houses, the organization of boycotts and nonimportation agreements signaled the creation of "modular" forms of politics that could easily migrate from place to place, group to group, issue to issue:

> Thenceforth, nonimportation and boycotting became the modular weapons of the American rebellion, employed most clamorously in the controversy over tea in Boston harbor. The effectiveness of the tactic was not lost on Britain: in 1791, the English antislavery association used a boycott on the importation of sugar from the West Indies to put pressure on Parliament to abolish the slave trade. From a parochial response to new taxes from the periphery of the British Empire, the boycott had migrated to its core.
>
> (Tarrow 1998: 38)

Tarrow rightly identifies the invention of quick-moving modular tactics as a hallmark of social movement activity and as a significant contrast with the more parochial attachments to local settings involved in Rough Music, effigy burning, and house sacking. But does the emergence of modular tactics qualify the American Revolution as a social movement?

We are still looking for times and places in which people making collective claims on authorities frequently form special-purpose associations or named coalitions; hold public meetings; communicate their programs to available media; stage processions, rallies, or demonstrations; and through all these activities make concerted displays of worthiness, unity, numbers, and commitment. As in Great Britain during the same period, the answer is clear: all the individual elements existed in the new United States of 1783, but they had not yet congealed into a distinctive, widely available form of popular politics. In Great Britain, the proliferation of interconnected associations from 1765 onward transformed popular politics and laid the basis for emergence of full-fledged social movements. But it still took decades before the full social movement apparatus became widely available to popular claimants.

Might antislavery mobilization, as Tarrow hints, constitute a crucial exception? During the 1770s and 1780s, jurists in both Great Britain and North America began to deliver rulings that challenged the legality of slavery. The Vermont constitution of 1777 banned slavery, while between 1780 and 1784,

Pennsylvania, Massachusetts, Rhode Island, and Connecticut took legal steps toward general emancipation. (New York did not join the move toward general emancipation until 1799, however, and blanket freeing of slaves did not occur there until 1827.) In both Great Britain and the American colonies, organized Quakers were creating antislavery associations during the 1770s. In fact, Friends congregations on both sides of the Atlantic were then expelling members who refused to free their own slaves.

In 1783, English Quakers sent Parliament its first (but by no means its last) petition for abolition of the slave trade. Britain's nationwide campaigns against the slave trade began, however, in 1787, with mass petitioning and formation of the Society for the Abolition of the Slave Trade. At that point, antislavery organizers worked chiefly within Quaker and Evangelical congregations; church services therefore overlapped with petition-generating meetings (Davis 1987; Drescher 1982, 1986; Temperley 1981; Walvin 1980, 1981). The initiative did not come from London but from the industrial North, especially Manchester. The 11,000 signatures on the Manchester petition of December 1787 represented something like two-thirds of all the city's men who were eligible to sign (Drescher 1986: 70). As Tarrow says, furthermore, antislavery activists introduced another weighty innovation: a general boycott of sugar grown with the labor of slaves, with perhaps 300,000 families participating in 1791 and 1792 (Drescher 1986: 79).

New petition drives surged from 1806 to 1808, in the midst of which both Great Britain (or, rather, the United Kingdom, which had formally joined Ireland with England, Wales, and Scotland in 1801) and the United States outlawed the slave trade. In 1833, after multiple mobilizations, Parliament finally passed an emancipation act applicable throughout its colonies. The United States remained fiercely divided on the issue of slavery. Yet by the 1830s, abolition had become the crux of a vast American social movement as well. Where in this sequence might we reasonably say that full-fledged social movements were flying?

We face a classic half-full/half-empty question. Somewhere between the Manchester petition of 1787 and the 1833 parliamentary banning of slavery in the British Empire, the full panoply of campaign, repertoire, and WUNC displays came together. When did it happen? Let us split the question into two parts: When did antislavery meet all the tests for a genuine social movement? When did the political form represented by antislavery become widely available for other sorts of claims? To the first part, we may reply that sometime between 1791 (the sugar boycott) and 1806 (the second great petition drive), British abolitionists assembled campaign, repertoire, and WUNC displays into a single political package; they thus have some claim to constitute the world's first social movement (Walsh-Russo 2017).

For the antislavery to become a model, however, we must allow another decade to elapse. On models drawn quite directly from antislavery, we then find workers, reformers, Catholics, and others regularly forming special-purpose associations, holding public meetings indoors and outdoors, adopting slogans and badges, staging marches, producing pamphlets, and projecting claims with regard to programs, identities, and political relations. For such a complex and momentous change, the quarter century from 1791 to 1816 looks like a very rapid transition indeed.

Might Francophiles then make a case for French priority? As the Revolution of 1789 proceeded, French activists certainly formed politically oriented associations at a feverish pace, made concerted claims by means of those associations, held public meetings, marched through the streets, adopted slogans and badges, produced pamphlets, and implemented local revolutions through most of the country (Hunt 1978, 1984; Jones 2003; McPhee 1988; Markoff 1996a; Woloch 1970, 1994). If such mobilizations had continued past 1795 *and* if they had become available for a wide variety of claims thereafter, we would probably hail the French as inventors of the social movement—or at least coinventors with their British counterparts. As it happened, however, the full array of social movement claim making did not acquire durable political standing in France for another half century, around the Revolution of 1848 (Tilly 1986: chap. 9). Even then, repression under Louis Napoleon's Second Empire delayed the full implementation of social movement politics through much of the country for another two decades.

More unexpectedly, Dutch eighteenth-century activists might also have some claim to have institutionalized social movements, at least temporarily. In what Dutch historians call the Fourth English War (1780–1784), Dutch forces joined indirectly in the wars of the American Revolution, taking a severe beating from superior British naval power. As the disastrous naval engagements continued, a sort of pamphlet war broke out within the Netherlands. Supporters of the Prince of Orange attacked the leaders of Amsterdam and its province Holland as the opposing Dutch patriots replied in kind; each blamed the other for the country's parlous condition. Drawing explicitly on the American example, patriots called for a (preferably peaceful) revolution. Earlier claim making in the Low Countries conformed to local variants of the older repertoire we have already seen operating in England and America (Dekker 1982, 1987; van Honacker 1994, 2000). But during the 1780s, petition campaigns began in earnest: first demanding recognition of John Adams as a legal representative of that contested entity, the United States of America, then proposing remedies to a whole series of domestic political problems.

Citizens' committees (possibly modeled on American committees of correspondence) soon began to form along with citizens' militias across Holland's towns. In a highly segmented political system, their incessant pressure on local and regional authorities actually worked. Between 1784 and 1787, patriot factions managed to install new, less aristocratic constitutions in a number of Dutch cities and even in a whole province, Overijssel. The Prince of Orange and his followers, however, still disposed of two crucial advantages: British financial support and military backing from the prince's brother-in-law, King Frederick William of Prussia. Late in 1787, a Prussian invasion broke the Netherlands' Patriot Revolution (te Brake 1989, 1990; Schama 1977).

As the French Revolution began nearby, those Dutch patriots who had not fled their country hoped, conspired, and even (late in 1794) made a poorly coordinated attempt at a coup. The next invading army arrived in January 1795, when French revolutionary forces established a Batavian Republic with active support from revived patriots. (Liberty Trees went up in Leiden and Amsterdam (Schama 1977: 194).) Despite governmental alterations on a French model, the new republic soon deadlocked between advocates of centralizing reforms in the French style and the customary federalism of the Netherlands. From 1798 to 1805, a quartet of faction-backed coups—unaccompanied by widespread popular mobilization—produced the major political changes. The republic gave way to a French satellite Kingdom of Holland (1806), then to direct incorporation into France (1810–1813).

The post-Napoleonic settlement created a bifurcated kingdom that until 1839 nominally included both the Netherlands and what became Belgium. From the French takeover onward, the Dutch state assumed a much more centralized administrative structure than had prevailed in the heyday of autonomous provinces. With the Batavian Republic of 1795, committees, militias, and patriots returned temporarily to power, only to be integrated rapidly into the new sort of regime, with French overseers never far away. Recognizable social movements did not start occurring widely in the Netherlands until after Napoleon's fall. Thus counterrevolution, reaction, and conquest wiped out another possible candidate for the social movement's inventor. Great Britain retains priority, in close interaction with its American colonies.

Arguments Revisited

With some solid history in hand, we can now revisit this book's organizing arguments to see where they are taking us. Here they are:

From their eighteenth-century origins onward, social movements have proceeded not as solo performances but as interactive campaigns. The tales of Britain and America we have reviewed leave little doubt that social movements emerged out of struggle engaging many parties, with each campaign centering on the repeated efforts of a shifting coalition to achieve a relatively well-defined set of political changes. At least in the early stages of social movements, coalitions between elite political figures (who enjoyed a degree of protection for their claims) and relatively organized segments of the working classes (who had the benefits of numbers, internal connections, and local grounding) played an exceptional part.

Social movements combine three kinds of claims: program, identity, and standing. The struggles we have witnessed always featured programs of political change, but they also included claims that the proponents of those programs enjoyed the capacity for autonomous, effective action and that participants had the political standing to speak publicly on the issues at hand. (So far, we have not yet encountered claims that others be *excluded* from political standing, but we will.) In the transition from the eighteenth to the nineteenth century, we see emerging a durable combination of the three sorts of claims in public meetings, petition drives, public declarations, demonstrations, and shared symbols of membership.

The relative salience of program, identity, and standing claims varies significantly among social movements, among claimants within movements, and among phases of movements. We have not yet examined enough variation among social movements to establish this argument conclusively. Yet we have already glimpsed the alternation between (1) supporting relief or parliamentary reform in British workers' movements after the Napoleonic Wars; (2) asserting that organized workers constitute a formidable, worthy force; and (3) complaining that they occupy an unduly marginal position within the regime.

Democratization promotes the formation of social movements. This part of our analysis has barely begun. Still, the American and British experiences, plus the aborted experiments of France and the Netherlands, establish a plausible correspondence between democratization and proliferation of social movements. These histories identify, moreover, significant connections of social movement operation with parliamentarization of public politics and with the rise of consequential, contested elections. The finer causal connections in both directions, however, remain open for exploration.

Social movements are most likely to emerge where parliaments must negotiate with local populations. In contrast, where economic growth and capital extraction can occur without such negotiation, as in the colonial contexts of slavery or serf labor, the ruling regime is likely to face other forms of contentious politics such as rebellions or coups.

Social movements assert popular sovereignty. The cases we've looked at also show how such assertions raise acute political issues: Who has the right to speak for the people? Does the right to speak include the right to attack the governing regime? When does the interest of public order override that right? Far more so than retaliatory rituals, popular rebellions, or even contested elections, social movements place these questions of rights at the center of popular politics. Through their often grudging toleration of the new synthesis among campaigns, repertoires, and WUNC displays, British and American authorities made themselves vulnerable to the claim that their critics, rather than they, genuinely spoke for the people.

As compared with locally grounded forms of popular politics, social movements depend heavily on political entrepreneurs for their scale, durability, and effectiveness. Rough Music or riding someone out of town on a rail could begin with little more than street corner encounters of local youths. Abolitionism, in contrast, could have gone nowhere without the religious officials, congregational leaders, and legislators who kept the issue in the press, constructed links between local groups of activists, planned public meetings, organized petition drives, and injected the issue of slavery into electoral campaigns. During the 1760s, London's John Wilkes and his lieutenants (as well as Boston's Samuel Adams and his confederates) pioneered major components of social movement claim making. But they still lacked the knowledge of campaigns, performances, and WUNC displays that British (and American) political entrepreneurs took for granted fifty or sixty years later.

Once social movements establish themselves in one political setting, modeling, communication, and collaboration facilitate their adoption in other connected settings. We have already noticed the generalization of social movement strategies across sectors in North America and, especially, the British Isles. We have also seen some precursors of international facilitation and collaboration in America, Britain, the Netherlands, and France; each borrowed some social movement innovations from at least one of the others. Antislavery in particular soon became an international undertaking (Walsh-Russo 2017). But the nineteenth century would bring far more extensive international facilitation of social movements, for example in the support lent to Ireland's anti-British activists by emigrants and sympathizers in England and America (Hanagan 1998).

The forms, personnel, and claims of social movements vary and evolve historically. This is perhaps the main conclusion our preliminary review of European and North American histories authorizes. Whatever else we see in struggles between 1765 and the 1830s, it certainly includes substantial variation and continuous evolution. As we have yet to see in detail, social movement claim making originated in challenges to national authorities, but it soon came into use not only in expressions of support for such authorities but also in claims on other authorities such as local elites, religious leaders, and capitalists. We are dealing with a political phenomenon deeply embedded in regional and national histories.

The social movement, as an invented institution, could disappear or mutate into some quite different form of politics. The point follows in principle from the previous arguments. We might even stretch our observations of reversals in France and the Netherlands into evidence that the elements of social movements need not endure forever and, indeed, prove vulnerable to authoritarian repression. As we will abundantly see later, the recent proliferation of international connections among activists may be creating new forms of bottom-up politics only vaguely resembling those we have encountered during the social movement's first half century. Still, we need a good deal more analysis before deciding what conditions are crucial, and what conditions fatal, for the survival of social movements. The next chapter's survey of the nineteenth century will advance that inquiry.

Note

1 Lesley Wood and Ernesto Castañeda edited this chapter, updating the language and citations.

3

NINETEENTH-CENTURY ADVENTURES

Charles Tilly[1]

On February 25, 1848, news of yet another French revolution, started in Paris on the previous day, reached Lyon. Several hundred weavers marched down into the city center from the silk-producing quarter of Croix-Rousse. Singing "La Marseillaise," they proceeded along the Rhône River, then crossed the city's central island to the Place des Terreaux and the Lyon city hall. Overwhelmed by the crowd, the military on hand asked the acting mayor to declare the republic from a city hall balcony. After he did so, members of the gathering entered the hall and chose an executive committee consisting of weavers plus a minority of bourgeois republicans. During the preceding July Monarchy (1830–1848), organized silk weavers had missed few opportunities to show their strength by marching in funerals and on authorized holidays. During insurrections of 1831 and 1834, they had also marched. But outside of crises and authorized public assemblies, they had until then generally avoided anything like the self-initiated parade of February 1848, if only because royal officials could take the very fact of their organized assembly as evidence that they were visibly violating the legal ban on workers' *coalitions*.

As the revolutionary regime settled into place, popular militias emerged from the organizations of workers and revolutionaries that had lurked in Lyon's political shadows. Political associations likewise multiplied, some of them new and some of them simply transforming clandestine cells or informal drinking clubs into legal entities. They often staged patriotic ceremonies that included the planting of Liberty Trees. Despite efforts of an increasingly conservative national government to restrain Lyon's radicals, militias and clubs assembled and marched through the city streets repeatedly between the February Revolution of 1848 and Louis Napoleon's coup d'état of December 1851. In its issue of March 14, 1848, for example, Lyon's left-wing newspaper *Tribun du peuple* reported:

> With four men carrying the liberty cap, a numerous troop of citizens crossed the city on the 12th. Following that holy emblem of our deliverance, the cortege marched in two files. Toward the middle, an equally significant emblem attracted great attention. It was a man bound with rough ropes held by citizens forming a square around him. He carried a pathetic faded flag hung with black crepe; it was the white flag, carried almost horizontally and poorly attached to its pole, resembling the coffin of a miserable criminal on his way out, to everyone's great satisfaction.
>
> (Robert 1996: 86)

The red cap stood for revolution, the white flag for legitimacy, the claim of the elder Bourbon branch (which had returned to power after Napoleon's defeat, but lost out in the revolution of 1830) to rule France. Within two weeks of the Parisian revolution, Lyon's citizens were regularly mounting or watching street demonstrations. Furthermore, demonstrators enacted the worthiness, unity, numbers, and commitment—the WUNC—of their cause by using widely recognized national symbols.

As of March 1848, then, had Lyon and France installed the social movement as a regular vehicle of popular politics? The question turns out to be both interesting and controversial. We must look closely at 1848 to determine whether the combination of campaign, repertoire, and WUNC displays had become readily available to a wide range of claimants. The best answer is yes, but only temporarily.

Speaking specifically of the demonstration rather than of the entire social movement apparatus, Lyon's historian Vincent Robert argues that despite a flurry of demonstrations under the Second Republic (1848–1851), demonstrations did not really become readily available ways of pressing collective claims until the great May Day mobilizations of the 1890s put them on the map. (Warning: the word *manifestation*, which Robert employs and which I am translating as "demonstration," did not actually displace such words as *cortège*, *défilé*, *démonstration*, and *rassemblement* in common French usage until after World War II (Pigenet and Tartakowsky 2003: 84).) Authorities themselves did not publicly recognize demonstrations as valid forms of political action, according to Robert, until just before World War I. At that point, Lyon's authorities began assigning police to protect and oversee demonstrations instead of routinely breaking them up as illegal assemblies.

Yet Robert recognizes protodemonstrations in Lyon as early as 1831. On January 19 of that year, some 1,400 workers assembled across the Saône River from Lyon's center and marched to shouts of "work or bread"; the authorities eventually arrested 15 participants (Rude 1969: 198–202). Further demonstrations occurred on February 12 (this time with a black flag of insurrection) and on October 25 (with about 6,000 participants) before the full-scale insurrection that began with a massive demonstration then took over the city from November 21 to 24 (Rude 1969: 208, 316, 357–596). In partial collaboration with Parisian rebels, Lyon's silk workers mounted another major insurrection in 1834. At least among Lyon's silk workers, demonstrations had already laid down a significant political history before the revolution of 1848. From that point forward, they occurred more frequently in times of relaxed repression or democratization, but still receded when governmental repression tightened again.

At least eight demonstrations crossed Lyon during the first month of the 1848 revolution. During March and April, the Central Democratic Club organized major demonstrations on behalf of radical democracy (Robert 1996: 94–100). Soon women's groups, political clubs, veterans of Napoleonic armies, schoolchildren, workers from the national workshops set up to combat unemployment were demonstrating in Lyon. Most of their demonstrations displayed solidarity with the new regime combined with statements of particular demands. They made *program*, *identity*, and *standing claims*, insisting that their participants and the people they represented had the right to public voice.

However, popular street marches and assemblies ceased under the weight of repression; for about fifteen years, demonstrations disappeared. During the later years of Louis Napoleon's Second Empire, a time of rapid industrialization in France, the regime began to relax some of its controls over workers' organizations and actions. In 1864, the empire granted a limited right to strike. In 1868, it became legal for workers to hold public meetings without prior authorization from the government. Later the same year an imperial edict permitted trade unions to organize, so long as they had their rules approved by authorities, deposited minutes of their meetings with the authorities, and allowed police observers to attend.

Backed by partial legality, Lyon's workers' demonstrations reappeared in abundance during the Second Empire's crisis year, 1870. As the police agent in charge of the Jardin des Plantes station reported on April 30:

> Yesterday evening a band of about two hundred people came down from the Croix-Rousse into my quarter, led by an improvised master of ceremonies who carried a stave and who preceded four torch-bearers with a sixteen-year-old carrying a red flag. . . . Of these individuals, who seemed to range from fourteen to twenty-five years of age, two-thirds were carrying staves. They sang the Marseillaise, the song of the Girondins, and then to the melody of the Lampions "Down with the Emperor! Long live the Republic!" On each side of the sidewalk, the band was followed by about thirty individuals thirty to forty-five years old who appeared to be workers and who seemed to be serving as protection. (Robert 1996: 168–69; the Lampion, literally a torch, comes from the name of an older revolutionary song including a three-beat chant on a single note.)

Between April and the new revolution of September 4, 1870, authorities and demonstrators played cat and mouse in Lyon.

A red flag of revolution flew at the Lyon city hall from September into the spring. The city established its own version of a radical, autonomous commune, which government forces crushed brutally in April 1871 (Aminzade 1993; Gaillard 1971; Greenberg 1971). Demonstrations reappeared during the new revolutionary interval, although at a slower pace than in 1848. Once the Third Republic's authorities restored top-down order, nevertheless, for two more decades Lyon's demonstrations consisted chiefly of adaptations within other sorts of events: anticlerical funerals, local celebrations of Bastille Day, official ceremonies, religious processions, and workers' delegations to municipal or state authorities. Legalization of trade unions in 1884 did not change the situation fundamentally. Only with the expansion of voluntary associations during the later 1880s did demonstrations again assume prominence in Lyon's public life.

As it did elsewhere in France (Tilly 1986: 313–19), May Day 1890 inaugurated a great series of annual workers' demonstrations in Lyon; perhaps 15,000 workers came out for that first great international display of workers' solidarity (Robert 1996: 270). In addition to workers, during the next two decades, many more groups demonstrated in Lyon: Catholics, anti-Catholics, anti-Semites, and many more, increasingly in cadence and coordination with national social movements. As Robert puts it, by World War I "the demonstration had become a normal form of urban political life, and a significant element in political life at large; even though the organization of a march depended on official permission, by then the authorities knew that it would be more dangerous to forbid than to authorize and that barring accidents it would occur peacefully" (Robert 1996: 373). Robert chooses to state his conclusion as a challenge to my own dating of repertoire changes in France. But in fact we agree: around the 1848 revolution, many of the older forms of public claim making began a rapid decline across the country, while for a privileged year or so the demonstration became a standard way of supporting programs, projecting identities, and claiming political standing in France.

After the revolution of 1848, it took another half century of alternation between relatively repressive and relatively permissive regimes for the demonstration to acquire the widespread availability it retained until the German conquest of 1940 and then regained with a vengeance after the Liberation of 1944–1945 (Duyvendak 1994; Fillieule 1997a; Tartakowsky 1997; Tilly 2003: 207–13). But that was also true for other components of social movements: formation of special-purpose associations and coalitions, organization of claim-making public meetings, multiplication of WUNC displays, packaging of these and other elements into sustained public campaigns. With these qualifications, we can date France's establishment of social movements as widely available forms of popular politics during the nineteenth century's final decades.

Meetings and Demonstrations in Belgium

What about France's neighbor, Belgium? Belgian historian Gita Deneckere has assembled a catalog of "collective actions" in Antwerp, Brussels, Ghent, and Liège spanning 1831 to 1918 from a wide range of archives, official publications, periodicals, and historical works. Her catalog includes about 440 occasions on which people gathered and made collective demands "in the socioeconomic field of conflict," which means largely workers' actions and actions concerning work

(Deneckere 1997: 10). Deneckere's narratives actually overflow the definition, however, since they include such events as patriotic resistance to the creation of a separate Grand Duchy of Luxembourg as part of Belgium's independence settlement of 1838–1839 (Deneckere 1997: 66–68).

Deneckere's selection principle still excludes widespread violence surrounding the Netherlands' separation of church and state in 1834, just as the uneasy union of north and south was breaking up, which eventually led to the Belgian Revolution. Similarly, it omits extensive struggles over relations between church and state between 1879 and 1884. Intense competition between organized French and Dutch speakers over language rights and political power likewise casts only faint shadows over Deneckere's chronology of collective actions (Carter 2003; Zolberg 1978). Nevertheless, within Deneckere's chosen field, her evidence demonstrates a great increase in performances attached to the social movement repertoire.

Deneckere's evidence reveals significant alterations in Belgian forms of contention between 1830 and 1900. Before the semirevolutionary mobilizations of 1847–1848, Deneckere's contentious events feature workers' assemblies and marches to present petitions, attacks on the goods or persons of high-priced food merchants, and work stoppages by people in multiple shops of the same craft. During the earlier nineteenth century, few junctions formed between ardent democrats and workers. As Deneckere puts it:

> The case for a new collective action repertoire had little appeal to workers before 1848. Concerted [radical] efforts to create a workers' movement that matched the structure of the young Belgian state had no effect whatsoever. Radical democrats received little or no response from workers. Nowhere did genuine labor leaders break with the organizational templates they already had in their hands.
>
> (Deneckere 1997: 68)

Workers' actions then frequently took the form of turnouts: occasions on which a small number of initiators from a local craft went from shop to shop demanding that fellow craft workers leave their employment to join the swelling crowd. The round completed, turnout participants assembled in some safe place (often a field at the edge of town), aired their grievances, formulated demands, and presented those demands to masters in the trade (often through a meeting of delegations from both sides), staying away from work until the masters had replied satisfactorily or forced them to return. Before 1848, we see little of the social movement repertoire in play.

Immediately after the outbreak of the 1848 revolution in France, Belgian republicans and radicals began calling for a fraternal revolution in their own country. But the government reacted quickly by, among other measures, expelling Karl Marx from the country on March 4, 1848. By the time of Marx's hasty exit, the liberal-dominated Belgian government had already taken steps to forestall revolutionary mobilization in Belgium. It did so chiefly by reducing wealth requirements for voting and officeholding, nearly doubling the Belgian franchise. The split between French and Dutch speakers in Belgium worked to the government's advantage because republicans and advocates of the French model came disproportionately from among the Francophones. This was a fact that raised doubts about democratic programs on the Flemish side, which was ever wary of plots to incorporate Belgium into France (Dumont 2002: chap. 3).

Between the political reforms of 1848 and the 1890s, the character of Belgian contention, as registered in Deneckere's catalog, altered considerably. For example, turnouts practically disappeared, as demonstrations and large-firm strikes became much more frequent and prominent. In the 1890s, regionally and nationally coordinated general strikes emerged as major forms of contentious action. Deneckere's catalog also reveals a significant shift during the later decades of the nineteenth century toward the demonstration as a site of public claim making. Crude counts from the catalog of Belgian public meetings, demonstrations, and petitions by decade indicate the extent of change. Table 3.1 presents the counts.

Working-class organizations lay behind a great many of the meetings, demonstrations, and petitions. Petition delegations soon disappeared as ways of making public claims, in favor of autonomously organized meetings and, especially, demonstrations. (The decline of public meetings results in part from an illusion: Belgian demonstrations often started from or included public meetings, but this tabulation accepts Deneckere's designation of a gathering as mainly meeting or mainly demonstration.) Organized workers increasingly made international connections: we first encounter the International Workingmen's Association in action, for example, during a Ghent demonstration of 1876.

Many of the later demonstrations occurred in the course of attempts to organize general strikes. As Deneckere says, workers and socialist leaders designed general strikes to be large, standard in form, coordinated across multiple localities, and oriented toward national holders of power. Participants commonly represented themselves generally as socialists or as workers at large, instead of emphasizing particular localities and trades as was previously common. Belgian workers began making nationwide program claims for socialism at large, identity claims as coherently connected workers, and standing claims that emphasized their improper exclusion from power. These new actions signaled a significant shift of repertoire. To our alerted eyes, they offer evidence that social movements established themselves in Belgian popular politics between 1848 and 1900.

Deneckere sees increasingly tight interdependence between popular contention and national politics. In the 1890s

> the correspondence between successive socialist mass actions and the parliamentary breakthrough to universal suffrage is too striking for anyone to miss the causal connection. On the basis of published and unpublished correspondence from ruling circles one can conclude that the general strike had a genuine impact, in fact more significant than contemporary socialists themselves realized. Time after time socialist workers' protests confronted power-holders with a revolutionary threat that laid the foundation for abrupt expansion of democracy.
>
> (Deneckere 1997: 384)

Table 3.1 Meetings, Demonstrations, and Petitions in Belgium, 1831–1900

Decade	Meetings	Demonstrations	Petitions
1831–1840	4	2	7
1841–1850	0	1	3
1851–1860	2	0	0
1861–1870	1	3	0
1871–1880	1	11	0
1881–1890	0	59	0
1891–1900	2	57	0

Source: Compiled from Deneckere 1997: 403–11.

Thus in Belgium, as in France, street politics and parliamentary politics came to depend on each other. Social movements provided a significant portion of the connective tissue between an increasingly relevant parliament and disenfranchised groups and popular concerns.

The history of the demonstration in France and Belgium, then, tracks the more general institutionalization of social movements in French and Belgian public politics. Over the nineteenth century, public demonstrations happened widely in Western democratizing countries and within a few colonies of those countries as well. With its eighteenth-century head start, Great Britain institutionalized demonstrations and other social movement performances (as seen in Chapter 2) well ahead of France and Belgium (Prothero 1997: 202–29). By the early nineteenth century, the public holidays, funerals, and other authorized assemblies that continued to attract French and Belgian political critics and claimants well into the century lost much of their appeal for British, Canadian, and U.S. claim makers. Elections were different, however: with an expanding franchise and rising demands on the part of disfranchised citizens, both election campaigns and parliamentary sessions increasingly became sites of claim making. In Britain, bills before Parliament frequently became the focus of social movement claim making. Parliamentarization promoted social movements (Tilly 1997).

Demonstrations nicely illustrate the historical origins of specific social movement performances. Despite their later generalization and diffusion across a wide variety of settings, issues, and claimants, demonstrations took shape differently in their places of origin. Initial settings contributed three features to demonstrations: 1) models of interaction, 2) legal precedents for assembly and movement, and 3) representations of relations between demonstrators and other political actors, including authorities and objects of claims. We have already seen the British demonstration adapting forms, legal precedents, and representations from delegations, petition marches, public holidays, artisans' parades, electoral assemblies, and authorized meetings. Military parades also provided some of the models, if not the legal precedents.

Where citizens' militias retained legal standing into the eighteenth century—as they did, for example, in the Netherlands, but not in France—the armed militia parade offered a model and a (risky) legal precedent. In Catholic countries such as France and Spain, religious processions made their mark, not only offering occasions for expressions of sentiment that authorities could not easily contain but also providing exceptional opportunities for WUNC displays. In nineteenth-century Ireland, demonstrations drew on a century or so of religious processions, fraternal order outings, artisans' holidays, and militia marches; that earlier history cast a sharp shadow on Irish demonstrations into the twenty-first century (Bryan 2000; Kinealy 2003; Tilly 2003: 111–27). Compared with tarring and feathering or drinking forty-five toasts, the street demonstration has modular qualities that facilitate its spread across the world. Those qualities, however, do not free it from history.

The same holds for other social movement performances: creation of special-purpose associations and coalitions, public meetings, solemn processions, vigils, rallies, petition drives, statements in public media, and pamphleteering. Even though they eventually cohered in a widely available repertoire that distinguished social movements from other forms of politics, each of these performances has a history that stamps itself on meanings and practices, sets limits on permissible and impermissible uses, varies somewhat from setting to setting, and produces internal changes within the performance itself.

Take one small but significant example from the reports on demonstrations we have already examined. The early demonstrations Robert describes for Lyon employed striking symbols such as the Liberty Cap, acted out politically significant tableaux, and featured stirring songs, but included little or no printed matter. By century's end, French demonstrators commonly marched under signs and banners broadcasting slogans and identifying the segments of the population they represented in words rather than pictures. Beneath that change lay not only advances in popular literacy, but also the relaxation of legal restrictions on political speech. Those shifts in the social and political context likewise affected the activities of special-purpose associations, access to the media, and the whole array of social movement performances.

Chartists

To see more clearly what happened once social movements institutionalized, let us return briefly to Great Britain—or rather to the United Kingdom, which incorporated Ireland with England, Wales, and Scotland in 1801. Once the struggles of the 1820s and early 1830s set social movements firmly on the political map, the United Kingdom, including Ireland, became a major creator of social movements. Antislavery organizing continued, as we have seen, up until the abolition of slavery in 1833. Social movements helped bring political rights to Protestant Dissenters in 1828 and to Catholics in 1829.

The next three years brought immense social movement mobilization on behalf of parliamentary reform, culminating in the Reform Act of 1832 (Tilly 1995: 284–339). The act did not enfranchise the many workers who joined that mobilization, but did greatly increase the voting of merchants and masters as it moved the system modestly toward representation proportional to the number of electors. Organized workers, too, increasingly employed social movement means—campaigns, repertoire, and WUNC displays—as they demanded relief and equal rights.

Workers and their radical allies complained bitterly, publicly, and rightly that the newly enfranchised bourgeoisie had sold them out by accepting the 1832 Reform Act. The legislation pointedly excluded wage workers and raised property qualifications in parliamentary districts that had previously given at least some prosperous workers the vote. Workers also complained when the newly constituted Parliament enacted its liberal version of political economy by passing a New Poor Law (1834) that authorized parishes to collaborate in Poor Law Unions. Those unions ended outdoor relief for able-bodied workers, sent them to workhouses if they did not find adequate employment, and made conditions within workhouses more punitive. The two issues generated separate social movements during the later 1830s. But they merged in the remarkable mass movement called Chartism.

Published in May 1838, the People's Charter issued from negotiation and compromise between radical and reformist leaders. It dropped, for example, radical demands for female suffrage and a ten-hour limit to the working day. It also omitted demands, popular among liberal reformers, for abolition of the Corn Laws that until 1846 provided U.K. grain producers with sliding-scale protection against competing imports and thereby increased the cost of daily bread. The charter itself took the predictable form of a petition beginning "Unto the Honourable the Commons of the United Kingdom of Great Britain and Ireland in Parliament assembled, the Petition of the undersigned, their suffering countrymen, humbly sheweth." After a preface dramatizing the misery of workers in the midst of plenty and singling out the Reform Act of 1832 for criticism, the charter went on to make these specific demands:

1. universal [that is, adult male] suffrage;
2. secret ballots [instead of viva voce voting] in parliamentary elections;
3. annual parliaments;
4. salaries for Members of Parliament;
5. abolition of property requirements for membership in Parliament; and
6. equal electoral districts across the country.

(Black 1969: 127–31)

The proposal first emerged from the reformist London Workingmen's Association that had formed in 1836. It soon drew support from an extraordinary variety of reformist, radical, and special-purpose associations throughout the United Kingdom.

Many existing workers' organizations attached themselves to the movement. An umbrella National Charter Association (NCA) originated in Manchester (1840) and soon had more than 400 branches, drawn especially from previously active local workers' groups. The NCA "was able to organize two million signatures to a petition in 1841 for the release of Chartist prisoners, and three million to a second petition for the Charter in 1842" (Prothero 1997: 222). Chartist leaders regularly spoke of their activities as a "movement." They also drew consciously on recognizable symbols. At a London Chartist demonstration in August 1842, for example, the police arrested two men carrying a large Union Jack and "a small blue and white printed silk, having on it the words, 'Reform in Church and State' and surmounted by a Crimson Cap of Liberty" (Goodway 1982: 108).

Chartists held General Conventions of the Industrious Classes more or less annually from 1839 to 1848. Although these conventions followed a two-decade-old radical program of forming a counter-Parliament to dramatize weaknesses of the existing body, to have held elections for a large national assembly would have directly challenged Parliament's legal claim to represent the nation. To evade prosecution, the national meetings henceforth brought together small numbers of delegates. Those delegates came, however, from voice-vote elections at mass meetings in localities across the country. Around these conventions flowed large demonstrations and multiple public meetings.

In Nottingham, for example, organizers sought to draw shopkeepers into their mass meeting in preparation for the 1839 convention by distributing a handbill declaring that

> we are far from thinking that the Retailers are a useless portion of society, their interest and our own is the same: unless the working classes are well paid for their labour, the Retailers cannot exist as a respectable body, but that they must share the same fate as the working classes. We therefore call upon you Fellow Countrymen to assist us in this righteous struggle . . . come forward to the assistance of the People's delegates. So shall the working classes form one phalanx which Despotism cannot penetrate.
>
> (Church 1966: 131)

Notice the bid to project WUNC: worthiness, unity, numbers, and commitment. We see Chartists combining program claims centered on the Charter itself, identity claims as the connected, worthy working classes, and standing claims protesting their exclusion from political power.

Not all Chartist activity took the form of WUNC displays. It ranged from peaceful meetings to open attacks on enemies. (Historians, in fact, often make a rough distinction between "moral force" and "physical force" Chartists on these very grounds.) Several abortive insurrections—summarily repressed and brutally prosecuted—arose within the Chartist movement. With the French Revolution of 1848, many Chartist demonstrations displayed French tricolor flags and called for revolutionary change. Lawyer-Chartist-poet Ernest Jones preached in 1848:

> I believe that we stand upon the threshold of our rights. One step, were it even with an iron heel, and they are ours. I conscientiously believe the people are prepared to claim the Charter. Then I say—take it; and God defend the right! . . . We'll respect the law, if the law-makers respect us. If they don't—France is a Republic!
>
> (Ward 1973: 200)

As in many later-nineteenth-century large-scale social movements, priorities in local demands and strategies varied wildly within Chartism. Yet, the center of gravity remained the collective placing of demands to equalize political rights in the United Kingdom.

After a last great burst in 1848, Chartism disintegrated as a national movement. Some activists moved into temperance, cooperatives, and local betterment programs or into educational, land, or property reform, while a minority stuck with local and regional Chartist associations (Price 1986: 56–67). The formal Chartist program as a whole did not become part of U.K. law until the twentieth century, and its more general populist demands failed utterly (Thompson 1984: 335–37). Nevertheless, the Chartist movement provided a seedbed and a template for the nineteenth century's major popular mobilizations. Later demands for an expanded franchise, female suffrage, disestablishment of the Anglican Church, and home rule in Ireland all followed some of the patterns set in place by Chartism.

A Glance at the Nineteenth-Century United States

While these democratizing events were taking place in the United Kingdom, similar processes were occurring throughout North America. In a pathbreaking study of American social movements between 1800 and 1945, William Gamson devised a shrewd cataloging strategy for that unruly world of campaigns, social movement performances, and WUNC displays. He and his research team went through about seventy-five historical reference works, tagging any named organization that participated in a wide variety of social movements and/or protest activities. From that listing of nearly 4,500 organizations they drew a random sample of 11 percent—467 organizations—from which they selected the fifty-three that detailed examination showed to be (1) seeking the mobilization of an unmobilized constituency and (2) making claims on an antagonist outside that constituency. Of the fifty-three, the twenty-seven organizations listed in Table 3.2 began their activity before 1900. Thus, they provide a rough calendar of nineteenth-century social movement initiation in the United States.

As I warned earlier, social movement organizations (SMOs) and social movements are by no means identical; movements are interactive campaigns, not organizations. SMOs sometimes outlast campaigns, and campaigns almost always involve multiple organizations, shifting coalitions, and unnamed informal networks. British Chartism shows us many previously mobilized constituencies (which Gamson's procedure excluded unless a new organization formed to mobilize them) joining in a vast social movement. Like the tracing of demonstrations alone, Gamson's organizational catalog therefore takes just one selective picture of American social movement activity.

Still, the picture flashes some striking highlights.

1. It portrays a remarkable acceleration of social movement initiation during the later nineteenth century. Only seven of the twenty-seven nineteenth-century organizations began acting before 1850, and well over half started up after 1875.
2. The sorts of organizations engaged in social movements shifted markedly. Before 1850 we see the predictable antislavery and social reform associations but only one workers' organization (the Union Trade Society of Journeymen Tailors) and one nascent political party (the nativist American Republican Party). After midcentury, groups trying to organize workers for either their own professional advantages or general political programs, from Chinese exclusion to socialist revolution, loom much larger.
3. Most of the challengers sought benefits or protection for special interests rather than generalization of political rights. In twenty-first-century perspective some of them—notably nativist mobilizations—look downright reactionary (see Hoffmann 2003; Kaufman 2002; Skocpol 1999: 72–75).

Table 3.2 William Gamson's Nineteenth-Century Challenging Groups and Their Program Claims

Year(s)	Group	Program Claims
1816–1834	North Carolina Manumission Society	promotion of voluntary manumission for slaves
1825–1830	Prison Discipline Society	prison reform
1831–1833	Society for the Promotion of Manual Labor in Literary Institutions	physical fitness
1832–1840	National Female Anti-Slavery Society	abolition of slavery
1833–1836	Union Trade Society of Journeymen Tailors	professional benefits
1833–1840	American Anti-Slavery Society	abolition of slavery
1843–1847	American Republican Party (Native American Party)	Protestant anti-Catholic
1858–1873	United Sons of Vulcan	benefits for ironworkers
1865–1872	Grand Eight Hour Leagues	legislation for eight-hour day
1869–1872	American Free Trade League	tariff repeal
1869–1876	International Workingmen's Association (First International)	socialist politics
1880–1887	Social Revolutionary Clubs (Anarcho-Communists)	economic reorganization
1880–1905	League of American Wheelmen	remove road restrictions on bicycles

1881–1912	United Brotherhood of Carpenters and Joiners of America	professional benefits
1881–1935	American Federation of Labor	legal and political support for labor movement
1882	League of Deliverance	opposition to Chinese labor
1885–1891	National Brotherhood of Baseball Players	professional benefits
1885–1934	Order of Railway Conductors	professional benefits
1886–1888	American Party	anti-immigration
1887	Progressive Labor Party	socialist political candidates
1888–1910	United Hebrew Trades	benefits for Jewish immigrant workers
1888–1935	International Association of Machinists	professional benefits
1892–1915	Brotherhood of the Kingdom	religion and social conditions
1892–1921	Amalgamated Association of Street and Electrical Railway Workers	professional benefits
1892–1933	International Longshoreman's Association (East)	professional benefits
1893–1932	American Proportional Representation League	PR against urban political machines
1896–1914	Brotherhood of the Cooperative Commonwealth	cooperatives and electoral power

Source: Gamson 1990: 277–85.

Across the nineteenth century, social movement claim making clearly became available to a widening variety of American interests. By the luck of the draw, Gamson's sampling procedure bypassed two of the most prominent nineteenth-century social movement issues, temperance and female suffrage. It also passed by most countermovements; for example, the widespread mobilization *against* abolitionism before the Civil War (Grimsted 1998; McKivigan and Harrold 1999). But it did capture municipal reform and the cooperative movement. Gamson's catalog portrays a quickening and broadening of social movement activity in the United States during the later nineteenth century.

Mary Ryan's history of public politics in New York, San Francisco, and New Orleans during the nineteenth century richly illustrates, and generally confirms, the impression of changes offered by Gamson's study. Despite giving greater prominence to ethnic and racial divisions, Ryan's roster of nineteenth-century organizations broadly resembles Gamson's. She reports, for example:

- activity of New York's Laborers Benevolent Union as a sort of Irish workers' protection society during the 1840s,
- appearance of a nativist American Party in New Orleans as early as 1856,

- formation of a Committee of Merchants for the Relief of Colored People in response to the New York draft riots of 1863,
- New Orleans' hosting of a Convention of Colored Men of Louisiana in 1865,
- San Francisco workers' parading as the Eight Hour League in 1867, and
- effective anti-Chinese agitation by the Workingman's Party of California in 1877,
- as well as racially, ethnically, and occupationally segregated organizations such as the Ancient Order of Hibernians and the Orange Loyal Association (Ryan 1997: 79, 82, 148–50, 173, 229, 262, 282, 290–91).
- But Ryan also marks the 1863 entry into public politics of New York's National Loyal Women League and of New Orleans' National Equal Rights League (Ryan 1997: 179, 262).

Her evidence reveals a wide range of program claims, a spectacular variety of identity claims, and repeated standing claims—including demands for the exclusion of other actors from political rights or even from the country as a whole.

Again, paralleling Gamson's observations, Ryan notes the increasing prominence of workers' organizations in her three cities' public politics after the Civil War.

> In 1877, when the great railroad strikes consumed smaller cities and towns, a variety of workers took to the streets of big cities for a common cause. Cigar workers announced their militancy on the streets of New Orleans and New York with particular vehemence and solidarity. The New Orleans press reported that they assembled in Congo Square and heard speeches in Spanish, French, and English. Similar work stoppages in New York won favorable notices on the sidewalks and in the press. Of "The Cigar Makers Street Parade" the *Tribune* observed, "The faces of the striking cigar-makers beamed with smiles of triumph as they assembled yesterday in front of Concordia Hall, to take part in the procession of the organization. Men, women, and children came singly and in groups from shops, each bearing a flag and banner with inscriptions." Those flags included the colors of Germany, Bohemia, and Austria and, like the language groups assembled in Congo Square, signaled a new mobilization within the urban public, that of "labor" in multiethnic array.
>
> (Ryan 1997: 256)

Ryan sums up the overall trajectories of nineteenth-century American urban politics as running "from differences toward dualism, from representation toward bureaucracy, from a citizenry toward a tax base, from voluntary associations toward social movements" (Ryan 1997: 259). As the number of public celebrations and manifestations in American urban spaces declined, disciplined claim-making—and often narrowly self-interested—social movements replaced it. The rise of the social movement, Ryan suggests, tamed the rambunctious street democracy of the early nineteenth century (see Vernon 1993 on nineteenth-century England).

Where, When, and Why Social Movements?

What do the nineteenth-century experiences of France, Belgium, the United Kingdom, and the United States add to our knowledge of conditions and causes for social movements? Quite a bit, actually. Most obviously, even these quick snapshots show us how much the fine grain of nineteenth-century social movement activity drew on local and regional culture: songs, slogans, symbols, costumes, and labels that took their meaning from previously existing practices and entities. Within the convergence on special-purpose associations, public meetings, and demonstrations that occurred in all four countries, we notice continued differentiation that attached claim-making campaigns, social movement performances, and WUNC displays to their immediate contexts and, thus, made them legible to local audiences. Modularity does not mean perfect uniformity: seen from one side a demonstration or a special-purpose association retained recognizable local cultural markers even if from the other its distinctive overall contours transferred easily from one setting to another.

The shift of repertoires we have observed in the four countries had profound implications for popular participation in public politics. House sacking, shaming ceremonies, forced illuminations, and direct attacks on malefactors declined rapidly as ordinary people moved to new forms of claim making and authorities applied more stringent repression to the old forms. The sheer effectiveness of social movement strategies by no means accounts for the change. The older repertoire's direct actions rarely produced political reform at the national level, but they often settled matters locally in a quick, decisive way. Ordinary people in North America, Belgium, France, and the British Isles lost some of their cherished, proven means of retaliation, coercion, supplication, and threat.

Segments of the population lacking connections with political entrepreneurs and special-purpose associations, furthermore, actually lost some of their political leverage. Gender, religious, and ethnic divisions, of course, patterned this exclusion. Before the time of Chartism, Great Britain's landless agricultural laborers had at least occasionally been able to exert collective pressure on farmers and local authorities through public shaming, appeals to local patrons, collective destruction of agricultural machinery, and coordinated withholding of labor; by the 1840s their means had dwindled to occasional arson, poaching, and clandestine attacks on animals (Archer 1990). Chartism itself recruited mainly from artisans and skilled workers rather than landless laborers. The repertoire shift produced a dramatic decline in the physical damage to persons and property wrought by collective claim making; most public performances in the social movement mode went off with no violence whatever, and such scuffling as occurred between police and demonstrators generally involved far less damage than had the old repertoire's attacks.

Why did that happen? On the whole, parliamentarization seems to have offered powerful spurs to the creation of social movements in all four of our cases. Remember the two main components of parliamentarization: (1) increase in the absolute power of representative institutions with respect to governmental activities such as taxation, war making, provision of public services, and creation of public infrastructure; and (2) increase in the *relative* power of representative institutions compared with hereditary rulers, great patrons, priests, and local holders of power.

In all four cases, the parliaments in question organized territorially, distributing across the national space. Not all parliaments do so; indeed, the Estates General that constituted France's closest approximation to a national parliament before the Revolution of 1789 specifically represented not French regions but the national memberships of three broad estates: clergy, nobility, and propertied commoners. Revolutionary struggles of 1789 and 1790 then converted the Estates General into a geographically representative national body (Lepetit 1982, 1988; Margadant 1992; Markoff 1996a; Ozouf-Marignier 1986; Schultz 1982; Tilly 1962; Woloch 1994). In France and elsewhere, such a territorial organization increased social and geographic proximity between national power holders and their constituencies. Rising absolute and relative impacts of parliamentary decisions therefore focused affected citizens on increasingly accessible potential targets of claims, their regions' representatives in the Parliament.

Parliamentarization also produced a further set of political effects that, on the average, favored social movement claim making:

- reduction in the political importance of long-established patron–client chains as major conduits for national politics;
- significant new opportunities for political entrepreneurs who could produce temporary links between public officials and multiple groups of aggrieved, connected citizens;
- accentuation of governmental claims to speak on behalf of a unified, connected people; and
- regular semipublic sittings of representative bodies that in turn became geographic and temporal sites for claim making.

In the nineteenth-century United Kingdom, United States, France, and Belgium, parliamentary sessions and deliberations focused many social movement campaigns. Just remember Deneckere's linking of "socialist mass actions" and Belgium's parliamentary move to manhood suffrage in 1893.

Nevertheless, we see significant differences between the relatively centralized political regimes of France and Belgium, on one side, and the more segmented political structures of the United Kingdom and, especially, the United States, on the other. Although the inventories at hand do not allow precise comparisons, they give a strong impression of social movements' greater focus on the national state in the centralized regimes. Workers in France and Belgium struck against individual employers but directed demands for rights, policies, and reforms to national authorities; repeated attempts of Belgian workers at general strikes aimed at the state rather than at employers. Parliament did draw a significant share of social movement claim making in the United Kingdom, but so did local and regional authorities. In the United States, leaders of cities and states drew a significant share of social movement claims. National political structures shaped social movement activity.

In a complementary way, the forms of organization already established on the ground also shaped social movements in the four countries. Such organizations as the League of American Wheelmen and the American Party formed precisely in the course of public claim making. Yet even when SMOs came into being in the course of social movement mobilizations, they fed on their organizational environments. Religious congregations, mutual benefit societies, fraternal orders, and ethnic associations, for example, recur as contexts for the coalitions and blanket associations that figured in U.S. social movements. Confrontations between Catholic organizations and their anticlerical opponents loomed much larger in France and Belgium. Even where close collaboration and emulation occur across settings, with the emergence of social movement activity elsewhere we should expect to find a similar grounding of its specific organizational forms in local environments. As a complex form of political interaction, we should not expect to find the social movement diffusing relatively unchanged.

Political Rights

Behind such differences, state-guaranteed political rights or their absence wielded a large influence. In the histories we have examined, rights to assembly, association, and speech mattered especially (see Anderson and Anderson 1967: chaps. 6 and 7 for a convenient review). Where regimes succeeded in abridging those rights seriously (as during the early years of France's Second Empire), social movements generally declined. Rights to assembly directly affected all the major social movement performances and their accompanying WUNC displays; unlike routines of the older repertoire that flowed out of routine authorized assemblies such as markets and holidays, social movement routines depended intimately on assembly.

Rights to associate proved crucial to the special-purpose organizations and crosscutting coalitions of social movements; clandestine organizations and informal networks could coordinate some forms of claim making, but legal rights to associate greatly facilitated mobilization and coordination of public claims. They also multiplied the number of political actors that a regime's denial of associational rights to any particular interest would threaten even when the actors in question opposed that interest; Belgian promoters of French and Flemish predominance both acquired an investment in the organizational forms their opponents deployed.

Freedom of speech obviously mattered centrally to the public making of claims in all its social movement forms: the meeting, the demonstration, the pamphlet, the media message, and all the rest. Among the cases surveyed earlier, Chartism provides the most dramatic examples; U.K. authorities scanned Chartist activities closely for signs of criminal conspiracy or attempted rebellion that they could prosecute but found themselves hamstrung with regard to restricting public expression. By the 1830s, the United Kingdom's popular activists were fully exercising rights to criticize their rulers and to propose radical political transformations.

This way of describing the situation, however, implies a false scenario: first a regime grants rights, then ordinary people take advantage of those rights. In fact, we have seen popular activists and political entrepreneurs from John Wilkes onward bargaining for rights to assembly, association, and speech. They generally did so by pushing against the limits that attached existing rights to certain populations, activities, organizations, or places. Wilkes's 1768 victory in court, which established powerful precedents in British law for the protection of political speech and influenced movements in America, provides a dramatic example.

Less visibly but more fundamentally, day-to-day bargaining in the course of contentious claim making pushed the boundaries of existing rights. Citizens who already exercised contained rights to assemble as taxpayers or as members of religious congregations dared to use taxpayers' meetings and church services for the formulation and expression of shared demands. Where members of the ruling classes were already employing similar means of assembly, association, and speech to pursue their own collective ends—as, for example, in prerevolutionary Boston—authorities had a more difficult time restricting the rights of ordinary people to exercise the same rights. That became especially true when dissident members of the elite drew popular followings or deliberately allied themselves with opponents of the regime.

The bargaining process speeded up enormously during nationwide political struggles and revolutions. It could proceed from bottom up or from top down. Bottom up, we see ordinary people increasing their access to assembly, association, and speech as divided elites fight with each other and sometimes reach out for popular followings. Top down, we see reformers or revolutionaries seizing control of central states and instituting rights as matters of principle and/or means of consolidating their power. Viewing the French revolution of 1848 from Lyon, we have seen both the bottom-up and top-down versions of rights extension occurring; workers and other claimants in Lyon took advantage of revolutionary divisions to emerge from the shadows into public politics, but the revolutionaries who captured the French state in February–March 1848 also instituted a legal program supporting assembly, association, and speech. The top-down intervention then promoted a temporary expansion of social movement activity in Lyon and other French cities. In 1870–1871, Lyon's radicals inverted the process: they seized power over the city against opposition from national authorities and for six months installed a commune whose citizens enjoyed extensive rights of assembly, association, and speech.

One political innovation that always proceeded from the top down greatly promoted the emergence of social movements: the institution of consequential, contested elections. As the histories of Britain and North America amply illustrate, even with narrow, uneven suffrage such elections could promote social movement activity. We should be reminded that only some property-owning white men were allowed to vote in America during this time. These early movements are part of the story of why some of the first social groups gained citizenship rights and participation and say in governmental affairs. Consequential, contested elections promoted social movement campaigns, performances, and WUNC displays in several different ways.

1. In a manner similar to official holidays, they almost inevitably involved public assemblies from which it was difficult for authorities to exclude nonvoters; those assemblies then became privileged occasions for the public voicing of claims.
2. They provided a model of public support for rival programs, as embodied in competing candidates; once governments authorized public discussion of major issues during electoral campaigns, it became harder to silence that discussion outside of electoral campaigns.
3. Elections magnified the importance of numbers; with contested elections, any group receiving disciplined support from large numbers of followers became a possible ally or enemy at the polls.
4. Candidates often had incentives for displays of popular support, including support from nonvoters; such displays fortified their claims to represent "the people" at large and to command wider support than one's electoral opponents (Morgan 1988).
5. To the extent that voting districts were geographical, both campaigns and polls offered opportunities for injecting local and regional issues into the public discussion.
6. Visible legal divisions between those who did and those who did not have the right to vote promoted claims by the excluded for rights denied as they made exclusion dramatically evident.

In Britain, North America, France, and Belgium, the nineteenth-century institutionalization of national elections promoted social movement activity. Expansion of the franchise then doubly facilitated social movement expansion: increased rights of political participation for the enfranchised, and increased incentives to collective complaints by the disfranchised.

Do Social Movements Equal Democratization?

Does all this then amount to a giant tautology: social movements = democratization (Giugni, McAdam, and Tilly 1998; Ibarra 2003; Markoff 1996b)? Certainly our historical cases argue for some general affinity between social movements and democratization. In fact, however, social movements and democratization remain logically, empirically, and causally distinct. Logically, proliferation of social movements does not entail democratization, since the campaigns, performances, and WUNC displays of social movements can in principle operate on behalf of inequality and exclusion rather than equality and inclusion; consider the movements in favor of expelling recent immigrants. Empirically, antidemocratic movements have formed repeatedly; we need look no further than the nativist mobilizations in William Gamson's catalog for the nineteenth-century United States.

Social movements and democratization also occur in partial causal independence; for example, in cases of conquest and revolution, new rulers sometimes impose democratic institutions suddenly in the absence of any previous social movement mobilization on behalf of democracy; think about occupied Japan and Germany after World War II. No necessary connection exists between social movements and democracy. The main generalization we can draw from our evidence so far runs rather differently: once democratization does occur, social movements (whether democratic or not) usually follow.

Ruth Berins Collier's book *Paths Toward Democracy: The Working Class and Elites in Western Europe and South America* (1999) compares democratization in Western Europe and South America and offers an opportunity to add a little more precision to these claims (for explication and critique of Collier's analysis, see Tilly 2001a). In a systematic effort to detect effects of middle-class and working-class participation in democratic transitions, Collier compares seventeen "historic" cases of democratization, mostly nineteenth-century, with

Table 3.3 Ruth Berins Collier's "Historic" Cases of Democratization, with Transition Dates

Country	Year(s)
Switzerland	1848
France	1848, 1875–1877
Denmark	1849, 1915
Greece	1864
Chile	1874/1891
Great Britain	1884, 1918
Norway	1898
Finland	(1906), 1919
Sweden	1907/1909, 1918/1920
Portugal	1911,1918
Argentina	1912
Italy	1912(1919)
Netherlands	1917
Belgium	1918
Germany	1918–1919
Uruguay	1918
Spain	1868, 1890, 1931

Source: Collier 1999: 23.

Key: date/date: elements of democratic rule arrived in segments; (date): arguable alternative to main date given; repeated dates: partial establishment followed by reversal(s) or long plateaus.

ten "recent" cases occurring from 1974 to 1990. Democratization, for Collier, means establishment of (1) liberal constitutional rule, (2) classical elections, and (3) an independent and popularly elected legislative assembly (Collier 1999: 24). Table 3.3 lists her historic cases, from Switzerland (1848) to Spain (three transitions, all reversed sooner or later, from 1868 to 1931). To sort out the interdependence of social movements and Collier's democratic transitions, we must decide which transitions to emphasize, date the availability of social movements in popular politics, and then match the two dates. As the history of France suggests, that will not always be easy; Collier's dates of 1848 and 1875–1877 for French democratic transitions clearly precede the date of durable social movement establishment indicated by the history of demonstrations, but 1848 certainly did bring France a temporary flowering of associations, meetings, demonstrations, and other social movement performances.

Drawing on Collier's own descriptions plus a variety of historical works, let me nevertheless offer a rough tabulation of Collier's cases. The tabulation distinguishes between instances in which social movement activity clearly proliferated before Collier's transition date and those in which substantial establishment of democratic institutions preceded the extensive growth of social movements. Table 3.4 presents the breakdown. Spain appears twice in the tabulation, with the abortive democratization of 1868 preceding any significant social movement mobilization but with the new transitions of 1890 and 1931 occurring after social movements had begun to proliferate, at least in the country's major cities (Ballbé 1983; González Calleja 1998, 1999). Other countries appear only once, but sometimes with multiple years representing subsequently reversed transitions, partial transitions, or alternative dates. Except for Spain, however, the multiple dates do not blur the decision concerning whether transition or social movements came first.

How do the countries divide? Although social movements preceded Collier's democratic transitions in twelve of the eighteen cases, in the other six, narrowly based democratic transitions promoted subsequent social movements where they had previously possessed little political standing or none at all. Regimes that early experienced top-down creation of liberal constitutions, contested elections, and popularly chosen legislative assemblies, on the average, put them into place before social movements developed fully; we have followed just such an experience closely for France. Aside from that obvious point, no strong difference in geographic location or previous type of regime differentiates the two sides.

There is one geographic exception, however: The Nordic countries—Denmark, Norway, Finland, and Sweden—concentrate early in the "Social Movements First" column. The Baltic region had long stood out from the rest of Europe for its exceptional combination of powerful (Lutheran) state churches with extensive citizenship rights. Denmark's early creation of a relatively democratic constitution (1849) resulted from the intervention of a young, reforming monarch in the wake of the 1848 revolutions. But even in Denmark, peasants, workers, and religious activists had been creating special-purpose associations

Table 3.4 Order of Social Movements and Democratic Transitions in Collier's "Historic" Cases

Social Movements First	Transition First
Denmark 1849, 1915	Switzerland 1848
Great Britain 1884, 1918	France 1848, 1875–1877
Norway 1898	Greece 1864
Finland (1906), 1919	Chile 1874/1891
Sweden 1907/1909, 1918/1920	Portugal 1911, 1918
Argentina 1912	Spain 1868
Italy 1912(1919)	
Netherlands 1917	
Belgium 1918	
Germany 1918–1919	
Uruguay 1918	
Spain 1890, 1931	

Sources: Alapuro 1988; Ballbé 1983; Birmingham 1993; Caramani 2003; Collier 1999; Deneckere 1997; Dolléans and Crozier 1950; Dowe 1970; González Calleja 1998, 1999; Lida 1972; López-Alves 2000; Lundqvist 1977; Öhngren 1974; Paige 1997; Rock 1987; Sabato 2001; Seip 1974, 1981; Skidmore and Smith 1984; Stenius 1987; Tilly 1986, 1995; Wåhlin 1986; Wircz 1981.

and deploying them in public politics for a century before then (Wåhlin 1986). Despite the previous chapter's placement of social movement invention in England and North America during the nineteenth century's first decades, then, the Nordic countries might have some claims to coinvention. Their eighteenth-century innovations, however, did not spread early or widely.

Norway, Finland, and Sweden hummed with social movements through most of the nineteenth century. Church-backed organizations provided the initial impetus, but secular liberals, religious opponents of state churches, advocates of cooperatives, supporters of folk nationalism, organized workers, and (especially after 1880) opponents of alcohol mounted vast campaigns, adopted social movement performances, and made regular displays of WUNC integral elements of their claim making (Alapuro 1988; Lundqvist 1977; Öhngren 1974; Seip 1974, 1981; Stenius 1987). In partial independence of democratic transitions, then, regional and national social processes sometimes promoted social movements.

Puzzling Switzerland

Given its reputation for intensive civic participation, Switzerland's appearance at the top of the "Transition First" list comes as a surprise. One might have thought that Swiss citizens were busy forming associations, staging demonstrations, and creating social movement campaigns well before 1848. The reality of the situation is a bit more complex. Far from easing into democracy as a consequence of age-old habits and culture, Switzerland fashioned democratic institutions as a contested and improvised compromise solution to a revolutionary crisis (for general historical background, see Bonjour 1948; Bonjour, Offler, and Potter 1952; Capitani 1986; Deutsch 1976; Gilliard 1955; Gossman 2000; Kohn 1956; Wimmer 2002: 222–68).

Swiss towns and cantons, especially in the highlands, did have a long history of civic participation, but in the circumscribed old-regime version of European peasant villages and city-states. Some subset of property-holding males and their sons typically formed an assembly that consented to major taxes and expenditures, elected the year's officers, and held veto power in the case of widespread dissent against official actions. But those proud electors generally excluded the propertyless, and often governed dependent territories whose residents had no say in public affairs (Böning 1998; Wyrsch 1983). Oligarchy would be a better name for the system than democracy.

The French Revolution shook Switzerland's economic and political ties to France. It also exposed Swiss people, especially its commercial bourgeoisie and its growing industrial proletariat, to new French models and doctrines. From 1789 onward, revolutionary movements formed in several parts of Switzerland. In 1793, Geneva (not a federation member, but closely tied to Switzerland) underwent a revolution on the French model. As the threat of French invasion mounted in early 1798, Basel, Vaud, Lucerne, Zurich, and other Swiss regions followed the revolutionary path. Basel, for example, turned from a constitution in which only citizens of the town chose their canton's senators to another giving urban and rural populations equal representation.

Conquered by France in collaboration with Swiss revolutionaries in 1798, then receiving a new constitution that year, the Swiss regime as a whole adopted a much more centralized form of government with significantly expanded citizenship. The new regime incorporated the territories of the cantons St. Gall, Grisons, Thurgau, Ticino, Aargau, and Vaud on equal terms with the older cantons but followed French revolutionary practice by reducing the cantons to administrative and electoral units. The central government remained fragile, however; four coups occurred in the period 1800 to 1802 alone. At the withdrawal of French troops in 1802, multiple rebellions broke out. Switzerland then rushed to the brink of civil war. Only Napoleon's intervention and imposition of a new constitution in 1803 kept the country together.

The 1803 regime, known in Swiss history as the Mediation, restored considerable powers to cantons but by no means reestablished the old regime. Switzerland's recast federation operated with a national assembly, official multilingualism, relative equality among cantons, and freedom for citizens to move from canton to canton. Despite some territorial adjustments, a weak central legislature, judiciary, and executive survived Napoleon's defeat. Survival only occurred, however, after another close brush with civil war, this time averted by Great Power intervention, in 1813–1815. In the war settlement of 1815, Austria, France, Great Britain, Portugal, Prussia, Russia, Spain, and Sweden accepted a treaty among twenty-two cantons called the Federal Pact (now adding Valais,

Neuchâtel, and Geneva) as they guaranteed Switzerland's perpetual neutrality and the inviolability of its frontiers.

The victors of 1815 did not give Swiss central authorities adequate means for managing their country's complexity. Switzerland of the Federal Pact operated without a permanent bureaucracy, a standing army, common coinage, standard measures, or a national flag but with multiple internal customs barriers, a rotating capital, and incessant bickering among cantonal representatives who had no right to deviate from their home constituents' instructions. At the national scale, the Swiss lived with a system better disposed to vetoes than to concerted change. At that point, social movements played no significant part in Swiss public life.

At France's July 1830 Revolution, anticlericalism became more salient in Swiss radicalism. After 1830, Switzerland became a temporary home for many exiled revolutionaries (for example Giuseppe Mazzini, Wilhelm Weitling, and, more surprisingly, future emperor Louis Napoleon), who collaborated with Swiss radicals in calling for reform. Historians of Switzerland in the 1830s speak of a regeneration movement pursued by means of "publicity, clubs, and mass marches" (Nabholz, von Muralt, Feller, and Bonjour 1938: II, 406). But that "movement" resembled the narrow, top-down mobilizations we have already observed in France and Belgium before 1848. A great spurt of new periodicals and pamphlets accompanied the political turmoil of 1830–1831 (Andrey 1986: 551–52). Within individual cantons, reformers began enacting standard nineteenth-century reforms such as limitation of child labor and expansion of public schools. Nevertheless, the new cantonal constitutions installed during that mobilization stressed liberty and fraternity much more than they did equality.

Between 1830 and 1848, Switzerland underwent a contradictory set of political processes. Although the era's struggles unquestionably activated many convinced democrats, they pitted competing conceptions of democracy against each other. They played out, furthermore, over a substratum of competition for control of the Swiss federation as a whole. The country's richer, more Protestant cantons struggled their way toward their own versions of democracy. Those cantons installed representative institutions that would be linked together instead of the de-centralized direct democracy of male citizens that had long prevailed in highland communities and cantons. Activists based in reformed cantons then used armed force to drive their unreformed neighbors toward representative democracy. They did so first in military raids across cantonal boundaries, then in an open, if short-lived, civil war, the Sonderbund War of 1847 (Bucher 1966; Remak 1993). Only after the liberal, wealthier side won the civil war decisively did negotiations resulting in a democratic constitution begin.

During the crisis, confessional qualifications for citizenship became even more salient. As astute observer Alexis de Tocqueville put it shortly after the civil war:

> Nowhere else has the democratic revolution that is now stirring the world occurred in such complicated, bizarre circumstances. One people composed of multiple races, speaking multiple languages, adhering to multiple faiths and various dissident sects, two equally established and privileged churches, every political question soon pivoting on religious questions and every religious question leading to political questions, really two societies, one very old and the other very young, married to each other despite the difference in their ages. That is Switzerland.
>
> (Tocqueville 1983: 635–36)

Switzerland as a whole actually dedemocratized between 1830 and 1847. Yet the settlement of 1848 clearly advanced democracy at a national scale beyond the level it had reached in 1798, 1803, 1815, or even 1830. Swiss democratization rapidly generated opportunities for social movements. Soon after 1848, Swiss citizens began creating a wide range of social movements closely tuned to the consultative institutions established by the constitutional peace settlement—for example, referenda at cantonal and national levels. They created the intensely participatory Swiss public politics we know today (Frey and Stutzer 2002: chaps. 8–9; Kriesi, Levy, Ganguillet, and Zwicky 1981; Steinberg 1996; Stutzer and Frey 2002; Trechsel 2000).

Social Movements in Argentina

Let us look at one more puzzling national placement concerning the historical context of social movements. The case of Argentina is important to discuss because it stands in the column of countries where social movements preceded democratic transitions. With the country's political history of caudillos, colonels, and repressive regimes, we might have expected Argentina to resemble Greece, Chile, or Portugal. In fact, the country's very uneven relationship between center and periphery left space for islands of social movement activity. At least in Buenos Aires, social movement politics became visible quite early. As Argentine historian Hilda Sabato summarizes:

> In the 1860s and 1870s, the people of Buenos Aires often mobilized in order to encourage, protest, or otherwise influence government action. Important demonstrations were staged, for example, in 1864, to support Peru in its conflict with Spain; to support the War of the Triple Alliance against Paraguay in the following year; to sympathize with Cuba in 1869 and 1873; to oppose the death penalty when Pascual Castro Chavarría was sentenced to death in 1870; to object to the official organization mounted on occasion of the yellow fever epidemics of 1871; to protest the restitution of the church of San Ignacio to the original owners, the Jesuits, in 1875; to resist the law of 1878 that imposed an additional tax on liquor, tobacco, and playing cards; to demonstrate for peace in the face of the revolutionary events of 1880.
>
> (Sabato 2001: 118)

Social movement activity continued into the 1880s. In 1889, Buenos Aires students formed an organization called the Youth Civic Union (*Unión Cívica de la Juventud*) to oppose government policies. The organization soon attracted nonstudent followers and evolved into a general civic union. In 1890, the union staged a Buenos Aires demonstration with 30,000 participants. Later that year a popular militia aligned with the union attacked government forces in a failed rebellion, only to discover that major politicians who had encouraged the attack had made a deal behind its back to change the government. The 1890s brought organization-based popular politics onto the national scene, but against a distinctive Argentine background of military and strongman politics.

Between 1890 and 1914, associational life flowered in Argentina. A broad, semi-conspiratorial movement of people who called themselves radicals connected numerous local middle-class political clubs with a hierarchy of party committees. They adopted standard social movement means, including mass meetings and demonstrations. Several anarchist federations organized workers in the Buenos Aires region. In addition to their own demonstrations on such occasions as May Day and New Year's Day, anarchists originated half a dozen general strikes in and around Buenos Aires between 1899 and 1910. When they threatened to sabotage festivities for the centennial of Argentine independence in 1910, however, the government began arresting anarchists as vigilantes and smashed their meeting places.

Meanwhile, Argentine socialists (who distinguished themselves sharply from the anarchists) initiated standard social movement campaigns for working-class credit, housing, education, divorce, women's suffrage, and an eight-hour day. Their Socialist Party, founded in 1894, brought together workers with professionals and some small manufacturers. By the time the party elected its first member of Argentina's Chamber of Deputies in 1904, social movement politics had taken firm root in the country. Thus, Argentine social movements unquestionably long preceded the democratic transition that Ruth Berins Collier marks at 1912, when the Sáenz Peña Law enacted suffrage and the secret ballot for men eighteen and over.

Collier's and my assignment of dates to Argentina brushes past a vexing problem that all of the cases actually hide: variability in access to both democracy and social movements within each regime. As of 1912, Buenos Aires had become a cosmopolitan capital of a large, prosperous country. But most of the country remained agricultural, significant regions still hosted indigenous populations that were little involved in national politics, and large parts fell under the control of great landlords, ranchers, and regional strongmen (Rock 1987: 179–83). In all our countries, the dates in question neglect great unevenness in access to democratic institutions and social movements. They mark essentially the time when some substantial segment of the national population first gained that access.

Internationalization of Social Movements

One more important observation emerges from the nineteenth-century national experiences this chapter has surveyed. Although the timing and character of social movements depended chiefly on the changing structure of national politics, international connections made a significant difference. We have already observed the close interaction between British and North American activists during the eighteenth century, in the social movement's very formative days. From early on, antislavery took a very international turn. Throughout the nineteenth century, international connections mattered in three different ways:

1. Social movements responded to changes produced by international contacts such as flows of migrants; American nativist movements provide a case in point.
2. Seeking to outflank national authorities, social movement entrepreneurs deliberately organized across international boundaries. We have glimpsed the International Workingmen's Association at work during the 1860s and 1870s, but we might also have traced the great influence of Irish exiles and sympathizers in nineteenth-century Irish nationalist movements.
3. International connections among rulers and claimants to rule also affected social movement activity, as rulers and claimants sought external validation of their politics. Claiming that your regime or your opposition movement represented a unified, committed people opened either side to demands for proof as a condition for international support. As the century wore on, furthermore, rulers' claims that their regime was a democracy and opposition's claims that the regime was *not* a democracy increasingly drew scrutiny and even intervention by outsiders.

Claims to legitimate rule, in turn, invited particular categories of oppressed peoples to adopt social movement strategies—campaigns, repertoires, and WUNC displays—on the way to gathering external support against their oppressors. The Indian National Congress, the first party in India that sought independence from Britain (founded in 1885), originated in just such an effort. During its early years, the Congress made its claims in the manner of an orderly British pressure group, by lobbying, petitioning, and drafting addresses; it acted as a social movement organization (Bose and Jalal 1998: 116–17; Johnson 1996: 156–62). Nevertheless, the spread and internationalization of social movements both greatly accelerated during the twentieth century. Our nineteenth-century story has concentrated very heavily on Western Europe and North America. The twentieth-century story will be different.

Note

1 Ernesto Castaneda and Lesley Wood lightly edited the language in this chapter.

4

TWENTIETH-CENTURY EXPANSION AND TRANSFORMATION

Charles Tilly[1]

Teleology and wishful thinking often coincide. We tell stories about the past in which all history conspired to produce our tolerable present and our glorious future. In 1962, on behalf of the Soviet Communist Party's Central Committee, the High Party School's Department of History of the International Working and National Liberation Movement applied the principle faithfully. It published two large volumes surveying the international working and national liberation movement from the eighteenth century to the recent past. The two volumes broke, significantly, at 1917, the year of the Bolshevik Revolution. Up to 1917 merited 644 pages; from 1917 to 1939, 634. Before 1917, they seemed to say, preparation; from 1917 onward, fulfillment. The past, for them, offered a vindicating vision of the future (Bogolyubov, R'izhkova, Popov, and Dubinskii 1962).

Each volume contained commissioned essays on major events, economic changes, workers' movements in industrial areas, and liberation movements in nonindustrial areas. It set down summaries for country after country, region after region. Here are titles of the two volumes' introductory and concluding chapters:

Volume I, chapter 1: Formation of a Producing Proletariat and the First Independent Appearances of Workers in England, France, and Germany.

Volume I, chapter 33: Workers' and National-Liberation Movements during the First World War.

Volume II, chapter 1: The World-Historical Significance of the Great October Socialist Revolution.

Volume II, chapter 27: International Workers' Movements 1917–1939. The Communist International.

We see unfolding an updated Communist Manifesto story of class formation and crystallization of popular action in militant movements, with the Bolshevik Revolution now figuring as the harbinger of worldwide collective action against tyranny. The second volume's final chapter concluded with this summary of conditions in 1939:

> Despite the impossibility of holding a Comintern congress in the conditions of the war's outbreak and the difficulty of maintaining contacts between individual parties and the Comintern's leading organs, the communist parties of most countries managed to offer correct analyses of conditions and interconnections of class forces and to work out correct tactical lines, to rally around themselves the broad popular masses in the battle for the interests of workers, for freedom and independence of their countries, for democracy, against reaction and Fascism. Here we have described the huge role played by the Communist International in the development of the world communist movement.
>
> (Bogolyubov, R'izhkova, Popov, and Dubinskii 1962: II, 625)

While to a twenty-first-century reader the forty-year-old party-line prose, with its "correct analyses" and "correct tactical lines," reeks of antiquity, it expresses a common inside view of social movement activity during the twentieth century: we are fulfilling history, and we will prevail.

Although they certainly stressed communist parties and the Comintern, these Soviet historians of 1962 took a broad view of relevant movements across the world. Their second volume's chronologies for 1935 and 1936 appear in Table 4.1. During those eventful years, the chronologies of major events included the emphatically noncommunist American New Deal legislation that finally authorized industrial (as opposed to craft) unions, antifascist action whether communist-organized or not, and electoral victories of Left coalitions in Spain and France. Unsurprisingly, the chroniclers omitted the lethal purges of the Soviet Communist Party, wholesale transfers of rural populations, and massive expulsions of suspected counterrevolutionaries from Moscow and Leningrad that Stalin was orchestrating during the same years. The absence of a truly cohesive account of what happened in the Soviet Union and the world during this period illustrates the danger of relying on one account when making historical analyses. If someone just read the chroniclers account, they would not have a truly accurate understanding of the social change and would be more likely to follow and believe the narrative arch of the teleological account.

For the part of the twentieth century up to 1939, the chronologies portray an international workers' movement sometimes facing setbacks, such as fascist countermobilizations and defeated rebellions, but generally gaining strength, increasing in international scope, and—after the fateful year of 1917—taking inspiration from the Soviet Communist Party.

The compilation's nineteenth-century chronologies enumerate several events already familiar to us from our own survey of the century. These events include the partial legalization of workers' organizations in England (1824), Lyon's workers' insurrections of 1831 and 1834, Britain's Chartist movement, the French revolution of 1848, and the formation of militant workers' parties, major strike waves in the United States from the 1860s onward and the foundation of the Argentine Socialist Party (1896). France gets a great deal of attention, partly because of its revolutionary tradition and partly because Marx, Engels, and Lenin wrote quotable analyses of the country's nineteenth-century political history. Outside of Europe and the United States, the chronologies also signal Latin American independence struggles (1810–1826), the Opium War of England and China (1839–1842), China's Taiping Rebellion (1851–1864), Indian rebellions against English rule (1857–1859), founding of the Indian National Congress (1885), creation of Sun Yat-sen's (Sun Yixian's) Society for the Regeneration of China (1894), Cuba's rebellion against Spain (1895–1898), formation of the Chilean Socialist Party (1897), and the Boxer Rebellion in China (1899–1900).

Yet some of the Soviet books' silences sound loudly, at least to ears tuned for social movements. Despite substantial chapters on English industrialization and the American Civil War, antislavery mobilizations make no appearance in the nineteenth-century history. Catholic emancipation, parliamentary reform, and female suffrage disappear from the British roster. In the United States, we

Table 4.1 Soviet Historians' Movement Chronologies for 1935 and 1936

1935	
July	Wagner Act, or law on industrial relations in the USA
July	Antifascist demonstrations in Paris and other French cities
July–August	Seventh Congress of the Comintern
1 August	Address of the Chinese Communist Party to the Chinese people calling for creation of a united anti-Japanese front
October	Conference of the German Communist Party in Brussels
October	Italian antifascist conference in Brussels
all year	Mass antifascist movement in Poland, with general strikes in Lodz, Cracow, and Lvov
1936	
January	Publication of the Popular Front program in France
February	Victory of the Popular Front in Spanish elections
May	Victory of the Popular Front in French elections
July	Fascist uprising in Spain. Beginning of the Spanish people's national-revolutionary war against fascist rebels and German-Italian interventionists
July	Beginning of international mass antifascist movement for the defense of the Spanish Republic

Source: Bogolyubov, R'izhkova, Popov, and Dubinskii 1962: IL 633.

hear nothing of nativism, temperance, and municipal reform. Argentina's Unión Cívica makes not a sound. The descriptions of the years 1847–1848 abound with revolutionary movements, but do not mention the Swiss civil war. Researchers of the Department of the History of the International Working and National Liberation Movement took their mandate seriously. They were not surveying all the world's social movements and political struggles but only those that bore somehow on the mission of bringing the world's workers into a communist-led collective fight for freedom.

Within that more restricted scope, what picture of nineteenth-century social movements does the Soviet survey project? From its retrospect of 1962, this Soviet study portrays a century of great promise: European and North American workers begin to show signs of class consciousness, and Latin American masses overthrow their Spanish masters. Soon Chinese, Indian, and Latin American peoples are beginning to resist other varieties of colonialism and make connections with the worldwide workers' movement.

As the Soviet movement history enters into the twentieth century, the Russian Revolution of 1905 adds Russia to the nineteenth-century revolutionary tradition, though it reveals a proletariat still unready to seize power. The Bolshevik Revolution then consolidates the nineteenth century's hopeful projects by offering a concrete model of proletarian revolution and a communist regime strong enough to lend muscle for workers' efforts everywhere. Between 1917 and 1939, we encounter a round of revolutionary struggles immediately after World War I: the founding of the Comintern, and the extension of progressive mobilization in Japan, Korea, Mexico, Indonesia, Iran, Turkey, Uruguay, Mongolia, Egypt, Hong Kong, Syria, the Philippines, and elsewhere, followed in the 1930s by formation of a far-reaching antifascist coalition. Soviet historians writing in 1962 knew, of course, that the German and Italian fascist regimes had collapsed in World War II and that a battered Soviet Union had emerged from the war on the winning side. Their vantage point helps explain the combination of teleology and wishful thinking that informed their history of movements up to 1939.

If the same group of experts had extrapolated their account forward through the remainder of the twentieth century, what features of the period from 1939 to 2000 would they have gotten right? They might have taken credit for having anticipated anticolonial mobilization, stressing how often leaders of independence movements styled themselves as socialists and drew encouragement from China or the Soviet Union. They might also have drawn some satisfaction from the formation of vigorous workers' movements in Japan, Korea, Brazil, and other rapidly industrializing countries. At least after the fact, they could probably have accommodated the American civil rights movement of the 1960s. They would, however, have encountered three very large surprises: proliferation of what Western observers eventually came to call new social movements, disintegration of almost all state socialist regimes, and the connections that later historians would start to make between new social movements, on one side, and opposition to state socialism, on the other.

The Social Movement Surge of 1968

In 1968, West Berlin, walled off from communist-run East Berlin, formed a western island in the midst of the solidly communist German Democratic Republic (for a sophisticated world survey of 1968, see Suri 2003: chap. 5). During 1968, nevertheless, West Berlin's Free University became the base for massive demonstrations against American involvement in Vietnam and against the West German government. Italy then hosted the most powerful communist party outside of state socialism. In Italy of 1968, not just communists but a wide variety of workers, students, Catholic churchgoers, and middle-class citizens—sometimes independently, sometimes in concert—started a round of claim making that continued into the early 1970s (Tarrow 1989).

Most famously, French students and workers joined in partially coordinated attacks on the regime of Charles de Gaulle and Georges Pompidou; they looked as though they might bring the regime down. In May 1968, the left-leaning magazine *Nouvel Observateur* published an interview of twenty-three-year-old French-German student leader Daniel Cohn-Bendit by none other than Jean-Paul Sartre. The interview opened with this exchange:

> JEAN-PAUL SARTRE: In a few days, with no call for a general strike, France was essentially paralyzed by strikes and factory occupations. All that because students took over the streets in the Latin Quarter. How do you analyze the movement you've started? How far can it go?
>
> DANIEL COHN-BENDIT: It grew beyond what we could have predicted at the start. Our objective is now to overthrow the regime. But it's not up to us whether that happens or not. If the Communist Party, the General Confederation of Labor, and the other national unions really shared our aims, there would be no problem: the regime would fall in a fortnight because it has no means of fending off a show of strength by the whole workforce.
>
> (Bourges 1968: 86)

History ruled otherwise: Pompidou's well-timed concessions to organized labor split the temporary worker–student alliance, and a June referendum brought a landslide for de Gaulle. However, the movement certainly shook France's regime.

The mobilization of 1968 extended far beyond Western Europe.

- In Canada, almost every university hosted its own uprising, and 40,000 Québecois students staged a general strike on behalf of becoming an independent socialist state (Westhues 1975: 392–94).
- In Mexico, student demands for civil liberties led to campus general strikes and swelling demonstrations reaching 100,000 participants or more. They led to the 2nd of October gathering at the Plaza de las Tres Culturas in Tlatelolco, at which the army and police killed hundreds of demonstrators and arrested more than 2,000.

- In state socialist Poland, students and intellectuals united in a campaign of meetings, demonstrations, and petitions on behalf of political rights and economic reform despite severe repression.
- In Pakistan, students launched a nationwide protest campaign against an ordinance that empowered the government to withdraw the degree of any student. Workers organized general strikes in solidarity (Katsiaficas 1988: 56).
- In Prague, dissident intellectuals spoke out against communist censorship and helped bring reformist Alexander Dubček to leadership of the Czechoslovak Communist Party. The 1968 Czech mobilization opened a season of liberalization that ended after dramatic resistance when Soviet-backed troops and tanks invaded the country in August.

The United States also participated energetically in 1968's movements:

- The American Indian Movement made its appearance on the national scene;
- Protests against the Vietnam War accelerated;
- The assassination of Martin Luther King Jr. incited collective attacks on property and struggles with police in mainly black neighborhoods of about 125 cities;
- Radical students at Columbia University and elsewhere shut down their schools;
- The Oakland-based Black Panthers distributed copies of Chairman Mao's writings on the University of California's Berkeley campus;
- The guerrilla image of Che Guevara (recently executed by Bolivian troops) became popular across a wide variety of dissident groups;
- A Poor People's March brought thousands of protesters to Washington;
- President Lyndon Johnson declined to run for a second term in the face of widespread opposition;
- The Chicago nominating convention of the Democratic Party generated a wave of demonstrations and street fighting; but
- Republican nominee Richard Nixon went on to beat Democrat Hubert Humphrey in a fiercely contested election.

Although the year's social movement organizers clearly fell far short of their announced objectives, 1968 marked a significant transition in American public politics and a substantial expansion in the range of social movement activity.

Reactions to 1968's conflicts in the United States and elsewhere developed the idea that "old" social movements on behalf of power for workers and other exploited categories had passed their prime. "New" social movements oriented to autonomy, self-expression, and the critique of postindustrial society, many observers thought, were supplanting the old. French sociologist Alain Touraine, a veteran analyst of workers' movements in Western Europe and Latin America, articulated some of the most influential ideas along this line and taught some of its most widely read proponents. Before 1968 ended, Touraine published a major statement under the title *The May Movement, or Utopian Communism.*

National liberation struggles were succumbing to the power of the world's dominant states, Touraine declared, while the Cold War had deadlocked the earlier open struggle between capitalism and socialism. The sheer power of governments, corporations, and mass media to produce stifling conformity, continued Touraine, had become the enemy of creativity and change.

Social movements of a new type, according to Touraine, held out the hope of breaking the bureaucratic stranglehold. The crucial task, he concluded, was

> to reveal what forces and social conflicts are operating in this new type of society, still too new to be aware of its nature and its problems. It is this new class struggle, between domination by the control apparatus and those who are experiencing change, that lends the May movement its importance, that makes it not the pivotal moment of a crisis but the beginning of new struggles that will be just as fundamental and lasting in our society as was the workers' movement in the course of capitalist industrialization.
>
> (Touraine 1968: 279)

Touraine's language promoted a comparison between resistance to state socialism and attacks on the rulers of capitalist democracies; both could forward liberation from oppressive systems of top-down control. Social movements of a new type could play vital roles in either setting.

Soon the term "new social movement" expanded to include mobilizations on behalf of feminism, homosexual rights, psychedelic drugs, indigenous peoples, the environment, and a variety of other causes that did not map easily into Touraine's own critique of postindustrial oppression. Activists and commentators began speaking of "identity" as the key, in contrast to the ostensibly instrumental aims of earlier social movements (Cohen 1985). They also began connecting new social movements with the creation of vibrant, autonomous civil societies in both capitalist and postsocialist countries (Cohen and Arato 1992). Reporting a massive French–Polish collaborative research effort on the Polish worker-based movement Solidarity, Alain Touraine and his colleagues asked:

> What is the aim of this social movement? Seize power, establish a proletarian dictatorship or the rule of workers' councils? Not at all. First because the agreements of Gdansk, which have from the start constituted Solidarity's fundamental law, explicitly recognize the party's leading role in the state. Second because militants themselves are trying to free themselves from the grip of power and not to win power. The repeatedly stated aim of Solidarity is to free society from the party's totalitarian domination.
>
> (Touraine, Dubet, Wieviorka, and Strzelecki 1982: 93)

Unlike their sedulously interest-oriented predecessors with their aims of wringing power and benefits from the existing system, ran the argument, identity-centered new social movements could recast the very framework of social life.

Craig Calhoun deftly punctured that balloon. In an article wittily titled "New Social Movements of the Early Nineteenth Century," Calhoun pointed out how regularly nineteenth-century mobilizations on behalf of ethnic minorities, women, religious revival, and workers' rights also stressed demands for autonomy and identity. We need to consider, concluded Calhoun, "the possibility that proliferation of NSMs is normal to modernity and not in need of special explanation because it violates the oppositions of left and right, cultural and social, public and private, aesthetic and instrumental that organize so much of our thought" (Calhoun 1995: 205; for similar doubts based on close study of Italian social movements, see Tarrow 1989: 194–95). In this book's terms, Calhoun was emphasizing how often identity claims accompany program and standing claims, sometimes becoming the focus of social movement activity. Social movements are always making new claims in at least one of these regards. When new political actors appear on the social movement scene, assertions of identity become crucial to the actors' impacts on constituencies, competitors, potential allies, and the objects of their program or standing claims. The distinction between "identity" and "interest" movement dissolves.

Crises and Transitions in 1989

Selected headlines from the 1989 *New York Times* (Table 4.2) tell stories that surely would have amazed the Soviet chroniclers of 1962. In terse summaries, we witness the flourishing of Poland's Solidarity movement; the installation of competitive electoral politics in most of Europe's state socialist regimes; lip service to democratization in even such hidebound authoritarian regimes as Albania's version of state socialism; mobilization leading to the destruction of the Berlin Wall; vast demonstrations in Budapest, Berlin, and Prague; a combination of social movement with civil war in Romania; and—perhaps most astonishing—a month during which students, workers, and city residents seized control of central Beijing's public spaces and even held back the army before a bloody military sweep (June 4) broke the movement. Yugoslavia began to tremble with demands for autonomies and distinctive regimes for its federated republics.

Social movements, long banned from the public politics of state socialism, seemed to be exploding the old socialist system. Among visible state socialist regimes, only Albania and Cuba managed to maintain close control. Even in Cuba a state visit of Soviet leader Mikhail Gorbachev (April 2–5, 1989) embarrassed Fidel Castro's regime, as Gorbachev chose the occasion to deliver a speech that renounced the policy of exporting revolution. This event reveals the disagreements even among large communist states and their leaders.

Confrontations in Beijing eventually brought a resounding defeat for democracy, but along the way they focused world attention on Chinese popular mobilization. Table 4.3 offers an abbreviated summary of events in Beijing alone; in fact, by June, students and workers all over the country were participating in one version or another of the Beijing events. When connected dissidents face authoritarian regimes, they commonly have three choices: bide their time in silence, engage in forbidden and clandestine acts of destruction, or overload the narrow range of tolerated occasions for assembly and expression. In the third case, criticism of regimes often occurs in the course of public holidays and ceremonies—Mardi Gras, inaugurations, funerals, royal weddings, and the like—when authorities tolerate larger and more public assemblies than usual. The Beijing events started exactly that way, with student memorials to the dead Hu Yaobang, a former secretary general of the Chinese Communist Party who had been quite unpopular with students while in office but who retroactively acquired the reputation of having been fired in 1987 for his excessive sympathy with student demands.

Students soon converted a ceremonial occasion into a mobilization having distinctive Chinese properties, yet in other regards greatly resembling social movement mobilizations elsewhere. When the government held a state funeral for Hu in Tiananmen's Great Hall of the People on April 22, some 50,000 students

Table 4.2 ***New York Times*** **Social Movement Headlines from the State Socialist World, 1989**

6 February	(Warsaw) Warsaw Opens Parley with Solidarity
26 March	(Moscow) Soviets Savor Vote in Freest Election since '17
2 April	(Havana) Gorbachev Begins His Visit to Cuba with Castro's Hug
4 May	(Beijing) Urging Chinese Democracy, 100,000 Surge Past Police
13 May	(Tirana) Albanian Leader Says the Country Will Be Democratized but Will Retain Socialism
13 May	(Beijing) China's Hero of Democracy: Gorbachev
17 May	(Beijing) A Million Chinese March, Adding Pressure for Change
4 June	(Beijing) Troops Attack and Crush Beijing Protest; Thousands Fight Back, Scores Are Killed
8 June	(Warsaw) Warsaw Accepts Solidarity Sweep and Humiliating Losses by Party
11 June	(Beijing) Democracy Movement: Over, for the Time Being
16 June	(Budapest) Hungarian Who Led '56 Revolt Is Buried as a Hero
15 October	(West Berlin) East German Movement Overtaken by Followers
4 November	(East Berlin) 500,000 in East Berlin Rally for Change; Émigrés Are Given Passage to West
20 November	(Prague) 200,000 March in Prague as Calls for Change Mount
25 November	(Prague) Prague Party Leaders Resign; New Chief, 48, Surprise Choice; 350,000 at Rally Cheer Dubček
26 November	(Budapest) Hungarians Hold First Free Vote in 42 Years, Shunning a Boycott
27 November	(Prague) Millions of Czechoslovaks Increase Pressure on Party with Two-Hour General Strike
4 December	(Prague) Protest Rallies Resume in Prague in Effort to Oust New Government
24 December	(Bucharest) Rumanian Army Gains in Capital but Battle Goes On

Source: Gwertzman and Kaufman 1991.

gathered at the square for the ceremonies. In an old, recognizable routine, groups of students regularly arrived at Tiananmen carrying banners representing the school units to which they belonged (Perry 2002: 313). Some of them reenacted old-regime rituals by kneeling on the Great Hall's steps to present a petition and ask humbly for a meeting with Premier Li Peng. Over the period from mid-April to the beginning of June, groups of students protested despite the presence of the government's armed forces; they marched despite prohibitions against assemblies,

Table 4.3 Chronology of the Beijing Student Movement, 1989

16 April	At death of Hu Yaobang, former secretary general of Chinese Communist Party, students post wreaths and elegiac couplets in Tiananmen Square and many Beijing colleges.
17 April	Students march to Tiananmen to memorialize Hu Yaobang.
20 April	Skirmishes between police and students at Xinhua Gate; some students begin class boycott.
22 April	Hu's funeral in Great Hall of the People; about 50,000 students march to Tiananmen to participate; numerous student actions include kneeling on the Great Hall's steps to deliver a petition and request a meeting with Premier Li Peng.
23 April	Students form Beijing Student Autonomous Union Provisional Committee.
26 April	*People's Daily* calls student mobilization "planned conspiracy," "turmoil."
27 April	About 100,000 students march to Tiananmen and protest the editorial. State Council announces willingness to meet with students.
29 April	Senior government officials meet with forty-five selected students from sixteen Beijing universities, but other students challenge both the dialogue and the student representatives.
4 May	Students march in commemoration of the May 4th Movement (of 1919).
5 May	Students form Beijing Student Dialogue Delegation. Most students end class boycott.
13 May	Three hundred students start hunger strike at Tiananmen, numbers eventually rising to 3,000 strikers, thousands of supporters.
14 May	High-level state delegation meets student activists; chaotic discussion ensues because of student divisions; students withdraw from the talks.
15 May	Mikhail Gorbachev arrives for a state visit; because of Tiananmen's occupation, government holds its official reception at the Beijing airport.
17 May	More than a million Beijing residents march in support of students and hunger strikers.
19 May	Government declares martial law, but residents and students block the troops. Students from outside Beijing continue to arrive in the city.
3 June	Military repression begins, with hundreds of people killed by government troops.
4 June	Troops encircle remaining 4,000 students at Tiananmen; students leave the square.

Source: Adapted from Zhao 2001: xxv–xxvi.

chanted slogans, staged hunger strikes, resisted orders to evacuate public spaces, and tossed bottles or shoes at the police. Such public contentious performances in China are quite significant because of the country's political structure, infamous for limiting free speech and any dissent against the government. Meanwhile, a state visit by Mikhail Gorbachev in mid-May embarrassed the regime's leaders (blocked from giving Gorbachev the customary state reception at Tiananmen) and encouraged students to call for Gorbachev-style reforms.

By that time, thousands of nonstudents had joined student activists in open challenges to the regime. As our two chronologies show, a million or more people marched through Beijing on May 17 in support of student demonstrators and hunger strikers. Demonstrators and their supporters blocked the 100,000 troops sent to clear Tiananmen during the nights of 19–20 May. Private entrepreneurs contributed money, services, and equipment such as battery-powered megaphones for student speakers. Despite considerable discouragement from student organizers (until mounting threats of repression changed the organizers' minds), substantial numbers of workers also provided aid and encouragement for the Tiananmen mobilization (Perry 2002: 318–23). Recent student arrivals from outside of Beijing, furthermore, increasingly swelled the crowds at the square. The mobilization was starting to overflow the square.

As martial law forces assembled in and around Beijing, residents often insulted and attacked the soldiers. But when troops began their assault on Tiananmen the night of June, 3, 1989, they brought in overwhelming force. On their way to retaking the city, soldiers killed about 250 people and only lost half a dozen of their own men. Between 4:30 and 6:30 a.m. on the 4th, the remaining students marched out of Tiananmen through columns opened by the military (Zhao 2001: 203–07). By the end of 1989, public mobilization of students and workers on behalf of civil liberties had entirely subsided across China.

Social movement mobilization in Eastern Europe had more durable success than in China. The *Annual Register* began its commentary on Eastern Europe's whirlwind year with a comparison to the French Revolution that had started exactly two centuries earlier.

> As we look back on 1989, the bicentenary celebrations of the start of the French Revolution in July [1789] seem like an historical overture to the actual drama of events in Eastern Europe, from October onwards, which by their range and speed gained a revolutionary label. Between the storming of the Bastille and the breach of the Berlin Wall, each an inaugural and symbolic incident of a far wider transformation of Europe, there was indeed a certain ancestral affinity. For the Declaration of the Rights of Man, which became the ideological manifesto of the French Revolution, was great-great-grandfather to the demand for personal freedom and political democracy which suddenly overwhelmed the fortress of authoritarian rule in East Germany, and then in Czechoslovakia, following more gradual but still radical reforms in Poland and Hungary, and followed in turn by reluctant changes in Bulgaria and by a triumphant uprising in Romania.
>
> (*Annual Register* 1989: 1)

Although the word "movement" recurred in the *Annual Register* accounts of particular countries' politics, the editorialist did not describe the events of 1989 as a social movement or a series of social movements. Indeed, the anonymous author invoked the authority of *Annual Register* founder Edmund Burke to warn: "He correctly foresaw that if you launch off from the claims of individuals, distinct from the societies to which they belong, you end with the despotism of a central authority as the incarnation of the sovereignty of the people" (*Annual Register* 1989: 3). One could hardly signal more emphatically the worrisome connection between social movement claim making and calls for popular sovereignty. Eastern European activists were making just such claims. As distinguished from the previous few decades' participation of East German, Russian, Chinese, Polish, Hungarian, Czech, and Romanian ordinary people in public politics, 1989 featured the combination of campaigns, WUNC displays, and performances from the social movement repertoire discussed in Chapter 1 to a startling degree.

Take the case of Czechoslovakia, where a repressive regime remained unshaken well into 1989. Regime forces ruthlessly dispersed a gathering in Prague to commemorate the anniversary of the Warsaw Pact's August 21, 1968 invasion of Czechoslovakia. After police and militia broke up a November 17 student commemoration of a student murdered by the Nazi government in 1939, students and theater groups used their national connections to call for a general strike. A new group called Civic Forum backed a declaration drafted by playwright Václav Havel that called for punishment of the repressive forces at the November 17 demonstration and demanded the establishment of civil liberties. An estimated three-quarters of the Czechoslovak population observed a two-hour strike on November 27. Then,

> when Prime Minister Adamec proposed a reform government on December 3, 1989, in which members of the Communist Party maintained a majority, Civic Forum rejected it and again threatened to strike. On December 7, the government capitulated and Adamec resigned. After two days of hurried negotiations between the civic movements and representatives of the Leninist regime, President Gustav Husák announced the formation of a Government of National Understanding in which members of Civic Forum had a majority, and then he himself resigned. With the nomination of Civic Forum spokesperson Václav Havel as president on December 30, 1989, the rapid demise of the Communist Party in Czechoslovakia was completed.
>
> (Glenn 2001: 8)

A stunning spread of social movement strategies accompanied and hastened the rapid collapse of a previously resistant state socialist regime.

At varying tempos, similar scenarios played out in much of Eastern Europe. Concentrating on the Soviet Union and its successor states, Mark Beissinger has taken the most comprehensive look at the deployment of social movement repertoire in Eastern Europe before, during, and after 1989. From a wide variety of sources he catalogued two sorts of events: public demonstrations of 100 persons or more, and "mass violent events" in which fifteen or more people gathered to attack persons or property (Beissinger 2002: 462–65). He points out that demonstrations and attacks did occur occasionally in the Soviet Union before Mikhail Gorbachev began his reform programs. In April 1965, for example, 100,000 people gathered in Yerevan, Armenia, to commemorate victims of the Ottoman expulsion and massacre of Armenians fifty years earlier (Beissinger 2002: 71). But under that repressive regime, both demonstrations and collective attacks by anyone other than state authorities remained very rare.

The arrival of reformer Gorbachev at the head of the Communist Party (1985), however, sparked an enormous expansion of claim making in the social movement style: not just mass demonstrations, but also special-purpose associations, strikes, press campaigns, and appeals for international support. (Those appeals often included demonstration signs in English rather than the local language in order to reach an international audience.) Although the earlier claims of Soviet social movements focused on political and economic reform, nationalist demands soon predominated. Russians themselves sometimes demanded special recognition within the Soviet Union; Boris Yeltsin first came to power as a Russian nationalist. But the bulk of the demands—as well as the mass violent events—were centered on recognition, autonomy, or independence for ethnically labeled subdivisions of the Soviet Union such as Estonia, Armenia, and Chechnya.

The relative timing of violent and nonviolent, nationalist and nonnationalist events tells a story of its own. Nonviolent demonstrations centering on nonnationalist claims reached their peak in 1989–1990, as a variety of claimants made bids to influence the form of government, the distribution of benefits, the provision of security, and related issues of civic participation. Nonviolent demonstrations concerning ethnic and national rights rose significantly in 1989, but they became even more frequent in 1991, before starting to dwindle. Violent attacks centered on nonnationalist questions never became frequent, but they did occur more often after 1989. The most dramatic shift occurred in nationalist violence. Despite secondary spurts in 1989 and 1990, it reached unprecedented heights in 1992 before tailing off rapidly (Beissinger 2002: 105, 284). Beissinger explains the sequence as a consequence of a political cycle: early risers, on average, either gained some advantages or demobilized peacefully. But those who persisted despite previous failures or arrived on the social movement scene late—especially if their program centered on political autonomy or independence—encountered rising resistance and engaged increasingly in claim making that incited or entailed violence. One can see some similarities in the more recent wave of protests in North Africa and the Middle East.

Grzegorz Ekiert and Jan Kubik prepared a similar catalog of "protest events" in Poland for 1989 through 1993. (An event qualified as a protest if participants made specific demands in nonroutine ways and if three or more people—from one person upward in the case of self-immolation and other "extreme" acts—took part.) In Poland, mass demonstrations accompanied the

1989 overthrow of the communist regime, but a new surge of demonstrations arrived in 1991, as a wide variety of claimants publicized their programs, identities, and political standings. On the 1993 calendar:

> In January, approximately 7,000 people demonstrated against the president and burned his effigy in front of his residence. In March, over 10,000 public sector employees marched through the streets of Warsaw demanding higher wages and increased state spending on education and health. In May, 4,000 farmers dumped stacks of hay in front of the government building, protesting the government's agricultural policies and demanding price controls, protective tariffs, and credit guarantees. In June, several thousand demonstrators clashed with police on the streets of Warsaw and ended the protest by burning the image of a red pig in front of the government building.
>
> (Ekiert and Kubik 1999: 108)

These were merely the most visible of the 250 Polish protest events Ekiert and Kubik uncovered for 1993. Considering Poland's exit from state socialism, the events stand out for their utter familiarity: despite specific idioms, such as a red pig to represent the former communist rulers, they greatly resemble demonstrations elsewhere across the democratic and democratizing world.

Were These Social Movements?

To what extent do the popular mobilizations of 1989 under authoritarian regimes therefore qualify as social movements? We tread on delicate, shifting ground. Across most of Eastern Europe, if not in China, social movements of a sort easily recognizable from our nineteenth-century survey eventually became widely available as means of political claim making. Looking at Poland or the Czech Republic today, we repeatedly see the combination of campaigns, WUNC displays, and performances in the social movement repertoire, such as mounting of demonstrations, releases to the press, and formation of special-interest associations devoted to specific public programs. We notice that many other groups, not just political dissidents, employ these means for making claims. But at what point in time and the political process can we reasonably declare that the social movement synthesis of campaign, repertoire, and WUNC display became widely available across groups, issues, and objects of claims? The question matters here for two reasons: first, because it bears on the general causal connections between social movements and democratization; second, because if in fact each regime invented its own social movements more or less independently, that fact would challenge the story of one-time invention and subsequent diffusion with adaptation that I have drawn from the eighteenth- and nineteenth-century histories in previous chapters.

Let us return attentively to the three test questions we have already applied to similar decisions:

(1) *Resemblance*: Does this particular campaign, performance, or WUNC display resemble those that commonly occur in full-fledged social movements?
(2) *Combination*: Does this particular campaign combine performances and WUNC displays in a recognizably similar manner to social movements elsewhere?
(3) *Availability*: In this setting, is the characteristic combination of campaign, performances, and WUNC displays now widely available for different issues, claimants, and objects of claims?

Once we pose the problem this way, it becomes fairly easy to recognize that, at their start, the state socialist mobilizations of 1989 all qualified under the first heading: with due allowance for such local idioms as kneeling on the Great Hall's steps and burning images of red pigs, they all involved some clear analogs to familiar social movement activities elsewhere. At that point, however, none had reached the third stage, that of making campaigns, performances, and WUNC displays widely available in popular public politics. All were located somewhere in the middle ground, early or late in the process of synthesizing campaign, performances, and WUNC displays into durable social movements pressing claims for regime change. To reach the third stage of having the campaigns, performances, and WUNC displays widely available, the movements would have needed to extend beyond their immediate spheres and origins.

All the countries involved had two sources of models for social movement action: their own earlier histories and their knowledge of social movements in the nonsocialist world. Before their moves into socialism, China, Russia, Poland, Hungary, East Germany, Romania, and Czechoslovakia had all passed through substantial twentieth-century periods in which at least some sectors of their population had engaged feverishly in the association building, meeting, demonstrating, communicating, and campaign planning of social movements. Those earlier efforts remained as available models. Through radio, television, electronic messaging, and occasional travel in both directions, many citizens of state socialist regimes received information about public politics in North America, Western Europe, and East Asia's capitalist countries. From at least the 1968 West Berlin student movement onward, East Germans in particular had widespread access to social movement models from West Germany. From syntheses of local history and available models, dissidents in the state socialist regimes of 1989 were starting to construct their own social movement sectors.

By that time, social movements had become regular features of public politics in a number of countries outside of Western Europe and North America. The upsurge of 1968 has already shown us Mexican students participating in social movement claim making. Elsewhere in Latin America, social movements likewise proliferated during 1989. In Argentina, for example, struggles over the transfer of power from Radical Raúl Alfonsín to Peronist Carlos Saúl Menem—Argentina's first peaceful change of presidential party since 1916—produced large mobilizations by trade unions, human rights groups, military veterans, and the Madres de la Plaza de Mayo (mothers whose family members had been abducted by the military who would meet in a public plaza in Buenos Aires wearing white headscarves). No social movements surfaced, however, in authoritarian Chile (still ruled by General Pinochet), Paraguay (where a coup toppled long-term dictator Alfredo Stroessner but replaced him with another general), or Cuba (where Fidel Castro's special version of state socialism included tight controls over popular expression).

All of these authoritarian countries had passed through earlier periods of social movement activity, but despots and dictators had shut that activity down. In Cuba, for example, social movements had flourished prior to Fulgencio Batista's coup of 1952 and continued intermittently in moments of regime weakness up to the Castro-led revolution of 1959. In 1955

> a series of developments marked the anti-Batista movement. *Auténticos*, *ortodoxos*, and other *políticos* regrouped and seemed to be better coordinated. University students elected new leadership and expressed renewed discontent. Toward the end of the year, independence war veteran Cosme de la Torriente formed the Friends of the Republic Society and called for a civic dialogue and a new round of elections. Except for the July 26th movement, every other opposition sector participated. Although Batista accepted the invitation, he would not concede to elections before their scheduled date of 1958. His intransigence bolstered those who argued that armed struggle was the only way to challenge his rule.
>
> (Pérez-Stable 1993: 56)

Despite calling itself the July 26th Movement, once it seized power in 1959, Castro's force rapidly suppressed opposition campaigns, performances, and WUNC displays (Pérez-Stable 1993: 52–81). In short, as of 1989, the Latin American map of social movements corresponded approximately to the map of relatively democratic regimes. Latin America's many authoritarian rulers still discouraged the combination of bottom-up campaigns, social movement performances, and WUNC displays. This shows that, freer and more democratic states allow for more opportunities for social movements to form.

By century's end, the basic generalization applied to the entire world: wherever relatively extensive democratic institutions operated, so too did social movements. What is more, wherever rapid steps toward democracy occurred—South Korea, Taiwan, South Africa, and elsewhere—those steps typically brought the flowering of campaigns, performances, and WUNC displays in the social movement vein. Sometimes, to be sure, it seemed that social movements had swept the whole world, democratic or authoritarian. Television, for example, occasionally showed the paraphernalia of demonstrations—gathering in public places, marching in ranks, shouting slogans, bearing signs, and so on—from remote corners of the earth. But it helps to recall our three-part test: (1) resemblance, (2) combination, and (3) availability.

By the year 2000, almost every country, at some point, met test 1 regarding resemblance, with supporters or opponents of the regime adopting one element or another from those in the social movement array. Since the vast majority of countries declared themselves democracies of some sort, the sheer presence of international mass media called forth at least some staged performances of popular public claim making by means of campaigns, social movement activities, or (especially) WUNC displays. Only a minority of regimes, however, unambiguously met test 3. In another substantial minority, some privileged sectors of the population could engage in limited social movement claim making, so long as they stayed within their prescribed limits and avoided offending the regime's most powerful actors. Students (who were often, of course, children of the ruling class) enjoyed that precarious privilege in a number of semiauthoritarian regimes.

Indonesia provides a clear case in point. Although contested elections began producing genuine government changes during the late 1990s, the Indonesian military retained great power in and behind the government, administered a number of rebellious areas, and used force widely with little fear of punishment. As of 2000, the New York-based democracy monitoring organization, Freedom House, rated Indonesia at the midpoint on its scales for political rights and civil liberties, labeling the regime as "partly free" (Karatnycky 2000: 235). After delayed announcement of results from a national election held in June 1999,

> on September 23, students in Jakarta put the government on notice that they would take to the streets if it took decisions that went counter to reform. That day, the parliament passed an army-backed bill on national security that would have given the army sweeping powers to declare states of emergency at the regional or national level. Pro-democracy groups and student organizations mobilized thousands in protest, and in the ensuing clash with security forces, four people were killed, including one policeman. On September 24, the government announced that it was suspending implementation of the law.
>
> (Human Rights Watch 2000: 193–94)

As this small opening for performances in the social movement style appeared in Jakarta, however, much of Indonesia engaged in a very different sort of politics, what Human Rights Watch calls "communal riots" involving religious factions, separatists, strongmen's militias, or all three.

Where peaceful protests did occur, furthermore, they did not much resemble the interactions of social movements. In February 1999, for example,

> in what was billed as a "national dialogue" on Irian Jaya's future political status, 100 prominent public figures from Irian Jaya presented President Habibie with a statement expressing the aspirations of the people of Irian Jaya for independence. The government rejected any discussion of independence, and in April, after participants in the meeting tried to disseminate the results of the meeting to a larger public at home, the Irian Jaya chief of police banned any further discussion. In August, news leaked out that five prominent Irianese had been banned from leaving Indonesia as of June 28. The ban, initiated by the military and imposed by immigration officials, was justified on unspecified national security grounds.
>
> (Human Rights Watch 2000: 195)

Although the Soviet Union and its successor states of 1989–1992 hardly qualified as entrenched democracies, Beissinger's analysis of claim making there makes it clear that the Soviet Union had come much closer to institutionalizing social movements by 1989 than had Indonesia by 1999.

In both cases, nevertheless, the international arena made a large difference to social movement performances and their suppression. The Soviet Union's demonstrators for political autonomy were addressing potential external supporters at the same time as they confronted Soviet authorities. Jakarta's students could take to the streets in part because of their membership in a national elite, but also in part because international television would broadcast their demands—and perhaps their struggles with the police—the very next day. On our three-step test, we might be able to place some Indonesian student mobilizations in test 2, but we could certainly not assign Indonesia as a whole to the list of countries that, as of the twentieth century's end, had fully institutionalized social movements.

Twentieth-Century Transmutations

In the minority of national regimes that had regularized social movement claim making by 2000, a century of substantial change in the character and distribution of social movements lay behind them. The more important twentieth-century trends included:

- routinization of (some) relations between social movement organizers and local authorities, especially police specializing in public order and crowd control;
- evolution of campaigns, social movement performances, and WUNC displays in response to changing means of communication;
- adoption of social movement campaigns by opponents of radical and reformist movements; and
- substantial adaptation of social movement campaigns, repertoires, and WUNC displays to local and national political cultures in countries outside the zone of early social movement development.

Over the century, impressive changes occurred in relations between social movement activists and authorities. At the twentieth century's end, many social movement participants still considered police and local authorities their enemies; they told repeated stories of brutality and repression. Yet compared to a century earlier, the legal environment had altered significantly. Where social movements occurred regularly, authorities might still require permits for meetings and demonstrations; demand that suspect organizations register; hound those organizations by means of surveillance, infiltration, conspiracy prosecutions, or tax assessments; limit access of dissidents to the media; shield public figures from attack; or avert their eyes from dirty tricks by a movement's opponents. As compared with shooting down demonstrators, incarcerating movement activists as subversives, and wholesale banning of dissident organizations, prevalent late-twentieth-century practices revealed a vast change in relations between activists and regimes in many places.

To recognize the change more clearly, we can crank the century's film back to Berlin at the start of the twentieth century. The case of Berlin shows the clash of street demonstrators and police as activist groups sought to have their demands met. German historian Thomas Lindenberger has done a splendid, detailed study of Berlin's "street politics" from 1900 to 1914. He speaks of the "little everyday war between police and public." As reference points for his wide-ranging study of street contention, Lindenberger assembled three substantial catalogs: of "little street wars," of industrial strikes, and of street demonstrations. In the case of street wars, Lindenberger prepared a catalog resembling those of Deneckere, Beissinger, Ekiert, and Kubik. His 405 "street disorders" collected from the neighborhood reporting in the daily *Vossische Zeitung* included occasions in which an estimated twenty or more people gathered in a public place and police intervened—whether or not the event began with a civilian–police encounter (Lindenberger 1995: 107–08). Official statistics, police reports, and periodicals supplied him with ample documentation on strikes. Extensive police reporting, plus the *Vossische Zeitung* and the socialist newspaper *Vorwärts*, also allowed him to prepare an exhaustive inventory of major street demonstrations through the period. Let us focus on the demonstrations.

In parallel with our news from nineteenth-century France, Lindenberger points out that, before the early twentieth century, most quasi-demonstrations occurred in the context of funeral marches and public holidays (Lindenberger 1995: 308–16). Like in France, May 1 became an unofficial workers' holiday, and the occasion for assertive gatherings, around 1890. But police generally broke up the frequent efforts of participants in indoor meetings to take to the streets at meeting's end. When the campaign for working-class voting rights began in 1906, however, the situation changed. From then until World War I, Berlin resounded with street demonstrations despite strenuous efforts of the city authorities and police to suppress them. "At least in the initial phase up to 1910, street demonstrations occurred against the background of a struggle against the police for control of the streets" (Lindenberger 1995: 386).

Table 4.4 describes the major demonstrations occurring in Berlin during ten weeks of 1910. They give a picture of a regime grudgingly making concessions to social movement activists, but using public order as grounds for containing or banning public performances such as meetings and demonstrations by regime opponents. Despite the presence of Social Democratic and Democratic Alliance deputies in the national legislature, the Berlin police kept a tight rein on street activities by both parties. As a consequence, the most frequent approach to demonstrating was to hold an authorized public meeting (with a police officer present to take notes and to call in reinforcements if necessary) and for people leaving the meeting to make their presence known briefly on the street under the watchful eyes of the police. At that point, we might think of Germany as making a stumbling entry into our test 3: widespread availability of social movement

Table 4.4 Demonstrations in Berlin, February–May 1910

13 February	Two hundred thousand participants in forty-two Social Democratic meetings across the city with subsequent street demonstrations involving tens of thousands.
15 February	Meetings of the city's women's movement followed by small demonstrations
20 February	Meeting of freethinkers with a short demonstration afterward.
27 February	Eight thousand participants in a meeting of left-liberal intellectuals followed by a demonstration involving a few thousand in front of the royal palace.
6 March	Demonstration announced in *Vorwärts* but forbidden by the authorities: a "right to vote stroll" shifted overnight from Treptow Park to the Zoo, where about 150,000 people demonstrated. Police went to both Treptow Park and the Zoo on foot and horseback, using bared swords against people in the gathering.
13 March	Five thousand participants in a meeting of the left-liberal Democratic Alliance, followed by a demonstration.
15 March	Forty-eight Social Democratic meetings across metropolitan Berlin without demonstrations, but with police decrees against any displays in public.
17 March	Social Democratic meeting in Spandau, followed by a demonstration.
18 March	Altercations between police and Social Democrats after a meeting at the cemetery of Friedrich Woods.
10 April	Three authorized open-air gatherings of Social Democrats and the Democratic Alliance in Treptow Park, Friedrich Woods, and Humboldt Woods with about 25,000 participants.
1 May	May Day celebrations after the authorized late-morning period had ended, but without police-demonstrator violence.

Source: Lindenberger 1995: 326–27.

campaigns, performances, and WUNC displays. Until it collapsed with the Nazi seizure of power (1933), the Weimar Republic that followed World War I offered wider scope to social movement claim making.

Leap forward to the later twentieth century. German authorities never stopped watching social movements closely; but after the repressive hiatus of the Nazi regime and World War II, they conceded an open legal space in German politics to conjoined campaigns, social movement performances, and WUNC displays. Summing up her comparison of "protest policing" in Germany and Italy between 1950 and 1990, Donatella della Porta concludes that

> in Italy as well as in Germany, from 1950 to 1990, protest control evolved toward more flexible forms based on a more liberal understanding of demonstration rights. In both countries, public order policies became more tolerant, more selective, more oriented toward prevention, more respectful of democratic procedures, and "softer," even though this evolution was hardly linear

> (both countries experienced "relapses," as it were, when political conflicts escalated into violent forms). We can add that, over time, cross-national differences seemed to diminish, probably because of international cooperation and cross-national flows of information involving both movement organizations and law enforcers.
>
> (della Porta 1995: 71; see also della Porta and Reiter 1998)

Social movements waxed and waned to the rhythms of a particular country's political history. The rise of regime-threatening social movements almost always stimulated attempts to repress them. But on the average and in the long run, authorities, police, and social movement organizers negotiated routines that provided broad opportunities for nonviolent campaigns, WUNC displays, and employment of the social movement repertoire. Whether this continues into the twenty-first century is an open question.

Movements and Media

From the eighteenth-century days of incipient social movements onward, newspapers, magazines, pamphlets, and other print media conveyed campaign messages, announced forthcoming movement activities, evaluated those activities, and provided news reports on their successes or failures. Nevertheless, twentieth-century alteration and expansion of communications media offered unprecedented opportunities and exposure to social movements. Radio, television, electronic messaging, opinion polls, and worldwide proliferation of the press all triggered shifts in campaigns, social movement performances, and WUNC displays.

As compared with direct attacks and person-to-person negotiation, broadcast of movement claims by means of public media reaches far more third parties. Those third parties include powerful figures other than the ones to whom activists are directing their claims. But they also include publics that will be making relevant judgments in elections, purchases, opinion polls, and other expressions of support; potential recruits to the cause; and, for that matter, allies of the target(s) who might reconsider their positions (Koopmans 2004). Thus, the broadcast of movement claims with regard to program, identity, and standing through such mass media as newspapers and magazines amplified the audience for social movements and WUNC displays.

Movement involvement with mass media also produces a sort of echo chamber in which activists hear how others are interpreting their claims to program, identity, and standing. Both the extent and the character of reporting, therefore, become objects of movement strategy. By no means, however, did twentieth-century social movements establish dominant or even equal relations with mass media. Movements attracted attention to the extent that their campaigns, performances, and WUNC displays became newsworthy: big, colorful, locally relevant, and/or oriented to issues already under widespread public discussion (Hocke 2002; McCarthy, McPhail, and Smith 1996; Oliver and Maney 2000; Oliver and Myers 1999; Scalmer 2002a; Tilly 2002b). This built-in asymmetry meant that activists could rarely count on media coverage, had little control over their portrayal in the media, and usually came away dissatisfied with the media treatment they received.

The most telling effect of new media was connecting activists with the circumscribed audiences reached by those media, and therefore to disconnect them from people not accessing the same media. Newspapers had a narrowing effect on social movement audiences so long as literacy was low and readership sparse. The internet, with its very unequal access—in 2017, only 15 percent of households in developing countries had internet access at home, while 84 percent of households in the developed world do—surely has a similar effect (International Telecommunications Union 2017). These dynamics are structured by age as well. In developed countries, 94% of young people aged 15–24 use the Internet compared with 67% in developing countries and only 30% in Least Developed Countries (LDCs) (International Telecommunications Union 2017). The internet reaches far beyond any activist's immediate circle, but it reaches very selectively.

Media differ significantly in asymmetry. Print media, radio, and television permit little feedback from recipients, despite letters to editors, op-ed columns, talk shows, and other gestures toward symmetry. Telephones and the internet, in contrast, permit greater symmetry between sender and receiver. Twentieth-century social movement organizers, for example, often used preestablished telephone trees to bring out participants in movement performances. As phone solicitation internet advertising, bots, and internet algorithms indicate, however, even that symmetry butts up against serious limits; it may equalize relations among parties that already define themselves as equal, but it also offers opportunities for well-organized purveyors to dominate the circulation of information.

Let us therefore avoid technological determinism: the mere invention of new *communications media did not single-handedly change the character of social movements. What often happened was that some social movement organizers adapted newly available media to an activity they were already pursuing; most such adaptations fizzled, but a few did so well that they produced changes in the organization that made them and offered models to other organizations that were pursuing similar campaigns.*

Father Coughlin

Take the example of Charles Edward Coughlin. The Canadian-born Catholic priest became one of the United States' most influential social movement leaders of the 1930s until the church silenced him, returning him to parish work in 1942. Born in 1891 and educated in Toronto, Father Coughlin first taught at Assumption College near Windsor, Ontario, across the river from Detroit. In 1923, he became assistant pastor of a parish in Kalamazoo, Michigan, before moving to a parish in downtown Detroit. Recognizing Coughlin's eloquence and organizing talent, Detroit's bishop soon made him pastor of a small village, then offered him appointment as head pastor of a church in Royal Oak, a northern suburb where the Ku Klux Klan had been burning crosses to intimidate Catholics. The KKK was attempting to create fear among religious minorities, immigrants, and Black communities.

At that point, commercial radio was a new medium, only in operation for six years. In 1926, as a fund-raising effort, Coughlin went on the radio in a broadcast that began as a children's program. His radio talks soon shifted to politics and economics in a populist vein. As Samuel Eliot Morison's general history of the United States described Coughlin:

> a consummate radio orator, his Irish humor attracted attention to his theories; and as a free-silver and paper-money man he appealed to the old populist faith that gold was the root of all evil and New York bankers the devils.
>
> (Morison 1965: 972)

Coughlin became so popular that the Columbia Broadcasting Service (CBS) took him national.

According to wildly varying estimates, Coughlin's Sunday afternoon broadcasts soon attracted ten million to forty-five million listeners (Brinkley 1983: 304). His Radio League of the Little Flower was soon financing not only Coughlin's Shrine of the Little Flower Church, but also a national movement promoting his version of social justice. From the start, he attacked the Soviet Union as a bastion of irreligion and a threat to sound family values. When he started attacking government policies and such eminent capitalists as Henry Ford, CBS dropped his show (1931), whereupon Coughlin created his own radio network. In 1932, Coughlin stridently opposed President Herbert Hoover's reelection campaign and by implication supported Franklin D. Roosevelt's presidential candidacy against the incumbent. (As a Catholic priest, Coughlin did not then dare to offer an explicit public endorsement of a presidential candidate. Later in his career, he overcame that scruple.) After Roosevelt's victory, Coughlin's organizations campaigned for creation of a national central bank, formed unions to compete with those he saw as tainted by communism, and joined with Huey Long to support the Bonus Bill for veterans of World War I. They engaged extensively in social movement activity.

Roosevelt soon disappointed Coughlin. By 1934, Coughlin was forming a National Union for Social Justice in explicit opposition to Roosevelt's New Deal because he believed that the legislation was not large-scale enough to bring the country out of the Great Depression. In 1935, Coughlin almost single-handedly blocked the Senate's endorsement of Roosevelt's proposal to enter the League of Nations' World Court (Brinkley 1983: 135–36). As the Union Party, his organization even backed its own populist third-party presidential candidate in 1936. After that party's resounding defeat in a Roosevelt landslide, Coughlin replaced the National Union with the isolationist, increasingly anticommunist Christian Front, named in explicit contrast to Europe's leftist Popular Fronts. His magazine

Social Justice carried the message to millions of Americans. It even began publishing the forged anti-Semitic *Protocols of the Elders of Zion*.

From that point on, Coughlin's weekly broadcasts became increasingly rabid on the subject of FDR's "communist conspiracy" and more openly anti-Semitic to boot. In 1940, Coughlin called for Roosevelt's impeachment on the grounds that transferring military equipment to Britain and continuing to support the Soviet Union constituted abuse of office. Once the United States entered World War II, the government had Coughlin indicted under the Espionage Act, canceled the second-class mailing privileges that played so important a part in his solicitation of funds, and thus gave Detroit's bishop a long-awaited opportunity; the bishop confined his diocese's increasingly intemperate irritator to parish work at Little Flower, where Coughlin served until 1966. Coughlin did not remain entirely silent, however; he continued to write anticommunist pamphlets up to his death in 1979.

Father Coughlin pioneered the use of radio as a vehicle of social movement organizing, and radio certainly did not disappear from the social movement scene with the departure of Father Coughlin. On the contrary, it continued to grow in importance during and after World War II. Radio news disseminated information about movement activities such as marches in the making and, more rarely, actually transmitted movement messages containing program, identity, and standing claims.

Conservative talk radio continues to be influential in the United States today, with conservative organizations sponsoring radio shows by Glenn Beck, Mark Levin, or Rush Limbaugh and gaining thousands of new members in the process (Vogel and McCalmont 2011). Although the liberal/progressive radio network Air America attempted to counter this influence, the network went bankrupt in 2010 (Stelter 2010). Nevertheless, from the 1960s television became an even more influential medium in the representation of American social movements.

My Columbia University colleague Todd Gitlin served as national president of a quintessential American 1960s social movement organization—Students for a Democratic Society (SDS)—in 1963 and 1964, remaining active in the organization until 1966. He then began withdrawing from SDS activities and, by the late 1960s, "grew steadily more estranged from the direction of the national organization" (Gitlin 1980: 294; for historical context, see Fendrich 2003). He concluded, among other things, that its interaction with the news media was driving the SDS to strike ineffectual radical poses that invited repression instead of promoting progressive change.

Instead of simply stomping off and fulminating, however, Gitlin eventually constructed a close study of interaction between this New Left organization and the media. His study concentrated on news coverage by CBS television and the *New York Times* from 1965 to 1970. Adopting an idea that entered sociology through Erving Goffman, Gitlin examined how interpretive "frames" in the news affected the telling of stories and the reflections of themselves received by activists. Gitlin concluded that media coverage encouraged the activists to remain newsworthy by means of innovations that did not necessarily advance their cause; to substitute what news media told them for direct observation of their actions' effects; to give disproportionate attention to eye-catching symbols, slogans, dress, and performances; and, in the absence of solid information about their own accomplishments and failures, to alternate between despair and hubris. (Recall Daniel Cohn-Bendit, about the same time, telling Jean-Paul Sartre that his movement can bring down the French regime if only workers' organizations will cooperate.)

For all his pessimism, Gitlin demonstrates two major points for our analysis: (1) that the sheer availability of a medium did not in itself alter movement campaigns, performances, and WUNC displays, and (2) that movement organizers themselves played an active part in integrating media access into their own campaign planning. The fact that media commitments often produce unintended and untoward consequences is an important part of the story. More recent analyses of media-movement interaction point in the same direction (see, e.g., Gerbaudo 2012; Granjon 2002; Hocke 2002; Oliver and Maney 2000; Tufekci 2017). However, even in our high-tech time, media do not in themselves cause social movements.

Annelise Riles uncovered use of an impressive array of media by activists as she coupled a survey of organizations participating in the United Nations Fourth World Conference on Women (Beijing 1985) with an ethnographic study of movement activity in Fiji after the conference. She found the organizations actively employing the internet, fax networks, telephones, satellite communications, and newsletters. She did discover some enthusiasts extending their information, contacts, and influence through these media (Riles 2000: 54–55), but for the most part activists did their work by ignoring the media or subordinating them to the maintenance of existing interpersonal relations.

Just as the prodigious expansion of smartphones seems to be serving primarily to facilitate communication among people who are already closely tied, Fijian feminists preferred those means that reinforced established connections. "Those working in bureaucratic institutions in Suva had numerous ways of sharing information at their disposal," Riles comments.

> They might walk across the street from one office to the next to meet face to face; at lunchtime, they were bound to encounter one another at one of Suva's handful of professional lunch spots. They could send letters, exchange faxes or memoranda, or send their drivers to deliver messages. They also could convene meetings and conferences. Yet the most popular means of day to day communication was the telephone. The telephone was useful precisely because it was regarded as personal (as opposed to institutional), private (in contrast to the collective office spaces in which face to face meetings take place), and informal. As described to me by networkers, as well as observed and practiced on my part, these were lengthy telephone conversations; it was not unusual for people to spend an hour or more on the telephone.
>
> (Riles 2000: 67)

In this bureaucratized setting, we might conclude that the activists had abandoned the mounting of campaigns, the deployment of social movement performances, and the creation of WUNC displays. That would be wrong: they continued to press women's issues in their relatively unresponsive environment. But they did so in the style of late-twentieth-century nongovernmental organizations.

Right-Wing Appropriation of Social Movement Forms

As twentieth-century social movements worked out partial accommodations with authorities and integrated new media into their repertoires, they also expanded to include a wider range of right-wing claim making. Although American anti-immigrant and proslavery mobilization remind us that nineteenth-century social movements did not always move in progressive directions, right-wing appropriation of social movement forms grew much more extensive during the twentieth century. It often occurred through countermobilization against reformist and radical movements as they began to threaten conservative interests. Europe's authoritarian mobilizations against labor, the left, and/or Jews in Germany, Italy, Spain, France, Romania, and elsewhere provide the most spectacular examples of this (Birnbaum 1993; Brustein 1998; Paxton 1995).

The case study of Marburg, Germany offers evidence of this countermobilization. Rudy Koshar's masterful study of organizational life in the university town of Marburg from 1880 to 1935 shows how Nazis entered a flourishing organizational landscape and used it to their own advantage. The number of voluntary associations in Marburg rose steadily from ten per thousand people in 1913 to 15.9 per thousand—one organization for every sixty-three people—in 1930 (Koshar 1986: 136). During that period, socialist trade unions were mostly losing strength, while veterans', housewives', and property owners' associations expanded enormously, and student organizations held their own. As the Nazi Party took root in Marburg from 1923 onward, it first drew its few members mainly from existing right-wing, nationalist, and anti-Semitic organizations. Its activists paraded, burned red flags, and shouted against left-wingers but had little influence on local politics until 1929. (Anheier, Neidhardt, and Vortkamp 1998 document a parallel 1929 surge of Nazi organizational activity in Munich; see also Anheier and Ohlemacher 1996 for national trends in Nazi membership.)

At the end of the 1920s, Nazis began speaking widely, proselytizing in the countryside, and engaging actively in electoral campaigns. They also infiltrated existing organizations at the university and in the community at large. Their anti-Semitic and anti-Bolshevik appeals reinforced well-entrenched political positions in Marburg. In contrast to prewar Berlin, many of Marburg's police belonged to the Social Democratic Party and thus split with conservative city officials, whose own response to Nazi organizing ranged from worried toleration to encouragement. "Deepening social roots," concludes Koshar,

> established the NSDAP [National Socialist Party, or Nazis] at the center of an evolving *völkisch* [racist-nationalist] polity. The success of Hitler's visit to Marburg in April 1932, which attracted 20,000 people from the city and countryside, was only partly due to the charisma of the *Führer*. It was also a direct outgrowth of the party's stance as a vehicle of popular involvement in local public life. Hitler was an attraction because the party was; the party was attractive in part because of its positive image in conversations in the marketplace, local stores, university classrooms, fraternity houses, meeting halls, soccer fields, and homes. Hitler's seemingly mysterious mass appeal could hardly have been so extensive without the unplanned propaganda of daily social life.
>
> (Koshar 1986: 204)

The party did not simply impose its will on the Marburg public, at least not before the Nazi seizure of power in 1933. It adapted to the local organizational environment, combining membership in existing non-Nazi associations with creation of parallel organizations under party sponsorship. By 1932 it was receiving half or more of the votes in Marburg's elections. It far outshadowed the city's communists and Social Democrats, with whom Nazi squads sometimes engaged in street fighting. On its way to power, it adopted the performances, campaigns, and WUNC displays of social movements at large.

International Adaptation of Social Movement Forms

The case of Marburg reveals the importance of local implantation for national social movements. The lesson is more general. As our glances at China, Indonesia, and Fiji have already shown, social movement campaigns, performances, and WUNC displays do not simply migrate intact from one political culture to another (Chabot 2000; Chabot and Duyvendak 2002; Scalmer 2002b; Wood 2012). Precisely because social movement organizers are most often addressing regional or national audiences on regional or national issues, they have no choice but to employ at least some familiar idioms, display some known symbols, and draw on existing organizational forms— however much they also innovate and borrow from elsewhere. The twentieth century's unprecedented spread of social movement activity across the world ironically produced both commonality and diversity. It produced commonality because social movement performances such as the demonstration or the creation of fronts, coalitions, and special-purpose associations provided models for emulators everywhere. It produced diversity because each region's organizers found ways of integrating social movement strategies into local conditions.

Indian Mass Mobilization

The case of India serves as evidence of the spreading of a social movement. The world's second-most populous country and most populous democracy, India, has hosted forms of social movement activity at least since the formation of the Indian National Congress in 1885. Mohandas Gandhi was a genius at organizing associations, marches, declarations, campaigns, and—preeminently—WUNC displays in his own version of the social movement style. He had become a veteran organizer of nonviolent opposition in South Africa. After a stop in England to organize an Indian corps for war service, Gandhi returned to India from his twenty-year South African sojourn in 1914.

Back in India, Gandhi supported the British war effort, which sent Indian troops to Europe, Mesopotamia, Palestine, Egypt, and East Africa. But he also played a crucial part in expanding the political role of the Indian National Congress and in forging its alliance with the All-India Moslem League. The Hindu–Muslim coalition often worked uneasily, since Muslim activists generally opposed dismantling the Ottoman Empire (still the world's leading Muslim power), which was, after all, a major aim of the British war effort. Indeed, in 1915 a conspiratorial Muslim Indian group sought German support for an uprising against the British in India and Afghanistan.

As World War I ground on, the Congress and the All-India Moslem League began demanding an elected Indian legislative assembly as a first step toward self-government. In 1916, they even agreed on a program that Indian nationalists had previously resisted: separate earmarked electorates for Muslim voters. In parallel with European events, the war's end brought an increase in popular mobilization. Gandhi led a campaign of strikes, demonstrations, and passive resistance as the colonial government struck back with repression. Authorities arrested Gandhi in April for violating an order to keep his organizing efforts out of the Punjab region. A low point arrived in April 1919, when a British general ordered his troops to fire on a large protest meeting in Amritsar, Punjab. As troops blocked the only exit from the meeting place, their volleys killed 379 demonstrators and wounded 1,200 more. The government then compounded its problems by declaring martial law and imposing severe punishments on participants. Those displays of colonial vengeance included public whipping and forced crawling through the streets. Widespread campaigns of condemnation in both India and Great Britain accelerated the introduction of moves toward self-government—or at least greater inclusion of Indians in the government of India.

The reform split the Congress, with Gandhi's group bitterly opposing Britain's partial measures. In 1920, the Congress launched a major campaign of noncooperation with British authorities and boycott of British goods. Indians rallied around the watchwords *satyagraha* (soul force), *hartal* (boycott), and *swaraj* (home rule), each of which had multiple religious, moral, and political overtones. The program included resignation from public office, nonparticipation in elections, withdrawal from school, and avoidance of law courts. It also involved spectacular actions such as a monster bonfire of foreign cloth, which Gandhi lighted in Bombay (August 1921). By that time, Indian nationalists were energetically creating their own distinctive forms of social movement claim making but directing them against the forms of British rule.

Meanwhile, militant Muslims organized their own campaigns to maintain the Ottoman sultan (emperor) as leader of the world's Muslims, to restore the Ottoman Empire as it was in 1914, and to reestablish Muslim control of all the faith's holy places in the Near East. The predominantly Hindu Congress hesitantly backed their Muslim allies' program. Although Gandhi and his followers insisted on nonviolence, in many parts of India people attacked landlords, moneylenders, and officials. Muslim attacks on Hindu landlords, in fact, led to wider Hindu–Muslim battles and repeated splits in the movement for self-government. As conflicts escalated in 1922, the colonial government imprisoned Gandhi, thus cutting short a great, turbulent civil disobedience campaign. Through repeated imprisonments, nevertheless, Gandhi continued to act as India's most visible social movement organizer until his assassination by a dissatisfied Hindu nationalist in 1948. He was, of course, an inspiring religious model, but he was also a consummate political entrepreneur.

Gandhi's disappearance by no means terminated Indian social movements. After Indian independence (1947), Hindu leaders continued to employ and invent distinctive versions of the social movement repertoire. Consider an extraordinary, turbulent campaign to build a Hindu temple on the site of a Muslim shrine and thus to assert Hindu historical, religious, and political priority. Ayodhya, Uttar Pradesh, India, long sheltered a sixteenth-century mosque, Babri Masjid. The first Mughal (and Muslim) emperor Babur is supposed to have built the mosque in 1528. Ayodhya attracted worldwide attention on December 6, 1992, when Hindu militants destroyed Babri Masjid, began construction of a Hindu temple on the same site, and launched a nationwide series of struggles that eventually produced some 1,200 deaths (Bose and Jalal 1998: 228; Madan 1997: 56–58; Tambiah 1996: 251; van der Veer 1996).

The campaigns behind that newsworthy event had, however, begun much earlier. During the nineteenth century, a platform marking the supposed birthplace of Ram, epic hero of the Hindu classic Ramayana, stood adjacent to the mosque. It represented the historical assertion that during his sixteenth-century conquest the Mughal emperor had demolished an ancient Hindu temple and built a mosque in its place.

The platform supplied the occasions for repeated Hindu–Muslim confrontations and for the program of building a Hindu temple on the site (Brass 1994: 241). Colonial authorities scotched the program. Shortly after independence, fifty to sixty local Hindus occupied the site one night and installed Hindu idols there. In response to Muslim demands, however, the newly independent (and avowedly secular) Indian government seized and locked up the mosque. During the 1980s, militant Hindu groups started demanding destruction of the mosque and erection of a temple to Ram. Just before the 1989 elections, Bharatiya Janata Party (BJP) activists transported what they called holy bricks to Ayodhya and ceremoniously laid a foundation for their temple.

The following year, President Lal Advani of the BJP took his chariot caravan on a pilgrimage (*rath yatra*) across northern India, promising along the way to start building the Ram temple in Ayodhya. Advani started his pilgrimage in

Somnath, fabled site of yet another great Hindu temple destroyed by Muslim marauders. "For the sake of the temple," he declared en route, "we will sacrifice not one but many governments" (Chaturvedi and Chaturvedi 1996: 181–82). Advani's followers had fashioned his Toyota van into a version of legendary hero Arjuna's chariot, an image familiar from Peter Brook's film *Mahabharata*. As the BJP caravan passed through towns and villages, Advani's chariot attracted gifts of flower petals, coconut, burning incense, sandalwood paste, and prayer from local women. Authorities arrested Advani before he could begin the last lap of his journey to Ayodhya, but not before many of his followers had preceded him to the city. When some of them broke through police barricades near the offending mosque, police fired on them, killing "scores" of BJP activists (Kakar 1996: 51).

Both sides represented their actions as virtuous violence—one side as defense of public order, the other side as sacrifice for a holy cause. Hindu activists made a great pageant of cremating the victims' bodies on a nearby riverbank, then returning martyrs' ashes to their homes in various parts of India. Soon the fatalities at Ayodhya became the cause of widespread Hindu–Muslim–police clashes. Those conflicts intersected with higher-caste students' public resistance to the national government's revival of an affirmative action program on behalf of Other Backward Classes (Tambiah 1996: 249).

The dispute continued into the twenty-first century, with militant Hindu leaders frequently vowing to build (or, as they insisted, rebuild) their temple on the Babri Masjid site. In 2003, the Uttar Pradesh state court ordered the Archaeological Survey of India (ASI) to bring its scientific expertise to bear on the site. ASI excavations identified fifty pillar bases plus other artifacts in patterns characteristic of North Indian temples. Instead of settling the matter with the cool calm of science, however, the new discoveries incited sharp disagreements among archaeologists as they brought cries of triumph from Hindu activists. Lal Advani himself declared that the ASI report "gladdens crores [tens of millions] of devotees of Lord Rama" (Bagla 2003: 1305). In 2003, one court dismissed the criminal charges against Advani that stemmed from his incitement of the 1992 attack on the Ayodhya mosque. However, in 2005, a high court put aside that dismissal. That same year, suspected Islamic militants attacked the disputed site using a jeep laden with explosives to blow a hole in the wall of the complex, killing five people (BBC 2005). In 2010, the Allahabad High Court announced its decision that two-thirds of the site should be controlled by Hindus and one-third by Muslims. Both sides argued that they would appeal the decision (Freedom House 2011).

These dramatic events could not have unfolded anywhere else than in India. Yet they combined a campaign (not only to build a Hindu temple but also to attract political support for the BJP), a series of social movement performances (associations, meetings, processions, and more), along with sensational displays of worthiness, unity, numbers, and commitment. In those regards, the political work of India's Hindu organizers resembled that of nationalist social movement leaders across the earth, complete with the strident nationalist claim that "we were here first." Just as Gandhi and his collaborators pioneered a distinctive Indian variety of social movement claim making oriented to the British colonial system and taking the British government itself as one of its targets, the BJP integrated visibly Hindu references into its campaigns, performances, and WUNC displays as it sought power within a nominally secular Indian state. Indian campaigns could hardly have made the distinctive duality of social movements—simultaneously local and international in their forms, practices, and meanings—clearer.

By the twentieth century's end, social movements had become available as vehicles of popular politics throughout the democratic and democratizing world. They had become available to programs that would have horrified many of the early-nineteenth-century social movements' pioneers. They had adopted cultural forms and technical means that no nineteenth-century social movement activist could have imagined. In Western democracies, at least, social movement organizers, authorities, and police had negotiated routines that greatly minimized the violence of social movement claim making. Organizers had also begun creating international alliances even more actively than their nineteenth-century predecessors had managed. However, that process brings us into the twenty-first century.

Note

1 Lesley Wood and Ernesto Castañeda updated the cases and language in this chapter.

5

SOCIAL MOVEMENTS ENTER THE TWENTY-FIRST CENTURY

Charles Tilly and Lesley Wood

In May 2007, local activists in southern China who were fighting the construction of a chemical plant in the city of Xiamen sent text messages from their cellphones. The local government "is setting off an atomic bomb in all of Xiamen," the messages read; it will cause "leukemia and deformed babies for our children and grandchildren, act! Participate along 10,000 people, June 1 at 8 a.m., opposite the municipal government building! Hand tie yellow ribbons! SMS all your Xiamen friends!" (*Asia Sentinel* 2007). Construction of the Tenglong Aromatic PX Co. Ltd. factory began in November 2006 in Xiamen's Haicang district, which has a population of 100,000. In March 2007, Zhao Yufen, a local researcher at the College of Chemistry and Chemical Engineering at Xiamen University, organized a petition to the Beijing parliament calling for the plant to be relocated away from residential areas. "Paraxylene is highly toxic and could cause cancer and birth defects," said Zhao in an interview with the Chinese newspaper *China Business* (Qiu 2008). Zhao's message was later taken up by bloggers. Lian Yue, who was quick to post critiques of the project on his blog, arguing, "*Environmental protection officials who can't protect the environment, what are the people of Xiamen supposed to do!* [sic]," subsequently prompting national debate. According to news reports in the *Asia Sentinel*, *Sydney Morning Herald*, and others, the text messages against the project then began to circulate. The *Sentinel* reported that by March, 29 the message was blocked amid claims it had reached a million people. Blocked words reportedly included "benzene," "demonstration," "atomic," and "leukemia" as authorities looked to thwart the spread of these messages aimed at recruiting participants in contentious performances.

Nevertheless, on June 1, tens of thousands of Xiamenes marched against the project and the company's pollution record in the region. Carrying banners and wearing yellow ribbons that read "people's livelihoods, democracy, people's rights, harmony," "reject pollution, protect Xiamen!," the crowd progressed through the streets. As the protesters proceeded, they uploaded photographs, video, and text messages onto blogs. Reports noted that local residents were bringing water to the demonstrators and that people were singing traditional local songs. When marchers reached the government offices, they chanted, "serve the people" and then broke through the police line, singing the Chinese national anthem. The march continued the rest of the day. Blog posts about the protests recorded thousands of hits, and when one site was blocked, another blogger picked up the information and distributed it further. The government began to counter the protesters with their own messages. One blogger reported receiving this message: "If you go through normal channels to give the government feedback, we guarantee we'll share your opinions and suggestions with environmental experts. . . . Source: 09599 Voice of China Mobile." In December 2007, the Chinese government announced that the plant would be moved to Guangzhou (Kennedy 2007).

Three months later, in March 2008, residents of Guangzhou and other nearby towns staged three days of protests against the decision to move the plant to their area. Building on the approach of the Xiamen residents, activists in the region went door-to-door handing out pamphlets (Cody 2008). On the first day of protests in Dongshan, 10,000 men, women, and children carried banners and after marching through the streets, the group staged a sit-in to block traffic on a main road. The next day when police and local officials attempted to disperse the protesters, the conflict escalated, leading protesters to throw stones at police vehicles and at the police station. In the demonstrations throughout the region, a dozen people were arrested and others injured. However, the protests appeared to have some effect. By Monday, the local government sent officials circulating through the area with loudspeakers to deny the reports that the chemical factory was about to be built near their community. A model for achieving success had been created and spread. By 2011, thousands of people used text messaging to organize protests demanding the closure of a similar type of plant in Dalian, Liaoning Province. Municipal officials quickly acceded to their demands and closed the plant (Bradsher 2011).

Across the country, more and more Chinese citizens engaged in public protest. According to China's Public Security Ministry, there were 10,000 protests in 1994. In 2007, there were more than 80,000, and in 2010 127,000 (*Asia News* 2011, *Economist* 2011).

So, would the twenty-first century finally bring social movements to the long-dreamed culmination of People Power across the world? Would new communication technologies carry the word swiftly through China, provide the means for activists and ordinary people to shift the tactical balance away from capitalists, military leaders, and corrupt politicians? Or, on the contrary, did the assembly of thousands in the streets there and elsewhere merely mark the last churning of popular politics in the wake of globalization's steamroller? The answer is not clear-cut. Technology analyst Howard Rheingold has spoken of electronically organized protests as "smart mobs": "people who are able to act in concert even if they don't know each other" (Rheingold 2003: xii). He stresses the enormous enthusiasm of people around the globe for text messaging.

Although China's figure of sixty-four mobile cellular subscriptions per hundred people in 2010 did not compare with the rates in developed countries (87 percent of population had subscriptions in 2010), the rate of cellular phone penetration has increased sharply over the past few years (International Telecommunications Union 2016; see Table 5.2). When one realizes that 90 percent of the world's population could potentially access cellular networks, satellite-backed cellular phones and text messaging begin to look like serious alternatives to fixed-line telecommunication, especially where poverty, political turmoil, or forbidding geography impede the creation of government-backed telecommunications infrastructure. In authoritarian China, text messaging has been an important new tool of social movements. This potential is leveraged when combined with 4G or 5G connections that allow cellphone users to post photographs, messages, and video clips to blogs and websites from their telephones.

This is made obvious by the way protesters used these new technologies in the 2011 "Arab Spring" uprisings in Egypt and Tunisia, as well as in Iran and elsewhere. *Newsweek*, among others, tagged these protests as Facebook revolutions (*Newsweek* 2011). In those uprisings, activists used mass texting, Twitter, and Facebook on their smartphones to update participants about the locations of protests and security officials, as well as to spread news, photos, and video clips to those involved and those observing the protests. As one Egyptian activist succinctly tweeted during the protests there, "We use Facebook to schedule the protests, Twitter to coordinate, and YouTube to tell the world." The use of these technologies did allow messages to spread more quickly and cheaply among protesters and those who knew them. The video and photographic capacity of the technologies facilitated the "newsworthiness" of the information being shared to mass media, who broadcast it further. Networks such as CNN and al Jazeera streamed live footage from the demonstrations, allowing viewers to observe directly the ebbs and flows of protest and their repression—and share in the emotions of protest as they developed. Such intense media coverage and surveillance may put pressure on authorities to avoid visible confrontation and to respond when images and footage generate international debate. Like the results of the first radio and television broadcasts of war and protest, the live streaming video and flood of photographs could make authorities increasingly aware of the perceptions of their actions toward protesters.

Cellular phones with text, image, and video messaging have become part of protest during the twenty-first century. At least superficially, these media have the populist attraction of not falling easily under governmental control. However, governments are adapting quickly to the new technologies, and they often try to stop their use by protesters. Since 2006, the international nongovernmental organization Reporters Without Borders have found an increasing number of governments, including Iran, China, Russia, Thailand, Pakistan, and Burma, who sometimes block the internet or particular websites (Reporters Without Borders 2011). Other governments block or interfere with SMS or cellular phones in various ways.

On January 28, 2011, the Egyptian authorities tried to stop activists from communicating by shutting down the internet. Immediately, activists turned to other media. For example, the *International Business Times* reported that We Rebuild, an activist group whose motto is "When countries block, we evolve," turned to landline phones, fax machines, and old-fashioned radios to get messages out of the country (Samuel 2011). Using dial-up networks, they connected protesters in Egypt with the internet, and then used software to re-route user traffic through a network of volunteered computers, making it possible to maintain anonymous communications. Protesters in Egypt also used satellite phones and even "old-fashioned" word of mouth, flyers, posters, and handbills to spread the news about the protests.

Even in countries such as the United States, political authorities have shut down communication tools in order to demobilize and disorganize protesters. On August 11, 2011 the San Francisco Bay Area Rapid Transit (BART) authority cut cellphone service in four of its stations in an attempt to disrupt anticipated protests against the police shooting of Charles Hill on July 3 (Norton 2011). Hill, a homeless man, was shot and killed by police officers at a station in San Francisco. He had two knives and the officers confronted him, eventually leading to his shooting. The situation revealed BART's failure to meet policy goals and trainings that were promised after the shooting of an unarmed Black man at a BART station in 2009 (Elinson and Walter 2011).

The Role of New Technologies

Undoubtedly, twenty-first-century social movement activists have integrated new technologies into their organizing and into their very claim-making performances. Serious questions, however, start there: Are new technologies transforming social movements? If they are transforming movements, how are they doing so? How do they produce their effects? How do new tactics and new forms of organization interact in twenty-first-century social movements? More generally, how and to what extent do recent alterations in social movements result from the changes in international connectedness that people loosely call globalization?

This chapter shows that significant changes in social movements are, indeed, occurring during the early twenty-first century. Internationally organized networks of activists, international nongovernmental organizations, and internationally visible targets such as multinational corporations and international financial institutions all figure more prominently in recent social movements, especially in the richer and better-connected parts of the world. Even domestically oriented movements, such as the campaign against the chemical plant in China, receive on average more international attention and intervention than their twentieth-century counterparts.

Yet this chapter (along with others) also issues four stern warnings.

1. **Avoid technological determinism**; recognize that most new features of social movements result from alterations in their social, economic and political contexts rather than solely from technical innovations.

2. Notice that, as they did during the nineteenth and twentieth centuries, twenty-first-century *communications innovations always operate in a two-sided way*: on the one side, lowering the costs of coordination among activists who are already connected with each other; and on the other, potentially facilitating governmental eaves-dropping and repression; and sometimes excluding those who lack access to the new communications, increasing communications inequality.
3. Remember that *most twenty-first-century social movement activity continues to rely on the local, regional, and national forms of organization* that already prevailed during the later twentieth century.
4. While noting that globalization is shaping the world distribution of social movements, *avoid the supposition that the confrontation of globalization and antiglobalization now dominates the social movement scene.*

Ignoring these warnings would blind you to the actual social changes that are affecting collective claim making worldwide as well as to the persistence of local, regional, and national issues in social movements.

Globalization

Let us first define globalization. For us, globalization means an increase in long distance interactions and transactions in relation to local ones. Any time a distinctive set of social connections and practices expands from a regional to a transcontinental scale, some globalization is occurring. Each time an existing transcontinental set of social connections and practices fragments, disintegrates, or vanishes, some deglobalization occurs. Only when the first sort of process is far outrunning the second does it clarify matters to say that humanity as a whole is globalizing.

Although there were waves of globalization before 1500, during the half millennium since that date, three main waves of globalization have occurred. The first arrived right around 1500. It resulted from the rapidly spreading influence of Europe, growth of the Ottoman Empire, and parallel expansions of Chinese and Arab merchants into the Indian Ocean and the Pacific. The Ottomans extended their control into southern Europe, northern Africa, and the Near East while Western Europeans were building commercial and territorial empires in Africa, the Pacific, and the Americas. Meanwhile, seafaring Muslim merchants continued to connect Africa, the Near East, and Indian Ocean ports. In Asia, European and Muslim commercial activity interacted with China's energetic expansion into Pacific trade under the Ming dynasty (1368–1644).

Ottoman expansion ended in the nineteenth century, and Europeans partly displaced Muslim merchants across the Indian Ocean and the Pacific. But Europeans and the Chinese continued their shares of the first post-1500 globalizing process into the twentieth century. Europeans began colonizing the more temperate zones of their empires in Africa, the Americas, and the Pacific.

Likewise, Chinese moved by the millions into Southeast Asia and the Pacific. One sign of the world's increasing connectedness was the large amounts of silver mined in Latin America that ended up in Chinese treasuries by the seventeenth century, drawn by the export of precious Chinese commodities to the West.

We can place the second major post-1500 wave of globalization at approximately 1850–1914. Consider the long-distance migrations between 1850 and World War I: 3 million Indians, 9 million Japanese, 10 million Russians, 20 million Chinese, and 33 million Europeans emigrated from their homes. During this period, international trade and capital flows reached previously unmatched heights, especially across the Atlantic. Improvements in transportation and communication, such as railroads, steamships, telephone, and telegraph, lowered the costs of those flows and speeded them up. Massive movements of labor, goods, and capital made prices of traded goods more uniform across the world and reduced wage gaps among countries that were heavily involved in those flows. This wave of globalization was often accompanied by exploitative adventures of northern companies, imperial armies, and by colonizing projects. The chief beneficiaries included Japan, Western Europe, and the richer countries of North and South America. For the world as a whole, globalization's second wave increased disparities in wealth and well-being between those beneficiaries and everyone else. Except for European settler areas such as Australia, those colonized by Europe did not generally share in the prosperity.

Migration, trade, and capital flows slowed between the two world wars. But as Europe and Asia recovered from World War II, a third post-1500 surge of globalization began. This time, intercontinental migration accelerated less than between 1850 and 1914. In comparison with 1850–1914, fewer economies felt acute labor shortages and labor organized more effectively to bar immigrant competition. Consequently, long-distance migration bifurcated into relatively small streams of professional and technical workers, on one side, and vast numbers of servants and general laborers on the other. The difference in wage earnings and potential for social mobility between developed and developing countries further increased inequalities between them. Because differences in wealth and security between rich and poor countries were widening visibly, potential workers from poor countries made desperate attempts to migrate into richer countries, either permanently or long enough to earn substantial money for their return home. Whole industries grew up around the facilitation of illegal, semilegal, and legal but brutal forms of migration into richer countries.

Flows of goods and capital accelerated even beyond nineteenth-century levels. Many of those flows occurred within firms, as multinational companies spanned markets, manufacturing sites, headquarters, and sources of raw materials in different countries. But international trade among countries and firms also accelerated. High-tech and high-end goods produced in East Asia, Western Europe, and North America became available almost everywhere in the world. Capitalists based in the richest countries invested increasingly in manufacturing in poorer countries where labor costs ran lower, often bringing clothing, electronic devices, and other goods produced in low-wage countries back to compete in their own domestic markets.

At the same time, political institutions, communications systems, technology, science, disease, pollution, and criminal activity all took on increasingly international scales. During the early twenty-first century, the third wave of post-1500 globalization was moving ahead full force.

The globalization waves of 1850–1914 and of 1950 onward differed conspicuously. Despite imperial outreach and the rising importance of Japan in this phenomenon, nineteenth-century expansion centered on the Atlantic, first benefiting the major European states, then increasingly favoring North America. Its twentieth- and twenty-first-century counterpart involved Asia much more heavily. As sites of production, as objects of investment, and increasingly as markets, China, Japan, Korea, Taiwan, India, Pakistan, Bangladesh, Indonesia, Malaysia, Singapore, Thailand, the Philippines, and other Asian countries participated extensively in global growth.

Another difference: during the wave of 1850–1914, economic expansion depended heavily on coal and iron. Consequently, capital and workers flowed especially to a limited number of smokestack regions, producing the characteristic grimy concentrations of industrial cities along waterways and rail lines. By the late twentieth century, oil, natural gas, hydroelectric generators, and nuclear reactors had largely displaced coal as sources of power in the world's richer regions. Post-1945 globalization featured such high-tech industries as electronics and pharmaceuticals. Those industries depended on important clusters of scientific and technical expertise, such as Paris-Sud and Silicon Valley, California. But with goods of high value and relatively low transport cost, they could easily subdivide production in accordance with the availability of labor and markets. Service and information industries pushed even further in the same direction: low-wage data-processing clerks in southern India, for example, processed information for firms based in New York and London, with fiber-optic cable and satellite connections transmitting data instantly in both directions.

Globalization in its nineteenth-century version consolidated states. It increased their control over resources, activities, and people within their boundaries as it increased their regulation of flows across those boundaries. Between 1850 and World War I, for example, the world's states regularized national passports and their firm attachment of citizens to particular states (Torpey 2000). In the process, uneasy but effective working agreements emerged among governments, capital, and labor at the national scale. This led to the creation of labor unions. Organized labor, organized capital, organized political parties, and organized bureaucrats fought hard but made deals. Those bargains eventually turned states from free trade toward protection of industries that combined large labor forces with extensive fixed capital. Chemicals, steel, and metal-processing industries led the way.

The variety of globalization found in the twentieth and twenty-first centuries, in dramatic contrast, undermined the central power of most states, freeing capital to move rapidly from country to country as opportunities for profit arose.

Post-1945 states also lost effectiveness when it came to containing accelerated flows of communication, scientific knowledge, drugs, arms, gems, or migrants across their borders. Even the predominant United States failed to block substantial flows of contraband, tainted capital, and unsanctioned migrants. The global economic crisis that has bankrupted states, corporations, and banks has not been contained by nation-states, even ones as powerful as the United States. Similarly, nongovernmental and supergovernmental organizations escaped partially from control by any particular state. The newly powerful nonstate organizations included multinational corporations, world financial institutions, the United Nations, political compacts such as the European Union, military alliances such as the North Atlantic Treaty Organization (NATO), and international activist groups such as Doctors Without Borders. An irony appears: the United States sponsored or at least supported the initial formation of many such transnational organizations. In their early phases, the United States often bent them to its national interests. Yet as the twenty-first century began, even the United States, the world's greatest financial and military power, could not simply order these organizations around.

Globalization and Social Movements

As a context for changes in social movements, we can see the operation of globalization more clearly by distinguishing among top-down connectedness, bottom-up adaptation, and a middle ground of negotiation. From the top down, globalization produces connections among centers of power, including commercial connections among financial nodes, coercive connections among military forces, cultural connections among religious or ethnic leadership clusters, and combinations of the three. From the bottom up, globalization looks different. It includes an increasing density of connections, such as long-distance migration streams, telephone calls across borders and oceans, remittances and gifts sent by migrants to their home villages (see Castañeda 2013; Tilly 2007b), and sharing of lore by social movement organizers. As critics often complain, it also certainly involves the spread of standardized consumer goods and services across the world.

In the intermediate zone of negotiation, people respond to opportunities and threats generated by top-down processes, employing bottom-up networks to create new relations with centers of power. That intermediate zone contains not only coordinated confrontations, such as the worldwide mobilization on February 15, 2003 against the American invasion of Iraq, but also globe-spanning trade in contraband, such as illegally acquired weapons, drugs, timber, and sexual services. The intermediate zone depends largely on connections produced by the top-down and bottom-up versions of globalization. For example, the more profitable forms of illicit trade use international financial circuits to launder their money, and international contacts among far-flung social movement activists often originate at conferences staged by international organizations.

Through these processes, global integration increases while simultaneously increasing categorical inequalities (Tilly 1998; Castañeda 2018). This becomes apparent when we look at the ways in which new communications technologies are affecting contentious politics. Although Howard Rheingold and many other technology enthusiasts claim that such technologies are entirely remapping social movement organization and strategy, it helps to recognize that from the start social movement activists have responded to mass media. We have already noticed how the vast increase of print media during the nineteenth and twentieth centuries gave new resonance to social movements long before the age of Facebook and Twitter. Radio and television played a similar role during the twentieth century. These new technological innovations are joining a long history of such media. Table 5.1 lists some crucial dates for technological innovations whose relationship with social movements can be considered.

We should take great care before adopting communications determinism in either its general or its particular form: generally by supposing that each of these innovations in itself transformed social life and political action, particularly by imagining that the internet and the cellular telephone afford so much greater communications power that they detach people from previously existing social relations and practices. In a thoughtful, comprehensive survey of internet

Table 5.1 New Communication Technologies

Year	Technology
1833	introduction of the telegraph
1876	introduction of the telephone
1895	Marconi's demonstration of radio
1920s	experimental television
1966	initiation of satellite communication
1977	first mobile telecommunications system (Saudi Arabia)
1978	first computer modem
1989	initial plan for World Wide Web
1995	public internet established in United States
1996	Wireless Application Protocol 2G digital GSM cellphones with SMS
1997	Google project initiated
1998	first downloadable content for cellphones
2001	first 3G cellular telephone network launched (Japan) Allows data streaming
2002	Friendster (social networking site) launched
2004	Facebook launched
2005	YouTube launched
2006	Twitter launched
2009	first 4G cellular telephone networks
2019	first 5G telephone networks

Source: International Telecommunications Union 2017. *ITU Yearbook of Statistics 2017* and International Telecommunications Union 2019.

use, Caroline Haythornthwaite and Barry Wellman argue that the internet is simply accelerating an earlier trend:

> Even before the advent of the Internet, there has been a move from all-encompassing, socially controlling communities to individualized fragmented personal communities. Most friends and relatives with whom we maintain socially close ties are not physically close. These ties are spread through metropolitan areas, and often on the other side of countries or seas. Mail, the telephone, cars, airplanes, and now email and the Internet sustain these ties. Most people do not live lives bound in one community. Instead, they maneuver through multiple specialized partial communities, giving limited commitment to each. Their life is "glocalized": combining long-distance ties with continuing involvements in households, neighborhoods, and worksites.
>
> (Haythornthwaite and Wellman 2002: 32)

Of course, these observations apply with greater force to rich Western countries than to the world as a whole. But they clarify the sense in which integration of communications innovations into existing social relations and practices extends projects that people already have under way and, especially, accentuates connections that were already in play but costly to maintain. The observations reinforce two crucial points that came up as we examined the adoption of new media such as radio in twentieth-century social movements. First, each new form of communications connection facilitates a specific set of social relations as it excludes those who do not have access to the relevant communications technology. Second, communications media differ dramatically in their degree of symmetry and asymmetry; newspapers, radio, and television exhibit massive asymmetry among participants, having few producers but many consumers, while digital communications redress the balance to some extent.

In similar ways, commercial relations and political relations both link communities and individuals in new ways and further isolate those not in the circuit. Looking chiefly at economic relations in a similar light, Viviana Zelizer astutely recognizes the existence of social relations she calls "commercial circuits." Each of those circuits includes four elements: (1) a well-defined boundary with some control over transactions crossing the boundary, (2) a distinctive set of economic transactions, (3) distinctive media (reckoning systems and tokens of value) employed in the pursuit of those transactions, and (4) meaningful ties among participants (Zelizer 2004). Cases in point include credit networks, mutual-aid connections among professionals in different organizations, and specialized currency systems. Such circuits create an institutional structure that reinforces credit, trust, and reciprocity within its perimeter but organizes exclusion and inequality in relation to outsiders. Circuits cut across the limits of communities, households, and organizations but link their participants in significant forms of coordination, communication, and interdependence. The idea extends easily to what we might call *political circuits*: not simply networks of connection among political activists but the full combination of boundaries, controls, political transactions, media, and meaningful ties. Social movements build on, create, and transform political circuits. In this regard, the communications media their members employ make a difference for precisely the reasons just mentioned: each medium in its own ways reinforces some connections, facilitates other connections that would otherwise be costly to establish or sustain, and excludes a great many other possible connections. Once in the club or involved in a political circuit, participants negotiate matches among media, transactions, and meaningful social ties as they establish and control boundaries between insiders and outsiders. *Instead of communications determinism, we find political participants actively engaged in organizational innovation.*

All the technological innovations listed earlier eventually became available to social movement organizers and activists. In general, they reduced communication costs as they increased the geographic range covered by social movement communications. They also tied social movement participants more firmly to other users of the same technologies as they separated participants from nonusers of those technologies This selection tended to reflect larger categories of racial, gender, and class inequality.

In their times, similarly, transportation breakthroughs such as intercity steam trains, electrical streetcars, and jet aircraft facilitated social movement contact at a distance but actually impeded contact with like-minded people who lived away from major transport lines. Neither in communications nor in transportation, however, did the technological timetable dominate alterations in social movement organization, strategy, and practice. Shifts in the political and organizational context impinged far more directly and immediately on how social movements worked than did technical transformations as such. As discussed in previous chapters, the presence of authoritarian or communist regimes, for example, greatly determined the capacity for social movements to succeed. Technical transformations are important, but far less than the political context in which these movements form and exist.

A little reflection on the world distribution of communications connections, in any case, dispels the illusion that the internet will soon allow for the coordination of social movements across the entire globe. Table 5.2 presents relevant data for an array of countries from relatively poor (e.g., Congo) to very rich (e.g., Norway). Note the wide disparities in the numbers of cellular telephones and internet connections. Mobile telephone ownership runs from those European countries whose average resident owns more than one telephone to the Congo, where fewer than seventeen people per hundred have one. Internet connections vary even more widely. Some small equalization among countries is occurring with respect to telephone access and internet connections. But when it comes to broadband internet connections that are essential for many online activities, rapid expansion of those services in richer countries is actually increasing worldwide inequalities. Within the internet, furthermore, inequality runs even deeper than these figures indicate; U.S. producers, for example, dominate the world's websites, making English the World Wide Web's lingua franca (DiMaggio, Hargittai, Neuman, and Robinson 2001: 312; International Telecommunications Union 2010).

Table 5.2 Communications Connections for Selected Countries, 2010–2016

Country	Fixed Broadband subs per 100 people, 2016	% increase 2010–16	Cellular mobile subscriptions per 100 people, 2016	% increase 2010–16	Internet users per 100 people 2016	% increase 2010–16
Australia	31	35	110	9	88	16
Canada	37	23	85	20	90	12
China	23	64	97	52	34	56
Congo (DRC)	0	−10	37	118	6	600
Czech Republic	29	93	118	−14	76	10
Iceland	38.5	10	121	11	98	5
India	1.4	55	85	39	30	275
Indonesia	2	150	148	61	25	127
Israel	27.6	10	129	−3	80	18
Kazakhstan	13	46	142	15	75	134
Norway	40	15	109	−3	97	4
Paraguay	3.6	500	111	21	51	155
Philippines	5.5	51	109	27	56	124
Saudi Arabia	10	104	149	−21	74	80
Swaziland	.5	500	74	19	29	163
United Kingdom	38.5	23.5	120	−8	95	12
United States	33	27	123	37	76	5
World	12.4	55	101	25	47	60

Sources: World Bank Data—International Telecommunication Union, World Telecommunication/ICT Development Report and database

Two conclusions follow. First, to the extent that internationally coordinated social movements rely on electronic communication, they will have a much easier time of it in rich countries than in poor ones. Second, electronic communications connect social movement activists selectively both across and within countries. Anyone whom a Norwegian organizer can collaborate with electronically in, say, India or Swaziland is part of a communications elite. In a more distant future, diffusion of high-tech communications facilities may eventually equalize social movement opportunities internationally. For the medium term, this important aspect of globalization is making the world more unequal.

Effects of New Technologies on Movements

Within the high-tech world, to be sure, organizers of international social movements have widely incorporated digital communications technologies into their performances. Websites, online petitions, blogs, social networking sites, e-mail, chat and video sites, and even the coordination of local actions by means of smartphones all speed up communications and increase the range of persons with whom any particular individual can maintain contact. Tough questions start there: Is the introduction of digital technologies into social movement practices transforming those practices more rapidly and extensively than did earlier communications and transport technologies such as the telephone, television, and long-distance buses? Are new sorts of relationships among activists emerging as a consequence? Are social movement campaigns, repertoires, and WUNC displays therefore changing character more dramatically than ever before?

There has been a great deal of work investigating the effect that digital media are having on international activism (Bennett 2003; della Porta, Andretta, Mosca, and Reiter 2006; della Porta and Caiani 2007; Diani 2001, 2003; Earl and Kimport 2011; Juris 2008; Tarrow 2005). Lance Bennett's exceptionally thoughtful and balanced review of the subject (Bennett 2003) argues that digital media are changing international activism in several important ways, including:

- making loosely structured networks, rather than the relatively dense networks of earlier social movements, crucial to communication and coordination among activists;
- weakening the identification of local activists with the movement as a whole by allowing greater scope for introduction of local issues into movement discourse;
- reducing the influence of ideology on personal involvement in social movements;
- diminishing the relative importance of bounded, durable, resource-rich local and national organizations as bases for social movement activism;
- increasing the strategic advantages of resource-poor organizations within social movements;

- promoting the creation of permanent campaigns (e.g., against austerity or for climate justice) with rapidly shifting immediate targets; and
- combining older face-to-face performances with virtual performances.

Bennett and other researchers on the question conclude that these changes, in turn, make social movements increasingly vulnerable to problems of coordination, control, and commitment.

We can see these problems up close if we look at the growing use of social networking apps by social movement organizations. In the lead-up to the 2011 protests against the Egyptian government, activists mobilized by using Facebook, forming a group called "We are all Khaled Said," which attracted hundreds of thousands of members. Although these "members" can access information, sign online petitions, or learn about events happening in the region, this online activity doesn't automatically correspond with offline engagement, collective strategizing, or sustained participation.

Even Bennett does not claim, however, that the trends he describes amount to established fact. Reflecting on the place of communications technologies in social relations at large as well as in earlier social movements, we should remain skeptical of straightforward technological determinism. Any influence these technologies have is mediated by preexisting cultures, practices, and competencies of users as well as their organizational routines (Garrett and Edwards 2007). Finally, it is likely that some of the changes Bennett detects result less from the adoption of digital technologies as such than from alterations in the political and economic circumstances of social movement activists (Diani 2001; DiMaggio, Hargittai, Neuman, and Robinson 2001; Sassen 2002; Tarrow 2005; Wellman 2000, 2001a, 2001b). Proliferation of international organizations, both governmental and nongovernmental; increasing prominence of transnational corporations and financial networks; diminishing capacity of most states to control flows of goods, persons, capital, or contraband; and expansion of communications among likely targets of social movement claims all contribute to the changes on Bennett's list. They all pose new challenges for social movement activists and they all encourage formation of new political circuits as bases of social movement mobilization.

Globalizing Processes and Mobilization

Now we need to broaden our scope from the dynamics around electronic communication to those that surround globalization. In principle, how might we expect the three currents of globalizing change—top-down, bottom-up, and in-between—to affect social movements across the world? We will use the example of the burgeoning international peasant movement Via Campesina, which formed in countries across the world. This network of small farmers and farmworkers from fifty-six countries emerged in 1993. The main goal of Via Campesina is "to develop solidarity and unity among small farmer organizations in order to promote gender parity and social justice in fair economic relations;

the preservation of land, water, seeds, and other natural resources; food sovereignty; sustainable agricultural production based on small and medium-sized producers." In order to "globalize the struggle against injustice and neoliberalism worldwide," the group organizes two annual global days of action and regular conferences among member organizations. On April 17, 2019 the global day of peasant struggle, farmers protested in twenty-nine countries simultaneously. Such an example helps us to think separately about the changing nature of campaigns, repertoires, and WUNC displays:

- Since top-down, bottom-up, and intermediate changes all increase connectedness among sites that share interests and, on the average, reduce the cost of communication among those sites, we might expect an increase in the frequency of *campaigns* involving similar or identical targets simultaneously at many different sites.
- As for *repertoires*, we might expect decreasing reliance on expressions of program, identity, and standing claims that require the physical copresence of all participants in favor of locally clustered performances connected by long, thin strands of communication. At the extreme, this trend would yield virtual performances requiring no physical copresence whatsoever, such as virtual sit-ins.
- When it comes to *WUNC displays*, we might expect an interesting bifurcation: on one side, ways of signaling worthiness, unity, numbers, and commitment that gain instant recognition anywhere in the world; and on the other side, increasingly localized WUNC codes that announce the relations of participating clusters to their local environments. Korean farmers wearing locally intelligible headbands but holding English-language signs up to television cameras at protests against free trade agreements illustrate the bifurcation.

(Via Campesina 2019)

The expected changes in campaigns and repertoires have almost certainly been occurring since the late twentieth century. In the absence of detailed event catalogs, the bifurcation of WUNC displays remains uncertain but plausible. If our speculation is correct, detailed comparisons of episodes will show that, as compared with more localized social movements, internationally oriented performances combine codes linking participants closely to their own localities and groups with other WUNC codes of worldwide currency, such as peace signs and chanting in unison.

Just as we should avoid simple technological determinism, we should guard against attributing every twenty-first-century change in social movements to globalization: coincidence does not prove causation. In particular, we should not allow the spectacular occasions on which activists coordinate their claim making across seas and continents to persuade us that the days of local, regional, and national social movements have faded away. Despite transnational connections, national governments are most often the subjects of claims. *International connections bind together people who continue to act mainly within bounded countries and who continue to take the governments of those countries seriously.* Many observers and participants describe all international connections as if they were global and, therefore, transcend the old politics of bounded, centralized states. In fact, states remain salient actors, targets, and sites of early-twenty-first-century social movements. The mobilization against the Egyptian government provides one example. The ongoing demands on national governments by youth movements for climate justice and against racism make the point even more emphatically.

Back to Egypt

Returning to our discussion of the 2011 protests in Egypt will help to clarify the place of social movements in twenty-first-century public politics—and provide some grounds for skepticism that new communications technologies are sweeping all before them. Like other countries in the region, Egypt gradually emerged from British and French rule during the first half of the twentieth century, while a British military presence lasted until 1954. At that point, the newly independent government nationalized the Suez Canal, and the ensuing war with Britain, France, and Israel resulted in Cairo being bombed. Although the 1960s and 1970s were relatively independent and prosperous years for Egypt, the ongoing strategic importance of the country in the region has meant that global powers, including the United States, Britain, and others, have consistently been involved in both the economic and political trajectory of the country, which limited the regime's accountability to its own population. After President Anwar Sadat signed a peace treaty with Israel in 1977 and was subsequently assassinated in 1981, Hosni Mubarak, also a former military officer, came into power. A state of emergency had existed since that time, during which corruption became endemic and security officials were allowed free reign to prohibit or disperse election-related rallies, demonstrations, and public meetings, and also to detain people indefinitely without charge. Amnesty International's 2010 report reads as follows:

> The government continued to use state of emergency powers to detain peaceful critics and opponents as well as people suspected of security offences or involvement in terrorism. Some were held under administrative detention orders; others were sentenced to prison terms after unfair trials before military courts. Torture and other ill-treatment remained widespread in police cells, security police detention centres, and prisons, and in most cases were committed with impunity. The rights to freedom of expression, association, and assembly were curtailed; journalists and bloggers were among those detained or prosecuted. Hundreds of families residing in Cairo's "unsafe areas" were forcibly evicted; some were left homeless, others were relocated but without security of tenure. Men perceived to be gay continued to be prosecuted under a "debauchery" law. At least 19 people seeking to cross into Israel were shot dead by border guards, apparently while posing no threat. At least 269 people were sentenced to death, and at least five were executed.

Nonetheless, many outside observers agreed with the Freedom House organization, which in 2010 generously ranked the country as "partly free" in terms of political rights and civil liberties. Such evaluations of course pay more attention to legal freedoms than they do to the accountability or responsiveness of the regime to its people's needs or demands.

Egypt had a steady growth in gross domestic product, but this growth has benefitted only a section of the population. The economy has long been dominated by the state, particularly by its military. The army holds monopolies in companies in a wide range of sectors including water, oil, hotels, cement, and construction. In 2010, forty percent of the population was estimated to live at or below the poverty line of $2 a day (Amnesty International 2011). Egypt was ranked as the ninetieth most unequal country, compared with the United States at forty-second place. The official unemployment rate was 9.7 percent, but the real figure, including underemployment, was quite possibly two to three times that.

In 1991, when an economic crisis and the first Gulf War were under way, Egyptian president Mubarak received a $372-million loan from the International Monetary Fund, part of $15 billion in emergency economic assistance. In return, Egypt agreed to overhaul its economy by slashing its budget deficit, freeing oil and other prices, and privatizing and deregulating many sectors. It introduced a sales tax and raised domestic energy prices (McCormick 2011, *New York Times* 1991). During 2004–2008, the country saw major economic reforms targeted toward attracting foreign direct investment (McCormick 2011: 3). However, the economic crisis slowed these reforms. Since 2007, life expectancy and adult literacy have declined, while infant mortality has increased (Amnesty International Reports 2007–2010). Significantly, the average cost of buying food shot up 32 percent from June to December 2010, according to the United Nations Food and Agriculture Organisation (FAO) (Schechter 2011).

Protests had been increasing over the previous years, with evidence of the spread of a social movement repertoire. Worker protests grew more frequent, rising from 97 in 2002 to 742 in 2009, the Land Centre for Human Rights reports (Awad 2010a). Since 2008, people have been demonstrating for pay increases, a minimum wage, and the need for price controls. Demonstrations were also held against police brutality and the Emergency Law. Two main social movement organizations have been central in the mobilizations: Kefaya (Enough), which trade unionists formed in 2004, and the April 6 group, formed after striking workers in the Nile Delta in April 2008 were brutally repressed. At that protest, police killed three people and arrested hundreds (including bloggers) after demonstrators pulled down posters of Mubarak (Saleh and Abdellah 2010). Both organizations linked key sites of economic struggle to pro-democracy claims (Amar 2011b).

These were not the only groups mobilizing. In the winter and spring of 2009, large-scale protests against Israel's invasion of Gaza were organized by the Muslim Brotherhood (17 January 2009). Outside of the large cities, in January 2010 there were large protests about the exclusion of some groups from political support. In the Sinai, Bedouins rallied against a lack of government support after a flood (*Reuters*, January 2010). That same month, Coptic Christians chanted about the lack of government protection for their community after six Copts and a Muslim policeman were killed near Luxor (*Reuters*, January 13, 2010).

Despite ongoing arrests and beatings of protesters, each of these events laid the groundwork for the social movement mobilization of January 2011. When police arrested and killed Khaled Said, mobilization increased, and opposition party members and public figures increasingly began to identify themselves with the burgeoning movement, partly in anticipation of the 2010 parliamentary election and the 2011 presidential vote.

When young protesters in Tunisia demonstrated their solidarity with an unemployed university graduate who was fined for selling vegetables without a permit—and who set himself alight in protest—activists and ordinary people identified with their struggle and saw parallels to their own situation. When protesters succeeded in forcing out the longstanding leader, they signaled a political opportunity to those critical of their own regime or its policies in encouragement of social movements.

What do the Egyptian struggles of 2011 tell us about twenty-first-century social movements?

First, they establish that despite a lack of civil liberties and political freedoms, experiments with institutionalized social movements are taking place in new locations. With plenty of local color, the marches, rallies, tent cities, and strikes clearly belonged to the international social movement repertoire; formed part of a sustained campaign to influence the government; expressed program, identity, and standing claims; and involved repeated displays of WUNC. As we have already observed for the latter part of the twentieth century, democratization and social movements across the world kept each other company during the early twenty-first century.

Second, the Egyptian struggles show that social movements can emerge in countries that are socially and geographically segmented. The majority of the participants in the pro-democracy protests across the region are young people, often educated ones, who are experiencing difficulty finding work. Geography also matters: most of the pro-democracy movement protesters live in the growing urban centers of their countries. However, away from the urban centers of Egypt, Tunisia, Iran, Syria, Libya, or Yemen, and away from the technologically linked youth, public politics does not involve social movements, but instead often involves religious leaders, bandits, hostage takers, patron–client networks, and guerrilla forces. Both authoritarian countries and authoritarian segments of partly democratic countries remained outside the world of social movements.

Third, international connections clearly mattered in the movement in Egypt. The *New York Times* reported that some Egyptian youth leaders attended a 2008 technology meeting in New York, where they were taught to use social networking and mobile technologies to promote democracy. Among those sponsoring that meeting were Facebook, Google, MTV, Columbia Law School, and the State Department. Economic ties, international nongovernmental organizations, and immigration patterns link Egypt to Tunisia, the United States, Gaza, England, and beyond. Bloggers transmitted news of the protests online, where international media picked up the stories. International media coverage (stimulated in part by electronic communication) meant that Egyptian activists had no choice but to act on the local and world stages simultaneously. Does that make the events of 2011 an instance or consequence of globalization? Not in the sense that intensification of international connections constituted or precipitated the mobilization against the government. At most, we can say that in the twenty-first century, even youth in cities in Egypt had integrated sufficiently into worldwide circuits of power and communication that their authoritarian rulers could not effectively control the domestic and international political activities of their citizens.

Fourth, the widespread use of mobile telephones, Facebook, Twitter, and YouTube is an important influence on the new movements. Concerned citizens were able to mobilize without forming bounded organizations and were able to communicate through their personal networks. As a result, their mobilization was broader, but possibly less predictable and durable.

Fifth, local culture and the state are still important. Egyptian crowds may have formed more rapidly or in larger numbers than before as a result of cheap, quick communications. But the overall contours of popular mobilization—at least as seen from this distance—greatly resemble those of earlier, pre-cellphone and pre-internet Egyptian contentious politics as well as earlier social movements elsewhere in the democratic and semidemocratic world: civil disobedience, the wearing of protest colors, assemblies in symbolically charged locations, the involvement of celebrities, and marches to government buildings.

So what? Our use of media sources limits our knowledge. Media reports help us greatly in specifying what sorts of actions we must explain, what major actors (individual and collective) appear in public, and which publicly avowed alliances form among actors. However, by themselves they do not answer the worrisome questions like to what extent did the popular mobilization exert an independent influence on the outcome? Without much closer observation of interactions among the campaign's participants, we cannot say for sure.

The most plausible reading of the evidence at hand, as we see it, runs like this: political entrepreneurs opposed to the regime mobilized dissatisfaction. Text messages, Facebook users, bloggers, and Tweeters amplified that dissatisfaction and spread the message to observers. The economic crisis, combined with the police killing of Khaled Said, provided the context. These factors, along with the recent ouster of Tunisia's leaders, signaled a political opportunity, and international connections provided the discourse of "rights talk" and "democracy" as a way of making claims. As a result, the marches and demonstrations emerged, and, without great fanfare, the social movement became more widely available through the region as a way of pressing popular claims.

Going International

Across much of the world, meanwhile, social movements are internationalizing. We have, of course, encountered international connections within social movements since the very start: remember the prominence of British symbols, such as

John Wilkes's number 45, in Charleston, South Carolina, in 1768? Abolitionism soon became a transatlantic movement with branches extending into a number of countries on both sides of the ocean. Through the nineteenth century, movements on behalf of temperance, women's rights, and Irish independence continued to generate cooperation around the Atlantic (Hanagan 2002; Keck and Sikkink 2000; Kish Sklar and Stewart 2007).

We are searching, then, not merely for examples of international social movement interactions but for indications of a significant change in the orientations of social movements. Figure 5.1 schematizes internationalization. It distinguishes between (1) *claimants* (for example, campaigners against the World Trade Organization) that make program, identity, and standing claims by means of WUNC displays integrated into social movement performances; and (2) *objects of claims* (for example, the World Trade Organization), whose response, recognition, or removal claimants seek. Over the two-century history of social movements this book surveys, both claimants and the objects or targets of their claims have ranged from local to regional to national to international. Most often, the two have operated at the same level: local claimants with local objects, regional claimants with regional objects, and so on. But an increasingly common pattern matched coordinated claims by multiple claimants at one level with objects at a higher level, as when abolitionists in Boston and Philadelphia joined to petition Congress for an end to slavery or when local Nazi activists in

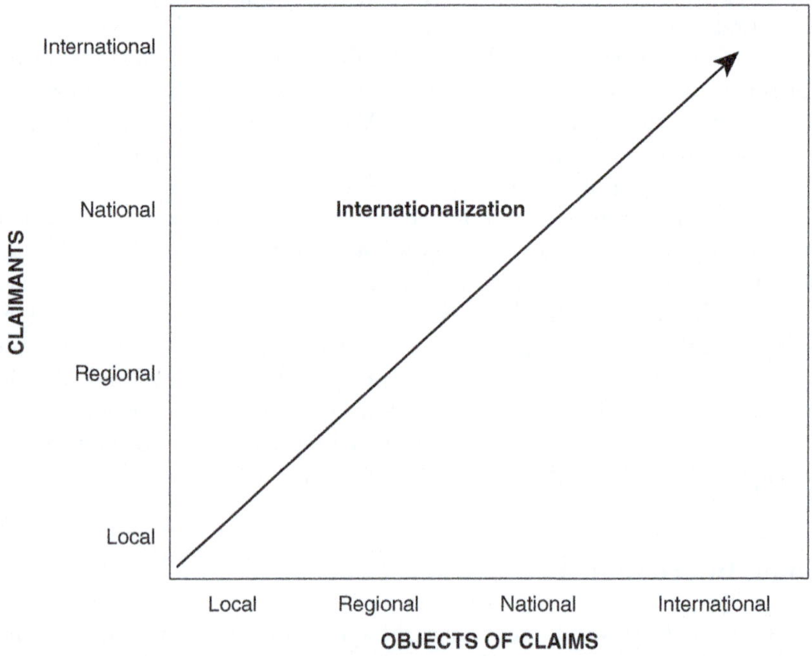

Figure 5.1 Internationalization of Social Movements

Marburg and other cities began coordinating their claims for Hitler's placement as German ruler.

Similarly, national-level claimants such as supporters of independence from the Soviet Union within USSR republics or Soviet satellite states in 1989 simultaneously targeted Soviet rulers and international authorities, including the European Union and the United Nations. The second case constituted a major step in the direction of internationalization. It fell short of the maximum—the upper right corner of Figure 5.1—because it mobilized people who spoke as regional and national claimants rather than actors who spoke decisively on behalf of an international "we." Nevertheless, the international construction of "we" became an increasingly familiar feature of twenty-first-century social movements.

Objects of claims also shifted their scale to the international level (Tarrow and McAdam 2005). As transnational corporations and national corporations operating in many countries—think of Nike, McDonald's, Coca-Cola, and Royal Dutch Shell—expanded and multiplied, they provided targets for multinational social movement coordination. Creation of international authorities such as the United Nations, the North Atlantic Treaty Organization, the European Union, and the World Trade Organization (WTO) likewise produced consequential actors whose influence, policies, and interventions attracted social movement claims from multiple countries (see, e.g., Deibert 2000; Wood 2004). When those actors held visible high-level meetings, the meetings themselves invited internationally coordinated protests of their policies. The most well-known of these "summit protests" took place in Seattle, Washington, against the World Trade Organization in November 1999. Jackie Smith describes mobilization around that meeting:

> On the evening of November 29, 1999, Seattle business and political leaders hosted an elaborate welcoming party in the city's football stadium for delegates to the World Trade Organization's Third Ministerial Conference. At the same time, thousands of activists rallied at a downtown church in preparation for the first large public confrontation in what became the "Battle of Seattle." Protesters emerged from the overflowing church and joined thousands more who were dancing, chanting, and conversing in a cold Seattle downpour. They filled several city blocks and celebrated the "protest of the century." Many wore union jackets or rain ponchos that proclaimed their opposition to the World Trade Organization. Several thousand marchers . . . progressed to the stadium, and around it formed a human chain—three or four people deep—to dramatize the crippling effects of the debt crisis. The protest deterred more than two-thirds of the expected 5,000 guests from attending the lavish welcoming event. The human chain's symbolism of the "chains of debt" was part of an international campaign (Jubilee 2000) to end Third World debt. It highlighted for protesters and onlookers the enormous inequities of the global trading system, and it kicked off a week of street protests and rallies against the global trade regime.
>
> (Smith 2002: 207)

Jubilee 2000 had originally formed as a coalition of United Kingdom non-governmental organizations oriented to questions of economic and social development. The coalition gradually began to focus on the cancellation of Third World debt. It pioneered the tactic of organizing "human chains" to represent the "chains of debt" around summit sites at a 1998 meeting of international financial leaders in Birmingham, England. It was one of many coalitions that brought together activists from a wide range of international political networks to sites where they shared strategies and analyses. The Battle of Seattle became a model for international organizers who targeted international institutions.

To understand the internationalization of claimants and objects of claims, we must recognize three other aspects of internationalization:

(1) proliferation of intermediaries specialized less in making claims on their own than in helping others coordinate claims at the international level,
(2) multiplication of lateral connections among groups of activists involved in making similar claims, and
(3) increasing coordination by repressive authorities of different countries and regions.

Human rights organizations such as Amnesty International and Human Rights Watch led the way for the first aspect, monitoring human rights abuses across the world, publishing regular ratings and reports on those abuses, intervening to call down sanctions from major states and international authorities on human rights abusers, but often providing templates, certification, connections, and advice to claimants. Movements of indigenous peoples across the world benefited substantially from that identification of themselves as participants in a worldwide cause, although their movements were in no way new. This aspect also includes foundations such as the National Endowment for Democracy or the Ford Foundation and groups such as Nonviolence International, who work to support particular types of social movement activity by providing resources to movements and organizations (Bob 2005). This aspect also includes the movement infrastructure provided by networks such as the Independent Media Center that have developed movement-run, media support for demonstrations through hundreds of sites worldwide.

Second, movement activists organized around similar causes—for example, environmentalism, women's rights, and opposition to low-wage sweatshops producing in poor countries for rich markets—have also created enduring connections across oceans and continents. As we have seen with Fijian feminist activists, some of those connections form initially at international meetings convened by international organizations such as the United Nations, others at summit protests. Still others form through electronic contacts mediated by discussion lists, websites and Twitter feeds. Such transnational networks appear to be the modular form within the global justice movement, and the more recent movements surrounding the economic crisis. These networks facilitate the diffusion of new ideas, create links between previously divided actors, and create new campaigns, frames, and identities (della Porta et al. 2006; Reitan 2007; Smith 2007; Tarrow 2005).

Third, in recent years, police and security professionals are converging at international conferences featuring workshops on crowd-control strategies, expert consultants are disseminating the latest "best practices," and officers are experimenting with new technologies of surveillance and border control in order to manage internationalized political protest. This has led to some convergence in crowd-control strategies (della Porta, Peterson, and Reiter 2006). For example, the security forces preparing for the 2008 protests against the Group of Eight (G8) in Japan publicly explained that they would meet to exchange information with the German officials who organized the security for the 2007 summit (12 August 2007, *Kyodo News*). One strategy that has spread quickly is the use of immigration controls with provisions against "hooligans" to limit the mobility of antiglobalization protesters to protest sites. Such repressive innovations correspond with changes in protest tactics and forms of organization.

Despite ample precedents, internationally coordinated social movement performances and international backing for regional and national social movement performances have occurred with increasing frequency since the final decades of the twentieth century. Activists and analysts became ever more likely, furthermore, to claim regional and national events for worldwide movements variously labeled antiglobalization, global justice, or global civil society (Bennett 2003; della Porta et al. 2006; Koopmans 2004; Rucht 2003; Smith 2007; Tarrow 2002, 2005).

This becomes apparent when we look at the events listed as part of a global movement around the economic crisis that began in October 2007. Launched on September 17, 2011, the Occupy Wall Street mobilizations began to attract media attention in the following month, and hundreds of cities and towns mobilized their own versions of Occupy Wall Street. A website called "United for Global Change" showed a short video that spliced footage from uprisings in Egypt for the end of Mubarak's regime and widespread corruption, with footage from Spain against the national government and banks, from Chile by students opposing corporate control of education, and from India against corruption to present a vision of a single unified movement, calling out, "People of the World Rise Up!"

On one hand, these events were clearly globally oriented and connected in that they were all connected to a larger economic crisis and global networks of multinational banks, corporations, and financial institutions, such as the International Monetary Fund, that created and facilitated the economic crisis. These brief images of chanting crowds represented in the video also articulate the connections between local concerns and global targets. However, within this "global uprising" these movements in Spain, Chile, Greece, and India were partly targeting nation-states, while others in each of those countries were less interested in making demands of authorities, even as they linked up with global movements. What was presented as a massive, simultaneous global upsurge was on closer inspection a convergence of distinct, albeit linked, waves of protest where diffusion was accelerated. Although tactics, slogans, identities, and frames spread increasingly rapidly, the movements themselves were rooted in distinct histories, polities, and economies as different as authoritarian Egypt, the media-saturated United States, the rapidly growing economy of India, and the complex politics of the European Union. In order to understand the similarities, differences, and confluences of these waves, we would need some additional information.

What do we see when we place the early twenty-first century in a longer time perspective? In the absence of comprehensive catalogs for social movements across the world (and with the tedious but essential warning that social movements by no means reduce to social movement organizations), we can get some sense of expansion from national to transnational over the last hundred or so years from looking at counts of foundings for international nongovernmental organizations. Those foundings ran at two or three per year during the 1870s and 1880s, and five or six per year during the 1890s, increasing to thirty or so per year before World War I. Founding of international nongovernmental organizations then declined during and after the war before rising to close to forty during the 1920s, declining again through World War II, then soaring to eighty, ninety, and finally above one hundred new foundings per year during the 1980s. The lack of resources and disruption in daily lives makes mobilization and organization of social movements especially difficult during wartime, which may explain why the creation of NGOs decreased during WWI and WWII. The number continued to increase; between 1996 and 2007 the number of international nongovernmental organizations rose from 15,108 to 21,443, averaging more than 500 new organizations a year (Boli and Thomas 1997: 176; for counts of existing international nongovernmental organizations 1900–2000, see Albrow and Glasius 2008; Anheier and Themudo 2002: 194).

The evidence displays striking correspondence between formation of international nongovernmental organizations and creation of governmental or quasi-governmental organizations such as the League of Nations, the International Labour Organization, the United Nations, and the World Bank; indeed, Boli and Thomas find that, year by year, the correlation between foundings of international nongovernmental organizations and foundings of intergovernmental organizations runs at 0.83 (Boli and Thomas 1997: 178). The Boli–Thomas data also reveal broad parallels between international nongovernmental organizations' founding and the rough timetable of globalization we proposed earlier.

Concentrating more narrowly—and, for our purposes, more cogently—on "free-standing nongovernmental associations that were specifically organized to promote some type of social or political change goal" and had members in at least three countries, Jackie Smith has pinpointed changes in the number of existing organizations (not the number of new foundings) from 1973 to 2003. Table 5.3 shows her counts of all such transnational social movement organizations (TSMOs).

The number roughly doubled during each decade from 1973 to 1993, then increased by another half between 1993 and 2003, and nearly doubled between 2003 and 2013. More TSMOs in Smith's catalog dealt with human rights and environmental issues than with peace, women's rights, development, global

Table 5.3 Number of Transnational Social Movement Organizations (TSMOs), 1973–2013

Year	Number of TSMOs
1973	183
1983	348
1993	711
2003	1,011
2013	1,767

Source: Smith 2018.

justice, ethnic self-determination, or right-wing causes. During the 1990s, however, organizations committed to ethnic issues declined as economic issues became more prominent. What people loosely call antiglobalization movements drew especially on organizations specializing in economic issues, but they often formed alliances with organizations focusing on human rights, the environment, and other prominent international social movement claims makers.

As the available data suggest, organizational bases of international social movement activity expanded approximately in time with proliferation of international connections in other regards (see also Keck and Sikkink 2000). However, this expansion reproduces patterns of inequality. Internationally active nongovernmental organizations operate disproportionately in cities and countries that also host major decision-making institutions. Even their meetings are concentrated in a small number of countries, with 48.5 percent of all meetings of international organizations held in the United States, France, Germany, the United Kingdom, Italy, Spain, the Netherlands, Austria, Switzerland, or Belgium (Albrow and Glasius 2008). Such sites facilitate the participation of local claimants more than they do more distant claimants.

Alas, we cannot rely on counts or descriptions of organizations—international or otherwise—as proxies for the campaigns, repertoires, and WUNC displays of social movements. Examining summit protests and global days of action will provide some clues about the ways in which social movements are mobilizing in the twenty-first century.

Although there had been protests against international financial institutions throughout the 1990s, shortly before the Seattle protests of 1999, the summits of international financial institutions began to draw large protests. Some of the larger ones were:

May 16–20, 1998: Group of 8 (G8) summit (Birmingham, United Kingdom) and World Trade Organization (WTO) ministerial meeting (Geneva, Switzerland); 2,000–3,000

June 18, 1999: G8 summit (Cologne, Germany); 800–1,000

November 30, 1999: WTO ministers (Seattle, United States); 50,000–70,000

September 26, 2000: International Monetary Fund and World Bank summits (Prague, Czech Republic); 12,000

July 18–22, 2001: G8 summit (Genoa, Italy); 50,000–60,000
June 2, 2007: G8 summit (Rostock, Germany); 80,000
June 25–26, 2010: G20 summit (Toronto, Canada); 10,000
July 7–8, 2017: G20 summit (Hamburg, Germany); 100,000.

These summit protests are coordinated by activists in international protest networks who work with local activists to set up the legal, training, and accommodations infrastructure, often through "convergence centers." These centers provide an accessible space for coordinating demonstrations, accommodations, independent media, first aid, and legal support for the demonstrators. Often, some of these activists organize a countersummit that provides an opportunity to critically discuss the issues of the summit, its participants, and their policies.

These summit protests can actually influence their targets as well as popular views of those targets. The *Annual Register* commented:

> Following what one reporter called its "fall from grace" at the ministerial meeting at Seattle in late 1999, the WTO spent 2000 in a period of "convalescence" or, in a less charitable characterisation, "paralysis." Little was achieved in resolving the complicated issues that had surfaced so dramatically at the 1999 session. Friction continued between developed and developing nations over the latter's demand for greater WTO influence. The economic powerhouses, most notably the EU, Japan, and the USA, still could not agree on a timetable and agenda for a proposed new round of global trade negotiations. And protests by antiglobalisation activists persisted, attacking, among other things, the perceived negative effect of WTO activity on labor standards and environmental protection and arguing that the poverty in many countries was being exacerbated, not ameliorated, by WTO decisions.
>
> (*Annual Register* 2000: 385–386)

Similarly, in September 2003, when trade representatives gathered in Cancún, Mexico to negotiate policy for international exchanges of foodstuffs, observers noted that street demonstrators and the newly formed Group of Twenty-One developing country food exporters had formed a formidable alliance which the European Union and the United States, with their extensive subsidies to farmers, could hardly ignore (Becker 2003). Still, the draft WTO agreement that emerged from the Cancún meeting made only minor concessions, mostly rhetorical, to the Group of Twenty-One and their backers on the street (Thompson 2003). In fact, the talks collapsed when the Group of Twenty-One withdrew in protest against the meagerness of rich countries' proposals. It would therefore take a much closer analysis to detect the precise impact of such action days on WTO behavior. But at a minimum, the international activist networks succeeded in shaping public discussion of that behavior.

In the years since the successes of Seattle and Cancún, summit protests have begun to decline in size. Some local and national activists have been critiquing these events for being cost-intensive, accessible only to a small section of the population, and increasingly irrelevant because of the intensive preparation by the police. Instead, they have been reemphasizing the importance of local and national protest. Locally organized, globally framed days of action coordinated to take place at the same time as global summits have increased in popularity.

A global day of action involves coordinated, simultaneous meetings, demonstrations, and press releases in sites that are generally organized relatively autonomously. These protests are mobilized by local, national, regional, and international organizations and networks of activists. These new global days of action began to increase in frequency with the global justice movement, sometimes involving over one hundred cities protesting on the same day.

The scale of those global days of action was dwarfed in 2003 when protesters demonstrated in more than 600 cities during the same weekend against the impending attacks of the United States on Iraq. Spread through preexisting formal and informal networks of activists, the practice of organizing global days of action has diffused to activists working on a host of issues. In the month of April 2018, this included the events listed in Table 5.4.

These few examples make clear that such events represent a diversity of issues, goals, causes, and scales. Despite similar websites that bring together the different actors, each one is tied to different networks, different types of organizing, and different scales of mobilization. For example, Earth Day is much broader in goals, and participation than the day seeking to protect Kurdish cities from the Turkish regime. Nonetheless, examining global days of action alone makes it impossible to tell whether such internationally coordinated actions were increasing as a share of all social movement performances anywhere. However, it certainly demonstrates the rise of geographically dispersed, simultaneous performances as a tactic of activists working at the local, national, and global levels.

Table 5.4 Global Days of Action: April 2018

April 14th – May 3rd	Global Campaign on Military Spending—Activities in 25 countries including rallies, press conferences, protests and online selfie campaigns.
April 17th	Rana Plaza Day—Global Week of Action (also known as Fashion Revolution Week) urging garment brands to make factories in Bangladesh safe by signing the 2018 Transition Accord. The day of action was promoted by trade unions, the Clean Clothes Campaign, and United Students Against Sweatshops.
April 22nd	Earth Day. One of the largest global days of action, that includes celebration, community work, and protest. According to the organizers, 1 billion people in 192 countries participate.
April 28th	Global Day of Action for Sur and Hasankeyf, against the ongoing destruction of the two antique cities Sur and Hasankeyf at the Tigris River in North (Turkish) Kurdistan by the Turkish government. The Kurdish diaspora, NGOs, and human rights groups organized events in 30 cities, including ten in Germany.

Source: Compiled from https://cleanclothes.org 2018; www.earthday.org/; http://demilitarize.org/; https://anfenglish.com/news/global-day-of-action-for-sur-and-hasankeyf-in-many-cities-26361.

Let us not confuse the increasing density of global networks with internationalization of protest targets and claimants. Even though movement participants are increasingly aware of their location within global movements—and understand the connections between different issues and movements—most of the time, they organize within national boundaries and against national or local targets. Doug Imig, Sidney Tarrow, and Maria Trif conducted some of the most precise analyses of internationalization, in this case within the European Union (EU) from 1984 to 1997. Imig and Tarrow scanned Reuters online news services to identify "contentious events" roughly equivalent to the contentious gatherings described in Chapter 2. They then asked which of the events (1) involved cross-national coordination among claimants and/or (2) directed claims to the EU or one of its agencies. Of the 9,872 events in the Imig-Tarrow catalog, only 490—5 percent—involved claims on the EU (Imig and Tarrow 2001: 32–34). Of those 490, only 84 involved international coordination; the other 406 gestured toward the EU but remained within national boundaries and directed their primary claims at authorities within their own countries. Between 1994 and 1997, it is true, the proportion of all events directly targeting EU agencies swelled from about 5 to 30 percent. Follow-up research by Trif and Imig showed that in 2002 some 20 percent of European events were transnational in coordination, but still only 5 percent were directed at EU agencies as such (Trif and Imig 2003). Donatella della Porta and Manuela Caiani (2007) found similar results when they used newspaper data, but, using 348 interviews with activists in Europe, argued that Europeanization was taking place through the building of networks and the framing of claims as European. At the beginning of the new century, a modest internationalization of Europe's social movement activity was finally starting to occur.

We can cast the evidence in two very different ways. Since the trend displays a recent increase in the proportion of international claimants and claims, we might project that trend forward into the twenty-first century, forecasting a vast internationalization of social movements (see, e.g., Bennett 2003; della Porta and Caiani 2007; Smith 2002). Plenty of anecdotal illustrations support such a reading, especially international mobilizations against the North American Free Trade Agreement, the World Trade Organization, and transnational corporations.

From another angle, however, the Imig–Tarrow results show us a late-twentieth-century European world in which most social movement claim making continued to occur within state boundaries. What is more, such international networks as Jubilee 2000, for all their spectacular efficacy at initiating one-time actions, including electronic petitions and simultaneous human chains, have generally fragmented or withered over time; on the whole, more centralized non-governmental organizations based near major world centers of power have proven more durable (Anheier and Themudo 2002). Since Western Europe and North America still contain the bulk of such centers and since their activists were almost certainly more heavily engaged in international social movement claim making than any other large regions of the world, serious worldwide internationalization still had a long way to go.

If Howard Rheingold and Lance Bennett have described the character of digitally mediated social movements correctly, indeed, supporters of democracy may actually want to cheer the current incompleteness of internationalization. Although successful grassroots networks like the international peasant movement Via Campesina offer hope, neither Facebook nor weakly linked networks enjoy the capacity for sustained political work on behalf of their programs that earlier centuries' histories have shown us as the accompaniment of social movement repertoires. Quick mobilization of millions in opposition to the G8 or McDonald's sensitizes their targets to public relations and encourages them to defend their perimeters. It does not obviously give ordinary people voice in the decisions of governments and powerful institutions. Indian activist-analyst Neera Chandhoke worries about a triple threat: that international nongovernmental organizations and global social movements will evade democratic accountability to the same degree that the WTO or the IMF evades it; that organizations and activists based in the global North will dominate international claim making to the detriment of organizations and people in poorer, less well-connected countries; and that the division between skilled political entrepreneurs and ordinary people will sharpen:

> We have cause for unease. For much of the leadership of global civil society organisations appears to be self-appointed and nonaccountable to their members, many of whom are passive and confine their activism to signatures to petitions circulated via e-mail. Also note that, whereas we see huge crowds during demonstrations against the WTO or in alternative forums such as the World Social Forum, between such episodes activity is carried on by a core group of NGOs. It is possible that participants in demonstrations are handed a political platform and an agenda that has been finalized elsewhere. This is hardly either democratic or even political; it may even reek of bureaucratic management of participatory events. It may even render people . . . consumers of choices made elsewhere.
>
> (Chandhoke 2002: 48)

Perhaps social movements are splitting: on one side, older styles of action and organization that sustain continuous political involvement at points of decision-making power; and on the other, spectacular but temporary displays of connection across the continents, largely mediated by specialized organizations, technologies, and entrepreneurs. If so, we must think hard about the effects of such a split on democracy, that faithful companion of social movements throughout their history.

6

DEMOCRATIZATION AND SOCIAL MOVEMENTS

Charles Tilly and Lesley Wood[1]

No social movements occurred in Kazakhstan in 2016. However, plenty of conflict occurred. There were large protests against land reforms that allowed foreigners to rent land, and hundreds were detained or imprisoned. Although opposition parties, unions and NGOs do exist, they are unable to operate freely. President (and Soviet holdover) Nursultan Nazarbayev has tailored the country's laws to consolidate his hold on government institutions. In 2010, Parliament passed a law confirming that Nazarbayev would enjoy lifetime immunity from prosecution (Human Rights Watch 2011). Weeks later, the president won 95.5 percent of the vote. Like previous elections, observers judged them to have fallen far short of international standards of free and open elections. Aware of the criticism, shortly before those elections Nazarbayev wrote an opinion piece for the *Washington Post* in which he described his plans for democratization:

> It took the great democracies of the world centuries to develop. We are not going to become a fully developed democracy overnight. But we have proved that we can deliver on our big ambitions. Our road to democracy is irreversible, and we intend to provide economic and political opportunities for our citizens. (Nazarbayev 2011)

Until recently, the Khazakh economy boomed, becoming a significant source of both oil and uranium. Partly as a result of this performance, and the country's strategic importance in the region, the country was awarded the 2010 chairmanship of the Organization for Security and Co-operation in Europe (OSCE). Despite this heightened international engagement, challenges for those seeking a more democratic regime in the country are great. Repeatedly, those who challenge the regime are arrested or attacked.

International observers argue that democracy has not yet come to Kazakhstan. The 2016 Human Rights Watch report argued that the government stifled the media, blocked access to websites, prosecuted and harassed opposition politicians, imprisoned activists, and suppressed demonstrations. In 2016, the U.S. State Department reported the following human rights problems.

> The most significant human rights problems were limits on citizens' ability to choose their government in free and fair elections; selective restrictions on freedoms of expression, press, assembly, religion, and association; and lack of an independent judiciary and due process, especially in dealing with pervasive corruption and abuses by law enforcement and judicial officials.
>
> The criminal and administrative codes that went into effect in 2015, as well as the trade union law, further limited freedoms of speech, assembly, and religion. Provisions of the criminal code prohibiting incitement of ethnic, religious, social, and other "discord" were particularly open to abuse.
>
> Other reported abuses included arbitrary or unlawful killings; military hazing that led to deaths; detainee and prisoner torture and other abuse; harsh and sometimes life-threatening prison conditions; arbitrary arrest and detention; infringements on citizens' privacy rights; prohibitive political party registration requirements; restrictions on the activities of nongovernmental organizations (NGOs); violence and discrimination against women; abuse of children; sex and labor trafficking; discrimination against persons with disabilities; societal discrimination against lesbian, gay, bisexual, transgender, and intersex (LGBTI) persons; discrimination against those with HIV/AIDS; and child labor.

Despite this knowledge, powerful actors continue to build alliances with the regime. In 2015, Kazakhstan and the EU signed the EU–Kazakhstan Enhanced Partnership and Cooperation Agreement, despite concerns of some European parliamentarians.

In this context, nothing much resembling a social movement goes on in Kazakhstan these days. Nor, for that matter, have the remaining fragments of the Soviet Union seen much social movement activity since 1989 (Barrington 1995; Beissinger 1993, 1998a, 1998b; Drobizheva, Gottemoeller, Kelleher, and Walker 1996; Kaiser 1994; Khazanov 1995; Laitin 1998, 1999; McFaul 1997; Nahaylo and Swoboda 1990; Petrova and Tarrow 2007; Smith, Law, Wilson, Bohr, and Allworth 1998; Suny 1993, 1995).

Breakaway Soviet Republic Belarus, for instance, looked as though it would produce an entire social movement sector during the early 1990s. Alexander Lukashenko won the Belarus presidency in a 1994 popular election as a crusader against "corruption." But as soon as he had consolidated his hold on the office, Lukashenko instituted censorship, smashed independent trade unions, fixed elections, and subjugated the legislature to his rule. Thus, his actions reversed the country's modest previous democratic gains (Mihalisko 1997; Titarenko, McCarthy, McPhail, and Augustyn 2001). Opposition leaders and journalists soon found themselves in danger of arbitrary imprisonment, torture, kidnapping, and murder (Human Rights Watch 2000: 249–53; Karatnycky 2000: 76–78).

The *Annual Register* ranks Belarus 127th on its Democracy index out of 167 countries. It explains that Lukashenko remains in office, despite widespread electoral irregularities. While repression had slowed since 2014, due to a desire for a better relationship with the West, in 2017, when the economy collapsed, and protests and police action accelerated. Initially there was tolerance, but soon, police began to arrest organizers. Then in March, 700 were arrested at a rally in Minsk (Ivanova 2017).

Although 2017 showed increased numbers of large-scale protests around both democracy and the economic crisis, organized partly through social media, unsanctioned protests, meetings, and assemblies remained illegal in the country. As that year came to an end, neither in the Soviet Union's old central territories (Russia and Belarus) nor in its Central Asian borderlands (Kazakhstan and neighboring countries) were social movements thriving.

False Expectations of Open Markets Leading to Democratization

We report this news because during the early 1990s, many observers of communist regimes' last days thought that the destruction of centralized superstructures in those states would rapidly open the way to social movements, which would then facilitate construction of a democratic civil society. Many analysts followed an analogy with the market's expected transformation of economic activity. Nevertheless, neither the growth of strong economies with large middle classes nor the normalization of social movements, nor democratization have come to pass through most of the former Soviet Union (Nelson, Tilly, and Walker 1998).

In fact, as of the end of 2019 most people in the world still lacked access to social movements as a way to voice popular claims. Despite Tiananmen and a variety of subsequent popular struggles, the quarter of the world's population living in China during the early twenty-first century had no regular recourse to social movements (Bernstein and Lü 2002). Where democracy fell short, social movements remained sparse.

Social Movements and Democratization

Previous chapters repeatedly identified a broad correspondence between democratization and social movements. Social movements originated in the partial democratization that set British subjects and North American colonists against their rulers during the eighteenth century. Across the nineteenth century, social movements generally flourished and spread where further democratization was occurring and receded when authoritarian regimes curtailed democratic rights. This pattern continued during the twentieth and twenty-first centuries: maps of full-fledged social movements and of democratic institutions overlapped greatly.

Yet, we have also learned that social movements do not necessarily espouse or promote democracy. Movements are more frequently organized around particular interests and grievances, than around demands for democratization as such. From early on, relatively democratic movements regularly provoked undemocratic countermovements, such as the United Kingdom's early-nineteenth-century opponents of Catholic rights. In more or less functioning democracies, furthermore, social movements recurrently pursue antidemocratic programs such as exclusion of immigrants, or racial, ethnic, and religious minorities. Sometimes they even pursue the abolition of democracy itself in the name of a totalitarian creed such as Mussolini's Fascism and Hitler's Nazism.

Circumstances in which democracy and social movements do *not* coincide set an especially perplexing challenge to the tracing of their causal connections. For example, Chapter 4 demonstrated that across the historical cases analyzed by Ruth Collier, democratization and social movements sometimes preceded and sometimes followed each other; neither depended entirely on the other's existence. Social movements occasionally form in democratic crevices of segmented or otherwise authoritarian regimes, as we have seen in China or Egypt. In moments of partial democratization—witnessed by many of the Soviet satellite states in 1989—social movements can form without necessarily becoming permanent features of the political landscape. It is clear that the relationship between democracy and social movements is more than mechanical. How does such a mechanism work?

The incomplete overlap of social movements and democratization poses three questions that are crucial both for explaining social movements and for gauging their futures.

1. What causes the broad but still-incomplete correspondence between social movements and democratic institutions?
2. To what extent and how does democratization itself cause social movements to form and prosper?
3. Under what conditions, and how, do social movements actually advance democracy? This particular question forces us to think about a further unpleasant question we have so far mostly avoided: Under what conditions, and how, do social movements damage democracy?

It is time to reflect on the social movements' history in search of answers to these pressing questions. In order to do so, we have to think about the character and causes of democratization before moving on to relations between democratization and social movements.

How Will We Recognize Democracy and Democratization?

Like almost all other regimes elsewhere in the world, former members of the Soviet Union generally claim to be democracies. Article 1 of the Kazakh constitution, for instance, reads as follows.

> *The Republic of Kazakhstan proclaims itself a democratic, secular, legal and social state whose highest values are an individual, his life, rights and freedoms.*
>
> The fundamental principles of the activity of the Republic are public concord and political stability; economic development for the benefit of all the nation; Kazakhstan patriotism and resolution of the most important issues of the affairs of state by democratic methods including voting at an all-nation referendum or in the Parliament.
>
> (Kazakhstan 2008; emphasis added)

Clearly, constitutions alone will not tell us whether regimes qualify as working democracies. Even today, visibly viable democracies remain a minority among the world's forms of rule.

How will we recognize democracy and democratization when we see them? Many widely used definitions of democracy concentrate on the character of relations among citizens: whether they are just, kind, considerate, egalitarian, and so on. Others stress legal criteria: contested elections, representative institutions, formal guarantees of liberty, and related political arrangements (for reviews of definitions and measures, see Collier and Levitsky 1997; Geddes 1999; Inkeles 1991; Lijphart 1999; Przeworski, Alvarez, Cheibub, and Limongi 2000: 55–59; Sorensen 2007; Vanhanen 2000). Here, however, let us insist that, like tyranny and oligarchy, democracy is a kind of regime: a set of relations between a government and persons subject to that government's jurisdiction. The relations in question consist of mutual rights and obligations, government to subject and subject to government.

Democracies differ from other regimes because instead of the massive asymmetry, coercion, exploitation, patronage, and communal segmentation that have characterized most political regimes across the centuries, they establish fairly general and reliable rules of law (Tilly 2004, 2007). According to Tilly, a regime is democratic to the extent that:

1. regular and categorical, rather than intermittent and individualized, relations exist between the government and its subjects (for example, legal residence within the government's territories in itself establishes routine connections with governmental agents, regardless of relations to particular patrons or membership in specific ethnic groups);
2. those relations include most or all subjects (for example, no substantial sovereign enclaves exist within governmental perimeters);
3. those relations are equal across subjects and categories of subjects (for example, no legal exclusions from voting or officeholding based on gender, race, religion, or property ownership prevail);
4. governmental personnel, resources, and performances change in response to binding collective consultation of subjects (for example, popular referenda make law); and
5. subjects, especially members of minorities or those with unpopular viewpoints, receive protection from arbitrary action by governmental agents (for example, uniformly administered due process precedes incarceration of any individual regardless of social category).

Thus, democratization means formation of a regime featuring relatively broad, equal, categorical, mutually binding consultation and protection. Note the word "relatively": if we applied these standards absolutely, no regime past or present anywhere in the world would qualify as a democracy; all regimes have always fallen short in some regards when it has come to categorical regularity, breadth, equality, consultation, and protection.

Democratization consists of a regime's moves *toward* greater categorical equality, regularity, breadth, binding consultation, and protection. **Dedemocratization** consists of moves *away* from them. Tensions often exist between different aspects of democracy. A move intended to increase the greater equality of protection and consultation in the long term might potentially challenge the breadth of protected consultation in the short term.

If democracy entails relatively high levels of breadth, equality, consultation, and protection by definition, as a practical matter, it also requires the institution of citizenship (Tilly 1999, 2006, 2007). Citizenship consists, in this context, of mutual rights and obligations binding governmental agents to whole categories of people who are subject to the government's authority. Those categories being defined chiefly or exclusively by relations to the government rather than by particular connections with specific rulers or to membership in categories based on imputed traits such as race, ethnicity, gender, or religion. It institutionalizes regular, categorical relations between subjects and their governments.

Citizenship sometimes appears in the absence of democracy. Authoritarian regimes such as fascist Italy institutionalized broad, regular, categorical, and relatively equal relations between subjects and their governments but greatly restricted both consultation and protection. Powerful ruling parties and large police apparatuses inhibited democratic liberties. Citizenship looks like a necessary condition for democratization, but not a sufficient one.

Our survey of the nineteenth century showed the United Kingdom, Scandinavia, the United States, Switzerland, and Argentina all instituting limited degrees of citizenship—still exclusive in many regards, but diminishing the political influence of patron–client ties, outright coercion, and membership in culturally defined communities—at least within the privileged circle of those who enjoyed any political rights at all. In these terms, democratization means any net shift toward citizenship, breadth of citizenship, equality of citizenship, binding consultation of citizens, and protection of citizens from arbitrary action by agents of government.

The Empirical Problem

What does our historical survey tell us about relations between democratization and social movements? Without far more extensive catalogs and chronologies of social movement claim making than are currently available, we have no hope of looking closely at point-by-point empirical relationships between democratization and social movements. Nevertheless, we can draw together threads from the earlier histories to think about the scale (number of simultaneous participants, localities, and/or actions) and scope (variety of programs, identities, sites, performances, and WUNC displays) involved in social movements. The nineteenth century showed us the French street demonstration coming into its own as authoritarian top-down controls weakened, while 1968 showed us French workers and students creating a temporary democratic opening on their own initiative. Similar partial stories in previous chapters suggest a broad sequence of this sort.

1. *Little or no democratization*: no social movements
2. *Incipient democratization*: campaigns, repertoires, or WUNC displays bearing partial resemblances to those of social movements, but no full-fledged combinations of campaigns, repertoires, and WUNC displays
3. *Further democratization*: social movement combinations in limited sectors (for example students in Indonesia) without general availability of social movement means to other claimants
4. *Extensive democratization*: widespread availability of social movement programs, repertoires, and WUNC displays across programs, identities, and localities
5. *Incipient international democratization*: internationalization of social movement claim making.

Figure 6.1 portrays the stages as overlapping ovals to emphasize that in any given regime at a particular point in time different political actors vary with regard to their involvement in different sorts of social movement activity. It also draws the "no social movements" oval very broadly to stress both that most historical regimes have lacked social movements and that historically, some relatively democratic regimes have operated without social movements.

According to Figure 6.1, at lower levels of democratization and through most of history, no social movements form at all. Earlier chapters have recognized that, taken separately, claim-making campaigns, individual social movement performances such as the public meeting or the petition drive, and concerted public WUNC occurred in a wide variety of regimes long before the mid-eighteenth century. But they have also documented the initial *combination* of campaigns, repertoires, and WUNC displays in Great Britain and North America between the 1760s and the end of the Napoleonic Wars. The figure incorporates a distinction that has likewise served us helpfully in earlier chapters: between (1) intermittent resemblances of particular claims, performances, or WUNC displays in the public politics of undemocratic regimes to similar claims, performances, or WUNC displays of regimes in which social movements regularly occur; (2) combinations of the three in particular political mobilizations within regimes that have not institutionalized social movements; and (3) full-scale availability of social movement campaigns, repertoires, and WUNC displays to a wide variety of claimants within a regime. Drawing on recent developments, the figure adds yet another level: (4) the internationalization of social movement activity.

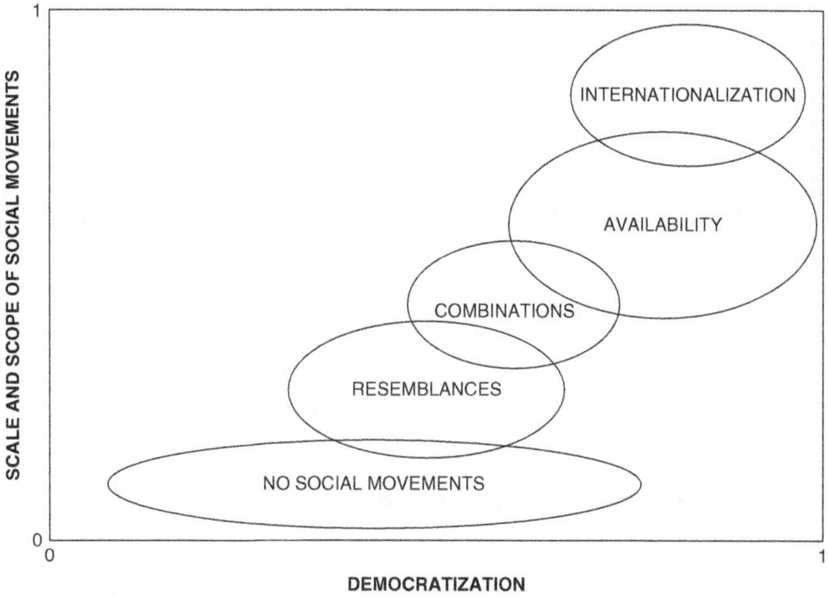

Figure 6.1 Scale and Scope of Social Movements at Different Degrees of Democratization

Overall, Figure 6.1 shows that in the course of democratization, resemblances generally precede combinations, particular combinations precede full availability of social movements, and availability within national regimes precedes internationalization. It also shows that availability and internationalization of social movements only take place within regimes that have extensive democratic institutions and practices—remembering of course that social movements are not the only form of contentious politics. Revolutions, ethnic and religious conflict, riots, strikes or militant nationalism are all types of contentious politics. In the absence of systematic evidence on the actual distribution of social movements across the world of the last two centuries, all stages of the argument take risks.

Stage 5 takes the greatest risks of all. The record of early-twenty-first-century social movements leaves open two possibilities that would blatantly contradict it. First, considering the political arena defined by international centers of power, it is not obvious that democratization is occurring internationally; categorically defined breadth, equality, consultation, and protection could actually be declining at the international scale as power shifts from states to international bodies and networks and as nationally grounded categories, breadth, equality, consultation, and protection thereby lose their impact. Second, as Chapter 5 suggested, internationalization of power relations might in fact be reducing the efficacy of social movements at the local, regional, and national scales as it narrows the scope of effective social movement action to just those groups and networks that can organize large international collaborations. That eventuality would oblige us to interpret internationalization as a reversal of the long-term trends that for more than two centuries favored broad correspondence between social movements and democratization. Internationalization could be bringing de-democratization.

What causes the strong but still incomplete correspondence between democratization and social movements? First, many of the same processes that cause democratization also independently promote social movements. Second, democratization further encourages people to form social movements. Third, under some conditions and in a more limited way, social movements themselves promote democratization. Before examining those three causal paths, however, we must review what causes democratization in the first place.

Why Does Democratization Ever Occur?

To put the matter very schematically, in currently undemocratic regimes, four social processes create favorable conditions for the establishment of political arrangements involving regular, categorical relations between subjects and governments; relatively broad and equal participation in decision making; binding consultation of political participants; and protection of political participants, especially members of vulnerable minorities, from arbitrary action by governmental agents. The four processes are:

1. Increases in the sheer numbers of people available for participation in public politics and/or in connections among those people, however those increases occur;
2. Equalization of resources and connections among those people, however that equalization occurs;
3. Insulation of public politics from existing social inequalities; and
4. Integration of interpersonal trust networks into public politics.

None of these constitutes democratization in itself, but all of them promote democratization, especially if they occur together. Let us consider each of the four in turn.

1. Increases in numbers and connections among potential political participants. Democracy has little chance to flourish when rulers form a small elite that governs through patronage, sale of state-controlled resources, and/or brute force. But circumstances such as defense against common enemies, calls for increased resources to support war or public works, demographic increase within the ruling class, expanding communications, and forceful demands for inclusion on the part of excluded parties all push rulers to expand the circle of participants in public politics. Ironically, when that happens, the overall proportion of the subject population connected and socially adjacent to those newly included also usually increases because others are then in a strengthened position to demand inclusion as well.

We have seen that sort of enlargement occurring with the British Reform Act of 1832, which brought merchants, smaller property owners, and masters into the governing coalition but excluded ordinary workers, many of whom had backed the Reform campaign. We have also discussed how Chartism gained its edge from the fact that its coalition partners in the pro-Reform mobilization of 1830–1832 acquired power but then enacted legislation regulating the poor while denying workers political rights.

2. Equalization of resources and connections among potential political participants. If overall inequality between categories—male and female, religious affiliations, classes, ethnic groups, and so on—diminishes for whatever reason, such equalization facilitates broad and equal involvement of category members in public politics, as it discourages their unequal treatment by governmental agents. Therefore, it boosts both protection and citizenship. Relevant resources and connections certainly include those provided by income, property, and kinship, but they also include literacy, access to communications media, and organizational memberships; when any of these equalize across the population at large, they promote democratic participation.

Equalization of resources and connections among potential political participants encourages both political competition and coalition formation. Together, competition and coalition formation promote establishment of categorically defined rights and obligations directly connecting citizens to agents of government in place of particular communal memberships and patron–client ties. Legal establishment of electorates provides the most visible examples, but a similar enactment of legally equivalent categories commonly occurs in the licensing of associations, authorization of public meetings, policing of demonstrations, and registration of lobbyists.

The very articulation of rules for these activities produces categories rather than particularistic arrangements and thereby encourages collective seekers of rights to argue on the basis of their similarities to members of privileged categories, rather than their valuable and distinctive properties. Women who struggled for political rights in Western countries during the nineteenth and twentieth centuries regularly pointed out that the rules and justifications backing male rights to vote and hold office provided no defensible rationale for excluding females from the same rights. For all the celebration of queer culture, LGBT movements often insist on their political similarities to previously excluded minorities and demand rights that are already available to other categories of the population, e.g. marriage.

Competition and coalition formation also inhibit the pursuit of control over governmental activities, resources, and personnel by means other than those categorically defined rights and obligations; blatant use of personal connections or brute force becomes corruption. Eventually the sheer expansion and partial equalization of the British ruling classes made it advantageous for dissident members of the new elite to join forces with excluded people as a makeweight against the old landed classes.

3. Insulation of public politics from existing social inequalities. Democratization does not depend on a top-down leveling of material conditions; the partial democracies of today's rich capitalist countries—all of which maintain extensive material inequalities—testify as much. Over the long run of democratization, indeed, erection of barriers to translation of existing inequalities by race, gender, ethnicity, religion, class, or locality into public politics has no doubt played a much larger part than any decree. Barriers arise to the direct translation of persisting categorical inequalities into public politics. For example, through the institution of the secret ballot and the creation of coalition parties that cross lines of gender, race, or class. If, those barriers contribute to the creation of a relatively autonomous sphere of public politics within which categorically defined breadth, equality, binding consultation, and protection have at least a chance to increase. Although many white male Americans in positions of power excluded women, blacks, and First Nations people from nineteenth-century public politics, adoption of a rigorously geographical system of representation, continuous movement of people to the frontier, and formation of patchwork political parties all blunted the direct translation of categorical differences within the white male population into public politics.

Despite residential segregation and gerrymandering, formation of heterogeneous political units and electoral districts similarly inhibits direct translation of categorical inequalities into public politics. It becomes politically risky for elected leaders to obviously favor only one section of the population. We saw a version of this representation effect in Great Britain, where the chiefly territorial allocation of parliamentary seats—by no means a democratic innovation back when barons and bishops forced the English king to hear their complaints, conditions, and demands—simultaneously gave voice to disfranchised British subjects and provided incentives for Members of Parliament to seek expressions of popular support for dissident positions. As Parliament gained power relative to the Crown and great patrons during the eighteenth century (once again no triumph for democratization in its own terms), the insulating effects of territorial representation increased. Similarly, broadly shared jury duty, military service, school enrollment, and responsibility for public works need not originate in democratic practices, but cumulatively tend to promote democratization by insulating public politics from existing social inequalities.

4. Trust networks and democratization. Trust networks figure more subtly, but no less potently, in democratization. As many democratic theorists have sensed, connections between interpersonal trust networks and public politics significantly affect democratization (Buchan, Croson, and Dawes 2002; Edwards, Foley, and Diani 2001; Hardin 2006; Jamal 2007; Landa 1994; Levi and Stoker 2000; Seligman 1997; Tilly 2005; Uslaner 2002; Warren 1999). Trust is the knowing exposure of valued future outcomes to the risk of malfeasance by others. Risk is threat multiplied by uncertainty. People frequently confront short-term risk without creating elaborate social structure; on their own they leap raging rivers, engage in unsafe sex, drive while drunk, or bet large sums of money. When it comes to the long-term risks of reproduction, cohabitation, investment, migration, or agricultural enterprise, however, people generally embed those risks in durable, substantial social organization. To that extent, they trust others—they make the reduction of threat and/or uncertainty contingent on the performance of other people they cannot entirely control. Such sets of relations to others constitute networks of trust.

When people commit themselves to risky, consequential, long-term enterprises whose outcomes depend significantly on the performances of other persons, they ordinarily embed those enterprises in interpersonal trust networks whose participants have strong incentives to meet their own commitments and encourage others to meet theirs. Such networks often pool risks and provide aid to unfortunate members. They commonly operate well because members share extensive information about each other and about their social environment, because third parties monitor transactions among pairs of members, and because exclusion from the network typically inflicts serious harm on members who fail to meet their commitments. Trade diasporas, rotating credit circles, skilled crafts, professions, lineages, patron–client chains, and religious sects often exhibit these characteristics. They couple easily with control over systems that generate inequality in work, community, and private life (Tilly 1998).

Through most of human history, participants in trust networks have guarded their networks jealously from governmental intervention. They have rightly feared that governmental agents would weaken them or divert them to less advantageous ends. Powerful participants who could not entirely escape governmental intervention have created partial immunities through such arrangements as indirect rule. Less powerful participants have characteristically adopted what James Scott calls weapons of the weak: concealment, foot-dragging, sabotage, and the like. Democratization, however, entails a double shift of trust. First, within the political arena, citizens must trust the organization of consultation and protection sufficiently to wait out short-term losses of advantage instead of turning immediately to nonpeaceful nongovernmental means of regaining lost advantages. Second, citizens build into risky long-term enterprises the assumption that government will endure and meet its commitments. Both are extremely rare circumstances over the long historical run. Within any regime that is not currently democratic, their realization faces enormous obstacles.

In those rare cases where it actually occurs, integration of trust networks into public politics operates within any of three channels: (1) disintegration of previously effective insulated trust networks, as when regional patrons lose their capacity to pay, feed, or arm their clients; (2) formation of commitments directly binding governmental agents and citizens, as when governments establish welfare agencies and citizens begin to rely on those agencies for absorption of long-term risks; or (3) formation of similar commitments between major political actors and their citizen members or clienteles, as when legally recognized trade unions become administrators of workers' pension funds. We witnessed a dramatic instance of integration in the Switzerland of 1848 and thereafter, as the peace settlement of a civil war provided different segments of the Swiss population far greater access and redress with regard to the national government than they had ever exercised before.

In these terms, how should we explain the partial democratization that the United Kingdom experienced after the 1760s? The four general causes of democratization—increases in numbers and connections among potential political participants, equalization of resources and connections among them, insulation of public politics from existing social inequalities, and integration of trust networks into public politics—all contributed to British democratization, but they contributed quite unequally. After years of feudalism and then mercantilism, the expansion of British capitalism enormously increased the numbers of potential political participants as well as connections among them (Tilly 1995: chap. 2). On balance, despite sharpening material inequalities, the resources and connections provided by concentrated workplaces, urban growth, intensification of communications, and accelerated domestic trade produced some equalization in resources and connections among potential political participants within Great Britain. As compared with depending chiefly on local landlords, parish priests, small masters, and other patrons for political intervention, Parliament's increasing centrality in the British system of power partially insulated public politics from existing categorical inequalities. Rapid growth of a propertyless, wage-dependent, and urbanizing working class, finally, combined with huge expansions of tax payments and military service to undermine old local and segregated trust networks in favor of direct connections between British subjects and their national government.

The same checklist helps explain why democratization remains distant in Kazakhstan. The flight of ethnic Russians from the post-Soviet country has depleted resources and connections, new inequalities have arisen between the small privileged segments of the national population and everyone else. President Nazarbayev and his allies have built the distinction between ethnic Kazakhs and others (not to mention the distinction between Nazarbayev's own clan and other Kazakhs) ever more sharply into public politics, and all but the privileged Kazakh elite have protected their trust networks more and more zealously from public politics. It would take a great reversal of all these processes for serious democratization to begin in Kazakhstan.

Processes that Promote Both Democratization and Social Movements

Some of the extensive historical overlap between democratization and social movements results from the fact that similar processes promote both of them. Recall the four main processes that promote democratization: (1) increases in the sheer numbers of people available for participation in public politics and/or in connections among those people, (2) equalization of resources and connections among those people, (3) insulation of public politics from existing social inequalities, and (4) integration of interpersonal trust networks into public politics. None of these qualifies as democratization in itself; none of them directly entails regular categorical relations, breadth, equality, binding consultation, or protection *within* public politics. Yet, all of them also promote the formation of social movements.

Increases in numbers and connections expand the pool of people that could, in principle, join, support, attend contentious gatherings or at least listen to a social movement campaign. They increase the likelihood that members of minority factions within the ruling class will seek allies outside the established range of powerful political actors. In Western history, dissident aristocrats and bourgeois alike recurrently sought to gain support outside their own circles; cautiously but consequentially, for example, Boston's property owners established alliances with Boston's property-poor workers against British royal power during the 1760s. Such reaching out provides opportunities for any organized group to gain credibility and power through displays of worthiness, unity, numbers, and commitment rather than through direct action or activation of patronage ties. Social movements facilitate just such displays, and indeed center on them.

Equalization of resources and connections increases the likelihood that people and groups having particular interests or grievances will join with those from other social settings in common campaigns, social movement performances, and WUNC displays. It makes coalition formation easier. Insulation of public politics from existing social inequalities facilitates the grouping of otherwise diverse participants in common claims with regard to programs, identities, and standing. Indeed, it makes possible the dramatization of diversity as a social movement's claim to attention. Finally, integration of interpersonal trust networks into public politics has a dual effect on social movements; it increases the stakes of potential participants in the outcomes of any new movement claims as it facilitates mobilization of already connected people.

The process of trusting public politics includes the following sorts of changes by average polity residents:

- creating publicly recognized associations, mutual aid societies, political parties, unions, congregations, and communities or seeking recognition for similar organizations that have existed underground;
- pursuing friendship, kinship, shared belief, security, and high-risk enterprises within such organizations;
- permitting family members to serve in national military and police forces;
- promoting careers of family members in public service, including government office;
- seeking (or at least tolerating) government registration of vital events such as births, deaths, and marriages, then using the registration to validate legal transactions;
- providing private information to public organizations and authorities through censuses, surveys, and applications for services;
- entrusting private contracts to governmental enforcement;

- using government-issued legal tender for interpersonal transactions and savings;
- purchasing government securities with funds (e.g., dowry) committed to maintenance of interpersonal ties; and
- relying on political actors and/or government agencies for vital services and long-term security.

Over the long historical run, such commitments of trust networks to public politics have rarely developed. Even in today's democratic countries, they have become common only during the last century or so. In addition to being consequential for individual lives and interpersonal relations, these commitments greatly increase the stakes of network members in the proper conduct of public politics. They create new collective interests. In these ways, they promote social movement activity at the same time as they advance routine democratic functioning outside of social movements. Thus, the same broad processes that promote democratization also promote the formation and proliferation of social movements.

How Democratization Promotes Social Movements

With their specific forms of associations, public meetings, demonstrations, and the like, social movements emerged from particular histories as historical products of their respective times and places. They then spread as models to other times and places. Yet some features of social movements give them affinities with democracy in general. In addition to the common causes of democratization and social movements just reviewed, democratization in itself promotes formation and proliferation of social movements. It does so because each of democracy's elements—regularity, breadth, equality, consultation, and protection—contributes to social movement activity. It also does so because it encourages the establishment of other institutions (e.g., political parties and labor unions), whose presence in turn usually facilitates social movement claim making. Let us take up each of these items in turn.

Formation of more regular and categorical relations between governments and subjects. To the extent that relations between governments and their subjects remain intermittent, mediated, coercive, and particular, incentives to join in collective, public claim making by means of social movement performances and WUNC displays remain minimal, indeed mostly negative. Through much of the recent history of China or Egypt, the previous chapter's survey suggests, people who dared to join in standard social movement claim making would threaten existing authorities, risk their lives, and condemn themselves to futility. Conversely, establishment of regular and categorical relations between governments and subjects—broadly speaking, of citizenship—in itself renders the making of rights-based claims feasible, visible, and attractive. At present, in some parts of China and Egypt, at least a modicum of citizenship seems to have developed, facilitating social movement claim making—but it is still too soon to be certain of the final outcomes, in the meantime protest coexists with repression and censorship.

Broadening of rights and obligations within public politics. We have long since noticed that firm rights to assemble, associate, and speak collectively, however they come into being, foster social movement activity. Similarly, broad obligations to vote, serve on juries, perform military service, pay taxes, deliberate on public services, and send children to school help create social connections and shared interests that promote participation in campaigns, social movement performances, and WUNC displays, bringing together socially disparate participants.

Equalization of rights and obligations within public politics. To the extent that public politics inscribes social inequalities in the form of differential rights to participate, receive benefits, or enjoy state protection, movement coalitions crossing such boundaries or representing identities not already written into law face serious barriers to organizing and acting publicly. To the extent that such legal reflections of social inequalities disappear from public politics, conversely, barriers to cross-category coalitions and newly asserted identities weaken. During the twentieth century, Indian leaders such as Jawaharlal Nehru strove mightily, and with partial success, to exclude caste, religious, linguistic, and gender differences from inscription into public politics. Thus, they simultaneously defended India's precarious democratization and promoted social movements. To be comprehensive in their approach, social movement activists sometimes seek legal inscription for their categories, as when representatives of indigenous peoples propose special rights for their constituents. When such claims succeed, they diminish the overall equality of protected consultation for the short term, but with the hope of increasing it in the longer term. The actions of particular movements influence the opportunities for other movements. Whether Hindu nationalists will overturn the democratic accomplishments of their more secular predecessors, matters enormously for the future of Indian democracy and Indian social movements.

Increase in binding consultation of subjects with regard to changes in governmental policy, resources, and personnel. Social movements benefit from consultation because social movement displays of worthiness, unity, numbers, and commitment gain weight from the possibility that movement activists or their constituents will actually acquire some say in governmental decision making. Most obviously, in systems where contested elections make a difference, mobilization and identification of supporters for a new social movement signal the presence of a constituency that an accommodating political party might be able to enlist in its own electorate.

Expansion of protections for subjects, especially members of vulnerable minorities, from arbitrary action by governmental agents. However protection and consultation expand, their combination provides new opportunities for the sorts of claim making in which social movements specialize. The installation of an intensely consultative regime in Switzerland after 1848 encouraged the proliferation of

Swiss social movements. Social movements thrive on protection because associations, meetings, marches, demonstrations, petition drives, and related means of action pose enormous risks in the absence of governmental toleration and in the face of massive repression. Secure rights of assembly, association, and collective voice promote social movements, just as their abridgment threatens social movements. Social movements disappeared after the rise of authoritarian regimes in Italy, Germany, Spain, and the Soviet Union.

Creation of complementary institutions. Democratization commonly fosters creation of crucial institutions that in their turn independently promote social movement mobilization. The most obvious and general of these are electoral campaigns, political parties, labor unions, other trade associations, nongovernmental organizations, lobbies, and governmental agencies committed to the support of specific constituencies rather than the general public. Such institutions generally facilitate social movements by providing vehicles for their mobilization, by establishing allies that back social movement claims without participating directly in movement campaigns, by locating receptive friends within government, and/or by reinforcing legal precedents for social movement campaigns, performances, and WUNC displays.

The connections are neither necessary nor universal. One-party regimes, for example, frequently stamp out social movements, just as corporatist regimes often build labor unions directly into the governing structure. On the average, formation of complementary institutions in the course of democratization further facilitates social movement activity. In the United States, the influence clearly ran in both directions: social movements that broke with existing political parties affected parties and other institutions as the operation of those institutions repeatedly provided support for social movements (Clemens 1997; Sanders 1999; Skocpol 1992).

The corollary also follows: when regimes dedemocratize, they offer less room to claims made in the social movement style. Italy under Mussolini, Germany under Hitler, and Spain under Franco all experienced sharp curtailment of what had been festivals of social movement activity under their previous regimes. To be more precise, these new authoritarian regimes selectively incorporated some performances from the social movement repertoire—notably the association, the march, the demonstration, and the mass meeting—but placed them so securely under central government control that they lost their meaning as autonomous assertions of WUNC. Noting that very process, political theorists of the generation following World War II mistakenly portrayed it as a transition from atomized mass society to authoritarianism. The first assumption (atomized mass society) was wrong, the second part (authoritarianism) right. Despite decreases in social control by the extended family and religious authorities, social groups, trust networks, and embeddedness have always existed including in cities and in modern times (Tilly 2005). In fact, Italy, Germany, and Spain made transitions from often undisciplined but burgeoning organized activity (some of it in standard social movement format) to highly coordinated central control in the form of fascist regimes.

When and How Social Movements Promote Democratization

A number of the same processes that promote democratization, then, also foster social movements, and vice versa. Democratization in itself further promotes social movements. That set of connections helps explain the affinity of social movements with democratization. It does not, however, answer the most difficult question with which we began: what about the *direct causal impact* of social movements on democracy and democratization? Precisely because of the broad covariation of democracy and social movements, reasoning from correlations will not resolve the problem. We have no choice but to close in on causal processes.

Which processes deserve our attention? In fact, the earlier survey catalogued the likely candidates: those processes that cause shifts from particularized and/or mediated to categorical and direct relations between citizens and government, broadening and equalization of relations among political actors, reduced penetration of social inequalities into public politics, and increasing integration of trust networks into public politics. The question now alters, however: which among our array of democracy-promoting processes do social movements themselves activate or reverse, under what conditions, and how? Remember that the great bulk of the social movements we have surveyed pursued particular interests rather than general programs of democratization. Remember also that a substantial minority of these movements organize around explicitly antidemocratic claims, such as the abridgment of rights for members of particular racial, ethnic, or religious categories. It will therefore not suffice to look for social movements that explicitly demanded democracy and to ask when and how they made gains. We must ask under what conditions and how social movement claim making actually promoted expansion of democratic relations and practices.

Once relatively high-capacity governments began practicing direct rule by means including representative institutions, (however narrow the representation) they set a powerful dialectic into motion. Governments bargained with legislatures for authorization to gather resources for pursuit of governmental activities, bargained with groups of citizens for the actual delivery of those resources, sought the collaboration of major political actors in the levying of resources and the execution of programs, and established procedures for recognition of political actors. However grudgingly or unconsciously, they thereby created incentives and opportunities for new or previously unauthorized actors to assert their existence and for minority factions within legislatures to form coalitions with outside actors. Electoral logic provides the most obvious example of such effects: coordinated public displays of WUNC signal the existence of potential voting blocs that could collectively influence outcomes of future elections.

Increasingly, political entrepreneurs inside and outside of legislatures discovered that they could add weight to their proposals, complaints, and demands by organizing public displays of popular backing for those proposals, complaints, and demands. It is unclear, for example, how large a role political parties, philanthropists, and conservative foundations played in the dramatic Tea Party displays against public healthcare in the United States. To the extent that such displays verify the presence of worthy, united, numerous, and committed sets of supporters, they constituted at once threats to institutionalized political processes and an effective tool for actors with demands of authorities.

Without a general conscious design, the organization of performances in the form of public meetings, marches, voluntary associations, petition drives, and pamphleteering promoted additional effects:

- establishment of standard practices by which political activists formed and broadcast collective answers to the identity questions "Who are you?" and "Who are we?" and "Who are they?";
- development of problem-solving ties among activists in the very process of preparing and executing public performances;
- incorporation of existing organizations such as churches and mutual aid societies into these new forms of political activity; and
- development of procedures by which governmental agents responded differentially to performances and identity claims—negotiating boundaries between legitimate and illegitimate performances, recognizing some actors while refusing to recognize others, applying facilitation or repression, co-opting, channeling, infiltrating, or subverting various groups.

Together, these additional effects established social movements as regular participants in public politics. Furthermore, they created new social ties among activists, between activists and their constituencies, and between activists and agents of government. Outside of any collective demands that activists made for democratization, the new social ties became crucial sites of democratization.

How so? The internal dynamics of social movements activated all three classes of democracy-promoting processes—processes that democratized public politics directly by broadening and equalizing collective political participation, processes that insulated public politics from existing social inequalities, and processes that reduced insulation of trust networks from major political actors. To the extent that social movement activism promoted establishment of recognized but autonomous collective political actors involving socially heterogeneous members and integrating their own distinctive trust networks, its democratizing effects increased. Conversely, to the extent that governments managed to destroy, deflect, disperse, ignore, or co-opt social movement coalitions and their trust networks, democratization suffered. After the profusion of French social movement activity during the 1930s, for instance, the German occupation of 1940–1944 rapidly closed down almost all visible social movements, which in turn contributed to the country's dedemocratization during those terrible years (Gildea 2002; Jackson 2001; Tartakowsky 1997).

In summary, proliferation of social movements promotes democratization chiefly in regimes that (1) have created relatively effective direct rule through a central administration rather than governing through privileged intermediaries or communal segments, and (2) have established at least a modicum of democratization, however that happened. The two conditions make it possible for the combination of campaigns, WUNC displays, and social movement performances to wield an impact on public politics, whereas their absence presents insuperable barriers to social movement effectiveness. In these circumstances, social movement strategies sometimes promote democratization directly by mobilizing effective claims on behalf of protected consultation. Despite the eventual dumping of working-class participants, Britain's social movement-based Reform mobilization of 1830–1832 did nudge the British regime toward greater categorically defined breadth, equality, binding consultation, and protection while establishing a precedent and model for subsequent prodemocracy mobilizations. The model of course was one that valued claim making in particular and limited ways.

As our historical surveys have shown, such explicit, effective prodemocracy social movements rarely form; far more often, social movement participants make claims on behalf of more particular programs, identities, or standing—claims that in themselves have no necessary connection with democratization. Blocking construction of a highway, supporting or opposing abortion, forwarding the rights of indigenous and undocumented people, and demanding better schools by social movement performances certainly take advantage of democratic liberties, but they do not present themselves as prodemocracy movements. Though, it could be argued that these actions show that freedom of expression and popular participation are alive and well.

Cumulatively, nevertheless, several kinds of social movement campaigns contribute to democratization. That happens, on the average, when they

- create coalitions that cross important categorical boundaries within public politics (example: visible members of the Coptic Christian Egyptians join with Muslim Egyptians in their efforts to oppose long-standing president Hosni Mubarak);
- form a pool of brokers with skills in coalition formation (example: in the nineteenth-century associations and church-based American activists brought together feminists, abolitionists, and supporters of temperance); and
- simultaneously establish connections within previously unmobilized and excluded categories of citizens (especially those embedded in segmented trust networks), and form alliances between those newly mobilized groups and existing political actors (example: Indian reformers recruit support from members of impoverished, stigmatized castes).

In short, social movements promote democratization when—either as explicit programs or as by-products of their action—they give people more power over the decisions that affect them. They do this by broadening the range of participants in public politics, by equalizing the weight of participants in public politics, by erecting barriers to the direct translation of categorical inequalities into public politics, and/or by integrating previously segmented trust networks into public politics. Great Britain during the late 1820s and early 1830s looks like a place where social movements promoted democratization in most of these ways. Conversely, social movements promote dedemocratization when they narrow the range of participants in public politics, increase inequalities among participants in public politics, translate existing categorical inequalities more directly into public politics, and/or insulate trust networks from public politics. Alas, India during the early twenty-first century looks like a place where polarized, segmented Hindu and Muslim social movement activity on behalf of their own ethnic group might actually be dedemocratizing the national regime. Anti-immigrant and white nationalists movements around the world also produce dedemocratization.

Taking such effects into account, we can hold out the hope that early-twenty-first-century mobilizations against global financial systems will promote a gradual democratization at an international scale by drawing a wide range of new, previously marginalized groups into international public politics. We can hope that in such countries as Egypt, Iran, and China, the standard democratizing processes—increases in the numbers and connections of people available for participation in public politics, equalization of resources, and connections among those people, insulation of public politics from existing social inequalities, and integration of interpersonal trust networks into public politics—will eventually promote both democracy and social movements.

At a world scale, nevertheless, we could equally worry that highly selective access to nongovernmental organizations and electronic communication will instead introduce fresh inequalities into international public politics and thus promote dedemocratization. Still, more access to technology and electronic communication, especially social media, allows more people to become informed and involved with various movements across the world. To the extent that global integration and neoliberal restructuring will mean that national governments lose the power to implement the programs that social movements demand, democracy will generally decline at the national level. Without a combination of vigilance and favorable developments over which democrats and activists themselves exercise only partial control, the future of democracy and of social movements remains insecure.

Note

1 Ernesto Castañeda edited for clarity for this fourth edition.

7

FUTURES OF SOCIAL MOVEMENTS

Charles Tilly and Lesley Wood[1]

Phoenix, Arizona, is located in the Sonoran Desert, where temperatures can rise to 120 Fahrenheit (49 degrees Celsius). According to the U.S. census, the city is home to more than 1 million people, 41 percent of the population identifying themselves as Hispanic. Arizona borders Mexico, and there are ongoing tensions about immigration and the rights of non-citizens. In 2004, the state of Arizona passed Proposition 200, a law that limited the availability of certain benefits to residents without current immigration documentation. The following year, the Minuteman Project was launched as "concerned citizens" formed armed patrols to monitor the United States/Mexico border to stop those trying to cross into the United States (Castañeda 2006, 2019; Shapira 2013). In 2006, members of Congress proposed bills that would limit the rights of undocumented immigrants to receive social services and support. These bills also included stipulations that made defending and supporting undocumented immigrants a crime. In response, there were massive immigrant rights marches across the country (Voss and Bloemraad 2011; Zepeda-Millán 2017).

Phoenix was one of the fastest growing cities in the United States growing from 983,403 people in 1990 to 1,552,259 in 2007, when the economic recession happened. Between 2007 and 2008, housing values in the area registered the largest decline in the country, over 30 percent of their previous value (Florida 2009). Unemployment increased, population growth declined, and tensions around immigration intensified. Democratic governor Janet Napolitano passed the State Employer Sanctions law, which levied penalties against businesses that hired undocumented immigrants. The law went into effect in 2008, at the same time that local sheriff, Joe Arpaio, increased his raids into Latino communities, detaining and deporting, at the police's discretion, anyone found without documentation. To add to the tension, on March 27, 2010, a rancher was killed near the border, and although suspects were not identified, the murder was blamed on undocumented immigrants or drug smugglers.

At the Federal level, Republicans framed the Obama administration as being "soft" on immigration enforcement. Arguing this, the new Republican governor, Jan Brewer (2009 to 2015), signed bill SB1070 in 2010. The law required police to question people about their immigration status if the police suspected them to be undocumented. Therefore, police could arrest day laborers while soliciting work if they were in the United States illegally, and police departments could have been sued if they did not actively enforce immigration laws.

From the date the bill was announced in early April, until it went into effect in July 2010, supporters and opponents of the bill rallied at the State Capitol building in Phoenix and marched through the city's streets. Sometimes they faced off against one another, chanting at each other across a line of caution tape. "We have rights!" shouted anti-SB1070 demonstrators. "No, you don't!" the pro-SB1070 group would shout in response (Daly 2010). Opponents of the bill chanted "Si, se puede," a phrase coined by Chicano civil rights leaders Dolores Huerta and Hugo Chavez that means, "Yes, we can." The use of a slogan in Spanish is especially significant in this context as demonstrators demanded a more inclusive society. The use of Spanish and the historical connection to the chant is also a continuation of a longstanding movement for Latino and immigrant rights in America. Others locked themselves to the doors of the Capitol building and were arrested for civil disobedience (Lemons 2010). The Phoenix Suns basketball team wore shirts that read "Los Suns" and explained that they were doing this "to honor [the] Latino community and the diversity of our league, the state of Arizona, and our nation" (Kerby 2010). Other opponents called for a boycott of the state, refusing to buy goods or services from Arizona or to visit the state. This boycott was endorsed by municipalities, individuals, and organizations across the country (AZ Central.com 2010). In response, a "buycott" was organized by the bill's supporters who encouraged spending at local stores and Arizona-based businesses (*Freedom's Wings* 2010).

A month after the bill was signed; more than 100,000 people marched in opposition to it (Flaherty 2010). The *Arizona Republic* reported: "Banging drums, chanting, singing, and waving American flags, the throng made its way toward the Capitol. Organizers, scattered throughout the crowds, picked up trash and provided water to the marchers." The following week, the Arizona Tea Party organized the "Phoenix Rising" rally inside a baseball stadium in support of the bill. Among the speakers was Sheriff Arpaio, known for his controversial raids of immigrant communities. He spoke to the crowd, and called July 29—the day SB 1070 was set to go into effect—the "magic day." He explained, "That's the day that—barring any legal holds—the law goes into effect. That's when I'm going to start enforcing that law." The crowd began to chant, "Joe, Joe, Joe!" enthusiastically. Rally organizer Daniel Smeriglio, head of the Pennsylvania-based Voice of the People USA, thanked the crowd for taking a stand. In a WUNC display, he said, "I know the heat is a deterrent, [but] we are here to say somebody did something and we stand with you. You represent the very best of America. That is why we are here" (Sexton, Madrid, and Gardiner 2010).

Randy Leever described an anti-immigrant rally in the small town of Palominas, Arizona, located right by the U.S.–Mexico border, a few months later. A crowd of between 500 and 800 conservative Americans gathered beside the 15-foot-tall border fence. Hundreds of small U.S. flags and nationalist messages were attached to the fence posts (Cooper 2010; Leever in Chron.com 2010). The rally was held on the land of Glenn Spencer, president of the border watch group American Border Patrol, whose property ends at the border fence. The United Border Coalition/United We Stand for Americans and Tea Party Nation organizations planned and sponsored the event. The rally attracted some big names: Arizona state senator Russell Pearce, who co-authored the state's immigration law, U.S. Senate hopeful J. D. Hayworth, and—the favorite among many attendees—Sheriff Arpaio. Leever reports,

> Some of the most salient points presented by a few of the speakers were greeted with loud applause and cheering. At one point, many of the crowd lined up at the fence and were chanting "USA, USA, USA," while waving American flags. (Leever in Chron.com 2010)

Down the highway from the rally was a group of 30 counterprotesters, who claimed that Arizona's immigration policies were racist and inhumane. Three of these protesters were able to get into the event and turned their backs to the stage as Arpaio began to speak.

Although the rally at the border attracted a great deal of attention, most of the marches and rallies about Arizona's immigration law took place at the state capitol buildings, the site of state power. Even a year after the bill was passed, supporters and opponents of the bill continued to march and rally there, sometimes at the same time. On April 22, 2011, hundreds of opponents and a few dozen supporters of the legislation rallied there, trying to out-chant one another and promote their position to authorities and the public (Cone Sexton 2011).

No one attuned to national and international news during the spring and summer of 2010 should have any trouble decoding these Arizona protests or their spin-offs in Alabama and elsewhere. North Americans and people across the world can easily recognize them as street demonstrations, a standard means of broadcasting support or opposition regarding political issues. In this case, demonstration and counterdemonstration represented opposition to, and support for, a law that will make migration from Mexico to the United States more difficult. While the people of Arizona took to the streets or gathered in baseball stadiums and plazas, hundreds of street demonstrations were occurring elsewhere in the world. Some of them were concerned with immigration and human rights, but most of them took up other locally urgent questions. In the early twenty-first century, the street demonstration looks like an all-purpose political tool – perhaps less effective in the short run than buying a legislator or mounting a military coup. Within democratic and semidemocratic regimes, demonstrations are an effective alternative to elections, opinion polls, and letter writing as a way of voicing public positions.

As the case of Arizona shows, the twenty-first-century demonstration has two major variants. In the first variant, outside the capitol buildings, participants gather, or rally, in a symbolically potent public location, where through speech and action they display their collective attachment to a well-defined cause. In the second, they proceed through public thoroughfares offering similar displays of commitment. Often, the two combine, as activists march to a rallying place, or as multiple columns converge from different places on a single symbolically powerful destination and/or then march again (such destinations include the Washington Mall, Trafalgar Square, and Tahrir Square). Increasingly, counterdemonstrators show up to advocate a contrary view and to challenge the demonstrators' claim to the spaces in question. Police or troops may station themselves along the line of march or around the place of assembly, and deliberately separate demonstrators from counterdemonstrators. Sometimes police or troops bar demonstrators' access to important spaces, buildings, monuments, or people. Passersby or spectators often signal their approval or disapproval of the cause that the demonstrators are supporting. Later, they may join the discussion in lunchtime arguments or online debates.

Hundreds of comments were posted online in response to coverage about the protests on May 29 on ArizonaCentral.com. Someone whose username was "Mr. Cynic" wrote:

> Regardless of the number of protesters that marched, the fact remains that 60 percent of the general public is in favor of the law. Vocal minorities are just that, and their cause is not helped when they have to import marchers from California and other states. Obama can fire up Eric Holder and send him to court and Al Sharpton can blather on all he wants. It will not matter in the long run because in this country, the majority still rules.

Despite his dismissal of the protesters, "Mr. Cynic" clearly understands that the demonstrators are trying to display the worthiness, unity, numbers, and commitment of their cause and themselves. His comments try to undermine such displays by arguing that the group is not worthy, nor united or committed. The contest for legitimacy that surrounds social movements is one that has serious consequences for public life.

Thanks to legal challenges by anti-SB1020, on June 25, 2012, the U.S. Supreme Court struck down three of the four provisions of S.B. 1070. Those that required legal immigrants to carry registration documents at all times; allowed state police to arrest any individual for suspicion of being an illegal immigrant; and made it a crime for an illegal immigrant to search for a job (or to hold one) in the state.

U.S. District Judge Susan Ritchie Bolton found Judge Arpaio to be in contempt of the law on July 31, 2017 (Cassidy 2017) with sentencing scheduled on October 5, 2017. This was a victory for immigrant rights' groups until 2017, when President Trump offered a presidential pardon to Arpaio

(Hirschfeld Davis, and Haberman 2017). This episode reveals the tensions between state and local laws and the federal government in the United States. It also shows how mobilization may be able to create change at one level, but fail at another.

Conclusions

As earlier chapters have shown, street demonstrations also have some identifiable kin: municipal parades, party conventions, mass meetings, inaugurals, commencements, religious revivals, and electoral rallies. Most citizens of democracies know the difference. Participants in such events sometimes bend them toward the forms and programs of demonstrations, for example by wearing ostentatious symbols or shouting slogans in support of a cause at a college commencement. Many of the same principles apply: the separation of participants from spectators, the presence of guards to contain the crowd, and so on. Considered as a whole, this array of gatherings exhibits (1) remarkable coherence, (2) systematic internal variation, and (3) type by type, impressive uniformity across places, programs, and participants.

Previous chapters linked street demonstrations firmly to a larger, evolving, two-century-old form of political struggle: the social movement. They documented the distinctive combination of campaigns, repertoire, and WUNC displays in a form of politics that were almost non-existent before the mid-eighteenth century, yet became available for popular making of claims across much of the world during the next two centuries. Successful movements helped to spread the ideas and tactics internationally. They also documented the marvelous duality of social movements: quite general and recognizable in their broad outlines, yet impressively adaptable to local circumstances and idioms. That duality comes across in the news from Arizona.

Historical Continuities and Innovations

Residents of Arizona might have been surprised to learn that their protests owe something to the violent victories of a dissolute demagogue in London during the 1760s, and to the anti-British agitation of a failed brewer in Boston at about the same time. But we now know that John Wilkes, Samuel Adams, and their collaborators really started something that would influence social groups across the world for many years. The people of Arizona are still using a twenty-first-century version of that innovation of the eighteenth and nineteenth centuries.

Let us indulge a historical fantasy: Suppose that John Wilkes and Samuel Adams time traveled intact from the 1760s to Arizona in May 2010 and watched the immigrant rights demonstrators. Conversing to see if they could figure out what these twenty-first-century people were doing and why they could say:

Wilkes: I've never seen anything like it.
Adams: You can say that again.
Wilkes: But it's something like a church service . . .
Adams: Or a workmen's parade.
Wilkes: Where is the audience? Who are they talking to?
Adams: And where are the troops or constables?
Wilkes: Still one thing's familiar: they're arguing about a people's liberty.
Adams: You know, it reminds me of an election campaign, with people wearing candidates' colors, holding flags, chanting slogans, gathering in central squares, and marching along major thoroughfares.
Wilkes: Except that it's so *civilized.* How do these people expect to make any difference?
Adams: Maybe we should ask them.

The fantastic encounter does not show Wilkes and Adams the full apparatus of social movements at work: the combination of multiple performances and WUNC displays in sustained, coordinated making of program, identity, and/or standing claims. Nor does it tell them about the many other activists outside of Arizona who are likewise joining social movements for and against the immigrant rights, often employing news releases, petitions, and public meetings in addition to street demonstrations. But this imaginary conversation does raise crucial questions about the present and future of social movements. Has the social movement lost its political effectiveness? Is the internationalization of power, politics, and social movement organization rendering amateur local, regional, or even national efforts obsolete? If the forms of social movements have changed so much over the last two centuries, what further changes might we expect to see during the rest of the twenty-first century?

How Can We Predict the Future?

Most likely the right answer to all these questions is: it depends. No doubt, it depends on which countries, which issues, which claimants, and which objects of claims we have in mind; for the moment, the futures of all social movements in Kazakhstan, for example, look dim, while social movements still seem to be enjoying active lives in Canada and Spain. Currently, movements protesting climate change are making little headway, while movements against police brutality are at least attracting energetic international support. More generally, we must distinguish among possible future trajectories for social movements on one side, and a number of different social movement scales on the other. Figure 7.1 schematizes the distinctions.

The figure builds in two main dimensions: one, directions of change from growth to decline; the other, scales from local to global. The diagram's "global" scale represents the possibility voiced by today's advocates of transnational activism, not merely that international actors and international targets will become routine in future social movements but that social movements will regularly coordinate popular claim making across the entire globe. Meanwhile, the diagram follows Chapter 5 by insisting that despite some internationalization, local, regional, and national social movements continue to occur during the early twenty-first century.

Figure 7.1 flattens into two dimensions a series of likely further changes in social movements we have seen occurring from their earliest days: changes in campaigns, repertoires, and WUNC displays. Surely the twenty-first century will bring a new program, identity, and standing claims—new issues for campaigns—that the century's first few years leave almost unimaginable; suppose, for example, that animal rights activists mounted campaigns to gain citizenship rights for the great apes. Someone will almost certainly invent new social movement performances and thereby alter the general social movement repertoire. WUNC displays will evolve as well, perhaps by adopting technologies that will broadcast instantly how many people are voicing support or opposition for a given social movement claim—thus giving new expression to the **N**umbers in WUNC. If social movements survive the twenty-first century, they will surely leave it much transformed with regard to campaigns, repertoires, and WUNC displays.

Despite neglecting such changes in social movements, the diagram implies a wide range of hypothetical possibilities. We might, for example, imagine a future combination of extinction of social movements at the local level, institutionalization at the national level, and expansion plus dramatic transformation at the global level. Or we could imagine that massive declines in state power will simultaneously activate linked regional and international movements, on the model of demands for indigenous rights or regional autonomy that seize power from states but also receive backing and guarantees from international organizations.

An overall shift to the right side within the diagram would mean that local, regional, and perhaps even national social movements gave way to international and global movements: extensive internationalization. A general shift to the left of the diagram—not much expected these days—would mean a decline of larger-scale movements in favor of a new localism. A net shift upward would signify general expansion and transformation of social movement activity. Vertical moves toward the middle would signal widespread institutionalization: the whole world involved in social movements at multiple scales, but with nongovernmental organizations, professional social movement entrepreneurs, and close relations to political authorities dominating the action. Below the midpoint, a general shift downward would represent decline or disappearance of social movements, likewise across the board. More plausible predictions would feature separate trajectories for social movements at different scales, for example, expansion and transformation of international social movements at the same time as local social movements contracted and institutionalized.

We must ground any predictions on the knowledge we have gleaned from examining two centuries of social movement history and the book's main arguments:

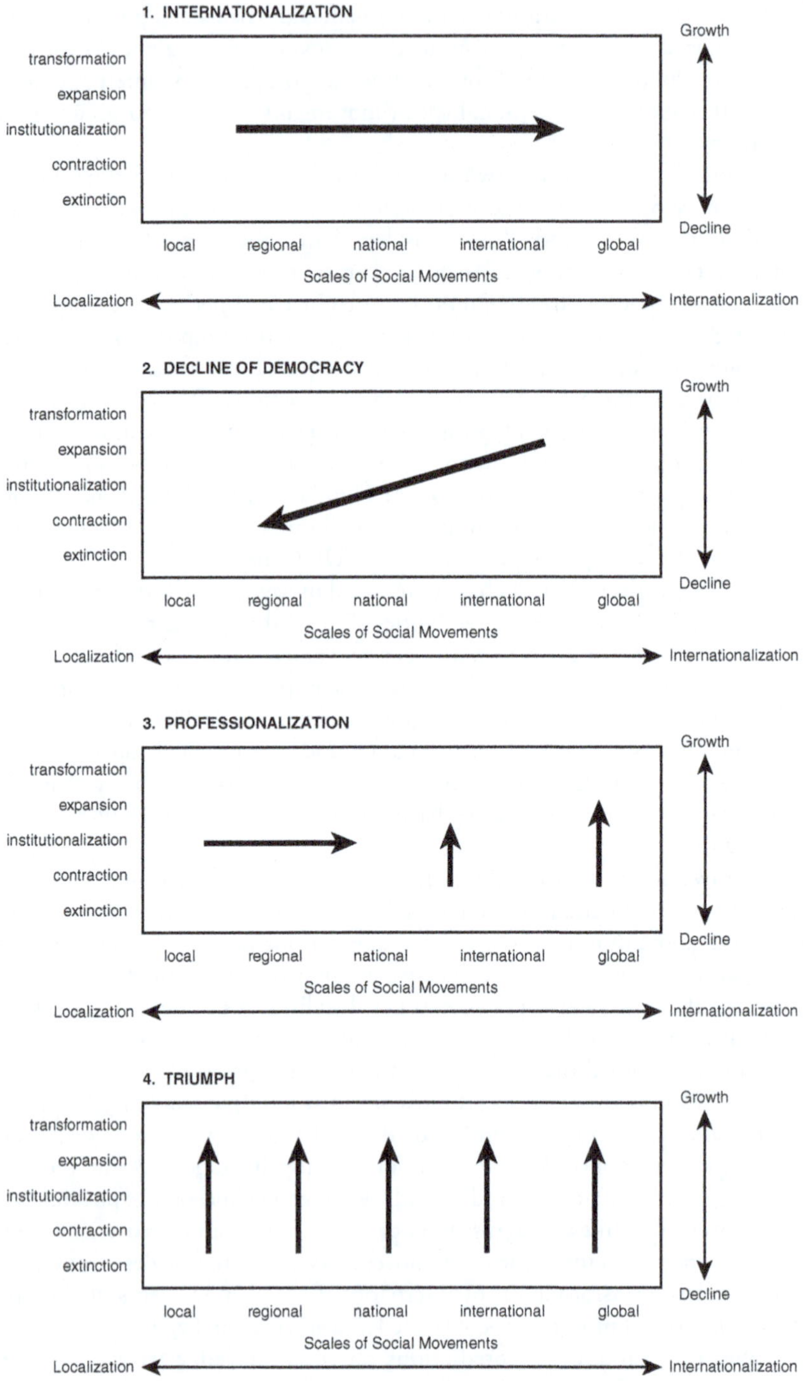

Figure 7.1 Possible Futures for Social Movements at Different Scales

From their eighteenth-century origins onward, social movements have proceeded not as solo performances but as interactive campaigns. By now, this observation should be self-evident. Thus, to predict future social movements involves thinking about changing relations among claimants, objects of claims, audiences, and authorities rather than simply extrapolating the most visible features of social movement performances. Think of, for example, the intricate interplay of movements, counter-movements, authorities, publics, and external powers across the fast-changing world in 1989 with the fall of the Soviet Union.

Social movements combine three kinds of claims: program, identity, and standing. Program claims involve stated support for or opposition to actual or proposed actions by the objects of movement claims. Identity claims consist of assertions that "we"—the claimants—constitute a unified force to be reckoned with. WUNC (worthiness, unity, numbers, and commitment) performances back up identity claims. Standing claims assert ties and similarities to other political actors, for example as excluded minorities, properly constituted citizens' groups, or loyal supporters of the regime. They sometimes concern the standing of *other* political actors, for example in calls for expulsion of immigrants or their exclusion from citizenship. The nineteenth-century United States showed us a dazzling (and sometimes depressing) array of program, identity, and standing claims with regard to which racial, ethnic, and gender categories deserved citizenship rights. Clearly, program, identity, and standing claims can evolve in partial independence from each other; standing claims, for example, depend sensitively on which political actors already have full standing, and which political procedures change an actor's standing. They thus depend on the rise or fall of democracy.

The relative salience of program, identity, and standing claims varies significantly among social movements, among claimants within movements, and among phases of movements. If institutionalization eclipsed identity and standing claims in favor of programs advocated or opposed by established specialists in social movement claim making, that eclipse would constitute a major change in twenty-first-century social movements. Professionalization of social movement organizations and entrepreneurs sometimes leads to new identity and standing claims. Yet, professionalization tips the balance away from identity and standing toward programs.

Democratization promotes the formation of social movements. Chapter 6 showed us that this apparently obvious statement hides a surprising degree of complexity. To single out the effects of democratization on social movements, we must separate them from common causes of democratization and social movements as well as from reciprocal influences of social movements on democratization. Once this is done, however, we see that predicting the future of twenty-first-century social movements depends heavily on expectations concerning future democratization or dedemocratization. In China and Egypt, we have to decide whether pro-democracy movements or ongoing state repression are more likely in the future.

Social movements assert popular sovereignty. Over our two centuries of history, the argument holds up well. The rise and fall of social movements in

France, for instance, neatly chart fluctuations in claims of popular sovereignty, so much so that France's authoritarian regimes took great care to suppress social movement campaigns, performances, and WUNC displays. Nevertheless, we have encountered two important qualifications to the general principle. First, professional social movement entrepreneurs and nongovernmental organizations sometimes represent themselves as speaking for "the people" without creating either deep grass roots or means for ordinary people to speak through them. Second, social movements have supported programs that, when realized, actually diminished popular sovereignty by implanting authoritarian leaders, charismatic cults, or programs of widespread exclusion. Any predictions concerning future social movements and their consequences will have to consider the possibility of reactive, exclusionary, nationalistic social movements and dedemocratization.

As compared with locally grounded forms of popular politics, social movements depend heavily on political entrepreneurs for their scale, durability, and effectiveness. We have certainly seen political entrepreneurs repeatedly in the midst of social movements. From Great Britain's Reform mobilization of the 1830s to recent mobilizations like Occupy Wall Street, entrepreneurs and their nongovernmental organizations have figured prominently in campaign after campaign. Indeed, the overall trend has increased the salience and influence of political entrepreneurs from opportunists to life-long core activists (Díaz Cepeda and Castañeda 2019). The future depends in part on whether that trend will continue, and which sorts of entrepreneurs will flourish in social movements.

Once social movements establish themselves in one political setting, modeling, communication, and collaboration facilitate their adoption in other connected settings. This observation has taken on new meaning as our analysis has developed, for connections of existing social movement settings with potential new settings are always only a fraction of all the new settings with which connections could, in principle, form. We have seen that selectivity most clearly in the connections facilitated by new communications media: generally lowering the cost of communications for people who have access to the system, but excluding others who lack that access. The same holds for interpersonal networks: expansion of social movement activity along existing networks excludes those who do not belong. Despite the engaging image of so-called Facebook revolutions, that play of inclusion and exclusion is likely to continue through the twenty-first century. As a consequence, some of our predictions will rest on estimates of who will connect with whom, and who will not.

The forms, personnel, and claims of social movements vary and evolve historically. As our whimsical vignette of Wilkes and Adams in Arizona suggests, social movement forms have undergone continuous mutation since the later eighteenth century and are still mutating. We have observed three distinguishable but interacting sources of change and variation in social movements: overall political and economic environments; incremental change in campaigns, repertoires, and WUNC displays within social movements; and diffusion of social movement models among sites of activism. To anticipate the future, we must specify how each of the three will change, not to mention how they will interact. For clues, we should pay particular attention to new sites of social movement action such as the 99 percent (Occupy Everywhere, see Chapter 10) protests, asking who does what on behalf of which claims.

The social movement, as an invented institution, could disappear or mutate into some quite different form of politics. We still have no guarantee that the social movement as it has prevailed for two centuries will continue forever. We must take seriously the possibility that the twenty-first century will destroy social movements as vehicles of popular claim making because the conditions for their survival have dissolved or because new forms of claim making have supplanted them. One dream of digital democracy proposes continuous, electronically mediated opinion polling and voting as a cheap, efficient substitute for associating, meeting, marching, petitioning, addressing mass media, and the rest of the social movement repertoire—a frightening prospect for lovers of social movements in something like their recognizable historical form. A case in hand, is that of Anonymous (discussed in Chapter 15).

Possible Futures

How can we apply these principles to the future? Figure 7.1 uses ideas and evidence in previous chapters to speculate about what could happen to social movements during the rest of the twenty-first century. It combines some of the more likely possibilities into four scenarios: internationalization, democratic decline, professionalization, and triumph.

–*Internationalization* entails a net shift away from local, regional, and national social movements toward international and global social movement activity.
–*Decline of democracy* would depress all sorts of social movements, especially at the large scale, but could leave pockets of local or regional social movement activity where some democratic institutions survived.
–*Professionalization* would most likely diminish the relative importance of local and regional social movements while shifting the energies of activists and organizers to national, international, and global scales.
–*Triumph,* finally, describes the glorious dream of social movements everywhere, serving at all scales from local to global as a means for advancing popular claims. Let us draw on implications of previous chapters to identify circumstances that would cause each of the four scenarios as well as reflect on likely consequences of each scenario for popular politics.

Internationalization. Many observers and activists of early twenty-first-century social movements assume that internationalization is already sweeping the field and will continue to a point at which most social movements will operate internationally or even globally. They project that environmentalists, feminists, human rights advocates, and opponents of global capital will increasingly join forces across countries and continents. Under what conditions might we now expect internationalization to dominate the futures of social movements? Considering the evidence of previous chapters (such as the Via Campesina movement discussed in Chapter 5), these are the most likely candidates:

- continued growth and impact by international networks of power and of organizations implementing them—financial networks, trade connections, multinational corporations, international governmental and regulatory institutions, intercontinental criminal enterprises;
- vulnerability of those networks to shaming, subversion, boycotts, or governmental regulation;
- expansion of connections among widely dispersed populations whose welfare those international networks affect, especially adversely;
- proliferation of organizations, brokers, and political entrepreneurs specialized in connecting those populations and coordinating their action; and
- formation of at least a modicum of democracy at an international scale—relatively broad, equal, consultative, and protective relations between citizens and agents of international governmental institutions.

Predicting that extensive internationalization of social movements will occur during the twenty-first century depends on implicit predictions that most or all of these conditions will apply. But Brexit, the Trump election, and growing nationalist movements point to a return to the nation-state as the site of protest.

If the scenario of internationalization prevailed, we might reasonably expect some further consequences for popular politics in the short and medium terms. First, given the minimum requirements of large-scale social movements for information, time, contacts, and resources, the existing elite bias of social movement participation would increase; the lowering of communication costs through the internet and cellphones surely would not override the increased coordination costs for a very long time. Second, for this reason and because of uneven access to communication channels, inequality between sites of active movement participation and all others would sharpen; relatively speaking, excluded people would suffer even more acutely than today from lack of means to mount effective campaigns, performances, and WUNC displays. Third, brokers, entrepreneurs, and international organizations would become even more crucial to the effective voicing of claims by means of social movements. All these changes point to declines in democratic participation; they would both narrow the range of participants in social movements and make participation more unequal.

Democratic decline. What if democracy declined as a result of causes outside of the social movement sphere: weakening of barriers between categorical inequality and public politics, segregation of new or existing trust networks from public politics, and so on? Because democracy always operates in connection with particular centers of power, a lot would depend on whether the decline occurred at all scales or only, for example, at the national scale. A plausible version of this scenario would have democracy suffering at the local or national level because it would take a political catastrophe to produce simultaneous dedemocratization across the world's thousands of local, regional, and national regimes. (Imagine rogue networks of bankers, soldiers, communications providers, or medical researchers, for example, who could decide which segments of the world population would—and would not—have access to their services.) The case of San Francisco shutting down cellphone use in the BART systems after protests from the killing of Charles Hill reveal such temporary loss of civil rights (see Chapter 13). In recent years, we have witnessed the election of people with anti-democratic dictatorial tendencies in Philippines, Eastern Europe, and beyond. Under most circumstances, democratic collapse at the large scale would still leave surviving democratic enclaves scattered across the world. We then might expect to find increasing differentiation of social movement practices across those surviving enclaves, as communication and collaboration among the world's social movement activists diminished and as local or regional activists adapted increasingly to their particular conditions.

Professionalization. In this scenario, professionalization leads to institutionalization, NGOization, and hence to declining innovation and radicalism of social movements. Committed populists often worry that social movement activists, already drawn disproportionately from prosperous, well-educated, well-connected segments of the population, will sell out the interests of truly disadvantaged people, establish comfortable relations with authorities, rely increasingly on support from the rich and powerful, and/or become social movement bureaucrats, more interested in forwarding their own organizations and careers than in the welfare of their supposed constituencies.

As compared with the early nineteenth century, some professionalization and institutionalization of social movements have unquestionably occurred in relatively democratic regimes: creation of protective legal codes, formation of police forces specializing in contained protection of social movement activity, establishment of negotiated routines for police–demonstrator interactions, creation of conventions for reporting on social movements in mass media, and multiplication of organizations specializing in social movement campaigns, performances, and WUNC displays. These changes have opened up full-time careers in social movement activism. Professionalization and institutionalization have proceeded hand in hand.

Up to the early twenty-first century, however, new issues, groups, tactics, and targets have repeatedly arisen at the edge of the established social movement sector. Many peripheral claimants failed, some quickly shifted to standard social movement practices, but a few brought their own innovations—sit-ins, occupations of public buildings and squares, teach-ins, giant puppet shows, cartoonlike costumes, new uses of media—onto the public scene. Predicting general professionalization and institutionalization of social movements, then, implies that opportunities for genuinely new issues, groups, tactics, and targets will diminish significantly. That could occur, in principle, either through declining incentives for popular claim making or through closing out of claimants who are not already part of the social movement establishment. But by definition social movements are truly disruptive and antiestablishment.

Triumph. What about across-the-board expansion of social movements at all scales, from local to global? Such a surprising future would require democratization of the many world regions currently living under authoritarian regimes, warlords, or petty tyrannies. It would also require a more general division of government and power such that local authorities still had the capacity to affect local lives and respond to local demands, even if international authorities gained power within their own spheres. It would, finally, mean that local, regional, and national activist networks, organizations, and entrepreneurs continued to act in partial independence at their own scales instead of subordinating their programs to those of international or global scope. Conversely, if widespread de-democratization occurred at all scales across the world, if centers of power increased their own protections against popular pressure, and if linking networks, organizations, and brokers either disintegrated or fell under authorities' control, a general decline of social movements would follow.

In the domain of social movements, we should be suspicious of *if–then* statements—if democratization, then social movement expansion; if internationalization, then sharpening inequality; and so on. Despite the ample documentation of previous chapters and generations of scholarly work, we have nothing like an *if–then* causal science of social movements. Flat predictions for the remainder of the twenty-first century involve even greater uncertainties. After all, they depend on a combination of three sorts of reasoning: (1) extrapolation of existing trends into the future, (2) *if–then* statements about the proximate causes of change in social movements, and (3) speculations about changes in the causes of those causes. To predict that the modest internationalization of social movements since 1990 or so will swell into a great wave, for example, we must assume that we have actually read that trend correctly; that the expansion of connections among dispersed populations affected by international power networks does, indeed, promote coordination of social movement activity among those dispersed populations; and that whatever causes the expansion of connections to occur will continue to operate through the century's many remaining years.

In the face of all this uncertainty, can we place any bets on the likely prevalence of one scenario or another? What combinations of internationalization, democratic decline, professionalization, and/or triumph are more probable? Throwing all if-then prudence to the winds, let us state a few guesses about the twenty-first century.

Internationalization: slower, less extensive, and less complete than technology enthusiasts say, but likely to continue for decades.

Decline of democracy: a split decision, with some democratic decline (and therefore some diminution in the prevalence and efficacy of social movements) in major existing democracies but substantial democratization (hence social movement expansion) in such currently undemocratic countries as China.

Professionalization: another split decision, with professional social movement entrepreneurs, nongovernmental organizations, and accommodations with authorities increasingly dominant in large-scale social movements but consequently abandoning those portions of local and regional claim making they cannot co-opt into international activism.
Triumph: alas, exceedingly unlikely.

"Alas" because, for all the reasons laid out in previous chapters, the triumph of social movements at all scales would benefit humanity, despite all the dangers of movements that many of us would oppose. The broad availability of social movements signals the presence of democratic institutions and usually promotes their functioning. It provides a crucial channel for groups, categories of people, and issues that currently have no voice in a regime's routine politics to acquire visible places in public politics. We should scan contemporary and future contentious performances and social movements carefully, in hope of refuting this pessimistic forecast (see Part II).

Note

1 Ernesto Castañeda revised this chapter.

PART II

Case Studies of Contemporary Social Movements

8

ANALYZING CONTEMPORARY SOCIAL MOVEMENTS

Ernesto Castañeda[1]

Beyond the predictions about the future of social movements that Charles Tilly presents in Chapter 7, an additional alternative for the future of social movements is stasis: Social movements keep being mainly driven by local concerns but are open to coalitions with both national and international activists and supporters. Social media help diffuse claims, programs, and agendas but offline social ties and relations are crucial for organizing, commitment, and mobilization. In some places, social movements in certain domains are seen as more legitimate than others (e.g. labor in France, race in the U.S.). In some places democratization will continue while in others, dedemocratization will increase the cost of activism but it may also increase the resolve of committed activists. As categorical groups that were once disenfranchised become integrated into decision-making processes and certain wealth accumulation, new marginalized groups will demand inclusion.

Defining Social Movements

Many people often think of social movements as synonymous with left activism; they may define activism as the way to show indignation at events seen as unfair, unethical, and immoral. Let us remember that the early use of the term "protest" gained momentum around the Reformation when it was used as an active and public critique of what some saw as shortcomings and deviations from religious ideals or some interpretations of the Bible. Thus, activist agendas can be fueled by religious beliefs as well as liberal ideas derived from the Enlightenment which include proselytizing-secularism.

In his book *Credit and Blame*, Charles Tilly (2008b) writes about the importance of morality and community in creating worldviews and mobilizing individuals. Yet, for Tilly, social movements are endeavors by categorical groups who share an identity and thus go beyond isolated individual decisions to engage in activism. Social movements are a type of contentious politics, which in turn are politics by non-electoral means; and thus, related to social change and to the public affairs understood as the issues affecting many members of a polity.

Charles "Chuck" Tilly dedicated much of his life to studying social movements and contentious politics through case studies and historical analysis. Through personal experience and social interactions with others, Charles Tilly was aware that sometimes altruistic political commitments motivate some lifelong activists (for a discussion of this, see Díaz Cepeda, Rubén, and Castañeda 2019). He was also aware that activists often fight each other over purity tests; and that critiques about compromising and selling out often weaken social movement agendas. From early on in his career, Tilly did not look to explain individual motivation. He was skeptical about the possibility of getting inside activists' heads. There were three reasons for this. The first reason was methodological. As a historical sociologist, most of his data came from archival research and secondary sources. He cared about common people who were already dead and thus could not be surveyed or polled (Tilly 1983). The second reason was theoretical. Tilly was not satisfied with the pseudo-Durkheimian theories with which Talcott Parsons and his students saw political violence as resulting from social disorganization, rapid change, decrease of morality, mob mentality, and individual rage. In this theoretical framework, political violence was always dangerous and to be avoided, thus condemning collective action and justifying the status quo. These were the dominant theories in the 1950s, while Tilly was a graduate student. But he saw these theories as intrinsically conservative and scientifically unsatisfactory. Without being a proponent of violence, Tilly saw how collective violence could bring up fairer regimes with the French and American revolutions as prominent examples of this regenerative property of revolutionary collective action. The third reason was ontological; Tilly argued that the proper unit of analysis for sociology should be neither individual nor "society" but actual meaningful networks and social relations (Castañeda and Schneider 2017).

Towards the end of his life, Charles Tilly wrote much about categorical inequalities, group exclusion, and exploitation, as well as the role of trust-networks and democratization. Thus, for Tilly, social movements are important not only because they raise attention to human rights violations and injustices against exploited and excluded individuals, but also because they often seek to end categorical inequalities. By this definition, social movements are collective enterprises and mostly about the rights and enfranchisement of the entire social groups, and not about individual redress.

For definitional purposes, Charles Tilly (Chapter 1) calls a series of contentious events a social movement when they combine these three elements:

1. *Social movement campaign*: a sustained, organized public effort making collective claims on specific authorities, e.g. national governments;
2. *Social movement repertoire*: combinations of culturally recognizable forms of popular protests, e.g. marches, rallies, demonstrations; and
3. *WUNC displays*: the coordinated public performance of Worthiness, Unity, Numbers, and Commitment by members and supporters of the movement.

This is a procedural definition. This definition is better suited for historical examples and long-ongoing movements because we can only know the duration of sustained campaigns after the fact. However, it does not tell us which movements will catch on or, even less so, which ongoing movements will succeed in the long run. This is not a weakness of the theory but a strength because ultimately, a movement's impact is contingent on a myriad elements (political context, political opportunity structures, international relations, historical commemorations among many others).

Social Movements as Part of a Comprehensive Theory of Social Change

In Part I, Charles Tilly presents an overview of social movements in a span of over two hundred years. Tilly's main purpose is not to provide an exhaustive account of any particular social movement, nor to create a list of the most important social movements in that time span. Rather, his intention is to make larger theoretical points about social phenomena. Tilly's argument is that **the social movement is a modern type of contentious politics**. He means "modern" not in the sense of "contemporary"—as is often used in everyday language—but in the historical sense, meaning that modern is something that appeared in world history after the end of the Middle Ages along with the rise of the nation-state and democratic arrangement between those governing and those governed. Tilly is one of the pioneers describing the historical dances and negotiations made between governments and those governed in modern Western Europe. The negotiations were contentious, dialogical, and dialectical. They were not the result of a pact between members of the elite and representatives of the people. States claimed to represent people of a delimited territory, and promised to defend them from outsiders, and built popular legitimacy to tax and enlist soldiers for the war effort (Tilly 1975) by providing protection and common goods. At the same time, states created cultural and educational institutions to form a common culture and identity for their citizens (Anderson 1983, Noiriel 2006 [1988], Weber 1976), as well as social welfare services and provisions in exchange for levies and allegiance to the state. In Tilly's metatheory, rights are not the result of enlightened ideas or enlightened rulers, but the result of contentious politics where excluded groups make their collective voices heard publicly while demanding inclusion and successfully challenge the authorities, forcing them to concede (Tilly 1992a). Violence or threats of violence are very common historically; only recently were civil disobedience and non-violent social movements used to gain rights for internally and externally colonized peoples.

For Tilly, social movements are but one type of contentious politics that are defined (Tilly 1986; Tilly and Tarrow 2015) as politics that occur outside of traditional, diplomatic, elite or electoral means, and also include the use of violence or culturally recognizable non-routine displays of public discontent: e.g., marches, strikes, boycotts, sit-ins. As Tarrow writes,

> Over the past decade and more, students of social movements have begun to employ the concept of "contentious politics." Coined by the late Charles Tilly in a series of works he began in the 1970s, the concept encompasses social movements but extends to a wider range of conflictual phenomena, including strike waves, civil wars, revolutions, and insurgencies. It shifts the focus from the subjects and objects of contention to the mechanisms that connect them to each other and to broader institutions and actors. Much questioned when it emerged, the contentious politics approach has ripened to influence work on intra-movement relations, on links between movements and parties, the radicalization of movements, civil war mechanisms, and escalation into revolutionary situations.
>
> (Tarrow 2015)

As Tilly writes in the preface to the first edition of this book,

> Although I did not speak much of "contenders" before the 1970s, did not explicitly define my subject as "contention" until the 1980s, and did not start theorizing about "contentious politics" until the 1990s, for half a century a major stream of my work has concerned how, when, where, and why ordinary people make collective claims on public authorities, other holders of power, competitors, enemies, and objects of popular disapproval. For many years I generally avoided the term "social movement" because it sponged up so many different meanings and therefore obscured more than it clarified. Preparing detailed catalogs of contentious events for periods from the seventeenth to twentieth centuries in Western Europe and North America changed my mind. The catalogs made clear that major shifts in the array of means by which ordinary people made collective claims on others—their contentious repertoires—occurred in those regions between 1750 and 1850; that despite considerable differences in timing from regime to regime, in each regime the shifts clustered together; and that within the cluster emerged a distinctive combination of campaigns, performances, and displays. Participants and observers alike eventually began calling that new form of politics a "movement." Why not pin down that change?
>
> Despite the current tendency to call everything from fads to established interest groups "movements," the emergence, transformation, and survival of that new, distinctive political form deserved historical attention. With some trembling about likely turf wars and definitional disputes, I decided to use the standard term "social movement" instead of inventing some substitute such as "full-fledged social movement" or "the type of social movement that first emerged in Western Europe and North America at the end of the eighteenth century." It certainly simplified the text.

Thus, Tilly's full-fledged social movements are more specific and limited in number than participants in some political actions would advertise. In other words, there is cache, and even legitimation, in participants calling a series of contentious performances a social movement. Nevertheless, it is an empirical and definitional question whether a series of contentious events amount to a social movement.

For Tilly, contentious politics, including full-fledged social movements, are important because when looking at the historical record, large-scale social mobilization and contention created democracy as we know it. These phenomena co-created the nation-state, the welfare-state, and largely peaceful domestic civil societies in the global north. At the same time, they created industrial Western Imperialism and a reduction of rights in the global south through colonial and client regimes. In the case of settler-colonial regimes such as the United States, Canada, and Australia, they reproduced the economic and socio-political arrangements of European societies among their white citizens.

The historical counter-factual to this international system, and our current international system of nation-states, would be the coexistence of city-states, federations of city-states (as in ancient Greece), coalitions between city-states and rural areas (as in Medieval Europe), and extensive multicultural Empires under military or Monarchic rule (as the Roman or Ottoman Empires) (Hanagan and Tilly 2011). In his famous bellic thesis, Tilly states that war makes states and states make war (Kaspersen and Strandsbjerg 2017). Tilly argued that the constant wars between polities reinforced the multi-city–agricultural land partnerships that united access to capital from urban commerce with the food staples and excessive populations from the countryside (Tilly 1992b). The need to tax and draft regular citizens resulted in an implicit agreement where residents grudgingly consented to a tax rate and pledged obedience to the capital city's rules in exchange for citizenship and accompanying benefits (Tilly 2007).

This leads away from monarchic regimes to democratic regimes and the symbolic correspondence between a national government and its people: e.g., the French revolution and the transfer of sovereignty from the King to the people. The democratic model then was imitated around the world and seen by many as the most legitimate form of government (Wimmer 2018). Thus, as Tilly writes in Chapter 1, "By the twenty-first century, people all over the world recognized the term 'social movement' as a trumpet call, as a counterweight to oppressive power, as a summons to popular action against a wide range of scourges. It was not always so. Although popular risings of one kind or another have occurred across the world for thousands of years," full-fledged social movements appeared in the West in the eighteenth century in nation-state electoral democracies as available tools to show public concern and gain a collective political voice. The spread of social movements is another example of "the demonstration effect" with the diffusion of this type of regime starting in early nation-state democracies and then being copied by activists and political entrepreneurs in other types of regimes.

Contemporary Social Movement Campaigns

Charles Tilly passed away on April 29, 2008. Since his passing, much contention has occurred across the world, including the Arab Spring. Lesley Wood incorporated contemporary movements, contexts, and technologies into the second and third editions of this book as she did for this fourth edition.

For this edition, I decided to briefly discuss some popular protests in recent years through case studies in the new second part of this book. The cases selected are used as examples. They are not meant to be exhaustive nor to represent the more important contemporary social movements. I am responsible for any mistakes in the analyses and categorizations done in this section. I believe that the case studies can help readers: 1) to think more abstractly about movements they often hear about in the media; 2) to know more about some of the cases that they may be less familiar with; 3) to carry out more in-depth research on these movements since there are still many unanswered questions around them; and 4) to use these case studies as models for what students could write about during a course on social movements.

When Tilly and I co-taught a course on "Contentious Politics, Social Movements, and Revolutions" at Columbia University in the early 2000s, Tilly instructed students to go in depth on a historical or contemporary case of their choosing by reviewing the existing academic literature, secondary sources, and creating event catalogues (Tilly 2005; Tilly 2008a) by looking at media coverage to create a timeline in order to describe what took place and how these events fit, or not, with the contentious politics analytical paradigm. This was also the approach to start carrying out social science research that Tilly took in graduate seminars, in his contentious politics workshop, and when advising graduate students and young scholars.

Inspired by this model, most of these case studies were written by my students during the span of one semester and then edited and added to by me and other students. These case studies are not meant to be exhaustive but used to test, push, and contradict Tilly's theoretical statements, given some recent developments across the world. Our sense is that his theoretical framework and historical context is still very useful. While we briefly make a case, we leave to the reader the "evaluation" of whether the cases described are social movements. We offer a conclusion at the end of each case in determining whether it meets Tilly's social movements criteria, but we keep this brief, so the reader can decide whether the cases fit the definitions and qualifications for being called social movements. Time will tell whether the categorization was appropriate.

As you finish reading this book, you may ask, what about environmental movements, the Women's March, #MeToo, Never Again, Indivisible, the Resistance, white nationalism, and other movements from right-wing groups or many other recent social movement campaigns? This could be your turn to review the news, to report on these contentious campaigns, to construct timelines and case studies; to attend marches and contentious events organized by these groups and to theorize about their origins and implications; to interview activists and participants and write about their drives and motivations; to discuss the roles of media and emotions; to dissect strategies and changes in public framings as well as the policy impacts of a specific social movement. After you have done some of this work, you can ask yourself whether these contentious events and social justice campaigns merit being called social movements, not only for public relations or political reasons but also for academic definitional purposes. Does your case study include WUNC displays? Does it provide modular contentious performances that can be replicated elsewhere? Is there a campaign around an issue or claim that is sustained through time? You can also then test and expand on the theories and definitions presented in this book and present modifications and correctives to these theories and typologies. Are restaurant confrontations, e.g. of officials in Trump's administration, a new contentious performance? Time will tell.

Doing rigorous research by studying social movements allows us to have a more comprehensive understanding of how various groups across the world, with their own histories, aim to create change and alter entire institutions and power arrangements. I hope that this book has given you the background, definitions, methods, and examples to conduct this research. While social movement research can be quite academic, it is necessary for various audiences to disseminate the knowledge acquired from such work to have a more thorough understanding of how and why groups create such movements. One of the goals of this book is for readers to share their findings with audiences inside and outside of academia to deliberate, discuss, debate, and think critically with others about these social movements and their implications for the future.

The timelines and general descriptions are meant as common starting places for discussion, research, and theory testing. Instructors may assign a subset of these cases or assign them to particular individuals or groups for class presentations. These case studies may also prompt researchers to update them and to look more closely at contentious dynamics, effects, and mobilization strategies in these movements. They will also allow the reader to contextualize future contentious performances. The next section presents some advice on what to do.

Pernicious Postulates about Social Movements and Producing Superior Stories

Charles Tilly (1984) wrote about eight "pernicious postulates," wrong conclusions, assumed in some popular social theories from the nineteenth century often unquestioned and reproduced by many contemporary authors. Tilly warned social scientists to avoid these false ideas when conducting research and generating social theory. Inspired by that list of postulates, I highlight some pernicious postulates about social movements to be aware of. Case studies are a useful way to start a narrative about a movement, but they may also be misleading if they are based on idealized understanding of previous social movements. Let me mention some caveats about social movements that go against popular descriptions of notorious social movements. I would invite readers to avoid, or be aware of, common theoretical and methodological assumptions by keeping the next points in mind.

1. Do not describe movements as clearly bounded, united, and coherent. Analysts often treat "the movement" as a single unitary actor, thus obscuring both (a) the incessant jockeying and realignment that always go on within social movements and (b) the interaction among activists, constituents, targets, authorities, allies, rivals, enemies, and audiences that makes up the changing texture of social movements; naming particular movements as discreet underplays the continuity of themes, actors, and performances between different movements. Do not limit research by only looking at contentious events explicitly sharing the same name.
2. Do not engage in methodological nationalism (Babones 2014; Tilly 1984; Wimmer and Glick Schiller 2002), by studying social movements only in relation to political borders or by thinking of a problem starting and ending in a national frontier. Social movements have always shared important transnational elements. For this reason, the case studies in Part II of this book do not limit themselves to one city, state, or even country; and many times, they move from one movement to the other. While this may make the research more difficult, it may better reflect influences and changes in terms of goals, claims, and targets. While many of the examples discussed in Part II take place in North America, it would be a mistake to fail to acknowledge their inspiration, and effects beyond this geographical region.
3. Do not overemphasize a theoretical perspective to the detriment of historical events and empirical data. Rather than looking to prove a theory or maintain an ideological commitment through research, let the data gathering and analysis surprise you and show patterns and dynamics that you did not anticipate and that had not been previously discussed. Focus more on processes and mechanisms rather than on normative and teleological statements. Event catalogs (Tilly 2002, 2005, 2008a) and the dynamics of contention agenda to analyze contentious politics are a good way to do this (McAdam, Tarrow and Tilly 1996; Tilly and Tarrow 2015), they emphasize methodological and analytical tools rather than prescribing results, policy, or moral implications.
4. The internet, Twitter, Facebook, and YouTube have become important spaces to hear about a social justice campaign, follow a movement, and even study some patterns, but as Tilly correctly warns, we should be careful not to fall into technological determinism. The invention of new communication systems and media does not single-handedly change the character of social movements.
5. Think about length and scope. A social movement is not the same as a political or PR campaign, a fad, slacktivism, or a hashtag alone. A march, no matter how large, does not a social movement make. A social movement lasts more than a few months.
6. Social movements are not necessarily about making visible, direct changes in policy or electing political leaders. Sometimes the end-goal is more about awareness or slowly shifting cultural practices or stereotypes about a marginalized group.

7. A social movement does not need to have identifiable leaders to be called a social movement. They are more about reducing categorical inequalities than about individual name recognition.
8. A social movement does not require a Social Movement Organization (SMO) to be called so. Having an institutionalized organization may help continue advocating for a specific population, but it is not a requirement nor a sole cause for success.

The case studies that follow illustrate some of these points. The case studies are often not presented in a linear or chronological way, they often revisit some main events from slightly different angles. They may include vignettes from participants, quotes from other scholars, and news story accounts in Tilly's fashion. Those interested in knowing more about these movements can read longer treatments by the many able social movement scholar experts. The goal here is to provide bird's-eye overviews next to each other for comparative analysis and theory testing.

In his later work, Charles Tilly wrote about the importance of narratives to construct meaning and make sense of the world in everyday life. He stressed the importance of storytelling and encouraged social scientists to use short stories as memorable ways to convey an empirical finding or theoretical insight. While folk stories are linear simplifications with few main characters, he used the term superior stories for accounts of reality that, among other elements, include multiple main actors, are not linear, do not exaggerate agency, individual volition, and planning, and include unintended consequences and indirect causes (Tilly 2006, 2008b). Keeping the eight points above in mind will increase the possibilities of producing superior accounts of social movements.

Note

1 This chapter was presented at the 2018 International Sociological Association meetings in Toronto and the 2018 Social Science History Association meetings in Phoenix. For helpful conversations and feedback, I thank Jack A. Goldstone, Bill Roy, Silvia Pedraza, George Steinmetz, Said Arjomand, Jeff Broadbent, Maarten Roy Prak, Donatella della Porta, Wayne Te Brake, Cecelia Walsh-Russo, John Krinsky, Mirjam Künkler, Chares Demetriou, Nick Toloudis, Mona El-Ghobashy, Randa Serhan, Aliza Luft, Yang Zhang, Anna Skarpelis, Dolores Trevizo, among other Tilly-scholars and colleagues, and especially Lesley Wood, Chris Tilly, Maura Fennelly, and Erica Lesto.

References

Anderson, Benedict. 1983. *Imagined Communities: Reflections on the Origin and Spread of Nationalism*. London; New York: Verso.

Babones, Salvatore J. 2014. *Methods for Quantitative Macro-Comparative Research*. Thousand Oaks, CA: SAGE Publications.

Castañeda, Ernesto, and Cathy Lisa Schneider. 2017. *Collective Violence, Contentious Politics, and Social Change: A Charles Tilly Reader*. New York: Routledge.
Díaz Cepeda, Luis Rubén, and Ernesto Castañeda. 2019. "Motivations and Activist Typologies: Core Activists in Ciudad Juarez." *Working paper*.
Hanagan, Michael, and Chris Tilly. 2011. *Contention and Trust in Cities and States*. Dordrecht, Netherlands: Springer.
Kaspersen, Lars Bo, and Jeppe Strandsbjerg. 2017. *Does War Make States? Investigations of Charles Tilly's Historical Sociology*. Cambridge, UK: Cambridge University Press.
McAdam, Doug, Sidney Tarrow, and Charles Tilly. 1996. "To Map Contentious Politics." *Mobilization: An International Quarterly* 1(1): 17–34.
Noiriel, Gérard. 2006 [1988]. *Le Creuset Français: Histoire De L'immigration, Xixe–Xxe Siècles*. Paris: Seuil.
Tarrow, Sidney. 2015. "Contentious Politics." in *The Oxford Handbook of Social Movements*, edited by D. D. Porta and M. Diani. Oxford: Oxford University Press.
Tilly, Charles. 1975. *The Formation of National States in Western Europe*. Princeton, NJ: Princeton University Press.
——. 1983. "Speaking Your Mind without Elections, Surveys, or Social Movements." *The Public Opinion Quarterly* 47(4): 461–78.
——. 1984. *Big Structures, Large Processes, Huge Comparisons*. New York: Russell Sage Foundation. (http://deepblue.lib.umich.edu/bitstream/2027.42/51064/1/295.pdf).
——. 1986. *The Contentious French*. Cambridge, MA: Belknap Press.
——. 1992a. "Where Do Rights Come From?" in *Contributions to the Comparative Study of Development*, edited by L. Mjøset. Oslo, Norway: Institute for Social Research.
——. 1992b. *Coercion, Capital, and European States,* AD *990–1992*. Cambridge, MA: Blackwell.
——. 2002. "Event Catalogs as Theories." *Sociological Theory* 20(2): 248–54.
——. 2005. *Popular Contention in Great Britain, 1758–1834*. Boulder, CO: Paradigm Publishers.
——. 2006. *Why?* Princeton, NJ: Princeton University Press.
——. 2007. "Grudging Consent." *The American Interest* September–October.
——. 2008a. *Contentious Performances*. Cambridge, UK: Cambridge University Press.
——. 2008b. *Credit and Blame*. Princeton, NJ: Princeton University Press.
Tilly, Charles, and Sidney Tarrow. 2015. *Contentious Politics*. New York: Oxford University Press.
Weber, Eugene Joseph. 1976. *Peasants into Frenchmen: The Modernization of Rural France, 1870–1914*. Stanford, CA: Stanford University Press.
Wimmer, Andreas. 2018. *Nation Building: Why Some Countries Come Together While Others Fall Apart*. Princeton, NJ: Princeton University Press.
Wimmer, Andreas, and Nina Glick Schiller. 2002. "Methodological Nationalism and Beyond: Nation State Building, Migration and the Social Sciences." *Global Networks: A Journal of Transnational Affairs* 2(4): 301–34.

9

THE MOVEMENT FOR IMMIGRANT RIGHTS

Ernesto Castañeda, Angelina Torres, Barbara Martinez, Madison Guare, and Emily Glover

This chapter describes a series of laws, policies, and changes in policy implementation that have targeted and often criminalized immigrants, and the resulting efforts to counter these policies and their effects throughout the United States.

In 2016, there were 23.6 million non-citizens from many parts of the world who were living in the United States (CPS 2018b), and around 11.3 million undocumented immigrants from many different countries (Passel et al. 2014). In 2016, there were more than 57 million Latin people in the United States, of which more than 37 million were born in the U.S. (CPS 2018a). One-fifth of all children in the U.S. have at least one parent that is an immigrant, and 4.5 million U.S. children have at least a parent who lacks immigration papers (Passel et al. 2014). These immigrants suffer from "liminal legality," meaning that they are living in the U.S. but they have limited rights and protections (Castañeda 2013a; Menjívar 2006). Legislative avenues have failed to regularize these immigrants (Zatz and Rodriguez 2015). Social movements have risen to demand that these residents' rights be respected and that as people living in the country they be fully included into American democracy. Teenagers who had lived most of their lives in the U.S. began to mobilize around the fact that they were unable to attend college or work in the U.S. because they had been born in another country (Castañeda 2013b; Gonzales and Chavez 2012; Gonzales 2015).

The Immigrant Rights Movement predates the campaigns to pass the DREAM Act. After an increase in deportations in the last years, the focus of these movements is to oppose deportations and provide sanctuary for immigrants (Délano Alonso 2017).

This chapter looks at the 1986 Immigration Reform and Control Act and subsequent immigration policies, up until President Trump's repeal of Deferred Action for Childhood Arrivals (DACA) in 2017. Moving beyond just looking at immigration legislation, this chapter describes how immigrants and allies in the United States organize to resist, protest, and ultimately form cohesive social movements for immigrant rights. As we discuss, local immigrant groups collaborate with one another and form a social movement that meets the three main criteria of having a social movement campaign, social movement repertoire, and WUNC displays.

Immigration Legislation

The 1986 Immigration Reform and Control Act (IRCA) provided amnesty and a path to citizenship for thousands of undocumented migrants in the U.S. and allowed them to petition to bring their family members, but it increased border surveillance and introduced penalties for hiring workers without papers; and did not provide mechanisms to legalize future newcomers.

In 1994, California had an estimated 1.3 million undocumented immigrants (Alvarez and Butterfield 2000). It was facing its worst economic crisis since the Great Depression. Some residents and opportunistic politicians like governor Pete Wilson equated these two phenomena and launched a revival of nativism with his support of Proposition 187 which aimed to limit the rights of undocumented immigrants and to restrict their access to public education, healthcare, and social services. The anti-immigrant Proposition 187 received the support of 59 percent of California voters.

This paved the way for the federal Illegal Immigration Reform and Immigrant Responsibility Act (IIRIRA) of 1996, passed by Congress and signed into law by President Bill Clinton. A legal scholar writes, "The title of the legislation set the tone: get tough on immigrants, stop illegal immigration, and blame immigrants for criminal and welfare problems"(Hines 2002: 40). IIRIRA put a greater emphasis on border security. Anti-immigrant policies and legislative proposals along with the lack of new amnesties pushed undocumented immigrants further into the shadows and made them increasingly afraid of being caught by immigration enforcement and separated from their family in the United States (Castañeda and Buck 2011; Castañeda 2013a; Hines 2002; Romero 2011).

In October 1996, thousands of Latinos protested on Capitol Hill in Washington DC

> This event, the first major Latino protest in the nation's capital, was organized by the National Coordinating Committee for Citizenship and Participation, also known as *Coordinadora '96*. This network of organizations first developed to fight [California's] Proposition 187, but later spanned across the United States.
>
> (Mohamed 2017: 58–59)

Immigrants asked Congress to protect their rights. Protesters displayed their U.S patriotism by singing the Star-Spangled Banner and waving both Mexican and

American flags during the march. Immigrants were attempting to depict their close ties to the U.S, and show that although they might be undocumented, they are a worthy component of American society. Estimates for the number of participants range from 25,000 to 100,000 (Mohamed 2017: 59).

"A Day Without Immigrants" Marches, May 1, 2006

On December 6, 2005, James Sensenbrenner (R-WI) introduced H.R. 4437: The Border Protection, Antiterrorism, and Illegal Immigration Control Act of 2005. The bill asked for more funds for border control, broader jurisdiction for the Department of Homeland Security, and for fingerprinting of non-citizens entering and leaving the country (many of these elements were later incorporated and enacted in other bills). It passed the House of Representatives on December 16, 2005, but the Senate did not vote on it. HR 4437 was very controversial since Title II Sections 201 and 203 sought to make undocumented status an "aggravated felony," a criminal offense, rather than a civil offense like getting a parking ticket. Furthermore, the ambiguous language could have made any person, agency or institution guilty of criminal behavior for helping undocumented people who had been previously deported. This worried the Catholic Church, social service agencies, employers, and regular people who often came in contact with undocumented individuals. The Bill would have also funded 700 miles of a double-layered fence along the border (Prieto 2018).

Opposition to the Sensenbrenner proposal fostered the massive Immigrants' Rights Marches of 2006 across the U.S., which were the largest marches in the United States history until that point (Voss and Bloemraad 2011). The campaign to support the march was dubbed, "The Day without Immigrants" in reference to a mockumentary by Jorge Arau and others entitled, "A Day without a Mexican" (2004). Events with similar names later occurred throughout Spain and France among other places.

The Immigrant Rights Movement has united many Latin people as well as other immigrants and allies all over the United States. In addition, the Spanish language media also played a vital role in calling people to participate in the 2006 march. In the U.S., popular Spanish-speaking radio hosts supported and promoted these record-breaking peaceful marches in 2006 (Mohamed 2017: 63). The Catholic Church was also active in organizing opposition to this law and in favor of immigrant rights (Castañeda 2018). The slogan "Today We March, Tomorrow We Vote" united different communities into one cause.

DREAMers as an Example of Immigrants' Humanity

DREAMers stress the fact that as minors they had little choice in immigrating without documents. They never chose to be undocumented. Many thought they were regular citizens until realizing they lacked a social security number.

Their situation calls into question the justice behind their status. Arguing it would be unjust to punish them for no fault of their own (Nicholls 2013; Nicholls and Fiorito 2015; Snow and Benford 1988).

The DREAMers presented themselves as first-class citizens, showing off their contributions to their communities, and playing into the American Dream narrative of hard work and pulling oneself up by the bootstraps. Working together in this movement, a number of young undocumented immigrants were able to name themselves "DREAMers" and work toward a common cause.

While figures vary on the number of undocumented immigrant youth and how many would be eligible for conditional residency, the capacity to bring 200,000 members to a rally in favor of the DREAMers cause, certainly speaks to the importance of the issue and the strength of the movement (Center for Immigration Policy 2012).

An important step in creating a new generation of activists was the creation of organizations and networks that could sustain protest activities that were visible across the various school groups (Nicholls 2013). Once the local groups began to come together in solidarity, then the claims and campaigns became familiar and available to other DREAMers. The creation of a national network of student organizations was also critical to the campaign of claim making and performances. Without a united group, it was difficult to juggle or claim the priorities of a vast collection of people. Members of an undocumented youth group in Miami would have different backgrounds than an undocumented youth group in San Francisco. The power of numbers caused DREAMers to refine their mission to a common cause and to state a bold claim on behalf of everyone. This also led to a spread of tactics and performances, as a coalition has more direct means of sharing news and information, and helping others recreate similar campaigns and contentious events. The repetition of the same tactics also increases their visibility to the public eye, similar to sit-in protests during the civil rights era (McAdam 1999).

DREAMers were able to learn from this nonviolent campaign and apply a similar strategy to challenge the sheriff of Maricopa County, Arizona. As discussed in Chapter 7, Joe Arpaio, Sheriff from 1993–2017, was responsible for some of the most intense racial profiling and abhorrent detention centers in the contemporary United States (Romero 2011). This was most evident in the existence of a "Tent City," approximately 6.5 km outside of downtown Phoenix holding upwards of 2,000 inmates (Lukinbeal and Sharp 2015). By showing the media the inhumane conditions under which prisoners were forced to live, the public began nonviolent but persistent protests against Arpaio. Thus, Arpaio became a recognizable embodiment of racism against immigrants in America.

The early tactics of the DREAMers were to frame themselves as the best and brightest, showcase themselves as non-violent, and to unite their voices and stories to grant legitimacy to the group through media. The group succeeded in creating a coalition, sharing information and education through the creation of student groups and mentors, and remaining persistent in conversations about immigration reform. The campaign of "undocumented, unapologetic, and unafraid" continues to act as an empowering rallying cry for DREAMers all through the United States as institutionalized in the Washington SMO United We Dream. The framing tactics used to enter the public eye served as an excellent springboard toward nonviolent protests, that then further explained the youth's discontent with their state of affairs and the injustice in their discrimination. United We Dream is becoming an influential Social Movements Organization joining the ranks of the NAACP, LULAC, the Human Rights Campaign and similar groups.

It is important to remember that the formation of a collective identity has to occur before a mobilization around this identity can occur (Tilly 2002, 2005). Thus, the tactic to advocate for immigrant rights around the identity of the DREAMer is somewhat independent of the DREAM Act.

The DREAM Act

Exceptional individuals such as Tereza Lee had success in getting personalized legalization passed to regularize their own status (Fuchs 2017; Kelly and Lei 2018) and inspired some congressmen to push for a more general solution. The Defense, Relief, and Education for Alien Minors (DREAM Act 2011) Act was first introduced in the Senate by Sen. Richard Durbin (D-IL), co-sponsored by Sen. Orrin Hatch (R-UT) in August 2001. The purpose of this bill was to provide some immigration relief (e.g., protection from imminent deportation and a path to citizenship for those satisfying certain specific criteria) for those who arrived in the United States without clearing immigration and customs or overstayed their visas through their parent's actions, at an age when they had no agency in their undocumented migration. To benefit from this legislative proposal, the person must have proof that they entered the United States before the age of sixteen and must have continuously lived in the country for at least five years. Potential beneficiaries in this original version of the bill must have graduated from a United States high school or obtained a high school equivalency diploma demonstrate good moral character, and pass criminal background checks and reviews. Candidates then have six years to continue to demonstrate moral character and either attend a higher-level educational institution or serve for two years in the military. Having fulfilled that, they would be granted permanent residency. This Act has faced intense resistance at multiple levels for nearly two decades. According to Congress.gov some of the times when DREAMER-related immigration legislation was voted on include:

August 2001—DREAM Act first introduced in the Senate (S.1291) by Sen. Orrin G. Hatch [R-UT]. Failed.

July 2003—Introduced by Hatch not passed (S. 1545).

November 2005—DREAM Act of 2005 introduced by Sen. Richard Durbin [D-IL].

April 2006—DREAM incorporated into Comprehensive Immigration Reform Act of 2006. Failed.

March 2007—STRIVE Act of 2007 introduced to the House (H.R. 1645) by Rep. Luis Gutierrez.
May 2007—DREAM incorporated into Secure Borders, Economic Opportunity and Immigration Reform Act of 2007. Failed.
May 2007—DREAM incorporated into Comprehensive Immigration Reform Act of 2007. Failed.
Oct 2007—DREAM Act proposed as stand-alone. Failed.
March 2009—DREAM Act proposed as stand-alone. Failed.
November 2010—DREAM Act proposed as stand-alone. Failed.
May 2011—DREAM Act proposed as stand-alone. Failed.
June 2011—Comprehensive Immigration Reform Act of 2011.
June 2012—President Obama proposes Deferred Action for Childhood Arrivals, Homeland Security announces it will not be deporting youth who apply and qualify for the stated measures.
April 2013—The comprehensive immigration reform bill S. 744, which passed the Senate with bipartisan support from sixty-eight Senators, included special legalization provisions for Dreamers. The corresponding bill (H.R.15) did not pass the House.
March 2017—Recognizing America's Children Act, introduced but not successful.
July 2017—American Hope Act of 2017 (H.R. 3591) introduced by Rep. Luis Gutierrez. Failed.

The bill failed to pass in its various iterations between 2001 and 2017. Meanwhile, immigrant youth began to form networks and organizations that advocated for their personhood and rights. Those who would have qualified to regularize through this legislation named themselves DREAMers. Many of them have spent the past decade mobilizing for an immigration reform that allows for their lawful residency in the United States.

Activists in favor of the DREAM Act have been effective in framing salient narratives (Snow and Benford 1988) to shift the popular perception of undocumented youth. DREAMers were able to create widespread sympathy by:

1. Embracing American symbols and marking the distance from foreign symbols and reminding people that the only country they knew and recognized as their home was the US.
2. Highlighting personal achievement, merit, and success by profiling valedictorians and successful students in newspaper articles, press conferences, and public demonstrations and sit-ins.
3. Countering the stigma of illegitimacy by self-absolving of the guilt of illegality.

The DREAMers created a series of groups, networks, and coalitions that gave some legitimacy to young "aliens" by sharing grievances and reframing themselves in the public light through non-violent protest (Nicholls 2013).

United We Dream, an organization born from this movement "began in the mid-2000s, when key national advocacy groups, led by the National

Immigration Law Center (NILC), developed an informal coalition of organizers and advocates to promote equal access to educational opportunities for immigrant youth" (United We Dream 2016). By 2006, when the Comprehensive Immigration Reform Act failed, local groups (the New York State Youth Leadership Council, the Student Immigrant Movement in Massachusetts, the University Leadership Initiative in Austin, TX, and the California Dream Network) came together to coordinate campaigns to mobilize and take action. Around the same time, United We Dream began to see a spread of student-run groups across U.S. campuses, with the creation of the DREAMers as a political identity and public group to join rather than stay as a disjointed set of secret lives and unheard voices.

For DREAMers, especially high-achieving students, the disappointment of not being able to continue their higher education and the risk of deportation constitute a shared experience. It is in the specificity of this shared grievance, that many of the 1.8 million undocumented immigrants that could benefit from reform were able to find a common voice (Gelatt and Pierce 2018).

When immigration reform failed again in 2009 and 2010, the DREAMers revised their tactics and continued to increase pressure on Congress through appealing to elected officials and the broader American public. They switched from lobbying to organizing rallies and sit-ins as modes of protest for their cause. Zimmerman (2011) suggests that the shift in tactics and modes reflects the transition

> from a movement that was initially focused on building support for the DREAM Act to one that has increasingly used direct action to bring attention to broader issues of immigrant, civil, and human rights as a strategy for social and policy change.

The DREAMers had now been named and identified; they had come together as a united group. Students occupied the office of Senator John McCain in Arizona, the floors of various Senators in DC, and various public offices throughout the United States.

The Trail of Dreams

On January 1, 2010, four Dreamers, Felipe Matos, Gaby Pacheco, Carlos Roa, and Juan Rodriguez set out to walk 1,500 miles from Miami to DC to call attention to their cause in a media campaign they called the Trail of Dreams. They reached DC on May 1, 2010 (Zatz and Rodriguez 2015: 82). Pacheco would become a national leader and one of the faces of the movement. This interstate march had a large symbolic impact on undocumented individuals and— among other actions and contentious performances—DREAMer activists credited this march for inspiring them to organize and to talk openly about their status with teachers and classmates.

Coming Out as Undocumented: Mobilization Grows

After the failure of the Dream Act to pass in Congress, undocumented youth used a new tactic from the movement for LGBTQ rights. Undocumented youth began to "come out of the closet." Indeed, some of the early undocumented youth activists were gay, and as journalist Jose Antonio Vargas says, he had to come out twice (Vargas 2011; Waugh 2013).

Young immigrants were now coming out publicly with t-shirts, press conferences, and a social movement campaign they called "Undocumented and Unafraid." Students made the point that they were not afraid of the consequences that might result from coming out publicly if it meant benefiting the movement (Zatz and Rodriguez 2015: 82). These immigrants were no longer shielding themselves from strangers as their parents did. They wanted their neighbors, friends, and classmates to realize their close connection with undocumented immigrants. Making undocumented immigrants more personable because they were no longer seen as mysterious "Others." Coming out of the shadows was an extreme shift in the movement that also increased mobilization and public support. It also created an identity around which to mobilize.

The incorporation of labels such as "undocuqueer" and the process of "coming out" as undocumented individuals allowed the movement to bridge with the LGBT community (Snow and Benford 1988) and build on their successful Human Rights Campaign for marriage equality and civil rights (Dorf and Tarrow 2014; Taylor et al. 2009). Many DREAMers see themselves as continuing a broader civil rights campaign (Zimmerman 2011).

The slogan "Undocumented and Unafraid" emerged in 2012 in an effort to further destigmatize undocumented immigrants and make them visible to the public eye (Nicholls and Fiorito 2015). The movement shifted from a quiet coalition working within legislative structure toward a loud and bold community that would not be ruled by fear. With the audacity of claiming themselves as unafraid, undocumented youth created a more pressing image and promoted a stronger reaction from the public differing from the more traditional and non-deviant claims of before. Likewise, "frame extension" was utilized by honing in more on the military service aspect of the bill where service would count to regularize their status; now including the showcase of DREAMers serving in the armed forces to appeal to conservatives, rather than highlighting only class valedictorians (Garcia Rodriguez 2014).

However, while the image of "good immigrants" was helpful in elevating DREAMers into the spotlight, the Act has not passed. Furthermore, the lobbying for the DREAM Act created a discourse of exceptionalism that further disenfranchised the parents of the DREAMers, adult undocumented DREAMers, who later started calling themselves "The Original DREAMers" trying to lose some of the remaining stigmas against "illegals." Many DREAMer activists have become aware of the exclusionary nature of the term and their campaigns and have stopped using the term DREAMer to identify themselves and have focused instead on decreasing deportations and defending the rights of non-citizens

(Schwiertz 2016). Furthermore, right-wing voters equate DREAMers with children and students and therefore are unsympathetic or feel duped when young adult migrants ask to benefit from the DREAM Act.

The lack of legislation has had many negative effects. For example, in 2011, workplaces and schools were frequently raided and as a result around 5,000 children were placed in foster care because their parents were detained because of their immigration status (Zatz and Rodriguez: 12–15).

Sentiments in certain communities started to change when the media depicted the separation of families; for example, mothers were taken from their nursing children (Zatz and Rodriguez 2015: 15). Mainstream media coverage humanized these immigrants and showed the grave need for a comprehensive immigration reform with pathways to citizenship. At the same time, the media was citing spokespeople from nativist and anti-immigrant organizations.

The Creation of DACA

A younger generation of undocumented immigrants became important members of the Latino Immigration Rights Movement. DREAMers participated in frequent and effective protest throughout the Obama administration and contradicted the commonly held stigma against Latinos (that they are uneducated delinquents). One protest consisted of Latino immigrants dressing in their graduation robes at the border (Zatz and Rodriguez 2015: 11). These groups of students focused on small wins in their movement by showing their contributions to society. Outsiders were now shifting their perspective and viewed DREAMers as determined activists (Garcia Rodriguez 2014).

DREAMers' campaigns made an impact in colleges all over the United States. Thousands of college students participated in a walkout to push their university to become "sanctuary campuses" for immigrants (Kauffman 2016). Demands varied from giving undocumented students financial aid to banning immigration officers from campus. Campaigns in universities are an important part of the Immigrants' Rights Movement. More college students than ever know someone that is a Latin immigrant, someone who is undocumented, or someone who is negatively affected by immigration policy.

Although DREAMers were unsuccessful in their goal of passing the DREAM Act, they put enough pressure on the Obama administration that in June 2012 President Obama instructed Homeland Security to produce a memo announcing Deferred Action on Childhood Arrivals to provide temporary residence and work permits to people aged thirty and younger who would qualify for the DREAM Act. Applicants need to renew their DACA status every two years to make sure they are actively following guidelines and have not committed a crime. This was not a permanent fix, but some formerly undocumented youth became "DACAmented" (Gonzales, Terriquez and Ruszczyk 2014). In a public statement, President Obama wrote,

> Over the years, politicians of both parties have worked together to write legislation that would have told these young people—our young people—that if your parents brought you here as a child, if you've been here a certain number of years, and if you're willing to go to college or serve in our military, then you'll get a chance to stay and earn your citizenship. And for years while I was President, I asked Congress to send me such a bill.
>
> That bill never came. And because it made no sense to expel talented, driven, patriotic young people from the only country they know solely because of the actions of their parents, my administration acted to lift the shadow of deportation from these young people, so that they could continue to contribute to our communities and our country. We did so based on the well-established legal principle of prosecutorial discretion, deployed by Democratic and Republican presidents alike, because our immigration enforcement agencies have limited resources, and it makes sense to focus those resources on those who come illegally to this country to do us harm. Deportations of criminals went up. Some 800,000 young people stepped forward, met rigorous requirements, and went through background checks. And America grew stronger as a result.
>
> (Obama, September 5, 2017)

The partial victory of the DREAMers to convince the executive branch to provide relief for deportation showed the results of their mobilization. The approval of DACA allowed around 553,000 "undocumented youths" to win a two-year relief from deportation.

DREAMers developed various methods to make their message strong, and have had a deep effect on the way U.S citizens view them to the point where a majority of Americans are in favor of DACA and the DREAM Act and even immigration reform (Blitz 2017; Washington Post-ABC News poll 2017). "Bound Dreamers" developed a strategy to align with advocacy organizations and other political allies to develop a sympathetic voice for immigrants (Nicholls and Fiorito 2015). This frame is used to eliminate stigmas associated with Latinos and is also used to stress the positive impact younger generations have on society. One DREAMer claimed, "We're basically debunking all the stereotypes, promoting ourselves as people with good character—to counter all the bad stereotypes of immigrants" (Nicholls and Fiorito 2015). These adolescents feel like Americans, they grew up in the U.S. and know it as their only home. "Bound Dreamers" use the best and the brightest as the face of their campaign to eliminate the stigmas (Nicholls 2015). Lastly, this group is focused on stressing that their illegality was not in their hands, many of them were brought to the U.S. as children. The campaign made by DREAMers has proved to be effective, and most citizens support DREAMers. The DREAMers' tactic to promote themselves in a positive light has affected policy and led to the creation of DACA. Some DREAMers have now finished college, medical school, law school, received PhDs, and become teachers, priests, and pastors and have been able to work thanks to DACA.

Ending DACA

However, on September 5, 2017, President Trump announced the end of DACA, arguing that Congress should be the one shaping the program and not the executive. After the announcement of the impending end of DACA, people have spoken publicly in favor of DACA and immigration reform, ranging from Silicon Valley top executives to Hollywood stars, Democrats and Republicans, immigration activists, and college presidents (Shear and Davis 2017). Protests have been staged outside of the White House, the Department of Justice, and in cities all over the U.S. in hopes that immigrant voices would be heard.

Public rallies have been essential to increase morale and make the movement visible to outsiders. DREAMers used public protests, like standing at the border in their graduation caps to send a broader message and create larger protests across college campuses. The Immigrant Rights Movement has been successful in making the argument to protect the human rights of undocumented people in the U.S. Public opinion polls across the nation show the widespread support to change U.S. immigration policy in a way that provides paths to citizenship to those currently here. Despite the Trump administration's decision to end DACA, the movement has become even stronger. People who initially opposed the DREAM Act and DACA are now speaking out in support. Republican legislators who previously voted against immigrant rights bills, now believe that children who were brought illegally through no fault of their own should not be forced to leave. Ultimately, DREAMers have become the voice and face of the Immigrant Rights Movement and continue to have a great effect on its progress.

Travel Bans

On January 27, 2017, Trump passed Executive Order 13769, calling to suspend the entry of people from Iran, Iraq, Libya, Somalia, Sudan, Syria, and Yemen for ninety days and from Syria indefinitely. This Executive Order resulted in an outbreak of protests across the nation.

Those previously in possession of a green card were denied re-entrance into the country, "creating pandemonium at airports along the eastern seaboard" (Kocher 2017: 166). Flights coming in from Africa, Europe, and the Middle East were affected immediately. Non-citizens from the countries on the list were held at airports, and, in most cases, sent back to their country of origin. Through news media and other social networking platforms, word quickly got out regarding many people's difficulties to enter the country. "Mass mobilization" was seen in protests, marches, and vigils nationwide as the notion of deportation was realized (Kocher 2017: 166).

Battery Park in Manhattan, New York, hosted around 10,000 protesters on January 29, 2017. Among the thousands of signs held up were slogans saying "Refugees welcome here" and "No hate, no fear" (Gordts, Miller, Abbey-Lambertz, and Wing 2017). Protesters demonstrated publicly their sympathy for refugees (Blitz 2017). In Boston nearly 10,000 people gathered at Copley Square for a #NoBanNoWall protest coordinated through social media (Gordts, Miller, Abbey-Lambertz, and Wing 2017).

In Washington, DC, protesters gathered in front of the White House with numerous signs expressing their disapproval of Trump's ban, as well as a large group shouting "shame" outside the gates of the White House (Gambino et al. 2017). Following this demonstration, an estimated 8,000 marched down Pennsylvania Avenue to the Capitol, where chants of "do your job" were heard (Gordts, Miller, Abbey-Lambertz, and Wing 2017).

Two days after President Trump signed the controversial executive order which banned immigration to the United States from seven countries, protesters gathered at the White House, as many had the weekend prior for the Women's March. As observer, Madison Guare writes,

> The crowds were held back from the White House itself by a tall and temporary chain link fence. There were people in trees and climbing walls. The crowd was made of all generations and ethnicities; it wasn't just college kids. After a sufficient amount of time spent by every person pushing the closest they could to the chain-link fence, the rally turned to a march.
>
> The crowd started walking down toward the Washington monument but turned to march to the Capitol and Trump hotel . . . We met a few women with a guitar and speaker, and they led the crowd in song. Slowly, This Land is Your Land began to drown out the "shame!" chants. It was a powerful thing to hear and feel the transition of the crowd's attitude.

Protest music plays an important role in these contentious events (DeMent 2017). In these contentious performances the chant of "No Ban, No Wall" is used to protest Trump's travel bans, and his proposal to expand existing border fences along the U.S.–Mexico border.

Airports reported additional protests, including Dallas-Fort Worth, Miami, Los Angeles, Detroit, and Portland (Gambino et al. 2017). Employees of major corporations, such as Google, staged walkouts worldwide against the ban (Bright 2017).

In Brooklyn, New York, the federal court granted an "emergency stay" for displaced refugees not immediately able to fly back to their country of origin. The acting Attorney General was fired within days for refusing to enforce the legal order designated to protect the citizens of the United States. This act sparked more movements speaking out against the Trump administration.

Because of the ban, international students, artists, biotech executives, researchers, and scientists have been limited in their mobility (Carroll 2017). Despite having valid U.S. visas, researchers around the world were stuck overseas (Nature 2017). Numerous universities united to protest the travel ban. Nearly 600 schools signed a letter to express the concern of higher education institutions nationwide for their current and prospective students (Redden 2017).

At Clemson University, three professors chose to oppose the Executive Order in a more personal way. Staging a six-day fast, on campus, they hoped to raise awareness and place pressure on not only Clemson's administration but also to inspire other universities to make stronger efforts in opposing the travel ban (Redden 2017). In doing so, they hoped to eliminate this order which blocked the opportunity of many international students to obtain a higher education in the United States.

The original travel ban produced constant protests, and courts questioned whether it was constitutional because it targeted predominantly Muslim countries. On March 6, 2017, President Trump released another Executive Order to replace order 13769. This new order includes countries that are not predominantly Muslim. Challenges and protests have decreased. Nevertheless, civilians nationwide united to voice their opinion on Executive Order 13769. These protests were effective in pushing Trump's replacement of the provisions of the original Executive Order. In its support of refugees and immigrants, these protests build on and strengthen the Immigrant Rights Movement. Social movements are a vital aspect of democracy, and instrumental in putting the brakes on unfair and unpopular governmental initiatives.

Keep Families Together

There was a public outcry in the summer of 2018 after the public learned about the consequences of Trump's so-called "Zero Tolerance Policy" to immigration, which included the separation of minors from their parents at the border even when families were reporting to border officers and asking for asylum. The mobilization and media pushback was such that on June 20, Trump signed an executive order ending the practice, but many families are still separated and contentious performances showing deep disapproval of these practices continue. Rallies happened across the country on June 30, 2018. On June 28, 2018, Democratic party activists and organizers of the women's march organized a civil disobedience sit-in in a Senate building, and hundreds of them were arrested. Participants used aluminum foil covers like those given to immigrants instead of blankets, sang, and chanted the following slogans:

We care, open hands up!
We disobey!
Abolish ICE!
Hey hey, ho ho all walls have gotta go from Palestine to Mexico. Hey hey ho ho all walls have got to go!
No Ban, No Wall!

Conclusion

Victories of the Immigrant Rights Movement include DACA after a decade of stagnation in successfully passing comprehensive immigration reform in the United

States. The movement continues under increased anti-immigrant rhetoric, threats of deportation, the criminalization of migration, and the misleading conflation of border security and stopping immigration and building a wall (Castañeda 2019). The Immigrant Rights Movement is likely to continue until amnesty is given to all people residing in U.S. territories and who call the U.S. home. Illegalization excludes and exploits around 3 percent of the people living in the United States. The Immigrant Rights Movement is related to civil rights and democracy because it is about decreasing categorical inequalities between citizens and non-citizens.

We will now briefly analyze the Immigrant Rights Movement in the United States using the Social Movements framework established in this book. The "social movement campaign" is apparent with the many immigrant rights activists' contentious performances and communication campaigns targeting politicians and policymakers who are in charge of the legislation that determines immigrants' statuses and rights. The "social movements repertoire" is also present. Immigrant groups and allies around the country have staged protests, marches, hunger strikes, and connected with the media to educate the public on their struggles and demands for justice. Supporters are using various forms of political action to maintain momentum, create awareness, and make their demands heard at the local, state, and federal levels. WUNC displays have also existed in several forms throughout the Immigrant Rights Movement in the United States. Wearing graduation gowns in protests at the border (Worthiness), having chants and common slogans on posters at rallies (Unity), leading protests with hundreds of thousands of participants (Numbers) and staging sit-ins at congressional offices risking arrest and deportation (Commitment) all reveal the cohesiveness of the movement across the country.

Since the passage of IRCA, immigrants and allies have collaborated across the country, especially during times of emergency such as after the repeal of DACA. The Immigrant Rights Movement is not solely known for being supported by popular progressive politicians such as Senator Kamala Harris (D-CA) or celebrities. Rather, the movement is made and organized by immigrants themselves; they are often the real leaders and protagonists of this movement. The amount of organization and protest performance for immigrant rights since the 1980s reveals the resilience of this social movements campaign. All of the criteria to be called a social movement have been met; thus, we can say that the Immigrant Rights Movement is a fully fledged contemporary and ongoing social movement with strong transnational links and actors.

References

Alvarez, R. Michael, and Tara L. Butterfield. 2000. "The Resurgence of Nativism in California? The Case of Proposition 187 and Illegal Immigration." *Social Science Quarterly* 81(1): 167–79.

Blitz, Brad. 2017. "Another Story: What Public Opinion Data Tell Us About Refugee and Humanitarian Policy." *Journal on Migration and Human Security* 5(2): 379–400.

Bright, Jake. 2017. "Trump's First Weeks in Office Have Politicized the Tech Industry", February 7. TechCrunch. Retrieved March 5, 2018 (https://techcrunch.com/2017/02/07/trumps-first-weeks-in-office-have-politicized-the-tech-industry/).

Carroll, John. 2017. "Biotech Bosses Protest Trump's Travel Ban", February 7. Science. Retrieved March 5, 2018 (www.sciencemag.org/news/2017/02/biotech-bosses-protest-trump-s-travel-ban).

Castañeda, Ernesto, and Lesley Buck. 2011. "Remittances, Transnational Parenting, and the Children Left Behind: Economic and Psychological Implications." *The Latin Americanist* 55(4): 85–110.

Castañeda, Ernesto. 2013a. "Living in Limbo: Transnational Households, Remittances and Development." *International Migration* 51(s1): 13–35.

——. 2013b. *Waiting for Real Reform: How Half-Way Measures Leave Immigrants in Limbo and Deprive America of Their Talents*. Cambridge, MA: Scholars Strategy Network.

——. 2018. *A Place to Call Home: Immigrant Exclusion and Urban Belonging in New York, Paris, and Barcelona*. Stanford, CA: Stanford University Press.

——. 2019. *Building Walls: Excluding Latin People in the United States*. Lanham, MD: Lexington.

Center for Immigration Policy. 2012. "Who and Where the Dreamers Are, Revised Estimates." Vol. Washington, DC: American Immigration Council.

CPS. 2018a. "Current Population Survey 2016 the Hispanic Population in the United States: 2016. Table 1. Population by Sex, Age, Hispanic Origin, and Race." Vol. Washington, DC: U.S. Census Bureau.

CPS. 2018b. "Current Population Survey 2018: Population by Nativity-Detailed." Vol. Washington, DC: U.S. Census Bureau.

Délano Alonso, Alexandra. 2017. "Sanctuary Campus: Resistance and Protection within and Beyond the University." *The Avery Review* 21.

DeMent, Iris. 2017, "A Year of Protest Songs from Athens and Beyond." Athens, GA: Flagpole. Retrieved March 5, 2018 (http://flagpole.com/music/music-features/2017/11/01/a-year-of-protest-songs-from-athens-and-beyond).

Dorf, Michael C., and Sidney Tarrow. 2014. "Strange Bedfellows: How an Anticipatory Countermovement Brought Same-Sex Marriage into the Public Arena." *Law & Social Inquiry* 39(2): 449–73.

Fuchs, Chris. 2017, "Original Dreamer Still Fights for Undocumented Immigrants 16 Years after First Dream Act", NBC News. Retrieved August 1, 2018 (www.nbcnews.com/news/asian-america/original-dreamer-still-fights-undocumented-immigrants-16-years-after-first-n740491).

Gambino, Lauren, Sabrina Siddiqui, Paul Owen, and Edward Helmore. 2017. "Thousands Protest against Trump Travel Ban in Cities and Airports Nationwide." in *The Guardian*.

Garcia Rodriguez, Marisa C. 2014. "Mediated Narratives on Citizenship, Immigration, and National Identity: The Construction of Dreamer Identities in Public Discourse Surrounding President Obama's 2012 Deferred Deportation Announcement." 3641212 Ph.D., The University of New Mexico, Ann Arbor. Retrieved from ProQuest Dissertations & Theses Global.

Gelatt, Julia, and Sarah Pierce. 2018. "The Trump Immigration Plan: A Lopsided Proposal." Vol. Washington, DC: Migration Policy Institute.

Gonzales, Roberto G, Veronica Terriquez, and Stephen P Ruszczyk. 2014. "Becoming Dacamented: Assessing the Short-Term Benefits of Deferred Action for Childhood Arrivals (Daca)." *American Behavioral Scientist* 58(14): 1852–72.

Gonzales, Roberto G., and Leo R. Chavez. 2012. "'Awakening to a Nightmare': Abjectivity and Illegality in the Lives of Undocumented 1.5-Generation Latino Immigrants in the United States." *Current Anthropology* 53(3): 255–81.

Gonzales, Roberto G. 2015. *Lives in Limbo: Undocumented and Coming of Age in America.* Oakland, CA: University of California Press.

Gordts, Eline, Hayley Miller, Kate Abbey-Lambertz, and Nick Wing. 2017. "Protests against Trump's Executive Order Don't Let Up", January 29. *The Huffington Post.* (www.huffingtonpost.com/entry/trump-executive-order-protests_us_588e2c36e4b08a14f7e69de4).

Hines, Barbara. 2002. "So near yet So Far Away: The Effect of September 11th on Mexican Immigrants in the United States." *Texas Hispanic Journal of Law and Policy* 8: 37–79.

Kauffman, Gretel. 2016. "The New Face of the Sanctuary Movement: College Campuses." in *The Christian Science Monitor.*

Kelly, Mary Louise, and Cecilia Lei. 2018. "The Original Dreamer Recalls All Pervasive' Fear as an Undocumented Child" *All Things Considered.* Washington, DC: NPR. Retrieved August 1, 2018 (www.npr.org/2018/06/20/622002025/the-original-dreamer-recalls-all-pervasive-fear-as-an-undocumented-child).

Kocher, Austin. 2017. "The New Resistance: Immigrant Rights Mobilization in an Era of Trump." *Journal of Latin American Geography* 16(2): 165–71.

Lukinbeal, Chris, and Laura Sharp. 2015. "Performing America's Toughest Sheriff: Media as Practice in Joe Arpaio's Old West." *GeoJournal* 80(6): 881–92.

McAdam, Doug. 1999. *Political Process and the Development of Black Insurgency, 1930–1970.* Chicago, IL: The University of Chicago.

Menjívar, Cecilia. 2006. "Liminal Legality: Salvadoran and Guatemalan Immigrants' Lives in the United States." *American Journal of Sociology* 111(4): 999–1037.

Mohamed, Heather Silber. 2017. *The New Americans? Immigration, Protest, and the Politics of Latino Identity.* Lawrence, KS: University Press of Kansas.

Nature. 2017. "Keep Science on Track." *Nature* 542(7640): 137.

Nicholls, Walter J. 2013. *The Dreamers: How the Undocumented Youth Movement Transformed the Immigrant Rights Debate.* Stanford, CA: Stanford University Press.

Nicholls, Walter J., and Tara Fiorito. 2015. "Dreamers Unbound: Immigrant Youth Mobilizing." *New Labor Forum* 24(1): 86–92.

Obama, Barack. 2017. Statement regarding DACA. September 5, 2017. Facebook.

Passel, Jeffrey S., D'Vera Cohn, Jens Manuel Krogstad, and Ana Gonzalez-Barrera. 2014. "As Growth Stalls, Unauthorized Immigrant Population Becomes More Settled." Vol. *Hispanic Trends Project.* Washington DC: Pew Research Center.

Prieto, Greg. 2018. *Immigrants under Threat: Risk and Resistance in Deportation Nation.* New York: New York University Press.

Redden, Elizabeth. 2017, "Professors Fast to Protest Trump Ban." Washington, DC: *Inside Higher ED.* Retrieved March 5, 2018 (www.insidehighered.com/news/2017/02/07/clemson-professors-fast-pressure-university-take-stand-against-entry-ban).

Romero, Mary. 2011. "Are Your Papers in Order: Racial Profiling, Vigilantes, and America's Toughest Sheriff." *Harvard Latino Law Review* 14: 337.

Schwiertz, Helge. 2016. "Transformations of the Undocumented Youth Movement and Radical Egalitarian Citizenship." *Citizenship Studies* 20(5): 610–28.

Shear, Michael D., and Julie Hirschfeld Davis. 2017. "Trump Moves to End Daca and Calls on Congress to Act." in *The New York Times* 5 September.

Snow, David A., and Robert D. Benford. 1988. "Ideology, Frame Resonance, and Participant Mobilization." *International Social Movement Research* 1: 197–217.

Taylor, Verta, Katrina Kimport, Nella Van Dyke, and Ellen Ann Andersen. 2009. "Culture and Mobilization: Tactical Repertoires, Same-Sex Weddings, and the Impact on Gay Activism." *American Sociological Review* 74(6): 865–90.

Tilly, Charles. 2002. *Stories, Identities, and Political Change*. Lanham, MD: Rowman & Littlefield.

——. 2005. *Identities, Boundaries, and Social Ties*. Boulder, CO: Paradigm Publishers.

United We Dream. 2016, "Our History." Washington, DC: United We Dream. Retrieved November 28, 2016 (https://unitedwedream.org/about/).

Vargas, Jose Antonio. 2011. "My Life as an Undocumented Immigrant." in *The New York Times*. New York 22 June.

Voss, Kim, and Irene Bloemraad. 2011. *Rallying for Immigrant Rights: The Fight for Inclusion in 21st Century America*. Berkeley, CA: University of California Press.

Washington Post-ABC News poll. 2017, "Immigration, DACA, Congress and Compromise. "October 20. Washington, DC: Washington Post. Retrieved April 18, 2018 (www.washingtonpost.com/page/2010-2019/WashingtonPost/2017/09/25/National-Politics/Polling/release_491.xml).

Waugh, Anna. 2013. "Gay, Undocumented and Unashamed." *Dallas Voice*. (www.dallasvoice.com/gay-undocumented-unashamed-10157604.html).

Zatz, Marjorie S., and Nancy Rodriguez. 2015. *Dreams and Nightmares: Immigration Policy, Youth, and Families*. Oakland, CA: University of California Press.

Zimmerman, Arely M. 2011. "A Dream Detained: Undocumented Latino Youth and the Dream Movement." *NACLA Report on the Americas* 44(6): 14–17.

10

CHALLENGING THE 1 PERCENT

The Indignados and Occupy Movements

Ernesto Castañeda[1]

Societies and social movements rarely stay within national borders. Nonetheless, we often engage in "methodological nationalism" (Wimmer and Glick Schiller 2002) when we study events and processes only occurring within the present-day borders of a political unit. The idea of societies mapping perfectly into current day political borders is a pernicious postulate that gets in the way of social science (Tilly 1984). Historically and today, movements are often transnational. Their claims, goals, tactics, and even activists move from place to place without regard to political borders. This chapter looks at the international roots of Occupy Wall Street and how this movement enlarged and spread beyond New York (Halvorsen 2012).

The Indignados

Spain's entrance into the European Union led to a boom in industry, tourism, and real estate particularly in Madrid, northern Spain, Catalonia, as well as Mediterranean beaches and Islands. After years of economic expansion, the economy contracted in 2007 due to a financial crisis. The government bailed out banks and established a set of austerity policies. Spaniards became outraged at the large and sudden cuts to social programs (Berglund 2017: 318; Hayes 2017; Mylonas 2014).

Unions organized a general strike on September 29, 2010, in opposition to proposed changes in labor laws (Peterson, Wahlström and Wennerhag 2015). The strike, related meetings, and marches brought together the activists. New groups such as Democracia Real YA! (Real Democracy Now), Juventud sin Futuro (Youth without a Future), No les Votes (Don't Vote for Them), and La Plataforma de los Afectados por la Hipoteca (Mortgage Victims Group) (Colau and Alemany 2012; de Andrés, Campos, and Zapata

2015; Suarez 2017) called on people across Spain to protest in their main local public squares on May 15, 2011. These "15M" organizers announced a #SpanishRevolution inspired by the then recent events in Tunisia and Egypt (Taibo et al. 2011).

Citizens were quick to blame the national government for their material woes. José Luís Sampedro, an influential figure for the movement, criticized the socialist government for not offering an alternative to the neoliberal policies that he considered "the cause of the economic and social problems facing Spain" (Hughes 2011: 410).

Over 15,000 people marched in Barcelona and Madrid on May 15. In Barcelona, the plan was to march to the Parliament of Catalonia and then to occupy one of the main public squares in the city: Plaza de Catalunya. In Madrid, the plan was simply to march to the large public square known as the Plaza del Sol. However, during the rally, someone called for people to spend the night in the Plaza del Sol (Abellán, Sequera, and Janoschka 2012; Romanos 2016; Taibo et al. 2011). In these and other cities, encampments were erected that night (Cabal 2011: 15). This proposal to camp in a public square resembled the tactic that was used in Tahrir Square in Cairo, Egypt and in previous movements like those against apartheid (Castells 2015).

Participants called this the 15M movement because it started with the contentious performances on the 15th of May. Nevertheless, the media did not take the movement seriously, calling participants *Los Indignados*, the Indignant or Outraged. The term was sometimes used in reference to a pamphlet by Stéphane Hessel, a Nazi concentration camp survivor and anti-Fascist French resistance fighter, who called people to become indignant at ongoing injustices and to become active in social movements (Hessel 2011). Some participants adopted this moniker with pride (Taibo et al. 2011). Others felt that the term was used to frame participants as irrational, emotional, angry, and without any clear demands nor legitimate complaints (Eklundh 2014).

Coverage in international media discussed the claims behind the movement and its complaints about high unemployment, cuts to social services, and corruption. Spanish corporate media dismissed the movement and framed it as dangerous, disruptive, and anti-democratic. It initially described the camp as dirty, insalubrious, and a public nuisance (Castañeda 2012: 313–14). Spanish pundits complained that the occupations were not useful or legal, and they called for the police to "clean the squares" (Sevilla-Buitrago 2015: 95). There were two other criticisms. Contrary to our discussions in previous chapters about the vitality of social movements within democracies, some Spanish pundits went as far as claiming that 15M was anti-democratic because it fell outside of electoral campaigning and/or because it lacked clear demands (Eklundh 2014). Yet, as we will discuss below, participants in the movement elaborated a set of demands, and made democratic processes central and innovated on techniques for assembly participation. Public opinion soon came to support the movement.

Demands Made

It was no coincidence that this social movement campaign started on May 15, just a week before the Spanish national elections on May 22. Amid an economic crisis, people saw no viable alternative between the economic proposals of the left or the right. Having been infected by neoliberal thinking, most large parties, including the then ruling socialist party, proposed more austerity policies. They were pressured by the International Monetary Fund (IMF), the European Union, the European Central Bank, and transnational investors and corporations to impose structural adjustments and budget cuts that would affect people in Spain, all in order for corporations and other large business entities to maintain access to foreign capital.

In 2011, the unemployment rate was 21 percent overall and 43.6 percent for people under the age of 24 (INE 2011). The college-educated population mobilized against an unequal system that failed to offer them jobs (Castañeda 2012: 309–10). Many of the people most active in the movement were young and chose not to vote that year because they were critical about the electoral solutions being offered to problems of unemployment, underemployment, poverty, homelessness, and exploitation of migrant labor. In contrast, as I observed in June 2011, people generated demands and discussed these problems in the makeshift community created in Plaza Cataluña in the heart of Barcelona. Collective debates occurred as participants created demands and proposals. General Assemblies were formed, allowing those present to vote on matters as they worked towards forming a consensus on demands and next steps through further debate and coming to compromises. Participants enacted direct democracy in part as a criticism of indirect, representative democracy. They also spoke against policies that many felt benefitted corporate interests over those of the people (Castañeda 2012:312).

On May 20 and 22, 2011 the movement's General Assembly in Madrid agreed to a list of demands (*cahier de doléances*), including to:

- Enact changes to electoral laws to include proportional representation.
- Provide Spanish constitutional rights such as housing, health, and access to secular public education.
- Abolish the Bologna Process to standardize higher education across the EU.
- Tax international capital transfers.
- Combat tax havens.
- Lower taxes for low-income earners.
- Provide high-quality public services and infrastructure.
- Provide cheap and efficient public transportation.
- Provide universal social services.
- Maintain public financing of scientific research.
- Have greater public control of banks.
- Not carry out surveillance or censorship of online communication.
- Guarantee freedom of information and free press.

- Organize referendums on the implementation of public policies with important implications for the quality of life of citizens, whether coming from the local, national, or European level.
- Reduce military spending.

(Cabal 2011: 10–16)

Subsequent assemblies and committees developed further detailed policy proposals. Therefore, the claim that the 15M had no list of demands is inaccurate.

Outcomes

A joint operation between the Barcelona Police Department (Guàrdia Urbana) and the Catalan Mossos d'Esquadra attempted to vacate the campers on May 27, 2011. The claim was to vacate the camp so that the plaza could be clean for sanitary reasons. The police brought down tents and destroyed private property. They used physical force to remove people sleeping in the plaza and peaceful protesters; 121 people were injured (Carranco 2011). Many onlookers and those following the coverage became angry at these police actions and provocations and started supporting the camp more vocally. Soon after, most of the Spanish public agreed with the demands of 15M; and ever since, most opinion polls show popular agreement with the movement demands (Assiego 2013; Calvo, Gómez-Pastrana, and Mena 2011).

An unlikely and largely unforeseen outcome of the Indignados campaign against established parties was the related formation of new political parties, most notably Podemos (Guedán 2016; Tormey and Feenstra 2015). A new leftist party that grew quickly and won many seats in congress and important posts in local government (Chironi and Fittipaldi 2017; Rodon and Hierro 2016), and reinvigorated electoral participation (Galais 2014). Former 15M participants started running for office. These new parties have won popular support. In 2015, Barcelona and Madrid elected activist women from the left as their Mayors. Progressive Manuela Carmena ran with the Ahora Madrid coalition. Ada Colau, a cofounder of PAH and active in 15M, also ran with a new party Barcelona en Comú—Barcelona in Common—in Catalan.

So while 15M was radically against unions and political parties, people such as Pablo Iglesias—a political science professor who became a spokesman and one of the leaders of Podemos—think that the best way to change institutions is to be within them (Guedán 2016: 28). Even some anarchists and libertarians have opted for electoralism and formed local parties such as Castelló in Movement (Ordóñez, Feenstra, and Franks 2018).

Precedents and Innovations

Where did this outburst of citizen democratic behavior come from? Much emphasis has been put on the role of social media in the 15M (Castells 2015);

> Some of the 15-M's main achievements are precisely its capacity to consolidate through the social media – where mobilisations are organised and disseminated – its ability to produce news in the new media and its effective impact on the mainstream media.
>
> (Casero-Ripollés and Feenstra 2012: 71)

While social media facilitated participation and communication, it did not cause the 15M movement. Research shows that the movement was inspired by previous workers' organizations and social movements such as the organization against evictions, Plataforma de Afectados por la Hipoteca PAH (Flesher Fominaya 2015; Peterson, Wahlström, and Wennerhag 2015), as well as the influence of the neoZapatista movement in Mexico and the Global Justice Movement (Rovira Sancho 2009), along with a culture of public assemblies in Spain (Flesher Fominaya 2015), and local struggles against various forms of inequality and xenophobia.

Activists in Barcelona have been busy since the 1990s organizing in support of the Zapatistas and immigrant rights, against economic globalization and small fascist neo-nazi gangs (Salas 2003). They have been successful in occupying (or squatting) vacant buildings to house students, artists, and poor residents. Likewise, the Indignados occupied public places in ways that linked local housing struggles to global justice mobilizations. Clearly, there were other reasons to occupy public spaces, such as Plaza Catalunya, including becoming visible to the media as well as to other citizens (Castañeda 2012: 313). These contentious performances were borrowed, not only from Tahrir, but also from sit-ins that protested university policies in the 1960s and from the shantytowns against apartheid in South Africa in the 1980s (Andrews and Biggs 2006; Soule 1997, 1999).

Occupy Wall Street

Shortly after the 15M encampments were cleared, activists camped in Zuccotti Park close to Wall Street in New York City's financial district. Launched on September 17, 2011, the camp called itself "Occupy Wall Street" and spawned a movement against inequality that "spread to over 100 cities in the United States and actions in over 1,500 cities globally" (#OWS 2018). In the midst of the global economic crisis, the movement criticized the increasing concentration of wealth and power in 1 percent of the population (Alvaredo et al. 2013; Atkinson, Piketty and Saez 2011; Stiglitz 2003), and the failure of elected politicians to respond.

Like in Spain, mainstream media first dismissed Occupy Wall Street (OWS) as disruptive, unfocussed, and undemocratic. Many pundits argued that these campers did not have a clear set of demands or provide real alternatives. As I have noted elsewhere, this is not only inaccurate, but implies that the claims of an aggrieved group can only be taken seriously if presented in standard formats, alongside recommendations or policy suggestions. This approach also implies that if presented in this standard fashion, political leaders will respond. These models of appropriate forms of political action come from narratives of successful historical social movements, as unified, one-issue movements with a charismatic leader at their helm. Thus, we have reconstructed narratives of Gandhi speaking for Indian independence, of Martin Luther King marching for civil rights, of Cesar Chavez unionizing farm workers, and of Mandela fighting to end apartheid while erasing important allies and rival leaders and tactical approaches around those social movement campaigns. We often retroactively frame what a movement was about—for example, the Civil Rights movement redefined by the Civil Rights Act. The perceived consensus and clarity of demands attributed to many historical social movements is often constructed after the fact (Castañeda 2014: 237). All movements face internal disagreements about goals and strategy (Snow and Soule 2010). At the time, journalists and observers dismissed the wisdom, justness, and legality of those movements. To expect contemporary movements to conform to the formula of a sanitized, stylized version of previous successful social movements is not helpful analytically (Castañeda 2014:237).

As shown above for 15M, Occupy also had clear demands. This criticism from the media may reflect the assumption that social movements are meant to have one main goal proclaimed by a charismatic leader. Critical media coverage of these movements portraying them as pointless, irrational, or unjustified is not unique to the Indignados. Similar criticism was made towards the Occupy movement and its members.

Occupiers came from a wide spectrum of society (Cordero-Guzman 2011). Occupy faced the challenge of engaging, attracting, reflecting, and trying to speak for the 99 percent of society (Ehrenreich 2011; Smith, Castañeda and Heyman 2012; Stoller 2011). OWS posed important questions about income inequality in contemporary America, about campaign finance, and about the limits of electoral democracy (Calhoun 2013; Castells 2015; Gitlin 2012). However, at 1 am on November 15, 2011, two months after it began, New York Mayor, Michael Bloomberg ordered the New York police to raid and evict the occupiers of Zucotti Park. They were not allowed back (Downie 2011).

Diffusion

15M and Occupy illustrate clear cases of what social movement scholars call diffusion, the spread of contentious performances and tactics. The Indignados were influenced by movements in Greece, Iceland, and North Africa (Castells 2015). When visiting the plaza Catalonia in 2011, I witnessed tactics from other countries, including Iceland, Chile, and Argentina. South American activists performed cacerolazos, a method of hitting pots and pans to demonstrate solidarity with fellow organizers (Castañeda 2012: 316–17). As discussed in previous chapters, this is similar to what in previous centuries was called Rough Music.

The sharing of such methods of protest reveals the dissemination of contentious performances within these social movements.

In turn, the 15M served as a model to the Occupy Movement (Romanos 2016). Micah White the activist and Adbusters writer who called for an Occupation of Wall Street, openly cites the Arab Spring and Spain as inspirations (#OWS 2018). Another activist states, "The Occupy Wall Street is the same movement as the Indignados" (Participant and scholar, Amalia Cardenas, personal communication). The OWS movements across the world (England, France, etc.) were influenced by activists' diffusion of information and tactics from various countries. Thus, the Occupy movement was global in its causes, implementation, and planning. Later, it would also influence contention in Gezi park in Turkey (Konak et al. 2015).

While the US media rarely mentions OWS and 15M in the same breath, occupying Zuccotti Park, a plaza close to Wall Street, was a logical conclusion and a strategic choice for the popular movements against austerity and financial speculation. Members of the Indignados movement created manuals and shared their notes from meetings, assemblies, and emails with fellow activists, including the Occupy Wall Street movement organizers (Castañeda 2015: 21). 15M participants set up websites such as "tomalaplaza," documenting the actions of the movement. Similar websites appeared in English, among them "TaketheSquare" and "TaketheSquare-International." These sites posted manuals for activists on how to camp. Volunteers translated these manuals into multiple languages. The manual on "How to Cook a Peaceful Revolution," available in Spanish, English, and many other languages includes a history of 15M until that moment along with recommendations for the everyday logistics of running a camp. News of the camps' actions spread through social media, grassroots and citizen journalism (DeLuca, Lawson, and Sun 2012; Suh, Bogdan, and Chang 2017). Thus, 15M provided a template for others to follow. 15M had multiple displays of Worthiness, Numbers, and Commitment (unity was harder to express when most of the population, part of the 99 percent, remained at the margins), with clear demands, and campaigns against cuts to social programs.

Participatory Democracy

Both M15 and Occupy experimented with different processes that aimed to expand participatory democracy. The occupied squares with their regular general assemblies, speaker-amplified speeches, and conversations, as well as user-generated mass media such as blogs, chatrooms, Facebook, and Twitter allowed for real deliberation among participants. Both mobilizations explicitly rejected a hierarchical static leadership structure. Participants could speak only for themselves and not for the movement as a whole. Decisions were made by consensus in large open assemblies. Committees around particular issues such as logistics, cleaning, political economy, health, and migration crafted communiqués and proposals and that would then be modified and voted by the assemblies. This horizontal organizational structure was purposely designed along the principles of deliberative or participatory democracy.

> Pundits complained about activists not going through sanctioned political channels such as voting or talking to representatives and elected officials directly. These outlooks imply a very limited definition of democracy, where popular voice only has a place during elections or through the legislative processes. This understanding of democracy could be called indirect or representative democracy, where the main role of the citizens is to vote, and then leave political decisions in the hands of those elected to govern. In this view, everyday government should be left in the hands of political parties, professional politicians, and policy experts. In this version of democracy, citizens can only show their discontent by voting parties and politicians in and out of office, through opinion polls, and by the consumption of critical media. In a modified version of this understanding of democracy, elected officials should represent the interests of their electorate, and their election represents an endorsement of their campaign proposals and views.
>
> (Castañeda 2014: 237–38)

This view heralds the mechanisms of representative democracy, in which the citizen votes and avoids the public sphere, as sufficient. In contrast, these movements challenge electoral systems where citizens rely exclusively on representatives to make changes that they want (Castañeda 2014: 237–38).

In part, the emphasis on participation was helped by the use of social media. This participatory impetus allowed diverse issues to be debated and then acted upon (Castañeda 2015: 12). This format:

> can revive the enthusiasm for direct democracy since citizens are quick to identify issues and to assign blame, leading them to believe that if the decision were put back in the hands of the citizens—and their network—they would solve the problem. This reinvigoration of public speech through private and relatively small overlapping networks has resulted in the diffusion of discontent and social movement strategies worldwide. Real-life ties, in-person meetings, marches, camps, and assemblies continue to be fundamental.
>
> (Castañeda 2015: 12)

Some critics have argued that the reason the Indignados or Occupy did not fully succeed in directly changing policy was due to this horizontal structure and lack of identifiable leaders and its reliance on assemblies for decision making. Regardless, the Indignados and the Occupy movements opened the conversation about growing economic inequality and popularized the discussion about the overwhelming concentration of wealth and political influence of the wealthiest 1 percent of the population.

Their demands and behavior are in support of increased democratization. As Charles Tilly (2007), Jacques Rancière (2006), Emmy Eklundh (2014), and others argue, democratizing processes must include groups that were previously excluded from rights and political decision making. Historically, social movements are a path through which the voiceless have demanded and gained recognition through non-electoral or institutional channels. Rights are gained through repeated demands (Somers 1994; Tilly 1992). The process for continuous democratization within nation-states is often slowed down around questions of membership. Representative democracies most often only include legal citizens, thus excluding non-citizens. Processes of exploitation, opportunity hoarding, and categorical inequality determine which individuals and categorical groups do not have recognized rights (Castañeda 2018; Tilly 1998). In Tilly's view of the reduction of categorical inequalities as part of increasing democratization, a fully democratic system would allow any local resident to have equal influence on political decisions, whether they were homeless or foreign-born. 15M and Occupy were partially successful in including people with different immigration and housing statuses as active members of the camps and movements (Smith, Castañeda, and Heyman 2012). In demanding political rights for all city residents, these populist movements extended the political participation of some middle class, poor, immigrant, and homeless individuals. As democratization increases, a challenge is how to incorporate diverse and differently positioned participants, without empowering movements that seek to exclude certain groups; to advance agendas that benefit working class citizens while protecting minority rights and containing homophobic, nationalistic, xenophobic, or eugenic agendas within and outside of social movements (Kaika and Karaliotas 2016).

The Indignados and similar movements challenge the limits of representative democracy and demand further democratization to include the interests of underrepresented groups (Tilly 2007). Indeed, the 15M movement largely resulted from regular citizens' frustrations for not being heard by any political party and being put second to corporate interests. Thus, 15M activists refrained from supporting any political party in the 2011 elections. To explain the movement Juan Carlos Monedero, a key participant, quotes El Roto, a graphic artist working for the Spanish newspaper *El País* who said, "*cuando los jóvenes salieron a la calle los partidos políticos, todos, súbitamente envejecieron*" "the youth took it to the street and suddenly all the political parties aged" (Guedán 2016: 15; Hughes 2011).

Despite the success of the 15M movement in mobilizing people, inspiring youth, and translating to the electoral scene by increasing options at the voting booth, neoliberal economic policies are still the default in Spain. In its multiparty system, the formation of new parties is easier than in the United States, and yet it requires forming governing coalitions. Despite the success of new 15M-inspired left and progressive parties, there had not been a national center-left majority coalition government. In the election of May 22, 2011, the conservative Popular Party (PP) won, and Mariano Rajoy continued to be Prime Minister until June 1, 2018, when he was ousted by Spain's parliament over a corruption scandal in the party. Podemos played a key role in bringing about a no-confidence vote and making Pedro Sánchez, from center-left PSOE, the Prime Minister (Pardo 2018).

Conclusion

Even when studied as discrete national cases, these two social movements campaigns shared at least four elements:

1. National media were initially unwilling to take them seriously;
2. They were incorrectly criticized for having no demands;
3. They enacted direct democracy; and
4. They were simultaneously deeply local and transnational in composition, influence, and in understanding the causes of their discontent originating in international finance and existing economic arrangements.

The Indignados and Occupy Movement meet several of the criteria for being Social Movements. The Indignados began with union organizing and large-scale marches throughout the country. The group formulated clear goals that were established through public deliberation, calling on the government to make structural changes to avoid disasters like the 2008 economic recession. As discussed, the 15M movement also went beyond local demands and called attention to issues on the global level. All of this action was done through various WUNC displays. The formation of groups such as Democracia Real YA! and the mobilization of over 15,000 people for marches in public squares illustrates the 15M movement's self-representation. Also, the Indignados greatly influenced the Occupy Wall Street movement in the United States, showing how the movement in Spain disseminated on a global level. Also, Carmena and Colau's successful mayoral campaigns give hope to 15M members that their demands will not be forgotten.

Activist Micah White argues that "protest is broken" because Occupy Wall Street failed at revolution—a change in legal regime—or to achieve power (White 2016). Yet, was Occupy a social movement or a global month-long contentious performance or PR campaign? For some astute analysts, OWS was more a "moment" than a real "movement" (Calhoun 2013; Gitlin 2012). The Occupy Wall Street protesters used handbooks made by 15M members and also decided to occupy public spaces, symbolically choosing ones located in Wall Street, Manhattan, the crux of financial growth. Despite the large gathering of people in Zuccotti Park, the Occupy Movement did not maintain its momentum in the following years. Yet, the Occupy Movement also met many of the Social Movement criteria; the group's demand to reduce the out of proportion concentration of wealth, political influence, and power held by the 1 percent was clearly made and articulated to the public and became a household phrase. Despite a polyphony of voices and agendas, clear demands were made, but the absence of sustained momentum makes the Occupy Movement seem less transformative than the Indignados Movement. The Indignados were successful in the creation of 15M movement, and in disseminating their methods of organizing to the Occupy Movement, as well as changing the electoral landscape in Spain and citizen expectations about the real representation of their interests and concerns. Another way to look at this could be to understand the Indignados in Spain and elsewhere, as well as Occupy

Wall Street and global encampments as contentious performances that are part of a larger "Anti-globalization" Movement, a Global Social Movement against the effects of neoliberalism—a movement that preceded these camps and that continues since the camps were evacuated (see Chapter 5).

Note

1 Jennifer Linsenmeyer and Maura Fennelly helped with research and editing.

References

#OWS. 2018, "About": Occupy Wall Street. Retrieved June 4, 2018 (http://occupywallst.org/about/).

Abellán, Jacobo, Jorge Sequera, and Michael Janoschka. 2012. "Occupying the #Hotelmadrid: A Laboratory for Urban Resistance." *Social Movement Studies* 11(3–4): 320–26.

Alvaredo, Facundo, Anthony B. Atkinson, Thomas Piketty, and Emmanuel Saez. 2013. "The Top 1 Percent in International and Historical Perspective." *Journal of Economic perspectives* 27(3): 3–20.

Andrews, Kenneth T., and Michael Biggs. 2006. "The Dynamics of Protest Diffusion: Movement Organizations, Social Networks, and News Media in the 1960 Sit-Ins." *American Sociological Review* 71(5): 752–77.

Assiego, Violeta. 2013. "La Voz Ciudadana." in *El Pais*. Madrid.

Atkinson, Anthony B., Thomas Piketty, and Emmanuel Saez. 2011. "Top Incomes in the Long Run of History." *Journal of Economic Literature* 49(1): 3–71.

Berglund, Oscar. 2017. "Contesting Actually Existing Austerity." *New Political Economy*: 1–15.

Cabal, Fernando. 2011. *Indignados: Toma La Calle 15.05.11*. Madrid: Mandala Ediciones.

Calhoun, Craig. 2013. "Occupy Wall Street in Perspective." *The British Journal of Sociology* 64(1): 26–38.

Calvo, Kerman, Teresa Gómez-Pastrana and Luis Mena. 2011. "Movimiento 15m: ¿Quiénes Son Y Qué Reivindican?" Vol. 4. *ZoomPolitico*. Madrid: Fundacion Alternativas.

Carranco, Rebeca. 2011. "La Carga Policial Desata La Indignación En Barcelona." in *El País*. Madrid: El País.

Casero-Ripollés, Andreu, and Ramón A. Feenstra. 2012. "The 15-M Movement and the New Media: A Case Study of How New Themes Were Introduced into Spanish Political Discourse." *Media International Australia* 144(1): 68–76.

Castañeda, Ernesto. 2012. "The Indignados of Spain: A Precedent to Occupy Wall Street." *Social Movement Studies* 11(3–4): 309–19.

——. 2014. "The Indignados and Occupy Movements as Political Challenges to Representative Democracy: A Reply to Eklundh." *Global Discourse*: 1–8.

——. 2015. "The Indignados and the Global Diffusion of Forms of Protest against Authoritarianism and Structural Adjustment Programs." Pp. 11–28 in *Waves of Social Movement Mobilizations in the Twenty-First Century: Challenges to the Neo-Liberal World Order and Democracy*, edited by N. Konak and R. Dönmez. Lanham, MD: Lexington Books.

——. 2018. *Immigration and Categorical Inequality: Migration to the City and the Birth of Race and Ethnicity*. New York: Routledge.

Castells, Manuel. 2015. *Networks of Outrage and Hope: Social Movements in the Internet Age*. Cambridge, UK: Polity Press.

Chironi, Daniela, and Raffaella Fittipaldi. 2017. "Social Movements and New Forms of Political Organization: Podemos as a Hybrid Party." *Partecipazione e Conflitto* 10(1): 275–305.

Colau, Ada, and Adrià Alemany. 2012. *Vidas Hipotecadas*. Barcelona: Lectio.

Cordero-Guzman, Hector R. 2011. "Main Stream Support for a Mainstream Movement: The 99% Movement Comes from and Looks Like the 99." Retrieved (occupywallst.org/media/pdf/OWS-profile1-10-18-11-sent-v2-HRCG. pdf).

de Andrés, Eva Álvarez, María José Zapata Campos, and Patrik Zapata. 2015. "Stop the Evictions! The Diffusion of Networked Social Movements and the Emergence of a Hybrid Space: The Case of the Spanish Mortgage Victims Group." *Habitat International* 46: 252–59.

DeLuca, Kevin M., Sean Lawson, and Ye Sun. 2012. "Occupy Wall Street on the Public Screens of Social Media: The Many Framings of the Birth of a Protest Movement." *Communication, Culture & Critique* 5(4): 483–509.

Downie, James. 2011. "Bloomberg's Disgraceful Eviction of Occupy Wall Street." in *The Washington Post*. Washington, DC.

Ehrenreich, Barbara. 2011, "Throw Them out with the Trash: Why Homelessness Is Becoming an Occupy Wall Street Issue." *TomDispatch.com*. Retrieved May 2, 2012 (www.tomdispatch.com/archive/175457/barbara_ehrenreich_homeless_in_america).

Eklundh, Emmy. 2014. "Who Is Speaking? The Indignados as Political Subjects." *Global Discourse* 4(2–3): 223–35.

Flesher Fominaya, Cristina. 2015. "Debunking Spontaneity: Spain's 15-M/Indignados as Autonomous Movement." *Social Movement Studies* 14(2):142–63.

Galais, Carol. 2014. "Don't Vote for Them: The Effects of the Spanish Indignant Movement on Attitudes About Voting." *Journal of Elections, Public Opinion and Parties* 24(3): 334–50.

Gitlin, Todd. 2012. *Occupy Nation: The Roots, the Spirit, and the Promise of Occupy Wall Street*. New York: itbooks.

Guedán, Manuel. 2016. *Podemos: Una Historia Colectiva*. Madrid: Akal.

Halvorsen, Sam. 2012. "Beyond the Network? Occupy London and the Global Movement." *Social Movement Studies* 11(3–4): 427–33.

Hayes, Graeme. 2017. "Regimes of Austerity." *Social Movement Studies* 16(1): 21–35.

Hessel, Stéphane. 2011. *Time for Outrage!* New York: Twelve.

Hughes, Neil. 2011. "'Young People Took to the Streets and All of a Sudden All of the Political Parties Got Old': The 15m Movement in Spain." *Social Movement Studies* 10(4): 407–13.

INE. 2011. *Encuesta De Población Activa Primer Trimestre De 2011*. Vol. Madrid, España: Instituto Nacional de Estadística Español.

Kaika, Maria, and Lazaros Karaliotas. 2016. "The Spatialization of Democratic Politics: Insights from Indignant Squares." *European Urban and Regional Studies* 23(4): 556–70.

Konak, Nahide, Rasim Özgür Dönmez, Ernesto Castaneda, Luis Ruben Díaz Cepeda, Gökçe Bayindir Goularas, Sam Halvorsen, Walter J. Nicholls, Mark Purcell, Helga Rittersberger-Tılıç, Beyza Ç. Tekin, and Rifat B. Tekin. 2015. *Waves of Social*

Movement Mobilizations in the Twenty-First Century: Challenges to the Neo-Liberal World Order and Democracy. Lanham, MD: Lexington Books.

Mylonas, Harris. 2014. "Democratic Politics in Times of Austerity: The Limits of Forced Reform in Greece." *Perspectives on Politics* 12(2): 435–43.

Ordóñez, Vicente, Ramón A. Feenstra, and Benjamin Franks. 2018. "Spanish Anarchist Engagements in Electoralism: From Street to Party Politics." *Social Movement Studies* 17(1): 85–98.

Pardo, Iñaki. 2018. "El Papel Clave De Podemos En El Desalojo De Rajoy." in *La Vanguardia*. Barcelona, España.

Peterson, Abby, Mattias Wahlström, and Magnus Wennerhag. 2015. "European Anti-Austerity Protests: Beyond "Old" and "New" Social Movements?". *Acta Sociologica* 58(4): 293–310.

Rancière, Jacques. 2006. *Hatred of Democracy*. London: Verso.

Rodon, Toni, and María José Hierro. 2016. "Podemos and Ciudadanos Shake up the Spanish Party System: The 2015 Local and Regional Elections." *South European Society and Politics* 21(3): 339–57.

Romanos, Eduardo. 2016. "Immigrants as Brokers: Dialogical Diffusion from Spanish Indignados to Occupy Wall Street." *Social Movement Studies* 15(3): 247–62.

Rovira Sancho, Guiomar. 2009. *Zapatistas Sin Fronteras: Las Redes De Solidaridad Con Chiapas Y El Altermundismo*. México, D.F.: Ediciones Era.

Salas, Antonio. 2003. *Diario De Un Skin: Un Topo En El Movimiento Neonazi Español*. Madrid: Ediciones Temas de Hoy.

Sevilla-Buitrago, Álvaro. 2015. "Outraged Spatialities: The Production of Public Space in the #Spanishrevolution." *ACME: An International E-Journal for Critical Geographies* 14(1): 90–103.

Smith, Curtis, Ernesto Castañeda, and Josiah Heyman. 2012. "The Homeless and Occupy El Paso: Creating Community among the 99%." *Social Movement Studies* 11(3–4): 356–66.

Snow, David A., and Sarah Anne Soule. 2010. *A Primer on Social Movements*. New York: W. W. Norton.

Somers, Margaret R. 1994. "Rights, Relationality, and Membership: Rethinking the Making and Meaning of Citizenship." *Law & Social Inquiry* 19(1): 63–114.

Soule, Sarah A. 1997. "The Student Divestment Movement in the United States and Tactical Diffusion: The Shantytown Protest." *Social Forces* 75(3): 855–82.

——. 1999. "The Diffusion of an Unsuccessful Innovation." *The ANNALS of the American Academy of Political and Social Science* 566(1): 120–31.

Stiglitz, Joseph E. 2003. *The Roaring Nineties: A New History of the World's Most Prosperous Decade*. New York: W. W. Norton & Co.

Stoller, Matthew. 2011, "The Anti-Politics of #Occupywallstreet": Naked Capitalism Blog, Aurora Advisors Incorporated. Retrieved 3/30/2012 (www.nakedcapitalism.com/2011/10/matt-stoller-the-anti-politics-of-occupywallstreet.html).

Suarez, Maka. 2017. "Debt Revolts: Ecuadorian Foreclosed Families at the Pah in Barcelona." *Dialectical Anthropology* 41(3): 263–77.

Suh, Chan S., Vasi Ion Bogdan, and Paul Y. Chang. 2017. "How Social Media Matter: Repression and the Diffusion of the Occupy Wall Street Movement." *Social Science Research* 65: 282–93.

Taibo, Carlos, Josep Maria Antentas, Esther Vivas, Juan Pablo Mateo, Antoni Domènech, Iván Giménez Chueca, and Juan Carlos Monedero. 2011. *La Rebelión De Los Indignados*. Madrid: Editorial Popular.

Tilly, Charles. 1984. *Big Structures, Large Processes, Huge Comparisons*. New York: Russell Sage Foundation (http://deepblue.lib.umich.edu/bitstream/2027.42/51064/1/295.pdf).
——. 1992. "Where Do Rights Come From?" in *Contributions to the Comparative Study of Development*, edited by L. Mjøset. Oslo, Norway: Institute for Social Research.
——. 1998. *Durable Inequality*. Berkeley, CA: University of California Press.
——. 2007. *Democracy*. Cambridge, UK: Cambridge University Press.
Tormey, Simon. and Ramón A. Feenstra. 2015. "Reinventing the Political Party in Spain: The Case of 15m and the Spanish Mobilisations." *Policy Studies* 36(6): 590–606.
White, Micah. 2016. *The End of Protest: A New Playbook for Revolution*. Canada: Alfred A. Knopf Canada.
Wimmer, Andreas, and Nina Glick Schiller. 2002. "Methodological Nationalism and Beyond: Nation State Building, Migration and the Social Sciences." *Global Networks: A Journal of Transnational Affairs* 2(4): 301–34.

11

THE MOVEMENT FOR CATALAN INDEPENDENCE

Ernesto Castañeda and Sebastian Megens-Sedor[1]

Starting from the establishment of the Spanish March in 795 up through the present day, this chapter looks at waves of mobilization for Catalan Independence through a historical lens. The 2017 vote on independence in Catalonia did not happen randomly; rather, it is the result of hundreds of years of cultural resistance and demands for an independent state. The political transformations, legislation, and public responses to the Spanish state will be discussed. Catalonian citizenry's support for independence and their commitment to making such demands has persisted for hundreds of years. Despite the opposition from the successive Spanish governments and from the Constitutional Tribunal from making this demand a reality, the Catalan call for independence remains a social movement.

One of the critiques of representative democracy made within the autonomous regions of Spain, such as Catalonia, during the 15M anti-austerity movements that began on May 15, 2011 (see the previous chapter) was the physical and moral distance between the people and politicians in Madrid. The continued effects of the economic crisis and the policies of both the Socialist Party (Partido Socialista Español PSOE) and then the conservative People's Party (Partido Popular PP), which is a major conservative political party within Spain, along with cases of corruption did not help to silence this critique. Another idea advanced by the 15M movement was the return of political and fiscal authority to local and subnational governments. These critiques of Madrid politicians has, in turn, been useful for the independence movements in Catalonia (Castan Pinos 2018; García 2016), and fueled referendums on Catalan independence. A large proportion of those who participated and sympathized with the 15M anti-austerity movement were in opposition to nationalism, which they saw as regressive, divisive, and dangerous; and thus, opposed Catalan independence. Nevertheless, the 15M or indignados movement had the unintended consequence of strengthening the Catalan mobilization for independence because it strengthened grassroots movements, increased social capital, and further legitimated calls for local governance.

In 2012, shortly after the 15M protests, there were massive protests held in support of Catalan independence, with estimates ranging from 600,000 to 1.5 million participants (García Barcia 2013: 399). In 2015, a coalition of pro-independence parties held a majority of the Catalan Parliament seats, despite having gained less than 50 percent of the popular vote. After this, the pro-independence wing of the Catalan Parliament moved towards an aggressive pro-independence agenda. Many residents of Catalonia saw this as a violation of their political will (Coscubiela 2017). Large Catalan cities, such as Barcelona, are global cosmopolitan cities with important percentages of the population originating from internal and international migration. The large number of newcomers has not threatened Catalan culture since public education is now provided in Catalan. Furthermore, many multi-generation Catalans are ambivalent. As a Catalan woman active since the fights against Francoism tells us,

> Many of us do not fit neatly, in the categories (often discussed in the media Spanish vs. Catalan nationalists) given the complexity of the topic. I do not feel Spanish, it is very hard if you were born in the midst of a Catalan family, from which you suckle a Catalan identity. Nonetheless, I feel a considerable rejection of nationalism in general, and even more to the Catalan nationalism that I have witnessed closely. . . . what I think is most questionable is the argument about an oppressed minority given that Catalans are hegemonic in Catalonia in terms of economic, political, and cultural power. Catalonia is also one of the wealthiest regions of Spain. Thus, things are more complicated . . . There is consensus, even amongst pro-independence parties, that they don´t have more than 47–48 percent support. This is key to understand the problem. The problem is not only between Catalonia vs Spain, the main issue is between Catalans themselves. Independentists by and large are part of the Catalan bourgeoisie and they hold the hegemony of symbols and the narrative. However, around 50 percent of Catalans do not support the movement.
>
> (Personal communication August 2018)

Despite it not being the priority for most people living in Catalonia, a referendum for Catalan independence was held on October 1, 2017, and the Spanish government attempted to stop it, calling it a "constitutional and democratic atrocity" (Jones 2017). The referendum went forward anyway, with 43 percent of the eligible voters participating. Anti-secessionist residents within Catalonia boycotted the referendum, and the national police used violence to deter some independentists from voting (Ordaz 2017). Among voters, the vote to secede won by a large margin. On October 27, 2017, the Catalan Parliament voted to move forward with independence through the "*llei de desconexió*," which was approved by 72 MPs out of 135, even though the Catalan Estatut (statute of autonomy, which is equivalent to the Catalan constitution) establishes that 90 votes—two thirds of the parliament—are required to approve any law that changes the terms in which Catalonia is run. Soon after, Catalan President,

Carles Puigdemont, declared independence for the region of Catalonia, building on centuries of mobilization by Catalan separatists (BBC 2017a).

When independence was declared on October 27, 2017, pro-independence crowds cheered and waved flags, including the Catalan separatist "Estelada" flag outside of the Catalan Parliament in Barcelona. Spanish Prime Minister Mariano Rajoy swiftly dissolved the Catalonia government, claiming that it was necessary to restore legality and to defend the nation, democracy, and the constitution (BBC 2017b). Spanish police arrested pro-independence officials in Barcelona. Crowds gathered in Plaça de Sant Jaume, the downtown square where the Generalitat and City Hall are located to decry these police detentions. Puigdemont and four of his ministers escaped to Belgium to avoid arrest. Puigdemont was later held in German custody. The government of Rajoy continued to request the extradition of Puigdemont and the other officials in order to try them in a Spanish court.

Prime Minister Rajoy called for new elections in Catalonia on December 21, 2017, to allow all Catalan residents to weigh in the issue of independence through party platforms. Although Ciutadans (Citizens), a pro-Spain party, won the most seats (37), pro-independence parties when grouped together, won the majority of the congressional seats (70) (Dewan 2017). The electoral law privileges rural areas like Girona and Lleida where most of the pro-independence vote comes from, over the more populated urban areas. These current events are just another episode in a long history of unsuccessful attempts at Catalan independence (Keating 1996; Sobrequés 2010).

From the outside, some people compare the declaration of independence with Brexit, while many others sympathize with the call for Catalan sovereignty. In a world history written by the victors of many national revolutions, the call for independence of a colonized people is still full of romanticism. But this view flattens the historical complexities such as the fact that many locals opposed political independence, that many common people failed to benefit from its promises, and that local elites often used independence to keep control (Bouton 2009; Tilly 1964). Many analysts point out that Catalan politicians and elites used the call for independence to divert attention from the revelation of large and ongoing corruption from Catalan leaders such as Jordi Pujol and others within his party, the Democratic Convergence of Catalonia (CDC) (Jones 2018a).

The Formation of the Catalan Identity

Let's look at the history of the region to understand the formation of this regional identity. In 795, Charlemagne established the *Marca Hispana*, also known as the Barcelona March, as a buffer zone between Franks and Moors (Griffith 2017; Sahlins 1989). Since the eleventh century CE, the County of Barcelona was part of the Crown of Aragon. The contested marriage between Fernando of Aragon and Isabel of Castile in 1469 resulted in the union of the Kingdoms of Castile and Aragón around the banner of Catholicism (García de Cortázar 2007). The merging of Castile and Aragon occurred after a failed war with Portugal and France, and only after Isabel had secured her contested claim to the throne. To legitimize their mandate over Castile and Aragon, the so-called Catholic Monarchs set into nation-building and expansion, resulting in the subjugation of the neighboring Christian Kingdom of Navarra in 1512, and the annexation of the Canary Islands as part of an agreement with Portugal (Castañeda 2018a: 85–86). Aragon later controlled a large European and Mediterranean empire. As part of Aragon, Barcelona and its hinterlands benefited from these military incursions and the resulting additional tributes.

Castile and Aragon formed a political union, but they kept much of their administrative independence. It was common to refer to Las Españas in plural at that time. Castile grew exceptionally through its access to the American colonies, while Aragon had little access to the Americans and it lost its colonies within Europe and around the Mediterranean. Thus, Castile and Madrid in particular became the dominant military and economic powerhouses in the peninsula (Sobrequés 2010).

A key event in Catalan history is the Reapers rebellion, a secessionist uprising of peasants (wheat reapers or *segadores*) against the Spanish crown, lasting from 1640 to 1652. Before the conflict, Castile was in war with France and it had been increasing taxes and quartering Castilian troops within peasants' houses (Guibernau 2012: 30). However, Catalonia favored France over Castile. The war required many men from Catalonia to fight against France, the locals did not support this cause, and they turned their anger towards Castile. A hymn developed during the Reapers war, *Els Segadors*, which was sung by the rebels, depicted the ongoing struggle between local peasants and imperial elites:

> Catalonia triumphant shall again be rich and bountiful. Drive away these people, who are so conceited and so arrogant. Now is the time, reapers. Now is the time to stand alert. For when another June comes, let us Sharpen our tools well. May the enemy tremble, upon seeing our symbol. Just as we cut golden ears of wheat, when the time calls we cut off chains.
>
> (The Reapers, Corcoran 2017)

The lyrics contain the notion that getting rid of people at the top would result in a stronger and wealthier Catalonia. As Spain was taxing Catalonia heavily, in addition to quartering troops and extracting additional men and resources for the war effort, it makes sense to believe that ridding the region of Spaniards would be beneficial to their circumstances. This tune was eventually incorporated as the Catalan nationalists' anthem. As scholar Daniel Hummel (2017) argues, the national anthem of any nation is meant to unify a diverse group of people, and to invoke emotions towards a specific national narrative. Thus, the establishment of this national anthem was an institutional calculation to help establish the Catalan identity. As such, the Reapers war and its hymn are an important part of the narrative of Catalan nationalism to this day (Corcoran 2017).

The next major milestone in Catalan nationalism was the Revolt of the Barretinas, which saw civil unrest from 1687 to 1689. The revolt emerged along rising nationalistic tensions, in addition to, once again, the quartering of soldiers and increased taxes upon Catalan citizens. As Spain was preparing for another war with France, they sent 2,400 soldiers to Catalonia, but as the Catalan forts were in ruins from the previous wars, Catalans were forced to quarter the soldiers in their homes. In addition to this, Catalans were forced to pay an additional military contribution tax to Spain. While all of this was occurring, Catalonia was enduring low food supplies, as natural disasters and crop destruction had occurred in the years prior (Davies 2011). This all culminated in Catalans protesting on city streets and in rural areas, and although many of the Barcelonan elites were not sympathetic to the cause, wealthy commoners were.

Many individuals partaking in the revolt refused to pay taxes, as they no longer supported the state of which they were considered a part. This led to 800 reapers marching on the small city of Puigcerda, with the message that no one should work, unless they were to receive a minimum wage of 4 *reales* (Kamen 1977: 219). This uprising inspired others to march and protest in other towns throughout the region (Dantí I Riu 1979: 90–94). People of Catalonia rallied together in recognizable and modular public protests in opposition to the Spanish crown's imposition of higher taxes and the quartering of troops. On April 6, 1688, a Catalonian militia marched on Mataro, a strategic port town, and rallied the population into a frenzy by ringing the church bells and crying out "Long live the land!" (Kamen 1977: 215–16). The people of Mataro were compelled to join the uprising, and the militia grew to 18,000 people. At this point, they marched onto Barcelona with demands for a reduced military contribution and the pardon and release of imprisoned members of the revolt. As the administration within Barcelona was aware that the city could fall at any moment, they gave in to the demands. The contingent was large enough for the administration to take their claims seriously.

On June 13, 1688, the populace took over the city of Manresa due to a disagreement on the payments of tithes. On June 14, 1688, rioters stormed an armory and armed all adult males, in an attempt to gain an edge on the city (Kamen 1977: 219). To appease the ongoing uprisings, the Viceroy of Catalonia put forth a donation to pay for some of those tithes.

It was not until the War of the Spanish Succession (1701–1714), which pitted Archduke Charles of Austria against Philip V of Spain in a contest for the Spanish crown, that Catalans witnessed another significant nationalistic movement. In 1705, still in the early years of the war, Archduke Charles Habsburg strategically captured Barcelona. Though the Treaty of Utrecht was signed, Catalonia continued their war efforts against the Franco-Spanish forces between April and July of 1713, in an effort to defend the Catalan constitution, which was implemented by the *Corts Catalanes* (Parliament). They held the force of law, and the King was not able to revoke the laws established by them (Dandelet 2003). This was in tune with Catalan nationalism, as they wished to retain their laws and culture, instead of being assimilated into the greater

Spanish state. Regardless, by 1714, outside forces recaptured Barcelona, the capital of Catalonia, and King Felipe V put forth the Nueva Planta decrees, which suppressed the institutions and privileges formed by the charters. He shut down Catalan universities and banned the use of the Catalan language in any formal administrative use. The issue of this decree forged various regions of Spain into a new, centrally governed Spanish state. Furthermore, one can see that the legislation put forth was an attempt to assimilate Catalans into Castillian culture, which resulted in a backlash and the resurgence of Catalan cultural and linguistic pride (Laitin 1989).

The capture of Barcelona by the Franco-Spanish forces on September 11, 1714, marked the end of the Principality of Catalonia as a political entity. The fall of Barcelona brought down its independently established judicial and legislative institutions. In recent years, September 11 is commemorated as the *diada*, the National Day of Catalonia; e.g., when FC Barcelona (the Barcelonan football club which is linked to Catalan Nationalism) plays against Real Madrid, Catalans typically come out in masses to support their team and wave the Estelada flag. Reminiscing on the loss of their autonomy in 1714; many Catalans shout "Independencia, Independencia" at 17 minutes and 14 seconds into the match (Chopra 2013). This contentious performance is a form of nation-building, as it creates unity around a national narrative.

Despite the ongoing internal and external struggles, the Catalan language and culture have experienced multiple *renaixenças* or rebirths. A *renaixença* occurred in the wake of European Romanticism, and it aimed to recover Catalan culture, literature, and language. After the Glorious Revolution of 1868, and amid the collapse of the First Spanish Republic, the renaixença obtained a political characteristic, and it became a movement for self-governance within Catalonia.

When Spain lost some of its remaining colonies of Cuba and the Philippines in 1898, there was a drastic increase in the number of individuals in favor of Catalan nationalism. Many made the argument that Catalonia was as much a colony as Cuba and also deserved international support for independence. In the following years, we see the founding of the first modern political parties within Catalonia.

In 1922, Francesc Marcià founded the political party Estat Catala, or Catalan State. The political party was pro-independence, and it used the Estelada as its symbol, officially making it the separatist flag of Catalonia. In 1932, during the Spanish Second Republic, Catalonia regained much of its autonomy. However, by 1939, it had already been taken back by Francisco Franco's nationalists. In the early 1960s, institutions, such as the Omnium Cultural, were created to promote the Catalan language and culture to combat the attempted destruction of Catalan culture during Franco's regime.

Following the death of Franco in 1975, Spain moved to restore democracy. Catalans began to recover many of their rights, and restore their cultural practices, and the center-right Catalan party, Convergence, was founded. By 1978, a new Spanish constitution acknowledged the right to Catalan autonomy, and to the autonomy of numerous other regions within Spain as well. However, many

Catalan nationalists objected to this, as the concept of Spain granting Catalonia some autonomy is incompatible with the idea of Catalan self-determination (Calamur 2017). Regardless, 88 percent of the Spanish citizenry, with 90 percent of Catalonians, voted in favor of the constitution. In 1979, the following year, the Statute of Autonomy of Catalonia was created, and it was approved by 88 percent of voters. In the wake of Catalan autonomy, many pro-independence political groups faded out, which created room for the far-left armed Catalan nationalist group, *Terra Lliure*, to launch attacks against Spain. Though the attacks were rare and their membership was small, *Terra Lliure* and similar groups caused chaos across Spain (Minder 2017).

From 1980 to 2003, Jordi Pujol, the founder of the Convergence Catalan party, won numerous elections based on a platform of moderate Catalan nationalism. With his moderate stance, he forged a strong relationship with Madrid, and negotiated increased autonomy for Catalonia. However, in return for increased autonomy, Pujol pledged allegiance to Spain and its constitution (Minder 2017). Though Pujol obtained greater autonomy for Catalonia, he never sought independence, which is mostly what angered separatists.

In 2005, the draft of a new statute of Autonomy for Catalonia gave the Generalitat of Catalonia the powers of self-governance and granted the Generalitat jurisdiction in numerous matters: health, education, the environment, culture and local governance. In 2006, the Spanish and Catalonian parliaments approved the new statute of autonomy, which was put forth for a referendum, and approved by 73.24 percent of the voters. It came into effect on August 9, 2006. However, there was a wave of opposition against the statute, and it was challenged in the Spanish Constitutional Court. In 2009 to 2011, non-binding independence referendums were held across Catalonia, with 94.89 percent of voters in favor of independence, because mainly only those in favor of independence participated in the referendums. On June 28, 2010, progressive and conservative judges reached a compromise and declared that portions of 14 of the 277 articles of the statute were unconstitutional, and that 27 required further interpretation (BBC 2017a).

After the court verdict was announced, Omnium Cultural and over 1,600 other organizations orchestrated a march on July 10, 2010, in order to denounce the decision. An estimated 1.1 to 1.5 million people flooded the streets (AFP 2010). At the time, it was one of the largest protests in Catalan history.

This protest triggered numerous other marches in the following years. As mentioned before, a particularly large Catalan independence demonstration occurred in Barcelona on September 11, 2012. It was organized by the Catalan National Assembly, another pro-Catalan independence cultural organization. With more than two million people in attendance, it is the largest march to have ever been held within Catalonia, except for the celebration of the restoration of democracy in Spain. Participants in the march were sporting the Estelada, as well as signs reading "Catalonia: A New EU State." At the end of the protest, Omnium Cultural put together a concert with Catalan bands and artists (Burgen 2012). Moreover, there were a series of public events promoting a Catalan independence.

The first Catalan Way event, on September 11, 2013, included a 250-mile-long human chain in support for Catalan independence. The Assemblea Nacional Catalana organized the contentious performance, and around 1.6 million people participated in the protest. To many, the chain has become a symbol of the unity of the Catalan people in attempting to achieve national sovereignty (BBC 2013). In 2014, the National Day of Catalonia had over 900,000 participants (Catalan National Assembly 2014). The same year, Catalan held a self-determination referendum, which showed that 80.76 percent of participants were in favor of an independent Catalan state, although overall participation was low and mainly those in favor showed up to vote (BBC 2014). On the 2015 diada, Omnium Cultural and Assemblea Nacional Catalana again held an event called the Free Way to the Catalan Republic, with an estimated 1.4 million people in attendance (RT 2015). A similar event, dubbed Go Ahead, Catalan Republic, was held on September 11, 2016 (Prim 2016). It was planned in the wake of pro-independent parties winning a majority in the Parliament of Catalonia, as some separatists hoped Catalonia would achieve independence by the end of 2017.

As noted earlier, the Catalan Parliament passed a measure on September 6, 2017, to hold an independence referendum. On September 7, the Spanish Court declared it unconstitutional (Calamur 2017). Regardless, on October 1, 2017, a referendum was held throughout Catalonia, asking participants if they were in favor of Catalonia becoming an independent state in the form of a republic. National Spanish police stormed polling stations and dragged away voters and many peaceful citizens trying to participate in the plebiscite were injured (Minder 2017). However, that did not stop the vote; over 92 percent of those that partook in the poll voted yes (Russell, Slawson, and Greenfield 2017). Madrid continued to threaten Catalonia, and stated that if Catalonia indeed declared independence, the Spanish government would do everything in its power to regain unity and punish the separatists. After the independence referendum, on October 27, 2017, the Catalan Parliament voted to create a sovereign Catalan Republic. Hours later, the Spanish prime minister announced that Catalonia would be stripped of its autonomy, effectively suspending the Catalan independence movement in its tracks (BBC 2017b).

After the dissolution of the Catalan government, numerous Catalan government officials, as well as the heads of the Catalan cultural institutions Omnium Cultural and the Catalan National Assembly, were jailed (Jones 2017b). Carles Puigdemont was put in custody in Germany, and in response to his arrest, there were massive street protests throughout Catalonia. Yellow ribbons were on display throughout Barcelona in solidarity with the political prisoners. Yet many argue that they were jailed because of their acts, not because their ideas.

The Catalan people were very much in opposition to the imprisonment without charges of their political and cultural figures. They believed that the Spanish government is increasingly oppressive and infringing their democratic rights, due to acts of brutality upon innocent Catalan people, policies leading to the loss of autonomy, and the re-introduction of political imprisonments to

Spain. Rajoy often stated that he was willing to use any measure necessary to preserve the unity of the Spanish state.

On May 11, 2018, Carles Puigdemont named Quim Torra as the candidate to be his successor as President of Catalonia, as Puigdemont was not able to govern effectively from exile. Torra is strongly pro-independence. In the past, Torra made xenophobic remarks against Spanish speakers in Catalonia (Jones 2018b). He is in favor of restoring laws that were suspended by the Spanish courts, and of drafting a constitution for a future Catalan Republic, both of which are popular stances within Catalonia. Yet, Torra won the election on May 14, 2018 and named several jailed political officials as members of his cabinet.

Using article 155 of the Spanish Constitution, the government in Madrid used the national police to scare individuals, and to revoke Catalonia's autonomy, depose government leaders, and take over the Catalonian government. Although more Catalans wish to gain independence, Spain can enforce its territorial integrity, making complete independence unlikely soon. Instead of independence, another alternative could be to establish new relationships with Madrid. This would lead to the reinstitution of autonomy, which would allow Catalonia to maintain its cultural and linguistic identity. The fall of Rajoy amid scandals on June 1, 2018, opened the door for dialogue and agreements between Madrid and Catalonia.

Within a Tillyian framework (Castañeda and Schneider 2017), the Catalan movement for independence could be seen as the result of an unsuccessful nation-building project by Spain in relation to Catalonia, and a series of unsuccessful military attempts at independence on the part of Catalans. A political arrangement had allowed cohabitation for a while, but recent polarization has activated social boundaries and national identities (Castañeda 2018b, Tilly 2005).

The claims for independence are further complicated by a less vocal but equally large number of Catalan residents, particularly in the large cities, who want to remain in Spain (Castañeda 2018a). This group includes internal and international immigrants, tourists, expats, cosmopolitans, and global entrepreneurs; as well as Catalans who benefit from remaining in Spain and see no real gains in independence at a time when they are fully integrated into the European Union and the global economy. At the same time, Catalonia is a successful producer of cultural nationalism since most of the children of Spanish and international immigrants in Catalonia grow to identify as Catalans first and speak both Spanish and Catalan.

This chapter covered hundreds of years of Catalans aiming for their independence. This case follows a movement through the longest period among the social movements showcased in this book. The collective claim has been apparent all along: a majority of Catalonians demand independence from Spain. The Reapers War in the 1640s featured a hymn of collective resistance against elites and exploitation, a voice of unity for the Catalan people. Similarly, a Catalan flag solidified a public display of nationalism independent from Spain. The chanting of "Independencia" at FC Barcelona matches is yet another public demonstration in favor of an independent Catalonia. Other displays like castells or human pyramids and massive street protests have been occurring for hundreds of years. A sizable number of Catalonia residents displayed Worth, Unity, Numbers, and Commitment (WUNC) in favor of independence. Despite Spain's power over Catalonia, the movement was able to bring about and win a referendum on independence. In 2017, 92 percent of engaged Catalonians voted for independence. The demand is clear, and the support is strong. The social movement is still unable to break away from the Spanish government's rule, but the people of Catalonia will not stop publicly displaying and demanding calls for an independent state. The lack of success in achieving a movement's stated goals does not mean it is not a social movement. In this sense, this is one of the oldest and longest running social movements discussed in this book.

Note

1 Amanda Sky and Neil Ross helped with research assistance.

References

AFP. 2010. "Catalan Protesters Rally for Greater Autonomy in Spain." in *BBC News*.

BBC. 2013. "Catalans Form Human Chain for Independence from Spain", September 11. BBC News. Retrieved February 15, 2018 (www.bbc.com/news/world-europe-24052713).

——. 2014. "Catalonia Vote: 80% Back Independence – Officials": BBC News. Retrieved February 15, 2018 (www.bbc.com/news/world-europe-29982960).

——. 2017a. "Catalonia Profile – Timeline" *BBC*, London: BBC. Retrieved February 15, 2018 (www.bbc.com/news/world-europe-20345073).

——. 2017b. "Catalonia Independence: Spain Takes Charge of Catalan Government," October 28. BBC News. Retrieved February 15, 2018 (www.bbc.com/news/world-europe-41785292).

Bouton, Terry. 2009. *Taming Democracy: "The People," the Founders, and the Troubled Ending of the American Revolution*. New York: Oxford University Press.

Burgen, Stephen. 2012. "Catalan Independence Rally Brings Barcelona to a Standstill," in *The Guardian*, September 11.

Calamur, Krishnadev. 2017. "The Spanish Court Decision That Sparked the Modern Catalan Independence Movement." *The Atlantic*, October 1.

Castan Pinos, Jaume. 2018. "Challenging the Nation-State's Territorial Integrity through Contestation: Secessionist Rallies in Catalonia." Pp. 69–92 in *Global Cultures of Contestation: Mobility, Sustainability, Aesthetics & Connectivity*, edited by E. Peeren, R. Celikates, J. de Kloet and T. Poell. Cham: Springer International Publishing.

Castañeda, Ernesto, and Cathy Lisa Schneider. 2017. *Collective Violence, Contentious Politics, and Social Change: A Charles Tilly Reader*. New York: Routledge.

Castañeda, Ernesto. 2018a. *A Place to Call Home: Immigrant Exclusion and Urban Belonging in New York, Paris, and Barcelona*. Stanford, CA: Stanford University Press.

——. 2018b. *Immigration and Categorical Inequality: Migration to the City and the Birth of Race and Ethnicity*. New York: Routledge.

Catalan National Assembly. 2014, "The Catalan Way 2014 Becomes the Biggest Mobilization in European History". Retrieved February 15, 2018 (http://catalanassembly.org/2014/09/18/catalan-way-becomes-the-biggest-mobilization-in-european-history/).

Chopra, Rakshit 2013, "The Role of Fc Barcelona in Fueling Catalan Nationalism," January 17. Sportskeeda. Retrieved February 14, 2018 (www.sportskeeda.com/football/the-role-of-fc-barcelona-in-fueling-catalan-nationalism).

Corcoran, Kieran. 2017, "Catalan Politicians Hailed Independence by Singing Their National Anthem—and the Lyrics Are a Brutal Swipe at Spain," October 27. Business Insider. Retrieved February 13, 2018 (www.businessinsider.com/catalonia-independence-national-anthem-is-rebuke-of-spain-2017-10?r=UK&IR=T).

Coscubiela, Joan. 2017, "El Discurso Que Ovacionó El Pp, Psoe Y C's," Barcelona: ESnoticia. Retrieved August 19, 2018 (www.youtube.com/watch?v=BbO9TBDFEnE).

Dandelet, Thomas James. 2003. "Philip V of Spain: The King Who Reigned Twice. By Henry Kamen. New Haven, CT: Yale University Press, 2001." *The Journal of Modern History* 75(2): 442–44.

Dantí I Riu, Jaume. 1979. "La Revolta Dels Gorretes a Catalunya (1687–1689)." *Estudis D'Historia Agraria* 3: 79–99.

Davies, Norman. 2011. *Vanished Kingdoms: The History of Half-Forgotten Europe*: Penguin Books Limited.

Dewan, Angela. 2017. "Separatist Parties in Spain's Catalonia Win Majority in Election": CNN. Retrieved March 1, 2018 (www.cnn.com/2017/12/21/europe/catalonia-election-results-independence-spain-intl/index.html).

García Barcia, Marta. 2013. "Catalonia: The New European State." *ILSA Journal of International & Comparative Law* 20(3): 399–421.

García, César. 2016. "Using Street Protests and National Commemorations for Nation-Building Purposes: The Campaign for the Independence of Catalonia (2012–2014)." *The Journal of International Communication* 22(2): 229–52.

Guibernau, Montserrat. 2012. *Catalan Nationalism: Francoism, Transition and Democracy*. London: Routledge.

Hummel, Daniel. 2017. "Banal Nationalism, National Anthems, and Peace." *Peace Review* 29(2): 225–30.

Jones, Sam. 2017. "Catalonia to Hold Independence Vote Despite Anger in Madrid." in *The Guardian* 6 September.

——. 2018a. "Catalonia Corruption Scandal: Court Orders Party to Repay €6.6m." in *The Guardian* 15 January.

——. 2018b. "Quim Torra Sworn in as Catalan President Amid Xenophobia Claims." in *The Guardian*. London 17 May.

Kamen, Henry. 1977. "A Forgotten Insurrection of the Seventeenth Century: The Catalan Peasant Rising of 1688." *The Journal of Modern History* 49(2): 210–30.

Keating, Michael. 1996. *Nations against the State: The New Politics of Nationalism in Quebec, Catalonia and Scotland*. London: Macmillan.

Laitin, David D. 1989. "Linguistic Revival: Politics and Culture in Catalonia." *Comparative Studies in Society and History* 31(2): 297–317.

Minder, Raphael. 2017. *Struggle for Catalonia: Rebel Politics in Spain*. London: Hurst & Company.

Ordaz, Pablo. 2017. "How the Independence Referendum Has Split the Catalan Police Force." in *El País*.

Prim, Sara. 2016, "Thousands of People Claim Catalonia's Independence in Five Cities across the Territory," Catalonia: Catalan News Agency. Retrieved February 15, 2018 (www.catalannews.com/politics/item/thousands-of-people-claim-catalonia-s-independence-in-five-cities-all-over-the-territory).

RT. 2015, "Gateway to Catalan Republic: 1.4 Million Rally for Independence in Barcelona," September 11. Retrieved February 15, 2018 (www.rt.com/news/315070-catalan-independence-rally-barcelona/).

Russell, Graham, Nicola Slawson and Patrick Greenfield. 2017, "Catalonia Referendum: 90% Voted for Independence, Say Officials – as It Happened." *The Guardian*. Retrieved February 15, 2018 (www.theguardian.com/world/live/2017/oct/01/catalan-independence-referendum-spain-catalonia-vote-live?page=with:block-59d132a6e4b03201709840e9).

Sobrequés, i Callicó Jaume. 2010. *Historia De Cataluña*. Barcelona: Editorial Base.

Tilly, Charles. 1964. *The Vendée*. Cambridge, MA: Harvard University Press.

——. 2005. *Identities, Boundaries, and Social Ties*. Boulder, CO: Paradigm Publishers.

12

SOCIAL MOVEMENTS IN CONTEMPORARY MEXICO

Ernesto Castañeda, Luis Rúben Díaz Cepeda, and Kara Andrade[1]

Protests led by young adults and students in Mexico have gained significant attention in recent years. This chapter looks at the origins of these movements, which were influenced by political corruption and the war on drugs. In particular, the formation of the student-led group #YoSoy132 against presidential candidate Enrique Peña Nieto, and the kidnapping and disappearance of 43 students. The students' kidnapping led to a series of contentious events assigning blame on the federal government. The use of social media helped garner not just awareness, but support beyond Mexico's borders. Whether or not this qualifies as a social movement under Charles Tilly's terms shall be determined after a brief analysis of the events.

In 2012, Enrique Peña Nieto (EPN) was on a Presidential campaign tour. He was a young politician who had been groomed to become President of Mexico by political elites and Televisa, the largest TV network in Mexico. EPN had been Governor of the state of México (2005–2011). He was running as the candidate of the PRI; the party had been in power from 1929 to 2000 and was planning a comeback in 2012 (Cadena-Roa 2017).

Social activists were concerned about the possibility of having the PRI win the presidency because this would mean the repression of the oppositional social movement organizations (SMOs), maintaining a neoliberal agenda, movement cooptation, and more social dominance by the *de facto* centers of power. Despite their desire to stop the PRI's candidate, Enrique Peña Nieto seemed to be on the road to the presidency as mainstream media constantly portrayed him as the sure winner of the election. Leftist organizations had been discredited, and students were not organized. People were acquiescent towards the election of EPN. No one predicted a social movement against his candidacy (Díaz Cepeda 2015: 46).

Yet, on May 11, 2012, at Universidad Iberoamericana, a Jesuit private university in Mexico City, whose middle-class student body was assumed to be friendly towards a PRI candidate, a spontaneous protest against Enrique Peña Nieto occurred. Students started the protest after EPN was questioned about and admitted that he had ordered the violent repression of protesters at San Andres Atenco, Estado de México, in May 2006, while he was governor (Kuri Pineda 2010). At his direction, over 200 protesters were incarcerated, including forty-seven women. Women participants reported they were sexually attacked by policemen as a form of political intimidation (World Organisation against Torture 2006).

After accepting his responsibility for Atenco, students booed EPN off the stage and out of the university. The next day, the campaign denied that the protesters were actual university students. Mainstream media downplayed the event and discredited the hecklers (Cadena-Roa and Serrano Campos 2013).

> To defend themselves from the accusations, despite fear of repression, students spontaneously started to tweet: "I am an Ibero student," "Nobody trained me," "I'm proud of my classmates." Also, in response to the accusations, a group of students created the Facebook event "Video for the truth," asking other students to send them a short video in which they identified themselves as UIA students and participants of the protest. Due to time limitations this group edited the final video and uploaded it to YouTube with only 131 students, but they received up to 230 videos as the days went by. The video became a world-trending topic in a matter of hours. After the video went viral, people and students from other universities and nonaffiliated people from civil society identified with the UIA students' demands and proclaimed themselves to be the 132nd protester, hence the name #YoSoy132.
>
> (Díaz Cepeda 2015: 47)

After this social media campaign, the students called for a meeting on May 16, 2012. On May 18 over a thousand students, mainly from private universities, marched to Televisa's headquarters to protest pro-Peña coverage and demand their right to information and freedom of speech (Díaz Cepeda 2015: 48).

Interest in this issue grew through social media coverage, and more than 15,000 people attended a march on May 23, 2012, in Mexico City. On May 26, a meeting with groups from public universities was organized in the historical Plaza de Tlatelolco. The group issued a statement declaring themselves "as a social, political, but not associated to any political party, pacifist, autonomous, independent, democratic [and] anti-neoliberal social movement that is looking for the transformation of the country through dialogue and social mobilization" (Muñoz Ramírez 2011). Over 100,000 people took part in an anti-EPN march on June 7. At their peak,

> they were able to call for a twenty-four-hour national college strike, a concert in the Zocalo with the attendance of over 50,000 people, and, in an unprecedented act, a call for a debate organized by them and not by the IFE, the body state office in charge of organizing federal elections. This debate was attended by all presidential candidates but EPN and was broadcast on a YouTube channel. The platform was not enough to support the immense number of people trying to watch the debate.
>
> (Díaz Cepeda 2015: 51)

Despite this growing social movement, EPN was declared the winner of the elections on July 1, 2012. After the election, #YoSoy132 participated in marches and other contentious events against EPN. Nevertheless, state repression increased, resignation set in, and the movement soon dwindled.

#YoSoy132's Impacts

A small-scale, loosely organized protest by a few students during a campus visit grew into a national movement that challenged México's political system and brought together groups demanding better democratic conditions. Luiz Rubén Díaz Cepeda explains how,

> A large part of its success was due to their ability to use social networks to bring together students from private and public universities. This was unprecedented; in México private university students do not usually protest, much less alongside students from the public universities. Also, even though #Yo Soy 132 primarily remained a student movement, it worked together with other workers' and farmers' social organizations to achieve their common goal. At their peak, #Yo Soy 132 was capable of organizing marches of more than 100,000 people. However, a year after their birth, and a few months after the presidential election, they lost considerable membership, which diminished their political power.
>
> (Díaz Cepeda 2015: 41)

Many have focused on the role that social media networks played in this movement. However, we argue that in fact, the student movement shows that the use of social media is necessary, but not sufficient for a social movement to be successful (Castells 2015; Díaz Cepeda 2015). We argue this based on evidence that the movement escalated after students from the private universities—Mexico Institute Technologic (Instituto Tecnológico Autónomo de México, ITAM) and Iberoamerican University (Universidad Iberoamericana)—first met face to face in Parque México with students from public universities such as Mexico National University (Universidad Nacional Autónoma de México, UNAM) (Muñoz Ramírez, 2011). The agreements reached provided the movement with the organizational structures and visibility of public universities that allowed people without regular internet access to learn about the movement. Delegates from universities from all over México attended assemblies held in UNAM's main campus, allowing them to create and reinforce solidarity networks.

The Mobilization around the 43 Ayotzinapa Missing Students

On September 26, 2014, around one hundred freshman students from the Ayotzinapa teachers' college Escuela Normal Rural Raul Isidro Burgos headed to the city of Iguala in the Mexican state of Guerrero (Gibler 2017). As in previous years, their goal was to raise funds and means of transportation for a trip to Mexico City to participate in demonstrations commemorating the Tlatelolco massacre of Mexican university students at the hands of the military on October 2, 1968 (Quezada 2018; Trevizo 2011; Soldatenko 2005).

The tragedy began when students non-violently took over five buses, a common practice that is often tolerated and that had never been repressed so swiftly and violently. However, in this instance, 80 miles south of Iguala during a pit stop, local police officers, and unidentified shooters opened fire on the five buses transporting the students. Six people—three bystanders and three students—were shot and killed, more than twenty students were wounded, and forty-three went missing. The next morning, the body of student Julio Cesar Mondragon was found in a road. Social movement organizations interpreted this as an intimidation technique.

As federal authorities began their investigations, local government immediately downplayed this event. Later, it was framed by the federal government as an exception that did not reflect the overall situation in Mexico, where violence was supposedly on the decline. However, social movement organizations (SMOs) challenged this discourse by claiming that the attack on the Ayotzinapa students, as well as the way the government conducted the investigations, were, in fact, exemplary of how corrupt the state had become. This can be seen in the chants that emerged a few weeks after the beginning of the movement: "It was the State!" and "Out with Peña!" A chant that was adopted not only by activists but also by regular people, such as the *Cariolla* or Stroller Contingent made up by mothers with their babies, was: "No, not the students! No, not our children!" Also, grandmothers shouted "Another 68, No More!" in reference to the tragedy that occurred a half-century ago (interview with Pérez) (Díaz Cepeda, Castañeda, and Andrade 2018).

The attack and the slow institutional response started a wave of mobilization that grew to the point where many people blamed the federal government for the attack, demanded the resignation of President Enrique Peña Nieto, and called for a new social contract.

Since the night of the tragedy, other students from the teachers' college Raul Isidro Burgos and their allies pressured local and state governments to bring the students back alive and started a cycle of mobilization. What happened to the disappeared students is still unknown nor have their bodies been recovered.

Accounts about the Bloody Night

Most sources agree on these basic facts: On the night of September 26, 2014, a group was attacked by policemen while in the city of Iguala, Guerrero. These were *normalistas*, the name given to college students attending the *normal rural* (a college for rural teachers) Raul Isidro Burgos in Ayotzinapa, Guerrero, in southwestern Mexico. Three individuals passing by and three students were killed, and forty-three other students, ranging in ages from nineteen to twenty-three years old, were kidnapped by the local police and then disappeared.

It is still not clear what happened to the missing students. On November 7, 2014, then-Attorney General Murillo Karam gave the following account: on the night of September 26, 2014, a group of *normalistas* from Ayotzinapa boarded two buses at the school and headed to the city of Iguala where they planned on commandeering three more buses, driving to México City. The *normalistas* arrived at Iguala at the same time that María de los Ángeles Pineda, wife of Iguala's mayor José Luis Abarca Velázquez, was celebrating an official reception. Afraid that the Ayotzinapa students would disturb the official event, Abarca ordered the local police to confront them. That night, Iguala police officers chased and shot the Ayotzinapa students; many students were hurt, and three were killed. In addition to them, a bus driver, a taxi driver and his female passenger were killed during the attack. Also, as mentioned, forty-three students were kidnapped by the Iguala police and were allegedly turned over to the *Guerreros Unidos*, a criminal group. Major newspapers indicated that the mayor and his wife were part of this criminal organization.

On January 27, 2015, the official version changed slightly. Karam said in a press conference that further investigations by the Attorney General's Office (PGR) had concluded that the *normalistas* were killed because they were mistaken for *Los Rojos*, a rival group of the *Guerreros Unidos*. In this version, the Iguala local police force was infiltrated by members of the former, and when one of the leaders mistakenly thought that *Los Rojos* were attacking Iguala, he ordered for them to be shot, incinerated in a garbage dump, and have their ashes thrown into the San Juan River. The PGR had recovered human remains and a few testimonies to support this claim, but the remains were too damaged to conduct DNA identity tests. Even though the details had changed, the narrative offered to the public was the same: it was an unfortunate event caused by corruption at the local police level.

However, Ayotzinapa students and many others contested this narrative. Journalists Anabel Hernández and Steve Fisher (2014) challenged the PGRs version. Based on several testimonies of surviving students, videos, and official documents, they argued that there were, in fact, three attacks; the first shots were fired around 10:00 pm when several police officers attempted to arrest the students when they were looking for a way out of Iguala. The *normalistas* resisted the arrest by throwing stones at the police cars and continued on their way. Moments later, a second attack happened. Several police officers used their police cars as a barricade and shot at the buses full of students. During this attack, one of the students, Aldo Gutierrez, was fatally shot in the head. Then the police took the forty-three students into custody, while other students ran for cover or were left behind. The third attack happened an hour later when an armed group shot at other students that had come to help the first student group and improvised a press conference. Daniel Solis, Yosivani Guerrero, and Julio Cesar Mondragon were killed in this attack. Mondragon was scalped and his facial skin cut by his assassins. His body was left in a public space, and a photograph was uploaded to the internet for anyone to see. Some journalists and activists interpreted this act as aiming to intimidate the students to leave and be quiet.

Another narrative was later advanced by an international group of experts assembled by the Inter-American Human Rights Commission. In this version, one of the buses taken by the students contained a hidden drug cargo, which was unknown by the students, and resulted in the high levels of violence against the students. A research team has reconstructed a timeline of events from different sources (Gallagher, Ruiz-Segovia and Martínez-Gutiérrez 2017). The truth is still unknown, but the disappearance of the students ignited a social movement in Mexico.

The Ayotzinapa Context

For many decades, Guerrero has been Mexico's most violent state with a long tradition of *cacicazgo*, where a few families have ruled the state as their personal chiefdom, attacking those that resist them.

Lucio Cabañas—a former student of the Raul Isidro Burgos teacher school—commanded guerrillas in the mountains of Guerrero. The federal army killed Cabañas and three other members of the guerrillas in 1974 while rescuing kidnapped senator and future governor Rubén Figueroa Figueroa.

A decade later, Rubén Figueroa Alcocer—son of the former governor—was elected governor in 1993. However, in 1996 he was forced to resign after being held responsible for the tragedy of Aguas Blancas in 1995, where police officers killed seventeen and injured twenty-three protesting peasants. Figueroa Alcocer was replaced by Ángel Aguirre Rivero as interim governor. Aguirre Rivero was again the governor at the time of the forced disappearance of the Ayotzinapa students. On October 23, 2014, Aguirre resigned under pressure from the Ayotzinapa movement. Guerrero is also a center of marijuana and heroin production, much of which is exported to the United States. Organized drug cartels found the ideal conditions for business in Guerrero's lawlessness. There have been growing clashes and conflicts of interest between public officials and drug trafficking organizations.

Guerrero has a history of poverty and repression, but also of resistance, where the students and teachers of Ayotzinapa have been in the forefront. The Ayotzinapa movement draws on the history of the teachers' colleges, which have existed in the state since the 1920s. These colleges were founded by Minister of Public Education José Vasconcelos, with the goal of educating peasants living in Mexico's countryside (Padilla 2009). Since their founding, these schools have a socialist and activist orientation and are active in the peasants' struggles for land distribution. However, they lost much of their funding from the federal government since the switch over to a neoliberal economic model in the 1980s. Students from these schools (*normalistas*) across the country are part of organizations such as the Mexican Federation of Socialist Peasant Students.

The teachers' college Raul Isidro Burgos is a male-only school with around 500 students, who have a reputation for using highly disruptive tactics to make their demands. Confrontations between these schools and the State have increased in recent times because, like the majority of the rural schools, they are fighting for their very existence against the state's clear intention to close these teachers' colleges. Ayotzinapa *normalistas* have been on the frontline of the defense of these institutions, and they have faced attacks and repression, including a protest in 2011 when two students were shot to death by federal police (McGahan 2014).

The Movement in Support of the Ayotzinapa Students

Initially, the events in Iguala did not gain national, much less international, attention. To understand this lack of awareness, it is important to remember that since 2006 when former President Felipe Calderon Hinojosa launched a war on drugs and took the army to the streets to perform patrolling functions, over 100,000 people have been killed, and over 30,000 people have gone missing (Campbell 2009; Gibler 2011; Muehlmann 2013). This strategy was discreetly continued by Peña Nieto with the same effects (Observatorio Nacional Ciudadano 2017). Under this context, the killing of three students, and the disappearance of another forty-three may not have been so newsworthy. Presumably, then, this case could have been another one in the long list of non-investigated crimes. However, the Ayotzinapa students were part of a vast network of SMOs which spread the news of the attack and brought public attention to the tragedy.

The parents of the kidnapped students got involved in the social movement right after the killings and kidnappings. However, the first organized reaction came from Ayotzinapa students and their activists' networks. The Ayotzinapa students are quite skilled at reacting when attacked, given their experience organizing social movement and communication campaigns. They quickly organized a press conference, and communicated the news to their allies, using social networks. They compiled a list of demands, which allowed them to give some direction to the mobilization. The day after the killings, the student body and staff of the Ayotzinapa School demanded the impeachment of Mayor Abarca and Governor Aguirre for the six murders and the return of the missing students (Hernández and Fisher 2014).

The attack against the Ayotzinapa students on September 26, 2014, was not the first case of violent disappearances. Nevertheless, people across the country paid attention and acted in solidarity. The growing popular support was due to *normalistas* and SMOs changing the official framing of the events. Enrique Pineda, a well-known social activist and founding member of the Ayotzinapa Solidarity Committee, told Luis Díaz Cepeda that, "the attack on the Ayotzinapa students, as well as the way the government has conducted the investigations, are not local nor isolated events—these acts are exemplary of how corrupt the state is." Active social organizers latched onto these events and brought them to national and then international attention as examples of the everyday violence against citizens and migrants exercised with impunity by both government armed forces and organized crime (Correa-Cabrera 2017).

Allied SMO campaigning around the forty-three are organized in three different groups. The first one is the National Popular Assembly (Asamblea Nacional Popular, ANP) based in Ayotzinapa and made up by local and national leftist organizations—such as Education Workers State Organization (Coordinadora Estatal de Trabajadores de la Educación, CETEG) and humans rights organizations such as Tlachinolla Mountain Human Rights Centre (Centro de Derechos Humanos de la Montaña Tlachinollan). In Mexico City, collectives and civil society organizations concerned by the events have organized the Ayotzinapa Solidarity Committee (Mesa de Solidaridad). In addition, college students from both private and public universities showed massive support all around the country for the forty-three kidnapped students.

Life-long activists came up with the idea of organizing "day of action" marches to bring awareness to the forced disappearances. From the beginning of the movement, the solidarity committee, in coordination with the parents and the ANP, decided to organize global action days. (See Chapter 5 for a discussion of Global Days of Action.) With all the discontent accumulated, the October 22, 2014 Global Action Day saw a mass demonstration in Mexico City.

Figure 12.1 Justice for Ayotzinapa. October 21, 2014, Global Action Day. Mexico City.

Source: Luis Rubén Díaz Cepeda © 2014.

Figure 12.2 "I think, therefore they disappear me. Responsible: the three levels of government." Graffiti on November 5, 2014, Global Action Day.

Source: Luis Rubén Díaz Cepeda © 2014.

The parents of the victims led this march, as they did in all the previous demonstrations. College students, union workers, multiple social organizations, and other non-affiliated supporters attended the march in large numbers. There were coordinated protests in twenty-two states on that day, as well as elsewhere in the world. Also, students at over eighty universities called for strikes. Some of them went on a twenty-four-hour strike, while others did it for seventy-two hours. In Guerrero, the ANP continued their plan of using highly disruptive tactics to bring the state government down.

During this day of protest, the chants of "It was the State!" and "Peña Out!" were no longer coming from isolated voices, but were almost unanimous. It was clear then that people no longer accepted the official storyline that this tragedy was a local exception, but instead was a symbol of the corruption of the whole government. The high spirits of that night made some people think that the scenario for a massive revolt capable of bringing the formal political system down was possible. However, experienced social activists were not so sure about this.

The most significant turnout was on November 20, 2014, when over 100,000 people took the streets of Mexico City to protest the students' disappearance. Many of these demonstrations honored not only the missing *normalistas*, but the thousands of people who disappeared in Mexico in the last decade and called for an overhaul of the entire Mexican political system. The demands reached as far as Europe and Asia (Dorfsman-Hopkins and Gómez Unamuno 2015). Groups in almost all countries in Latin America joined this Global Action Day. For a while, global action days happened every month, which kept the movement alive.

Precedents

It built on the memory of the October 2, 1968 Tlatelolco massacre of student protesters. To this day, the exact number of students killed, injured, and disappeared on that date in 1968 is unknown; the estimate goes from one hundred to three hundred people. Since then, October 2 has been a symbolic day of resistance.

Four decades later college students organized once again to demand further democratization (Ortega Ortiz 2008). In 2012, the student movement #YoSoy132 (#I Am 132, see above), inspired by the 15M and Occupy movements (for more on these movements, see Chapter 10), began when students confronted the Institutional Revolutionary Party's (PRI) candidate Enrique Peña Nieto—later to become president of Mexico—regarding his policies as governor and also critiqued the Mexican media's biased coverage of the 2012 general election. First, they spread their complaints using videos uploaded to YouTube; then they used Facebook and Twitter and content went viral in Mexico. Later, this support translated into massive street demonstrations, where a new generation of politically aware youth rose up.

Just as in *#Yo Soy 132* (Guillén 2013), the use of social networking sites was vital to deliver information about what happened in Iguala to a broader audience. Within days, the case of the 43 missing Ayotzinapa students went beyond local organization networks and gained national and international attention. The traditional protest of October 2 in Mexico City was the perfect scenario for the emerging movement to gain momentum and for possible allies to meet each other. The Tlatelolco commemoration reunites most of the leftist organizations of the country, and in 2014, some SMOs tied their demands with the ones from the parents of the Ayotzinapa students. Protests were not limited to that October 2 march, but they spread throughout Mexico City and other states in Mexico, the United States, and some countries in Europe.

Our research indicates that many of the young students that participated in #YoSoy132 also participated in the Ayotzinapa movement and used their social media know-how to promote the 43 media campaign. Both movements reflect the growing trend towards non-partisan movements, grassroots organizing, and self-governance parallel to the vigilante self-defense and community police movements in Guerrero and Michoacán that arose in 2013 (Andrade 2015a, 2015b; Andrade, Castañeda, and Díaz Cepeda 2017; Díaz Cepeda, Castañeda, and Andrade 2018).

Unlike previous victims, who did not belong to any social organization, Ayotzinapa students were highly politicized, and hence were part of an extended network of SMOs, which supported the efforts of the parents to find their sons. This network acted quickly and organized local protests the very next day after the events. They also reported the attack to other social organizations, as well as national and international news reporters, hence gaining national and, later, worldwide attention. By doing so, they broke the media's self-censoring, which the government relied on to hide inconvenient information. The government tried to frame the events in Iguala as a local issue, blaming criminal groups. However, thanks to their "know how," and information campaigns, the students and their allies defeated this false narrative. On the contrary, by showing that local police officers had participated in the attack and the federal forces, at the very least, had failed to protect the students, they started to show how the federal government was also responsible.

By breaking the media siege, Ayotzinapa students and their networks reached a broader audience. Within this audience, there were a vast number of people that were also discontented with the EPN administration who later joined the movement. As social movements scholar Sidney Tarrow (2011: 166) would say, a larger number of allies encouraged people to participate further. With more support, Ayotzinapa shifted in scale, growing a local to national, and later, an international, concern.

Figure 12.3 Photo of a Zapatista poster demanding the location of the 43.

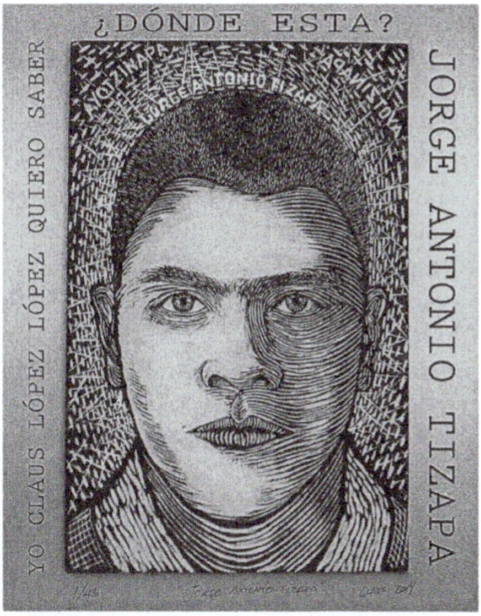

Figure 12.4 Illustration of disappeared student Antonio Tizapa by Claus López.

Source: #IlustradoresConAyotzinapa Shared by Creative Commons. http://centroprodh.org.mx/43x ayotzinapa/index.php/project/jorge-antonio-tizapa-legideno/

Figure 12.5 Picture of posters of some of the missing students at a presentation of the experts' report at the Wilson Center in Washington, DC in 2016.

Source: © Castañeda.

Internationalization

The events in Iguala have troubled not just Mexicans, but others around the world, as can be observed in the numerous books and articles from different disciplines, about the topic (i.e., Díaz Cepeda 2016; Gibler 2017; Martín Beristain 2016; Reed-Sandoval 2016). The forced disappearance of the students and the failure of local authorities and the federal government to respond to the crime have prompted activism in Mexico and beyond. From staging "die-ins" at many campuses to candlelight vigils and protests in many international cities, including forty-three cities in the United States, to crowdsourced projects such as the painted portraits of each student and many Twitter-hashtags such as #Ayotzinapa, #AyotzinapaSomosTodos, #EselEstado, #NoSomosUnNúmero, #YaMeCanse, #yanoscansamos, #UStired2, #YaMeCansé, #PorEsoPropongo, #IlustradoresConAyotzinapa and many others, the initial local campaign grew into a global movement in less than a month. Protests have taken place throughout Mexico, the United States, Europe, and Latin America showing solidarity with the parents, teachers, and students in demanding an end to impunity in Mexico.

The Ayotzinapa movement is an organic movement with no hierarchical organization, but rather a web of activists and organizations. This structure allowed activists, SMOs, and sympathizers to break the media siege and reach potential members from the United States, South America, and Europe. For example, grassroots activists such as Miguel Ángel Jiménez Blanco filed reports about the events in Iguala via WhatsApp to his international journalist contacts (Andrade, Castañeda, and Díaz Cepeda 2017).

Transactional Protest

Right after the killings in Iguala, a group of Mexicans stood in front of the Mexican Consulate in New York to protest the disappearances of forty-three individuals. Don Antonio Tizapa was part of this protest. Antonio Tizapa looked at the pictures of the students brought by another member of the community, only to realize that his son was one of the disappeared.

Mr. Tizapa has been vocal in events in the United States in support of the return of the forty-three disappeared students. He has joined forces with Amado Tlatempa, who has been living in New York for over ten years. Two of Amado's cousins are among the forty-three missing. He told Castañeda in an interview that his cousins joined the teachers' school because they were very poor, and the school offered them food, housing, and the prospects for a stable job afterward. Amado runs marathons in the United States along with Don Antonio to raise awareness for the 43. Don Antonio conducted a hunger strike in front of the Mexican Consulate in New York on December 24–26, 2016. As of 2018, there is still no news of his son's whereabouts.

Government Reaction

The Mexican government downplayed the events in Guerrero and framed them as exceptional and not reflective of the overall situation in the country, boasting that drug violence was supposedly on the decline. In the first years of his administration, Peña Nieto claimed a decrease from the violence that the country experienced from 2006 to 2012, when 23,000 people disappeared, and approximately 70,000 were killed (Martínez Toyes and Arellano Quiroga 2012; Rosen and Zepeda 2016; Velázquez Vargas and Martínez Canizales 2012). However, as the Ayotzinapa movement made clear, the killings did not end with President Calderon's administration but continued with EPN. During the first twenty months of the EPN administration, there were over 57,899 homicides; and 2017 had a record high of 31,174 homicides, according to the Mexican Public Security National System.

The Mexican government tried to close the case and silence the mobilization by attempting to prove that the students were dead and stated outright that the parents and everyone else should just get over it and move on. The parents were suspicious of the Attorney General, yet they collaborated with the investigation, and also investigated on their own. Whenever the parents had a lead, they asked the federal police (PFP) to go with them. However, on the occasions when the federal police refused to accompany them, they self-organized and with the support of the Union of Organized People from the State of Guerrero (UPOEG) they looked for their sons, at times with the media in tow (Andrade, Castañeda, and Díaz Cepeda 2017, CNN 2014). In these searches, they found many clandestine graves in places where the federal police had supposedly already searched. This increased people's distrust of the federal investigation.

The changing versions and lack of evidence made people suspicious and served to fuel the growing movement. Then the government used a worn playbook of tactics to discredit and repress SMOs. On the one hand, the government accused students of being involved in drug trafficking. However, since "most of the students were still in their teens, in their first semester at the school, and came from impoverished communities that a majority of Mexicans can identify with" (Goldman 2014), the population did not believe them to be criminals. Also, there is video evidence, as confirmed by the federal investigation, that the policemen kidnapped the students. The footage also proves that the students were not armed and that they did not fire back, as some had argued at one point. At the same time, by the end of 2014, the government started to repress mobilization efforts through targeted and random arrests. Arguably, these arrests were made with the intention of intimidating people and reducing mobilization. Police repressed later protests under the excuse that mobilizations of support and protests were a threat to the stability of the country because at the end of a few of the marches in Mexico City anarchists burned trashcans and crashed businesses' windows.

Results

Despite all the support and political pressure, the most important demand of the parents of the disappeared, to have their sons returned alive, has still not been met. Mayor Abarca was charged with kidnapping, but never tried or convicted. Governor Aguirre resigned but was not charged or prosecuted, and the Office of the Attorney General has refused to investigate the army. Perhaps, the most important victory of the parents has been that the federal government accepted that the Human Rights Inter-American Court (CIDH) help in the investigation of the case. The groups of experts appointed by the CIDH had the goal of overseeing Mexico's actions to protect the injured students and to find out what happened to the missing students.

In April 2016, this group issued a 605-page report stating that the government's official version of the students' disappearance was riddled with flaws and mentioned many instances when the Mexican government created roadblocks in their investigation of the case. Peña's administration responded by ending the collaboration with CIDH on July 2016, as they did previously with Argentine investigators. However, thanks to several demonstrations and a sit-in that took place in front of the U.S. State Department, the parents and their allies created enough political pressure on the Mexican federal government to sign a new agreement with this group of experts.

Failures and Questions about the Future

#YoSoy132 did not prevent EPN from being elected, but it energized youth in Mexico, used social media effectively, and connected activists in the physical world. Interestingly, there was little organized opposition and fewer protests against the further privatizations and neoliberal structural reforms implemented by Peña Nieto's government (Cadena-Roa 2017).

The whereabouts of the students, what actually took place in Iguala, and who was involved remain a mystery. Similarly, many clandestine graves were located during the search for the disappeared students, and the criminals behind those murders are unknown (CNN 2014). What is certain is that neither the parents nor much of the Mexican population accepted the version presented by former Attorney General Murillo Karam on January 27, 2015. The ultimate goal of the Ayotzinapa movement, to find the students, and later demands, to have the President resign and draft a new constitution, were not met.

Nonetheless, the visibility of the movement in the international diplomatic circles among foreign leaders, including the Pope and international parliaments, deflated the bubble about the supposed "Mexican moment," a public relations campaign engineered through the international press at the beginning of the Presidency of Enrique Peña Nieto, and the return of the PRI to power after eight years of hiatus to a 71-year rule, framed Mexico as experiencing a renaissance. The case of the Ayotzinapa 43, arguably, played a role in the election defeats that the PRI suffered in 2016 when it lost seven out of twelve state elections for governor, including the states of Durango, Quintana Roo, Veracruz y Tamaulipas where it had ruled since the end of the Revolution—and may well have also contributed to PRI's defeat in the 2018 presidential election that swept a center-left party to power. In yet another action, the Popular Citizen Constituent Assembly (Asamblea Popular Constituyente, APC) a parallel social movement founded by Bishop Vera and Father Solalinde among others, organized a citizen constitutional assembly on February 5, 2017, the hundredth anniversary of the current Mexican constitution.

Movement Test

Would movement scholars call this a movement? The organizing strategies and tactics of those protesting the Ayotzinapa disappearances do meet many of the criteria Charles Tilly used in determining what makes a social movement. The Ayotzinapa had a campaign with clear goals: to achieve justice for the forty-three missing students, an end to police corruption, and more transparent politicians who represent their constituents. The movement did not solely start from the one event when the students were kidnapped; instead, Ayotzinapa formed through the Mexican government lack of accountability for decades. These grievances pushed various groups to join together and demand justice. The collective organized activities around the forty-three disappeared students showed solidarity and aimed to blame the authorities.

Seeing Ayotzinapa as contentious politics means recognizing the organized activities of disruption, violence, as well as conventional forms of contention in modern Mexico—mass protests, blocking of roads, taking of tolls—and "sustained" tactics that years later keep their grievance visible to the public. There are also "dense social networks and connective structures" that "draw on consensual or action-oriented cultural frames" for solidarity and mobilization (Tarrow 1998: 10, 95) both inside Mexico and beyond into the United States and dozens of other countries. All of these add to the social movement repertoire of Ayotzinapa. Numerous twitter hashtags, protests at the Mexican consulate in New York City, and the parents of the kidnapped students leading investigations are just a few of the political actions the group took in making their demands heard.

WUNC displays are also present in this movement. The parents of the forty-three students led protests and demanded the government to solve the crimes, showing the Worthiness of the group. Unity in the cohesive march on Global Action Day also shows the group's ability to assemble thousands of people in protest. The Numbers of this movement are vast; popular twitter hashtags, 500,000 people taking part in marches, and spreading awareness across national borders all took place. The Commitment to the movement is also strong; student strikes and sit-ins in front of the U.S. State Department show that participants are willing to make sacrifices for the organization.

The Ayotzinapa movement was discovered not only in the actions of one or two organizations, but in the spread of contentious actions to different arenas, and in the changes in understanding of what happened. Communication technology played a vital role in the acceleration of the movement and its tactics. The role of communication in this case aligns with Jo Freeman's (2003: 22–24) three propositions: (1) "the need for a pre-existing communications network or infrastructure within the social base of a movement" which makes "spontaneous" activity possible, (2) this communication network must be "*co-optable* to the new ideas of the incipient movement"; and (3) the presence of one or more "precipitants" or immediate catalysts that spark the fire for the "spontaneous action" to occur.

The power of Ayotzinapa's campaign was its prowess to use the tools available to them to reach the hearts and minds of others, who before these tragic events did not even know that Ayotzinapa existed. The movement worked to find the students but also pushed for accountability within Mexico's governing structures. The Ayotzinapa mobilization directly challenged the Mexican state for its inability to provide security to its citizens. It is part of a larger movement against the nefarious effects of the war on drugs. Philosopher Javier Sicilia and members of the Catholic Church have been visible actors in this movement. Activists in Ciudad Juarez, Chihuahua, have been at the forefront of organizing against the militarization of the war on drugs (Díaz Cepeda and Castañeda 2018; Staudt and Mendez 2015). Nevertheless, this is an issue that goes beyond local cities, states, and party-affiliation of those in government and thus likely to continue. Disappearances have not stopped, and over 200,000 people have been killed since the start of the war on drugs in 2006 (INEGI 2018; Matrogiovanni 2014). Yet these are not the only problems that SMOs are protesting, as there are around 600 land conflicts in Mexico between transnational companies and indigenous communities (Trujillo, Lorena and Composto 2014; Trujillo, Lorena and Fini 2016) and teachers' unions—such as are State Coordinating Committee of Education Workers of Guerrero, or CETEG—are fighting for better working conditions. The effects of the neo-Zapatista and indigenist Zapatista Army of National Liberation (EZLN) and the Popular Assembly of the Peoples of Oaxaca (APPO), a broad resistance coalition (both located in states near Guerrero), are still resounding (Estrada Saavedra 2016a, 2016b). In Mexico, contentious events and social movements are an integral means by which organized groups make political claims and get access to resources, and this will not be changing in the near future. Activists will likely continue to demand answers about the missing 43 Ayotzinapa students and work for systemic change in Mexico.

Note

1 Monica Villacorta, Araseli Lara, Lesley Buck, and Maura Fennelly helped prepare this case study. Chris Tilly and Lesley Wood provided valuable feedback. All errors remain our own.

References

Andrade, Kara. 2015a, "The Life and Death of Miguel Angel Jiménez, Organizer in Guerrero, Mexico," Washington, DC: Pulitzer Center on Crisis Reporting. (http://pulitzercenter.org/reporting/life-and-death-miguel-angel-jim%C3%A9nez-organizer-guerrero-mexico).

——. 2015b, "Whatsapp and Murder in Mexico." *Latino USA*: NPR. (http://latinousa.org/2015/12/11/whatsapp-and-murder-in-mexico/).

Andrade, Kara, Ernesto Castañeda, and Luis Rubén Díaz Cepeda. 2017. "Interview with Activist Miguel Ángel Jiménez Blanco." *Interface: A Journal for and about Social Movements* 9(1): 590–600.

Cadena-Roa, Jorge, and Daniela Serrano Campos. 2013. "Yosoy132 and the Return of the Pri." Pp. 123–26 in *The Future We the People Need: Voices from New Social Movements in North Africa, Middle East, Europe and North America*, edited by W. Puschra and S. Burke. New York: Frederich Ebert Stiftung.

Cadena-Roa, Jorge. 2017. "Los Movimientos Sociales En La Segunda Alternancia." Pp. 143–68 in *Los Indignados Mexicanos: Insurgencia Juvenil Frente Al Regreso Del Pri a La Presidencia*, edited by H. Varela Guinot and J. L. Hernández Avendaño. Mexico: Colofón.

Campbell, Howard. 2009. *Drug War Zone: Frontline Dispatches from the Streets of El Paso and Juárez*. Austin, TX: University of Texas Press.

Castells, Manuel. 2015. *Networks of Outrage and Hope: Social Movements in the Internet Age*. Cambridge, UK: Polity Press.

CNN. 2014. "Policías Comunitarios Buscan a Más Desaparecidos En Guerrero: Integrantes De La Upoeg Iniciaron Nueva Búsqueda De Fosas En 4 Municipios Guerrerenses: Iguala, Cocula, Chichihualco Y Taxco." Mexico City: Expansion. Retrieved May 13, 2016 (http://expansion.mx/nacional/2014/11/18/policias-comunitarios-buscan-a-mas-desaparecidos-en-guerrero).

Correa-Cabrera, Guadalupe. 2017. *Los Zetas Inc.: Criminal Corporations, Energy, and Civil War in Mexico*. Austin, TX: University of Texas Press.

Díaz Cepeda, Luis Rubén, and Ernesto Castañeda. 2018. "Motivations and Activist Typologies: Core Activists in Ciudad Juarez." *Interface: A Journal for and about Social Movements* 10(2).

Díaz Cepeda, Luis Rubén. 2015. "#Yo Soy 132: A Networked Social Movement of Mexican Youth." Pp. 41–58 in *Waves of Social Movement Mobilizations in the Twenty-First Century: Challenges to the Neo-Liberal World Order and Democracy*, edited by N. Knoak and R. O. Donmez. Lanham, MD: Lexington Books.

——. 2016. "Addressing Ayotzinapa: Using Dussel's Analectic Method for Establishing an Ethical Framework for Complex Social Movements." Pp. 215–28 in *Decolonizing the Westernized University: Interventions in Philosophy of Education from Within and Without*, edited by R. Grosfoguel, R. Hernández, and E. R. Velázquez. Lanham, MD: Lexington Books.

Díaz Cepeda, Luis Rubén, Ernesto Castañeda, and Kara Andrade. 2018. "Activists' Communication and Mobilization Tactics to Find Ayotzinapa's 43 Disappeared Students." in *Protest and Pr*, edited by A. Adi. London: Routledge.

Dorfsman-Hopkins, Marcela, and Aurelia Gómez Unamuno. 2015, "Global Support," Ayotzinapa's 43 Disappeared Students. Retrieved February 26, 2018 (https://blogs.haverford.edu/disappeared-students/international/).

Estrada Saavedra, Marco. 2016a. *La Comunidad Armada Rebelde Y El Ezln: Un Estudio HistóRico Y Socioló́Gico Sobre Las Bases De Apoyo Zapatistas En Las CañAdas Tojolabales De La Selva Lacandona (1930–2005)*. Mexico, DF: El Colegio de México.

—— ed. 2016b. *El Pueblo Ensaya La RevolucióN: La Appo Y El Sistema De DominacióN OaxaqueñO.* 1st ed. ed. Ciudad de México: Centro de Estudios Sociológicos, El Colegio de México,.

Freeman, Jo. 2003. "The Women's Movement." Pp. 22–31 in *The Social Movements Reader: Cases and Concepts*, edited by J. Goodwin and J. M. Jasper. Malden, MA: Blackwell Publishers.

Gallagher, Janice, Camila Ruiz-Segovia, and Paula Martínez-Gutiérrez. 2017. "Ayotzinapa Timeline.Org." Retrieved January 22, 2018 (www.ayotzinapatimeline.org/).

Gibler, John. 2011. *To Die in Mexico: Dispatches from inside the Drug War*. San Francisco, CA: City Lights Books.

——. 2017. *I Couldn't Even Imagine That They Would Kill Us: An Oral History of the Attacks against the Students of Ayotzinapa*. San Francisco, CA: City Lights Books.

Goldman, Francisco. 2014. "Crisis in Mexico: Could Forty-Three Missing Students Spark a Revolution?" *The New Yorker* (www.newyorker.com/news/news-desk/crisis-mexico-forty-three-missing-students-spark-revolution).

Guillén, Diana. 2013. "Mexican Spring?# Yosoy132, the Emergence of an Unexpected Collective Actor in the National Political Arena." *Social Movement Studies* 12(4): 471–76.

Hernández, Anabel, and Steve Fisher. 2014. "Iguala: La Historia No Oficial." *Proceso*, December 13.

INEGI. 2018, "Indicadores Sociales," Mexico City: Instituto Nacional de Geografía e Informática. Retrieved May 1, 2018 (www.beta.inegi.org.mx/app/indicadores/?ind=1002000030#divFV6300000264#D1002000030).

Kuri Pineda, Edith. 2010. "El Movimiento Social De Atenco: Experiencia Y Construcción De Sentido." *Andamios* 7(14): 321–45.

Martín Beristain, Carlos. 2016. *El Tiempo De Ayotzinapa*. Tres Cantos, Madrid: Foca.

Martínez Toyes, Wilebaldo L., and Jaime A. Arellano Quiroga. 2012. "Movilidad Poblacional: Efecto De La Violencia E Inseguridad En Ciudad Juárez." in *Seguridad Y Violencia En Ciudad Juárez, México*, edited by M. Limas Hernández. Ciudad Juárez, Chihuahua: Universidad Autónoma de Ciudad Juárez.

Matrogiovanni, Federico. 2014. *Ni Vivos, Ni Muertos*. Ciudad de Mexico: Grijalbo.

McGahan, Jason. 2014. "Anatomy of a Mexican Student Massacre." in *The Daily Beast*, Vol. 2015.

Muehlmann, Shaylih. 2013. *When I Wear My Alligator Boots: Narco-Culture in the U.S.-Mexico Borderlands*. Berkeley, CA: University of California Press.

Muñoz Ramírez, Gloria. 2011. *#Yo Soy 132 Voces Del Movimiento*. Mexico, DF: Ediciones Bola de Cristal.

Observatorio Nacional Ciudadano. 2017. "Reporte Sobre Delitos De Alto Impacto." Vol. 4(9). Mexico City: Observatorio Nacional Ciudadano Seguridad, Justicia y Legalidad.

Ortega Ortiz, Reynaldo Yunuen. 2008. *Movilización Y Democracia: España Y México*. Mexico City: El Colegio de México.

Padilla, Tanalis. 2009. "Las Normales Rurales: Historia Y Proyecto De Nación." *El Cotidiano*, pp. 85–93.

Quezada, Sergio Aguayo. 2018. *El 68: Los Estudiantes, El Presidente Y La Cia*. Mexico City: Ediciones Proceso.

Reed-Sandoval, Amy. 2016. "Ayotzinapa: An Attack against Latin American Philosophy." Pp. 215–28 in *Decolonizing the Westernized University: Interventions in Philosophy of Education from Within and Without*, edited by R. Grosfoguel, R. Hernández, and E. R. Velázquez. Lanham, MD: Lexington Books.

Rosen, Jonathan D., and Roberto Zepeda. 2016. *Organized Crime, Drug Trafficking, and Violence in Mexico: The Transition from Felipe Calderón to Enrique Peña Nieto*. Lanham, MD: Lexington Books.

Soldatenko, Michael. "México '68: Power to the Imagination!" *Latin American Perspectives* 32(4) (July 2005): 111–32.

Staudt, Kathleen A., and Zulma Mendez. 2015. *Courage, Resistance and Women in Ciudad Juárez: Challenges to Militarization in Ciudad Juárez*. Austin, TX: The University of Texas Press.

Tarrow, Sidney. 1998. *Power in Movement: Social Movements and Contentious Politics*. New York: Cambridge University Press.

——. 2011. *Power in Movement. Social Movements and Contentious Politics*. New York: Cambridge University Press.

Trevizo, Dolores. 2011. *Rural Protest and the Making of Democracy in Mexico, 1968–2000*. University Park, PA: Pennsylvania State University Press.

Trujillo, Navarro, Mina Lorena, and Daniele Fini, eds. 2016. *Despojo capitalista y luchas comunitarias en defensa de la vida en México: Claves desde la Ecología Política*. Puebla, México: Instituto de Ciencias Sociales y Humanidades Alfonso Vélez Pliego, Benemérita Universidad Autónoma de Puebla.

Trujillo, Navarro, Mina Lorena, and Claudia Composto. 2014. "Claves de lectura para comprender el despojo y las luchas por los bienes naturales en América Latina." In *Territorios en disputa: despojo capitalista, luchas en defensa de los bienes comunes naturales y alternativas emancipatorias para América Latina*, edited by Mina Lorena Navarro Trujillo and Claudia Composto. México: Bajo Tierra.

Velázquez Vargas, María del Socorro, and Georgina Martínez Canizales. 2012. "La Inseguridad En Ciudad Juárez Desde La Percepción De Los Ciudadanos." In *Seguridad Y Violencia En Ciudad Juárez, México*, edited by M. Limas Hernández. Ciudad Juárez, Chihuahua: Universidad Autónoma de Ciudad Juárez.

World Organisation against Torture. 2006. "State Violence against Women in Mexico: The San Salvador Atenco Case." Vol. *Alternative Report to CAT 37th session*. Mexico.

13

BLACK LIVES MATTER AND THE MOVEMENT FOR BLACK LIVES

Aleshia Faust, Dillon Johnson, Zaria Guignard, Samir Adechoubou, Catherine Harlos, Maura Fennelly, and Ernesto Castañeda

This chapter discusses Black Lives Matter (BLM), which appeared in 2013 after the acquittal of George Zimmerman, the man who shot and killed unarmed Trayvon Martin, a Black adolescent in Florida. Since then, BLM has organized chapters across the country and the world. Rallying cries like "I can't breathe" after the killing of Eric Garner and Colin Kaepernick "taking a knee" during the national anthem are just a few of the examples of the movement's various tactics in attempting to achieve their goals. BLM aims to end systematic racism and oppression in America. BLM has movement campaigns, repertoire, and WUNC displays and a network and chapters like a Social Movement Organization. The transformation of BLM being used as a hashtag and then growing into an international social movement organization will be discussed. Some activists make distinctions about whether someone belongs to BLM or to the Movement for Black Lives and distinguish between each. In this chapter we do not make distinctions because from the point of view of many outside observers and participants, these actions are all directed against ending disproportionate police violence against communities of color. Similarly, the Civil Rights Movement was actually a disjointed collection of different activist, organizations, and groups with different goals, strategies, and politics. Yet, looking back, this collective action is commonly referred to as a single movement since it all revolved around and contributed to increasing the citizenship rights of Black Americans.

Trayvon

Trayvon was a quiet seventeen-year-old who attended a local public high school and was active in sports. He was middle class and had a strong support system;

"With parents that wanted to expose him to the world, Martin had experiences that included skiing, horseback riding and a trip to New York City to take in the sights" (Biography 2016). He took an Honors level English class with some of his friends, even though math was his favorite. He was interested in aviation and wanted to be a pilot one day (Biography 2016).

On February 26, 2012, Trayvon Martin left his dad's fiancé's house in Sanford, Florida to go to a local 7–11 for snacks. Around 6:30 pm, the cameras in the shop show that Trayvon had bought the snacks and left the store. Trayvon then started to head home. George Zimmerman, a Neighborhood Watch volunteer, "called Sanford police to report what he considered to be suspicious behavior by Martin" (Alcindor, Bello, and Copeland 2012; Berry and Stovall 2013: 592). Against the dispatcher's advice, Zimmerman decided to get out of his car and follow Martin. Trayvon's friend saw Zimmerman staring intently at him and called him to tell him to run. After Trayvon started running, Zimmerman sped up and tried to catch him. Trayvon thought he was no longer in Zimmerman's sight, and Zimmerman thought that he had lost Trayvon, but the call between Trayvon and his friend went dead after a lot of scuffling was heard. Zimmerman had shot Trayvon Martin in the chest. By 7:30 pm Trayvon Martin was pronounced dead (Berry and Stovall 2013), less than a hundred yards from the house where he was staying (Biography 2016). Police did not arrest George Zimmerman on the scene. Instead, the police brought him into custody for questioning and released him because he claimed he was using self-defense against an unarmed teen. In fact, it was "only after social media outrage and civil rights protests alleged racial profiling and discrimination did Governor Rick Scott appoint a special prosecutor, who brought the charges against Zimmerman six weeks after the shooting" (McCoy 2014: 15). A month later, Zimmerman was charged with second-degree murder and manslaughter. On July 13, 2013, Zimmerman was found not guilty in the killing of Trayvon Martin. Jurors ignored what to many people seemed like concrete evidence about the culpability of Zimmerman. Many people expressed dismay and took to the streets after the decision was announced. Partly, out of this demand, we saw the birth of the Black Lives Matter movement.

#BLM

In July 2013 as Alicia Garza heard of the acquittal of George Zimmerman, she posted on Facebook, "***Black people, I love you, I love us, Our lives Matter.***" These words would have a tremendous impact in starting a form of cyberactivism that used the hashtag #BLM in which participants shared reasons why Black Lives Matter. The stories shared told how many Black individuals felt that their lives did not matter in the eyes of their fellow Americans.

Alicia Garza, a labor organizer in Oakland, alongside her friends Opal Tometti and Patrisse Cullors created the hashtag, a website and an activist network. According to the Black Lives Matter homepage,

> #BlackLivesMatter is an online forum intended to build connections between Black people and our allies to fight anti-Black racism, to spark dialogue among Black people, and to facilitate the types of connections necessary to encourage social action and engagement.
>
> (BLM 2018)

This open and honest discussion among Black people all around the United States allowed for the connection of stories and shared experiences. Black communities across the country had similar stories of marginalization and feelings of exclusion, and the tagging gave them a collective voice. BLM gave voice to the Black community and allowed for the creation of a new activist Black identity.

In 2014, another tragic event catapulted the BLM movement forward. Michael Brown, an eighteen-year-old Black resident of Ferguson Missouri, was shot and killed by officer Darren Wilson. People felt that the officer had no reason to shoot, and suspected that he would not suffer any consequences. Busses were rented to get individuals to Ferguson to protest this tragic event. The BLM founders were some of these Freedom Riders. There were massive and peaceful protests by residents, local groups, and outside supporters. Some fires and looting occurred. The police used tanks, tear gas, and other violent means to repress the people in the streets. The amount of violence used by law enforcement against unarmed civilians furthered racial tensions. Many individuals protesting in Ferguson felt that police officers and courts acted as if Black lives did not matter.

Hashtag or Movement?

In a panel discussion in DC on October 19, 2016, Alicia Garza shared how BLM came into existence,

> There [are] a lot of misconception[s] about Black Lives Matter because it is used for so many things and it becomes really confusing and in a lot of ways that is both intentional but then also sloppy. So, BLM was initiated by myself, Patrisse and Opal in 2013 after Trayvon Martins' killer was acquitted. We set up BLM as a space for Black folk to have further conversation about what we can do to fight back against what we called anti-black racism and state sanctioned violence. We made [it] very clear that this fight was not about just Black men but in fact it was about forging political space where we could be whole people . . . One of the things that we have continued to battle specially in the age of social media is the question of is BLM just a hashtag? Is it a social media phenomenon? Can social media create a movement? Did you guys make a movement or is BLM an organization?

Early on, it was hard to know what the impact of this hashtag would be. Many questioned whether this was just a trending hashtag, a fad, or budding social movement. BLM started on social media and remains the most active online.

Researchers analyzed over 40 million tweets, 100,000 websites, and 40 interviews of BLM activists in 2014 and 2015 (Freelon, McIlwain, and Clark 2016). They found that right after the killing of Michael Brown, the volume of mentions of the BLM movement spiked tremendously, with "over 55 times more tweets and over 13 times more unique users" than before Michael Brown became a household name (Freelon, McIlwain and Clark 2016: 42). There were 12,589,097 #BlackLivesMatter Tweets from August 9 to August 31, 2014 (Freelon, McIlwain and Clark 2016: 42). These scholars note that it was the online and in-person protests around the death of Michael Brown that really made BLM into a social movement.

Online activity was an essential factor in the formation of the BLM movement, although it is important to remember that the three women founders had real-life friendships and organizing experience. In the days and weeks following Brown's death, the hashtag #Ferguson also became widely used on Twitter and was the centralizing word used during the protests related to his death. Twitter saw an uptick of over 2 million tweets per day related to Ferguson. Such a high volume of tweets all related to a single event, according to social media researchers, had not happened before. The word Ferguson, with or without the hashtag, became the most popular term between June 2014 and May 2015, with over 21.6 million tweets using the word. The phrase BLM was the third most used keyword all over Twitter in that same time period (McLaughlin 2016).

Following the grand jury's decision to not indict the officer who had killed Michael Brown, #BLM started to be widely used on Twitter. The average tweets per day reached 3.5 million, a majority of which used the phrase BLM or Ferguson. By December 2014, #BLM was used in over 100,000 tweets a day, becoming the central phrase for the budding movement.

> As its usage rose, other hashtags associated with complaints about the police died out. Remember #HandsUpDontShoot and #NoJusticeNoPeace? McIlwain said #BlackLivesMatter became dominant because it's durable in many social justice situations, such as decrying municipal courts for dubious fines on residents, many of them African American. "it's a very simple principle and it's not tied to any specific action. While it's focused on police shooting, it doesn't only incorporate that," he said. "Something about it has broad resonance."
>
> (McLaughlin 2016)

So #BLM became a motto, symbol, and name for a social movement against police brutality, but also functioned to express demands for dignity and social justice for all Blacks.

Timeline

Here are the some of the grievances and killings that were protested by the movement. All of the victims listed in this timeline were people of color (ABC 2016).

February 26, 2012: Trayvon Martin, a 17-year-old adolescent, is shot and killed by George Zimmerman. Zimmerman is later acquitted of any charges. The Black Lives Matter movement officially started when Zimmerman is later acquitted of murdering Martin.

November 23, 2012: Jordan Davis, 17, and three friends are approached at a gas station in Jacksonville, Florida by Michael Dunn about the volume of their music. Dunn shoots their car and kills Davis.

November 2, 2013: Renisha McBride is shot dead in Detroit.

July 17, 2014: Eric Garner, 43, is killed by an NYPD officer after being put in a chokehold on a sidewalk in Staten Island, New York. A video shows Garner gasping for air and saying, "I can't breathe." The phrase becomes key in campaigns by the BLM movement. Large protests erupt in New York streets after a grand jury fails to indict the officer Daniel Pantaleo.

August 5, 2014: John Crawford, 22, is killed by police for holding a toy gun outside a Walmart store in Ohio.

August 9, 2014: Unarmed Michael Brown, 18, is killed by police officer Darren Wilson in Ferguson, Missouri.

August 11, 2014: Ezell Ford is killed by officers of the Los Angeles Police Department.

October 20, 2014: Laquan McDonald, 17, is shot 16 times by police officer Jason Van Dyke for holding a three-inch knife in Chicago, Illinois.

November 23, 2014: Tamir Rice, 12, is shot by police for carrying a toy weapon in Cleveland, Ohio.

December 20, 2014: Rafael Ramos and Wenjian Liu, two New York Police Department officers are shot dead in Brooklyn.

April 12, 2015: Freddie Gray, 25, runs away after seeing police in Baltimore, Maryland. Police ignore his requests for his inhaler. He dies on April 19 from injuries to his spinal cord incurred while transported by police.

July 13, 2015: Sandra Bland, 28, is inexplicably found hanged while in police custody in Texas for a minor traffic violation.

November 16, 2015: Jamar Clark, 24, is shot by Minneapolis police while handcuffed. BLM coordinates protests outside the police station for 18 days. No charges are filed against police officers.

November 20, 2015: Akai Gurley is shot by NYPD officers in the stairwell of a Brooklyn apartment building.

July 5, 2016: Alton Sterling, 37, is shot five times while pinned to the ground in Baton Rouge, Louisiana as recorded in video.

July 6, 2016: Philando Castile is shot in his car by a police officer in Minnesota while Castile's girlfriend Diamond Reynolds live streams the incident on Facebook.

July 22, 2016: Charles Kinsey is shot while lying on the ground unarmed with his arms raised in the air pleading with Miami police officers not to shoot.

You can find more detailed times of police shootings, contentious performances, and related events online (ABC 2016; Anon 2015; BLM Timeline 2016; Eleframe 2018).

Goals

The Black Lives Matter Network wishes to bring an end to the war on Black bodies as Back folks are continuously targeted and placed at a disadvantage in the American context. BLM also wishes to bring awareness to police violence against women, queer and trans folk who have been excluded from our collective stories of who we are (BLM 2018).

Women have been crucial in this movement, and in response to concerns that only Black male victims were recognized, the #SayHerName campaign, "was created to raise awareness about the number of women and girls that are killed by law enforcement officers" (Khaleeli 2016). BLM is raising awareness not only about police brutality against Black men, but about violence that hurts Black bodies, regardless of their gender and sexual orientation or identity. For example, BLM has brought much attention to the high suicide and homicide rates affecting transgender individuals.

BLM supporters argue that to claim that Black Lives Matter, can be inclusive of all Black Lives, not just heterosexual males. Many organizations and networks come together in the name of Black Lives. For example, at the University of Missouri, students protested against a hostile racial climate on campus using #Mizzou #BLM. Campaign Zero aims to gather comprehensive data on police attacks against Black bodies and to provide solutions to end this violence.

The Movement for Black Lives targets policies that negatively affect Black people and seeks to alter the dynamics that perpetuate categorical inequalities. According to the Movement for Black Lives homepage, this platform was created,

> in response to the sustained and increasingly visible violence against Black communities in the U.S. and globally, a collective of more than 50 organizations representing thousands of Black people from across the country have come together with renewed energy and purpose to articulate a common vision and agenda.
>
> (The Movement for Black Lives 2016)

The Movement for Black Lives is a form of collective action where many Black organizations developed a holistic list of demands that they released on August 1, 2016. The demands included the following: end the war on Black people, reparations, economic justice, community control, invest–divest demands, and developing political power (The Movement for Black Lives 2016). These demands are far from being achieved.

According to the Black Lives Matter website, the whole point of BLM is to "build local power and to intervene in violence inflicted on Black communities by the state and vigilantes" (BLM 2018). This statement does not differentiate between violence carried out by state and non-state actors because the consequences are the same. This movement is trying to reduce systemic racism, racial profiling, police brutality, and racial inequality.

The hashtag Black Lives Matter is accessible and holds a lot of symbolic weight, which is why it is used by activists addressing various problems facing Black communities. Actions differ within different states and cities based on the respective BLM chapter's priorities. BLM affiliates have organized over 2,326 demonstrations, ranging from sizes of ten to thousands of people (Eleframe 2018).

Critics and Responses

By 2018 there were at least fifty recognized chapters of BLM across the United States as well as chapters in Canada, the UK, and France. While there is a central committee, these different chapters work on what they see as the most pressing needs in their community. This leads to the criticism that the BLM movement is too decentralized because each chapter acts as its own entity. Yet, given that the chapters decide the ways in which they wish to act, each chapter can be successful in its own sphere of influence. However, individuals outside of major cities, where most chapters are located, are less likely to participate. When individuals post or organize protests using the BLM hashtag, the public may assume that a BLM chapter and/or BLM as a whole supports these actions. Like the Indignados and #YoSoy132, in practice, BLM is a decentralized movement.

When #BLM came about, some people had adopted the ideology that we lived in a post-racial society because of the election of Barack Obama in 2008 (Bonilla-Silva 2017). However, this belief fails to recognize that the violence against Black bodies based solely on their race is a part of both American history and contemporary life.

Critics have also argued that the BLM has further perpetuated racial divisions, but BLM says it speaks about issues that non-Blacks underplay or are unaware of. People claiming to feel erased when the statement Black Lives Matter is mentioned have come up with #AllLivesMatter, #BlueLivesMatter, along with many similar hashtags focusing on other identities. The BlueLivesMatter hashtag has also gained a lot of attention because of the killing of police officers. For example, on July 7, 2016, a sniper murdered five police officers at a Black Lives Matter protest in Dallas. Some have blamed BLM for influencing these shooters.

The movement's response was to denounce these violent acts but also reiterate that all lives matter but that Black folks are being disproportionally targeted by aggressive policing and not given proper justice. This lack of justice suggests that Black lives do not matter in comparison to White lives and therefore, we need to focus on creating a culture where the same value is given to people of all backgrounds.

Protesting at Sporting Events—Taking a Knee

During the 2016 NFL preseason, Colin Kaepernick, a quarterback for the San Francisco 49ers, sat on two different occasions while the national anthem was being sung; but the public did not take notice until August 26, 2016, when someone took a photo of him sitting on the bench. This led to widespread criticism and critiques of his actions. Two days later during a press conference, he elaborated on what he was trying to get across.

> I'm going to continue to stand with the people that are being oppressed. To me, this is something that has to change. When there's significant change and I feel that flag represents what it's supposed to represent, and this country is representing people the way that it's supposed to, I'll stand.
>
> This stand wasn't for me. This is because I'm seeing things happen to people that don't have a voice, people that don't have a platform to talk and have their voices heard, and effect change. So I'm in the position where I can do that and I'm going to do that for people that can't . . . If we have these real conversations that are uncomfortable for a lot of people. If we have these conversations, there's a better understanding of where both sides are coming from.
>
> (Sandritter 2016)

Initially, his message became lost in criticisms that labeled him as unpatriotic, Un-American, misguided, or ungrateful. Yet in the same statement, Kaepernick also said:

> I have great respect for the men and women that have fought for this country. I have family, I have friends that have gone and fought for this country. And they fight for freedom, they fight for the people, they fight for liberty and justice, for everyone. That's not happening. People are dying in vain because this country isn't holding their end of the bargain up, as far as giving freedom and justice, liberty to everybody. That's something that's not happening. I've seen videos, I've seen circumstances where men and women that have been in the military have come back and been treated unjustly by the country they fought for, and have been murdered by the country they fought for, on our land. That's not right.
>
> (Sandritter 2016)

As one young Black male co-author asks, Why all the outrage? Is it because he is an outspoken African American man? Is it because he is an athlete and he would diverge fans from their entertainment with his "political views"? Do people just not care about the issues he is trying to bring light to? Or is this related to white nationalism? White nationalists bombarded Kaepernick with criticism, but nonetheless, he continued.

Eric Reid another NFL player joined the protest. These two men met and attempted to construct a more productive way of protesting, so they communicated with Nate Boyer, a former football player and Green Beret, to try to find a middle ground for their actions. Boyer suggested taking a knee would be more respectful in the eyes of the military (Boyer 2017). From that moment on,

Kaepernick began taking knees instead of sitting. Still, he was labeled "unpatriotic." Kaepernick was not only talking about making changes; he has donated over a million dollars towards charities that focus on racial issues.

Kaepernick introduced a new contentious performance to the repertoire, one that could be reproduced elsewhere. Soon not only were NFL players the only athletes protesting. On September 4, 2016, professional soccer player Megan Rapinoe took a knee during the national anthem to express solidarity with Kaepernick claiming that "she knows what it means to look at the flag and not have it protect all of your liberties" (Sandritter 2016). From Howard University cheerleaders, WNBA, NBA, to youth league players from different walks of life who believed in his message, people were partaking in the movement by kneeling. After the 2016 season, Kaepernick decided to opt out his contract, which officially made him a free agent so therefore he could sign with any team he pleased. Some fans wanted the NFL to ban these protests and punish or fire Kaepernick. Some claim that due to these actions, the NFL ratings plummeted, affecting the NFL financially. Months passed, and no teams showed interest in signing Kaepernick because they argued he would be a distraction, that he did not care about playing, or that he just was not a good player despite his stellar record with San Francisco (Rosenberg 2017).

Kaepernick's argument is rooted in the critique of differentiating between "legitimate" and "illegitimate" violence and thinking that the legitimacy of a killing depends on the person shooting (Tilly 2017). In this situation, we have state actors being able to shoot using their discretion, and implicit biases, without having to worry about consequences.

BLM Protest during Trump's Inauguration

Fieldnotes by Catherine Harlos

On January 20, 2017, some friends and I gathered a couple of blocks from the Inauguration checkpoint. It was chilly and dark—just past 7:30 in the morning. The Movement for Black Lives crowd was circling around the action's leaders, who were Black folks from Black Lives Matter DMV as well as Baltimore's Black Youth Project. The crowd was quite diverse, with a sizable amount of white folks. I guessed they were from the white racial justice group Showing Up for Racial Justice (SURJ) (later, I was proved right). I wasn't surprised to see a good amount of white folks, as I knew many of my friends who are people of color were terrified at the idea of protesting an event swarming with ominous "Make America Great Again" Hats.

The rally began with several of the core leaders/organizers leading typical Black Lives Matter chants—"Black lives, they matter here! Trans lives, they matter here!" The organizers emphasized that the African American community has always been in a crisis state—these dimensions of power and oppression are not new, they said, and if they seem new to you, that means you are coming from privilege. While men spoke as well, the pre-action speeches were led by Black women. One read a powerful and moving poem about being a Black woman, and another gave a critical speech reminding white folks to stay in their lane, de-center themselves, and be cognizant of their space. One particularly powerful line was about how "we [the Black folks present] come from the neighborhoods that you [the white folks in the audience] roll up their windows while driving through." She stressed the importance to be plugged into and actively following Black-led movements, even if you are in SURJ. These messages were critical for white people like me to hear and adhere to while protesting in order to strive for collective liberation. The speeches and rallying cries ended with Assata Shakur's words.

It is our duty to fight for our freedom.
It is our duty to win.
We must love each other and support each other.
We have nothing to lose but our chains.

We took off marching and chanting toward the check-point. Once we arrived, young Black men—members of Black Youth Project/BLM—chained themselves to the checkpoint. Organizers reminded us that they were putting their lives in danger to resist the inauguration. We all chanted and cheered, clapping, and repeating "I got your back!" I felt a wave of emotion beyond words watching these young men my age put so much on the line to resist. It was both beautiful and devastating. White folks formed a crowd around the chained young men, and one of the Black women leading called out for queer Black folks to come make a space in the front.

A tall white man yelled, "Green and yellow SURJers over here!" Having no idea what that meant, but knowing that green and yellow usually mean low-medium risk of arrest and SURJ is where it's appropriate for white folks to go, I took off. We crouched down and listened to his directions. He told us we were going to link arms and sit in front of the fence in order to block people from entering the parade. Once he gave us the go, we bolted forward as a group and infiltrated the line of Trump supporters. Collectively, we sat down and linked arms.

Immediately, the Trump supporters erupted in angry exclamations. We began to sing songs such as "There Is More Love Somewhere," "This Little Light of Mine," and "This Land is Your Land." One white woman who had a very sweet voice led the singing – the line was mainly, but not exclusively, white women.

A white man got particularly enraged, calling us names and videotaping us. The women next to me and I angrily challenged him, but the white man organizing this part of the action told us to ignore this man. We continued on singing as he called us unemployed, screamed at us, and threatened that when Trump became president, the police would handle us accordingly. At one point, he was screaming in our faces "WHY DO YOU WANT TO TAKE AWAY MY RIGHTS?" It is almost as though you could have substituted "rights" for "white privilege."

Chants mixed into our singing—"This checkpoint is closed!" we exclaimed. Police officers were present, and troops gathered behind us, complete with camouflage trucks. BLM organizers cheered us on and assured us that the chained young men were doing okay so far as they were out of our sight. Our main SURJ organizer warned us that the action had now escalated to "red" level, meaning there was a high chance of arrest. My friend Elli and I decided to stay—we had never been in a successful human blockade before. People began to hand us coffee, hot tomato soup, and nuts. I got a coffee merely to warm my hands.

After a while, we were told to stand up and form a multi-layer blockade facing both sides of the fence. I joined the one closest to me—we were three lines thick, with people of color joining in. Things seemed to be escalating. And they did. White men rammed themselves into us trying to get through, even though they could walk to another entrance to get in. But our presence thoroughly disrupted their day, thus aggravating them. I was terrified thinking that the people in the front line were going to get knifed.

Finally, after a good couple of hours, one of the core BLM organizers told us to disband; our mission was complete. Emotional and exhausted, Elli and I tearfully smiled and made our way to the nearest fast-food restaurant. After sandwiches and bathroom breaks, we set off for the main J20 Resistance gathering in McPherson square. On our way, we heard eerie cheering and music right at noon. We were miserable. However, it comforted us to know that the cheering seemed to come from a very small crowd indeed.

Upon our arrival, we gathered posters, booklets, and flyers in a large tent hosting a variety of local leftist/anti-racist organizations—Black Youth Project, Democratic Socialists, Empower DC, etc. We asked around and found out that a rally started in about an hour. To kill time, we read through our leaflets, ate hot potatoes given to us by other protesters, and marveled at the growing crowd of typical leftist protesters (elderly people who apparently were wearing the same protest garb they wore in the '60s, people with long hair, young people wearing all black and ski masks, etc.). By the time the rally started, there was a crowd of several hundred.

Many leaders and artists spoke and performed, including Black women working to fight incarceration and environmental racism, a transgender singer and activist, Michael Moore, and the Indigenous Youth Council. With them was a Tribal leader from the Standing Rock Sioux tribe, as well as other Native organizers and political leaders. They spoke about how water is life, and how they want our help in protecting the water for their children and families. There was also prayer. Many of the spectators—myself included—broke down in tears.

By now it was almost 5:00 pm. I was exhausted, freezing, and starving. I said farewell to my friends and went over a block to call a Lyft home. However, at this moment I ran into Elli and Sophie, who had been using a nearby bathroom.

"What's that?" Elli said, pointing. We looked down the street, and there was billowing black smoke and tiny orange flames. We all looked at each other and began to run towards the fire. I put on a mask that could cover my eyes and mouth in case of tear gas. Many other protesters ran towards the flames as well. Closer to the fire was chaos. People were visibly frightened, running in every direction. Folks looked disoriented. We heard that cars had been set on fire. Troops were clustered in the streets, and helicopters circled noisily above us. We peered closely at the smoke—staying close, but not too close.

Suddenly, a loud booming sound filled the air. It sounded like a bomb. Hundreds of people were screaming and running away from the noise. Elli, Sophie, and I ran for our lives. I was screaming. Thankfully, someone shouted out that it was a police flash grenade. Catching our breaths, we grumbled with frustration at the police. I had almost had a heart attack.

We inched closer again, trying to figure out what was going on. I later found out that anti-capitalists had set a limo on fire—powerful symbolism. We felt like the scene was apocalyptic as more helicopters circled above us and more troops watched us walk. Just as before, something scary happened swiftly. "TEAR GAS!" someone roared. Again, we took off, shrieking and sprinting. I moved my mask in front of my eyes and mouth. We could see the billowing tear gas hanging in the air, a smaller yet more menacing cloud than the black smoke from the burning car. More cracks and booms ensued. At this point, we decided it was time to go. Elli had on contact lenses and did not want to ruin her eyes in the tear gas. We ran towards the bus and left. (Co-author, Harlos' fieldnotes)

Thus, BLM participated in demonstrations during Trump's inauguration, successfully blocking an entrance to the Washington Mall for ticketed guests to witness the inauguration with the support of organized white allies acting as human shields, and Black activists chaining themselves to security barricades. This was a contentious performance full of symbolism and commitment. These peaceful protests barely made the mainstream media, but the burning car did—thus the importance of first-hand testimonies from observers and participants in contentious performances.

This recollection also shows the connections between different movements #BLM, Standing Rock, and the so-called Resistance. It also shows the problem with dealing only with media reports to reconstruct timelines and event catalogs and supports the need for ethnographic work to get an inside view into a movements tactics, repertoires, and actions.

Conclusion

This chapter describes the growth of the Black Lives Matter and related collective contentious performances adding up to a movement. BLM meets many of Charles Tilly's criteria for being a social movement, consisting of multiple social movement organizations. In terms of including a "social movement campaign," BLM goes beyond just one event. Although it was formed after the killing of Trayvon Martin, BLM aims to end racial oppression for all Black Americans and continues to garner attention after other events such as the shooting of Michael Brown and Eric Garner. Although social media has been vital to BLM disseminating their message, it does not determine the group's existence. Public displays of protest in the movement's repertoire include marches, sit-ins, and kneeling during the national anthem. Common rallying cries like "I can't breathe" also publicly express the members' suffering and calls for justice. Although Colin Kaepernick garnered a lot of national attention for not standing during the national anthem at NFL games, he is not the sole face of BLM; rather, he worked on spreading the organizations' message towards making a more equitable America. The WUNC displays are apparent in marches, songs sung at Trump's inauguration, and determination to participate at any time towards BLM's goals. The organization's mission also goes beyond achieving justice for Black Americans as it also focuses on women and LGBTQ rights. The movement aims to make systematic changes in the country that will create a better society for those oppressed and acts largely through contentious politics. Thus it seems to meet all of the criteria to be called a social movement in Tilly's sense.

References

ABC. 2016. "Timeline: The Black Lives Matter Movement: Where Did It All Begin?," Sydney Australian Broadcasting Corporation Premium News. Retrieved July 14, 2018 (https://search.proquest.com/docview/1803644010/fulltext/BE5F284ED595 40CDPQ/1?accountid=8285).

Alcindor, Yamiche, Marisol Bello, and Larry Copeland. 2012. "In Wake of Trayvon Martin's Death, America Is Soul-Searching." in *USA Today*.

Anon. 2015. "Blm Timeline (2012–2015)", Georgetown. (https://repository.library.georgetown.edu/bitstream/handle/10822/1040691/Black%20Lives%20 Matter%20Timeline%20.pdf?sequence=1).

Berry, Theodorea Regina, and David O. Stovall. 2013. "Trayvon Martin and the Curriculum of Tragedy: Critical Race Lessons for Education." *Race, Ethnicity and Education* 16(4): 587–602.

Biography. 2016. "Trayvon Martin": A&E Television Networks. Retrieved February 7, 2018 (www.biography.com/people/trayvon-martin-21283721).

BLM. 2018. "Black Lives Matter—About": Black Lives Matter. Retrieved February 7, 2018 (https://blacklivesmatter.com/about/).

BLM Timeline. 2016. "Black Lives Matter Interactive Timeline (2012–2016)," Las Vegas: UNLV. (https://courses.online.unlv.edu/courses/WMST/WMST113/Black LivesMatter/dist/).

Bonilla-Silva, Eduardo. 2017. *Racism without Racists: Color-Blind Racism and the Persistence of Racial Inequality in America*. Lanham, MD: Rowman & Littlefield.

Boyer, Nate. 2017. "Ex-Green Beret Nate Boyer Writes Open Letter to Trump, Kaepernick, Nfl and America": ESPN. Retrieved February 7, 2018 (www.espn.com/nfl/story/_/id/21003968/nfl-2017-ex-green-beret-nate-boyer-writes-open-letter-president-donald-trump-colin-kaepernick-nfl-united-states-america).

Eleframe. 2018. "At Least 2,326 Black Lives Matter Protests and Other Demonstrations Have Been Held in the Past 1,299 Days." Retrieved February 7, 2018 (https://elephrame.com/textbook/BLM).

Freelon, Deen, Charlton McIlwain, and Meredith Clark. 2016. "Beyond the Hashtags: #Ferguson, #Blacklivesmatter, and the Online Struggle for Offline Justice." Vol. Washington, DC: Center for Media & Social Impact, American University.

Khaleeli, Homa. 2016. "#Sayhername: Why Kimberlé Crenshaw Is Fighting for Forgotten Women." in *The Guardian*. 30 May.

McCoy, Yavilah. 2014. "Trayvon Martin: Reflections on the Black and Jewish Struggle for Justice." *Tikkun*, January 1, pp. 14–21.

McLaughlin, Michael 2016, "The Dynamic History of #Blacklivesmatter Explained: This Is How a Hashtag Transformed into a Movement": *HuffPost*. Retrieved February 9, 2018 (www.huffingtonpost.com/entry/history-black-lives-matter_us_56d0a3b0e4b0871f60eb4af5).

Rosenberg, Michael. 2017. "Colin Kaepernick Can Be an Activist and a Football Player": *Sports Illustrated*. Retrieved February 8, 2018 (www.si.com/nfl/2017/08/15/colin-kaepernick-national-anthem-protests-charlottesville).

Sandritter, Mark. 2016. "All the Athletes Who Joined Kaepernick's National Anthem Protest": SBNation.com. Retrieved February 8, 2018 (www.sbnation.com/2016/9/11/12869726/colin-kaepernick-national-anthem-protest-seahawks-brandon-marshall-nfl).

The Movement for Black Lives. 2016. "Platform": The Movement for Black Lives. Retrieved February 8, 2018 (https://policy.m4bl.org).

Tilly, Charles. 2017. "Pernicious Postulates." in *Collective Violence, Contentious Politics, and Social Change: A Charles Tilly Reader*, edited by E. Castañeda and C. L. Schneider. New York: Routledge.

14

MASS INCARCERATION AND PRISONER RIGHTS

Carly Miller, Emily Johnson, Maura Fennelly, and Ernesto Castañeda

Unequal Incarceration

Besides Black Lives Matter, we have also seen movements around another issue disproportionally affecting Blacks: incarceration. Michelle Alexander, author of *The New Jim Crow: Mass Incarceration in the Age of Colorblindness*, and others argue that African Americans today are still being treated as second-class citizens through systemic oppression within the justice system. Although explicitly racist laws are unconstitutional, the practices of the justice system disproportionately affect the Black community in a negative manner. The argument is that after the Civil Rights movements of the 1960s, Richard Nixon declared the War on Drugs to target the Black community. Alexander states that "in the drug war, the enemy is racially defined" (Alexander 2012: 98). Due to the War on Drugs, measures such as harsh mandatory minimums for drug offenses and "three strikes" laws have resulted in a wave of mass incarceration, disproportionately affecting African Americans—followed by Latinos—who face unequal punishments for minor crimes. According to the NAACP website,

> African Americans are incarcerated at more than five times the rate of whites. . . . African Americans and whites use drugs at similar rates, but the imprisonment rate of African Americans for drug charges is almost 6 times that of whites.
> (NAACP 2018)

These statistics reveal severe discrepancies in how our justice system treats individuals of different races throughout the country (Escobedo 2015). The United States currently incarcerates more individuals than any other nation in the world; with only 5 percent of the world's population, the U.S. has 25 percent of the world's prison population (Lee 2015). Formerly incarcerated individuals are disenfranchised in a variety of different ways. They are kept from voting polls, face numerous barriers to employment, and do not have the same access to social services in comparison to their counterparts without a criminal history (NAACP 2018). Broad criminal justice reform has moved to the top of the agenda of many activists pushing for social change.

Despite the lack of national awareness and social media attention, several prisoner groups have formed across the country and staged protests in their respective prisons. Unpaid and underpaid labor, poor living conditions, and other grievances pushed prisoners to mobilize and communicate. Family members, contraband cellphones, and social media allowed prison groups to share with people in other prisons their methods and tactics in planning strikes and other forms of protest. The prisoners' status influences the lack of public awareness on the matter. Still, the prisoners' mobilization meets many of the criteria for it to be considered a social movement.

Prison Protest Timeline

The following timeline displays some significant actions taken within prisons, but also policy changes and historical events that interact with the movement.

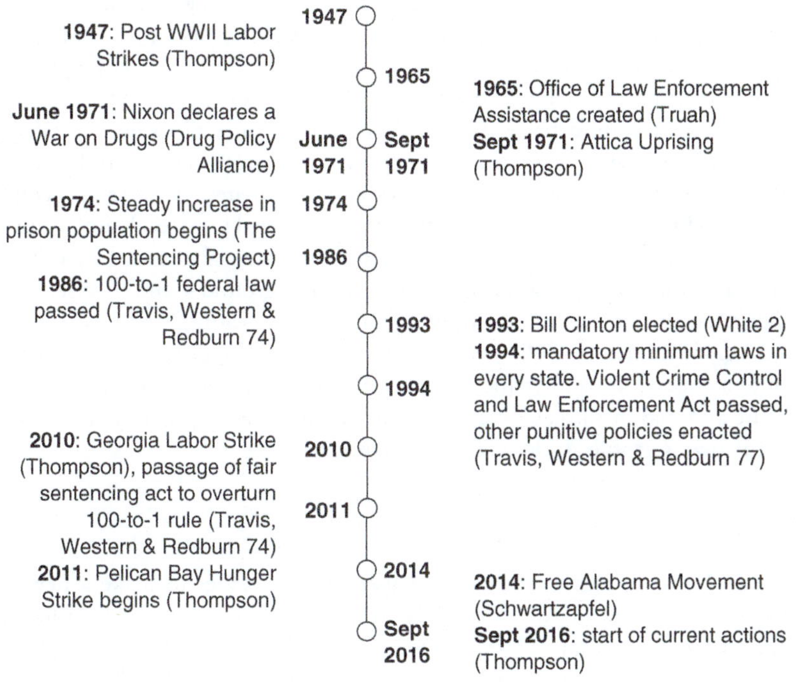

Figure 14.1 Timeline of prison protests

Source: Drug Policy Alliance 2018; Schwartzapfel 2016; T'ruah 2014; The Sentencing Project 2017; Thompson 2016; Travis, Western, and Redburn 2014.

Prison Strikes

Strikes and movements in prisons are not a new phenomenon. This timeline depicts some of the key moments in the prisoner rights movements. The application of punishment and conceptions of criminal justice have changed through history, as has public opinion regarding punishment. In recent years, the more liberal and rehabilitation-oriented methods of crime control are being more seriously considered. Discriminatory policies like Stop and Frisk and theories such as "the broken windows theory" that have led to the over-criminalization of minorities are increasingly being discredited. These policies are sold to the public as methods to create safer communities, but they have often led to people of color being unnecessarily stopped, harassed, and even arrested by police officers.

2010 Georgia Work Stoppage

In 2010, thousands of prisoners in Georgia called for better living conditions and refused to perform their jobs (Wheaton 2010). Quickly, prisoners in Illinois, North Carolina, Virginia, and Washington followed suit. This multi-prison protest was coordinated through banned cellphones. Some inmates reported that organizers had spent months "building a web of disparate factions and gangs—groups not known to cooperate—into a unified coalition using text messaging and word of mouth" (Nicolich 2011: 11). In fact, the Georgia protest appeared to be the first prison movement to incorporate technology to "orchestrate a grassroots movement behind bars" due to the delicate nature of using contraband cellphones. One inmate noted that these groups "had come together and set aside all differences, whites, blacks, those of us that are affiliated in gangs" (Nicolich 2011: 11). This created a collective identity of victimized inmates. Elaine Brown, former Black Panther leader and advocate for prisoner rights stated that "their general rage found a home among them—common ground—and they set aside their differences to make an incredible statement" (Wheaton 2010). Ms. Brown played a significant role in this movement. She boiled the prisoners' complaints down to a concise list of demands but made it clear that the protest was organic in nature and that the inmates reached out to her to act as a figurehead (Wheaton 2010). Brown's profile attracted external support.

The Free Alabama Movement

The Free Alabama Movement of 2014 used similar tactics to make a new set of demands. Inmates in Alabama declared that the prison system is "running a slave empire" (Eidelson 2014). Here, the shift has focused on the exploitation of unpaid or underpaid labor in prisons. The strikers wanted educational programming, rehabilitation, better living conditions, an end to overcrowding in prisons, as well as an end to life sentences without parole. These demands were put together into a bill entitled Alabama's Education, Rehabilitation, and Re-Entry Preparedness Bill. One inmate at the St. Clair Correctional Facility and the founder of the prison-based group "Free Alabama Movement," Melvin Ray, stated, "the only weapon or strategy . . . that we have is our labor, because that's the only reason that we're here" (Eidelson 2014). Prison labor includes laundry, kitchen, chemical work, license plate production, and furniture making. This labor was entirely unpaid, and in 2012 the Senate passed a bill to let private businesses employ prison labor.

The prisoners organized work stoppages and in secret posted cellphone videos on the movement's website detailing the abuses taking place in the facility. In the videos inmates walk the outsiders through dilapidated and dangerous facilities with issues such as exposed livewire and blocked fire exits.

The National Prison Work Stoppage

The Incarcerated Workers Organizing Committee, a group of the Industrial Workers of the World Union, planned the strike "against prison slavery." They connected with the families of inmates as well as previous movements such as the Free Alabama Movement and the Free Ohio Movement (Kim 2016). The National Lawyers Guild endorsed the protest (Lewis 2016). Here again, we see an outside mobilizing group used to propel group action and attention. Inmates were concerned about harsh parole systems, the lack of educational services, overcrowding, and medical neglect. However, "the issue that has unified protesters is that of prison labor" (Speri 2016). Annually, over two billion dollars are generated with the labor of more than 900,000 prisoners (Spross 2016). Inmates make park equipment, tires, laundry supplies, clothes, nameplates or food equipment for major companies including IBM, Boeing, Macy's, Microsoft, and AT&T for little or no pay (Spross 2016). The Thirteenth Amendment declares, "Neither slavery nor involuntary servitude . . . shall exist within the United States." However, there is one crucial clause in the amendment, which allows the use of involuntary servitude as a punishment for crime (Kim 2016). The Amendment is often used to justify unpaid or heavily underpaid prison labor.

On September 9, 2016, the beginning of the National Prison Work Stoppage was planned to occur on the 45th anniversary of the Attica Uprising, a landmark prisoner protest. Over 24,000 inmates protested. They stopped their work, but also used other forms of resistance in at least twenty-nine prisons spanning across at least twelve states (Washington 2016). In South Carolina, preemptive measures were taken leading up to the strike. Inmates were isolated, and by September 5, the whole system was on lockdown (Washington 2016). In Florida's Holmes Correctional Institution approximately 400 inmates refused to work and took over damaged buildings. Ultimately, riot squads entered and used gas canisters against the protesters. In Michigan, the protest reached a violent level, and the state sent in armed officers to regain control. A hundred inmates in California participated in a hunger strike. A protest in Texas received the most attention due to lead organizer Malik Washington, who was placed in solitary confinement on September 15 in an attempt to stop his communication with others (Speri 2016). The prison was put on lockdown through October 2.

By October 6, the Justice Department said it would investigate Alabama Prisons to make sure their conditions were humane (Washington 2016). This was a glimmer of hope amongst the repression of the protests. Some inmates lost visitation privileges, were placed in solitary confinement, were denied phone use, and lost canteen privileges. Prisons were sent into complete lockdowns after the protests (Kim 2016).

Outside of the prison, efforts were made to propel this movement forward. Organizers took to the streets with signs and flyers as an attempt to spread the word about the current state of the prison system (Lewis 2016). Prisoners wrote letters and used contraband cellphones to send out new information (Schwartzapfel 2016). The Incarcerated Workers Organizing Committee blogged about their organizing, and about the conditions in prisons. Other blogs such as "Support Prisoner Resistance" and "Dying to Live" also updated outsiders on the events inside the prisons. One inmate utilized Twitter by claiming the handle "@Prisonslavery1" as a means to share what was happening day to day during the strike (Lewis 2016).

This was crucial because the strike received scant coverage in the mainstream local media, and these protests did not make national headlines either. There are many reasons for this, including the way that officers and prison officials have the authority to limit information flow inside and outside the prisons, making accurate coverage impossible. The inmates are at the mercy of the guards and cannot share the truth about the protests behind bars (Washington 2016). Prison administrators possess the ability to deny the existence of ongoing protests within a facility, which can lead to false information being given to the media. These denials challenge the validity of statements made by prisoners who may appear to be lying against the word of the prison administration.

Yet there was some coverage on activist blogs and Facebook groups, followed by some smaller national outlets in early September (Kim 2016). The Incarcerated Workers Organizing Committee came out with a statement that again compared this unpaid labor with slavery, "they may have replaced the whip with pepper spray, but many other torments remain" (IWOC 2016). Included in this statement was a call to action directed at the public. "We need support from people on the outside," it stated, "a prison is an easy-lockdown environment, a place of control and confinement where repression is built into every stone wall and chain link . . . the only protection we have is solidarity from the outside" (IWOC 2016). Today there is not much coverage or conversation in the media discussing prison protests despite their considerable size. Yet, movements against police brutality, mass incarceration, and prisoner rights are likely to continue in the future.

Social Movement Test

The prisoner rights movements across the U.S. used limited resources to create a campaign with clear goals. Demands for better living conditions, resources, and the end to unpaid labor are all clearly articulated and common across the prison populations in the United States. Demonstrations in the form of hunger strikes, refusal to work and protests all show the cohesive repertoire of the movement. WUNC displays are also present although they happen inside prison walls and thus rarely reach public officials or the general public. The National Prison Work Stoppage illustrates the cohesiveness and unity of the various prison participants; 24,000 prisoners participating in resistance in one month alone is tremendous considering the minimal resources the members have. This linking together and planning is significant considering that the members lack constant access to cellphones and other forms of communication. The Incarcerated Workers Organizing Committee also assists in informing the public about the goals these prisoners are attempting to achieve. Risking prison lockdowns, the denial of privileges, and even solitary confinement offer proof of the prisoners' commitment to achieving a more just prison system. These prisoner protests will likely continue in the future, and inspire other prisoners to protest. The prisoner rights movement is a cohesive and sustained social movement despite the limited media coverage.

References

Alexander, Michelle. 2012. *The New Jim Crow*. New York: New Press.

Drug Policy Alliance. 2018. "A Brief History of the Drug War." New York: Drug Policy Alliance. Retrieved February 10, 2018 (www.drugpolicy.org/issues/brief-history-drug-war).

Eidelson, Josh. 2014. "Inmates to Strike in Alabama, Declare Prison Is 'Running a Slave Empire'": Salon. Retrieved February 10, 2018 (www.salon.com/2014/04/18/exclusive_prison_inmates_to_strike_in_alabama_declare_they%E2%80%99re_running_a_slave_empire/).

Escobedo, Tricia. 2015. "What's Going on with Prison Reform in America?": CNN. Retrieved February 9, 2018 (www.cnn.com/2015/10/21/us/prison-reform-overview/index.html).

IWOC. 2016. "2016 Prison Strike Call to Action." Incarcerated Workers Organizing Committee. Retrieved May 20, 2019 (https://incarceratedworkers.org/resources/2016-prison-strike-call-action).

Kim, Tammy E. 2016. "A National Strike against 'Prison Slavery.'" *The New Yorker* (October 3).

Lee, Michelle Ye Hee. 2015. "Does the United States Really Have 5 Percent of the World's Population and One Quarter of the World's Prisoners?" *The Washington Post*. April 30, 2015. Washington, DC.

Lewis, Cora. 2016. "Prisoners in 24 States Plan to Strike Friday": BuzzFeed. Retrieved September 10, 2018 (www.buzzfeed.com/coralewis/prisoners-in-24-states-plan-to-strike-friday?utm_term=.hgK3pVvzpJ#.th394KDM4y).

NAACP. 2018. "Criminal Justice Fact Sheet", Washington, DC: NAACP. Retrieved February 9, 2018 (www.naacp.org/criminal-justice-fact-sheet/).

Nicolich, Meredith. 2011. "Nonviolent Prison Strikes." *Fellowship* 77(1–3): 11.

Schwartzapfel, Beth. 2016. "A Primer on the Nationwide Prisoners' Strike." New York: The Marshall Project (www.themarshallproject.org/2016/09/27/a-primer-on-the-nationwide-prisoners-strike).

Speri, Alice. 2016. "45 Years after Attica Uprising, Prisoners Are Rebelling Again": *The Intercept*. Retrieved February 10, 2018 (https://theintercept.com/2016/09/16/the-largest-prison-strike-in-u-s-history-enters-its-second-week/).

Spross, Jeff. 2016. "Why No One Knows About the Largest Prison Strike in U.S. History," October 18. *The Week*. Retrieved February 10, 2018 (http://theweek.com/articles/655609/why-no-knows-about-largest-prison-strike-history).

T'ruah. 2014. "The Evolution of Incarceration." *Digital Initiatives*. Canton, NY: St. Lawrence University (www.engagingthenorthcountry.org/node/287).

The Sentencing Project. 2017. "Fact Sheet: Trends in Us Corrections." Washington, DC: The Sentencing Project. Retrieved February 10, 2018 (https://sentencingproject.org/wp-content/uploads/2016/01/Trends-in-US-Corrections.pdf).

Thompson, Christie. 2016. "Do Prison Strikes Work? Amid a Current Prison Work Stoppage, Here Are Five Strikes and How They Turned Out." New York: The Marshal Project. (www.themarshallproject.org/2016/09/21/do-prison-strikes-work).

Travis, Jeremy, Bruce Western, and F. Stevens Redburn. 2014. *The Growth of Incarceration in the United States: Exploring Causes and Consequences*. Washington, DC: National Academies Press.

Washington, John. 2016. "At Least 24,000 Inmates Have Staged Coordinated Protests in the Past Month. Why Have You Not Heard of Their Actions?". *The Nation*.

Wheaton, Sarah. 2010. "Inmates in Georgia Prisons Use Contraband Phones to Coordinate Protest." In *The New York Times*. New York: *The New York Times*.

15

ANONYMOUS

Digital Vigilantes

Justin Ezra, Michael Valenti, and Ernesto Castañeda

The loosely organized hacktivist group "Anonymous" first appeared in major news outlets in 2008 after it targeted the Church of Scientology (Olson 2012). Anonymous is a set of individuals who engage in a diverse repertoire of collective action that uses the internet to combat those they believe are damaging the common good (Coleman 2013). This chapter looks at the formation and growth of Anonymous. The group's tactics and involvement with various political issues, including the Arab Spring and the 2016 U.S. presidential election will be discussed. Yet preliminary analysis done seems to indicate that Anonymous is not a Social Movement Organization (SMO).

Anonymous History

In 2003, Christopher Poole, a fifteen-year-old American, launched 4chan. The website was started as a discussion-imageboard about anime (Japanese animated dramatic movies, popular with U.S. male teens); users post an image with text, and other users can respond in a similar fashion. Posts stay on the website for a couple minutes or some weeks depending on the board and speed of discussion in the section of the website that it was posted on (Dewey 2014). 4chan's demographics were mainly young, college-educated men primarily based in the United States. The website grew in popularity and membership through board /b/, a board with no overarching discussion and self-described as random.

Today, 4chan is an online discussion board that is composed of over fifty topic-based forums where individuals post photographs with outrageous or funny comments (Kushner 2014). The concept of Anonymous came into existence when the imageboard 4chan had the "anonymous" name option, keeping users unnamed while posting text or images on the site. What made 4chan different from other online discussion boards was that anyone who did not use a username would appear with the default screen name "Anonymous" whenever they posted or commented on one of the forums (Klein 2015). Poole hoped that providing anonymity would keep the site irreverent in nature. Some of the first and highest regarded memes and internet sensations originated on 4chan including LOLcats, Chocolate Rain, RickRolls, Impossibru! man, Rule 34, and YOLO.

Something very relevant to 4chan users was the pursuit of "lulz." Lulz is derived from the acronym LOL which stands for "Laugh Out Loud," and having many people comment the most lulz on a post, the equivalent to getting many likes or views on a social media site (Jordan and Taylor 2004). This pursuit of lulz kept the nature of 4chan extremely irreverent especially for the most famous forum titled: /b/ (Kushner 2014). The forum /b/ took the lulz to the extreme as the posts in the forum often included puerile jokes and images, many of which were pornographic or offensive in some way. Most of the individuals who went to forum /b/ would use pseudonyms and very often the default screenname Anonymous (Knappenberger 2012). Interestingly, a certain community began to form on the /b/ forum, and many on the forum realized this, so they began to partake in collective and coordinated online "trolling." Trolling is doing something online, often in the form of a post, that is deliberately offensive or provocative with the aim of upsetting an individual or a group while trying to elicit a response (Knappenberger 2012). The /b/ community from 4chan began partaking in bigger coordinated trolling schemes which eventually led this online community to call themselves "Anons" in reference to their Anonymous screennames (Klein 2015). An Anonymous culture formed in the community on the /b/ forum, and moved away from trolling and began to get involved in activism, and vigilante campaigns online (McDowell 2015). Anons began to get attention on social media and other online discussion boards who called the collective community on /b/ "Anonymous."

In 2006, the first attack organized on 4chan was against the Finnish social network/game Habbo Hotel. Some Anonymous users felt that dark-skinned avatars were banned more often than white avatars.

> A group of 4chan users calling themselves /b/lockers decided to raid Habbo Hotel by forming blockades around the entrances of [virtual pools] popular hangouts, exploiting a technical issue that wouldn't allow avatars to walk through each other when entering and exiting premises.
>
> (YF 2017)

This led to the closing of the pools which annoyed users. The raiders branded themselves a part of "Anonymous" (YF 2017). This "raid" garnered Anonymous their first news story from the Los Angeles-based local Fox News station. The sensationalist news story branded Anonymous as "hackers on steroids," "domestic terrorists," an "internet hate machine," and called many of their attacks random or done for destructive purposes (Schuman 2007).

While the beginning of Anonymous may be shrouded with a sense of mystery, the group has grown since its beginnings to create more organized raids and attacks to fight for some of their loosely held beliefs and ad hoc purposes. The online collective is a very loose group, but they are able to perform acts to bring attention to issues of the day. Anonymous is now involved in online social justice issues and internet rights, particularly, freedom of information. However, due to contradictions and conflicts within the collective, their activism has decreased.

Virtual Contentious Performances

Anonymous is not a formal organization, there are no explicit hierarchies, and there are no membership applications, hirings, or initiations (McDowell 2015). Those who are members of Anonymous or follow the collective are mainly connected through social media, but the essential way in which Anonymous is linked with one another is through Internet Relay Chats (IRCs) which are a type of online chat room. Often Anonymous will have their own IRC servers and this is where much of the strategizing communication occurs.

When Anonymous finds an issue they believe is unjust, they take action in the form of an "operation." Operations start when a member of anonymous uses social media or an IRC to lay claims or pronounce a cause/movement that must be attended to. Before action is taken on behalf of any claims or movements, the strategies or methods as to how one can participate are communicated via social media and IRCs. So, anyone at any time can become a part of Anonymous and use social media, IRCs, and other forms of communication to pronounce operations and lay claims to act for a "good cause."

These "digilantes" (digital vigilantes) or "hacktivists" (hacker activists) are highly regarded by some for their swift and timely action upon injustice (McDowell 2015). Because Anonymous is a loose collective of activists there is not a concrete and continuous agenda, often having multiple operations at the same time.

In general, the people who participate in Anonymous are highly knowledgeable about computers. Campaign participants utilize their coding and programming skills to call attention to companies, governments, groups, and individuals whom they see as putting others in harm's way or partaking in illegal activities. The actions most often used by Anonymous are "Doxing" or "doxing," which is a type of hack that leaks emails and disseminates private information (such as telephone numbers and house addresses) to the public, and Distributed Denial of Service attacks (DDoS).

DDoS attacks are what Anonymous use when they want to take down websites. A DDoS attack "floods a site with so much data that it slows down or crashes" (Kushner, 2014). Imagine a bus or train stop where there is a consistent number of individuals waiting in line and boarding the bus or train. A DDoS attack would be the equivalent of sending thousands and thousands of people to that bus or train stop to flood the line to the point where the bus or train stop can no longer operate, and those who actually needed to use the bus or train can no longer do so. DDoS attacks are frequently accompanied by the use of botnets, which are a set of compromised computers that are connected to a central command server from which the botnet owner can use the resources from all the compromised computers to run multiple DDoS attacks (Coleman 2013). Even though Anonymous has millions of members across the globe, the "heavy lifting of the actual hacking was done by a few people in the background giving the masses the Low Orbit Ion Cannon (LOIC) to assist in the attacks" (Coleman 2013). A LOIC is a public mechanism that can be distributed using a link that assists in a DDoS attack by furthering the amount of traffic towards a website. Thousands of Anonymous members use a LOIC at the same time, while more skilled members use botnets to carry out DDoS attacks.

Anonymous uses other tactics besides hacking. Those who affiliate with Anonymous write press releases and manifestos, design propaganda that spreads through social media, make videos that accumulate millions of views on YouTube, and partake in massive communication methods such as flooding a company with millions of emails or jamming a company's phone service by having hundreds of people call or order hundreds of pizzas in the name of an individual, group, or company requiring them to pay for the food (Jordan and Taylor 2004).

Anonymous is also known for their protests and gatherings to which most protesters wear the Guy Fawkes mask from Alan Moore and David Lloyd's 1989 comic book and the 2005 movie *V for Vendetta,* the masks became synonymous with Anonymous (Knappenberger 2012).

Scientology

In January of 2008, a video of Tom Cruise advocating, and praising Scientology appeared online. It was quickly made fun of on 4chan. The Scientologists tried to ban the distribution of the video claiming copyright protections. As a protest, the video quickly went viral and soon it was all over the internet. Because the video was copyrighted, the Church of Scientology demanded it to be taken down and began to take legal action against websites that refused to take the video down. The Anonymous community from the /b/ forum saw the church's actions as censorship and the community decided to do something about it, thus deciding that extreme measures were to be taken (InfoSec Institute 2011). Next, an Anon went to YouTube and issued a "press release" against the church with a computerized voice-over. The video would receive over two million views within a few weeks. This video was the first time that Anonymous gained support, members, and followers outside of the /b/ forum (Coleman 2013). This video was also the first time Anonymous made an open public statement backing up an operation. That video established a model used by members of Anonymous when making videos and calling for people to understand, join or support operations.

At this point, Anonymous was no longer just a community or culture, for tens of thousands decided to partake in the operation attacking the Church of Scientology (Chen 2014). Anonymous had soon outgrown the /b/ forum and needed platforms where thousands to millions could communicate and coordinate (Kushner 2014). They chose social media and IRCs. The IRC servers that Anonymous began to use were an apt example of a "free space"—a place where alternative identities can be forged, skills are developed, and associative ties are nurtured, all of which, under the right circumstances might be mobilized for collective action (Coleman 2013). This "free space" gave Anonymous the opportunity to coordinate electronically, mobilize, and unify. Thus, the attacks on the Church of Scientology began. Anonymous DDoS attacked the church multiple times, shutting down their website and almost causing permanent damage (Chen 2014). Hundreds of others used other means of collective action such as clogging up the email and phone service of the church, while others sent orders from many different food delivery services, which cost the church thousands.

What really forged an Anonymous identity and their representation in the public's imagination was when many people participating in this campaign took to the streets and protested in front of Church of Scientology buildings across the United States in March of 2008 (Massa 2016). This was the first time when thousands of Anonymous participants came together in person to protest in the physical world. It was also during this first protest when they decided to use the Guy Fawkes mask to hide their identities and to continue their anonymity in real life (Knappenberger 2012). The mask then became the symbol of Anonymous.

Anonymous continued to conduct small operations throughout 2009, gaining more and more supporters. IRCs and social media facilitated the movement to continue as a loose collective because operations could be coordinated and communicated with extreme precision without any organizational bureaucracy or formal structure.

Operation Payback

While Project Chanology (the operation against the Church of Scientology) brought Anonymous to the foreground, the most well-known Anonymous attack was "Operation Payback." Operation Payback unofficially came to fruition after the Motion Picture Association of America admitted to hiring "an Indian software company, AiPlex, that openly admitted to launching DDoS attacks against The Pirate Bay," a massive internet piracy site (Bakioğlu 2016: 40). The fact that other organizations were using DDoS attacks as a tool against a piracy site greatly frustrated Anonymous, who viewed The Pirate Bay and similar sites as a legitimate way for people to spread and share information. Anonymous began DDoS attacks and interrupting the services of many pro-copyright websites such as the MPAA, the Recording Industry Association of America, AiPlex, as well as many other websites associated with the previously stated websites. Disrupting the services of these pro-copyright corporations through DDoS attacks caused havoc, but it was just the beginning of Operation Payback.

In late 2010, many companies from the financial sector and e-commerce sector including MasterCard, PayPal, Visa, and Amazon had stopped processing donations to WikiLeaks, a freedom of speech vigilante organization commonly used by whistleblowers (InfoSec Institute 2011). WikiLeaks releases hundreds of thousands of diplomatic (often controversial) documents that had been kept secret. Anonymous considers websites such as WikiLeaks extremely valuable to the public, and the collective was infuriated by the companies that had effectively cut off their ability to accept donations. An Anon made a video on YouTube and officially declared "Operation Payback" against those companies (Klein 2015).

The anti-corporate spirit of this campaign quickly gained popularity. Veterans of Anonymous guided and directed many newcomers in IRCs as to how they could contribute to the attack on MasterCard, PayPal, Visa, Amazon, and other companies (Delio 2014). This was the first time that the masses used LOICs to compliment the dozens of DDoS attacks by experienced hackers (Kushner 2014). The companies were hard-hit. Visa claimed damages of up to five million dollars. Operation Payback gave Anonymous public media attention, and they were discussed as a movement (Knappenberger 2012).

Operation Payback had consequences for Anonymous. Copyright and piracy laws stayed exactly as they were before, and WikiLeaks did not recover their banking and credit card connections. Sixteen people were arrested in 2011 on suspicion of either using a DDoS attack or hacking PayPal (Sengupta 2011). These arrests took place in the U.S., Britain, and in the Netherlands where a sixteen-year-old was arrested for being a member (Sengupta 2011). Of these arrests, thirteen defendants pleaded guilty to carrying out the attack against Paypal and faced up to ten years in prison along with a $250,000 fine.

A litigious case came up a little bit later regarding attacks against Koch Industries' websites. A thirty-eight-year-old man was arrested and pleaded guilty to taking part in the attack and was sentenced to two years in jail and given a $183,000 fine (Vaas 2013). He admitted to taking part in the attack for one minute and was probably one of the thousands of people taking part in the attack. Members of Anonymous can participate in an attack for only a brief period and still be arrested and charged. Those who were arrested could have been large players or somebody who randomly saw a post on 4chan and participated for a minute as they clicked on a link for curiosity. There is no way to tell why they participated or how much of an impact that person had within the group. Still, many members of Anonymous were not satisfied with the results of Operation Payback, and they felt they should expand their scope globally to help with the injustices that were occurring across the world.

Within Anonymous, some members saw themselves as pursuing political change, some hoped for anarchic or utopian results. Members who participated in Operation Payback had varying beliefs as to why they were targeting the anti-piracy groups. Some members said that "piracy is 'the next step in a cultural revolution of shared information . . . [it's] the beginnings to an information singularity; a beginning of true 'equality of opportunity,' regardless of wealth or capacity" (Bakioğlu 2016: 43). Other members described more realistic goals saying that "'Nobody would listen to us if we said piracy should be legal, but when we ask for copyright lifespans to be reduced to fair lengths, that would sound more reasonable" (Bakioğlu 2016: 43). These members are fighting the same battle in the same way but have different ideas of what the long-term goals of Anonymous should be. According to people who participated in the past, campaigns have participants who are the anarchists, older members who focus on annoyances and wreaking havoc, as well as new members who join in for a moment just to cause chaos and say they were part of Anonymous. The lack of organization and the ease at which random people can take part in Anonymous's actions make a common message or intent murky at best.

Going International

Shortly after the Tunisian Revolution began in December of 2010, many in Anonymous saw the Tunisian Revolts as a chance to fight authoritarianism and censorship. "Operation Tunisia" began with the intentions to help bring down the Tunisian dictator Zine El Abidine Ben Ali (Raza 2016). In the usual Anonymous fashion, a YouTube video was posted with the details of the operation. The traction that this video gained was bigger than any previous video Anonymous had posted. Social media took the operation internationally, and Anonymous' numbers went up to the millions (Raza 2016). Anonymous took down most Tunisian government websites with DDoS attacks combined with LOIC attacks (Kushner 2014). Members of Anonymous did whatever they could to clog the government servers, and finally, one hacker took over the President's website and put up an image of a pirate ship. Not long after, the people of Tunisia prevailed, and Ben Ali left office. Furthermore, Anonymous announced more operations and took similar collective action in Libya, Bahrain, Morocco, and Egypt (McDowell 2015).

"Operation Egypt" was a defining moment for Anonymous. Not too long after the Arab Spring revolutions occurred, the Egyptian government attempted to shut down all internet access within the country. Anonymous helped protesters find alternative ways to use the internet and provided special virtual care packages that included valuable information to protesters on how to protect themselves from tear gas, police brutality, and other violence that could occur on the ground (Knappenberger 2012). These special care packages were translated into Arabic and were file shared via social media or encryption software throughout Egypt. The collective actions of Anonymous in helping the Arab Spring Revolution became the first massive online demonstration conducted on the internet (Coleman 2013). Anonymous provided crucial infrastructure through IRC servers and social media websites (Coleman 2013). The Arab Spring sculpted Anonymous into a truly global entity as Anonymous helped to connect with activists in different countries and aid in their respective political and social movements. Anonymous became much more than just a hacktivist network and became part of social and political movements around the globe.

Path, Division, Consequences

After the Arab Spring, Anonymous continued as a political actor. In early 2011 it took part in the Occupy Wall Street movement, attacked the homophobia of the Westboro Baptist Church, and performed attacks against Sony, child pornographers, the FBI, the state of Israel, and more. The group seemed to have officially moved on from the havoc of their early days in Habbo Hotel to act on a left-wing political agenda loosely based on their original support of freedom of information rights.

Anonymous has been active alongside other social movements, addressing topics of racism and police brutality after the shootings of Michael Brown in Missouri (McDowell 2015). They have attacked the KKK and have taken down their websites multiple times. Furthermore, Anonymous, alongside WikiLeaks, provided damaging information to the public on both Hillary Clinton and Donald Trump during the 2016 Presidential Election.

Anonymous has always lacked a single identity that most members can agree with. Alinta Krauth (2012: 27) believes that Anonymous operates as a pseudo-direct democracy. For Anonymous this means that there is an easily identifiable split among members, there are "meme-creating protesters given to a certain amount of internet hyperbole on the one hand, and hopeful rallyists with low technical sophistication on the other" (Krauth 2012: 28). This split is most apparently seen in the 2016 election where some Anonymous Facebook groups denounced Donald Trump while others denounced Hillary Clinton, but these Facebook groups all claim to be the official Anonymous group. The fighting among Anonymous groups showed the internal disagreements that activist groups can experience (Szoldra 2016).

Some critique Anonymous because it lacks "a general goal or cause for its activism; its goals and targets seem to change from one action to another" (McCarthy 2015: 440). Anonymous often lacks clear goals and has contradicted its own actions many times. While their first fights were for freedom of information and anti-censorship, they fought this by censoring websites such as Paypal and entities such as the Church of Scientology, and they continue to do so by using weapons such as DDoS attacks and doxing. Even the group's attack on homophobia, child pornography, and Israel all halt the flow of information and increase censorship of the internet. Anonymous seems to prefer to fight on whatever front or injustice is popular that day or anything that seems to violate their beliefs regarding the internet or freedom of information, even if that means contradicting their beliefs around freedom of speech.

LulzSec

Anonymous has been relatively quiet since the 2016 election. Nevertheless, there has been a sub-group of Anonymous called LulzSec which has gone on vigilante hacking campaigns against many groups and individuals. Some do not even consider LulzSec a part of Anonymous because they have moved away from the regular ethics and operations frequently used by Anonymous (Coleman 2013). LulzSec has attacked governments, corporations, groups, and individuals using extreme forms of hacking just for the "lulz." This deviates from regular Anonymous style, but many in Anonymous have participated in LulzSec, and the media has not separated the two movements (Klein 2015). To some Anonymous is a social movement, to some, they are vigilante watchdogs, to others they are criminals and cyberterrorists. For some, Anonymous is working for social justice, while for others Anonymous is wreaking havoc. Anonymous has also used different tactics at different times and it is constantly evolving.

Social Movement Test

The U.S. government views Anonymous more as criminals than anything else (Raza 2016). However, let us suppose that in a time of crisis with another country, say North Korea or Russia, Anonymous would help the U.S. government in the conflict. Would they still be considered criminals or cyberterrorists even if they use hacking to help their own country? It is important when analyzing Anonymous to approach the collective movement from multiple perspectives and to not jump to any preconceived conclusions.

Using Charles Tilly's basis for a social movement as the synthesis of campaign, repertoire, and WUNC displays Anonymous can only loosely be considered a social movement. To begin, Anonymous members do participate in a social movement campaign by continually making claims to an authority of some sort. To the second point, Anonymous' repertoire, for the most part, is diverse, but their most effective campaigns/operations consistently include the DDoS attacks, doxing attacks, other forms of virtual obstruction, and short-term social media posts. These repertoires can be copied by others, but there are high legal and technical entry barriers. Anonymous produces WUNC displays online and in the real world showing its Worthiness, Unity, Numbers, and Commitment but these vary in strength depending on the operation. In terms of worthiness and commitment, it does appear that many of the people taking part in Anonymous' actions deem it to be worthy as they are taking part in illegal actions that risk serious consequences such as jail time; not to mention the members of the collective are continually taking part or representing Anonymous both in public and online. The unity and commitment aspects of Anonymous vary because members of the collective will only take part in the operations that resonate with them, and collective action usually takes place randomly when coordinated on IRCs and social media sites often making it difficult to unify all members who claim to be in Anonymous or support the collective. In terms of numbers, it is hard to estimate how large Anonymous really is because it is a loose collective. At times, there have been millions of people participating in the movement, other times it has only been a couple hundred or thousand people. Many of their operations could have been carried out with only a couple dozen members using botnets to employ DDoS attacks and doxing attacks. The attacks would have been successful regardless of the other thousands of members using other methods in complement to the botnets and doxing attacks. So, even though Anonymous has many members, the most complex work is only done by a relatively small number of individuals. Another issue is whether Anonymous' methods break ethical and legal codes or is this a new type of civil disobedience? It is not easy to determine whether it is acceptable to take over or damage intellectual property (websites) even if Anonymous is protecting citizens and assisting them in endeavors of freedom and democracy (McDowell 2015). This may be a new tactic in the repertoire of contentious politics. Contentious politics includes the use of disruptive techniques to obtain a political goal; often these techniques are not peaceful or legal (Tilly 2016). Given all this, Anonymous is indeed a political activist collective, and depending upon the campaign at hand it can be part of a larger social movement.

Anonymous engages in contentious politics; its displays are neither good nor bad; it depends on whose side one is on and what perspective one wishes to take in analyzing the collective acts. Some see Anonymous as a vigilante collective, political activist group, a social movement, watchdogs, trolls, revolutionaries, criminals, or cyberterrorists. Anonymous could rightly be considered a Social Movement Organization (SMO), even while Anonymous did not start with the goals to become an SMO and its lack of headquarters, hierarchy, and leadership makes it hard for politicians and media to comprehend. Yet, to the degree that people participating in a chat decide together what to do beyond personal ego and fame, this group engages in truly democratic exercises, and activism about the causes decided collectively by those participating. In the end, Anonymous has launched many rather successful social movement campaigns and introduced new contentious performances.

References

4chan. 2003. "4chan.Org." (4chan.org).

Bakioğlu, Burcu S. 2016. "The Gray Zone: Networks of Piracy, Control, and Resistance." *Information Society* 32(1): 40–50.

Chen, Adrian. 2014. "The Truth About Anonymous's Activism: A Look Behind the Mask Reveals a Naïve Techno-Utopianism." *The Nation*.

Coleman, Gabriella. 2013. "Anonymous and the Politics of Leaking." Pp. 209–28 in *Beyond Wikileaks: Implications for the Future of Communications, Journalism and Society*, edited by B. Brevini, A. Hintz, and P. McCurdy. London: Palgrave Macmillan.

Delio, Michelle. 2014, "Hacktivism and How It Got Here": Wired. Retrieved April 21, 2018 (www.wired.com/2004/07/hacktivism-and-how-it-got-here/).

Dewey, Caitlin. 2014. "Absolutely Everything You Need to Know to Understand 4chan, the Internet's Own Bogeyman." in *The Washington Post*. Washington DC.

InfoSec Institute. 2011, "A History of Anonymous." Retrieved April 21, 2018 (http://resources.infosecinstitute.com/a-history-of-anonymous/#gref).

Jordan, Tim, and Paul A. Taylor. 2004. *Hacktivism and Cyberwars: Rebels with a Cause?* London: Routledge.

Klein, Adam G. 2015. "Vigilante Media: Unveiling Anonymous and the Hacktivist Persona in the Global Press." *Communication Monographs* 82(3): 379–401.

Knappenberger, Brian [Director]. 2012. *We Are Legion: The Story of the Hacktivists.*

Krauth, Alinta. 2012. "Anonymous in Portmanteaupia." *Social Alternatives* 31(2): 27–32.

Kushner, David. 2014 I. "The Masked Avengers." *The New Yorker.*

McCarthy, Matthew T. 2015. "Toward a Free Information Movement." *Sociological Forum* 30(2): 439–58.

McDowell, Abby. 2015. "Anonymous: The Hacktivist Social Justice Movement": Medium. Retrieved November 30 2017 (https://medium.com/communication-new-media/anonymous-the-hacktivist-social-justice-movement-8c0deb57fd04).

Massa, Felipe G. 2011. "Out of Bounds: The Anonymous Online Community's Transition to Collective Action." in *Academy of Management Annual Meeting Proceedings*. San Antonio, TX.

Massa, Felipe G. 2016. "Guardians of the Internet: Building and Sustaining the Anonymous Online Community." *Organization Studies* 38(7).

Olson, Parmy. 2012. *We Are Anonymous: Inside the Hacker World of Lulzsec, Anonymous, and the Global Cyber Insurgency*. Boston, MA: Back Bay Books.

Raza, Ali. 2016, "The Anonymous Group: What Is It and How Big Is It": Hackread. Retrieved April 21, 2018 (www.hackread.com/anonymous-group-what-is-it-and-how-big-is-it/).

Schuman, Phil. [Director]. 2007. *Fox 11 Investigates: Anonymous.*

Sengupta, Somini. 2011. "16 Arrested as F.B.I. Hits the Hacking Group Anonymous." *New York Times*. New York.

Szoldra, Paul. 2016. "The Anonymous Attack on Donald Trump Is Setting Off a Hacker Civil War." *Business Insider*, March 16.

Tilly, Charles. 2016. "Joseph Strayer Revisited." In *On the Medieval Origins of the Modern State*, edited by Joseph R. Strayer, vii–xvii. Princeton, NJ: Princeton University Press.

Vaas, Lisa. 2013. "Man Fined $183k after Joining Anonymous Ddos of Koch Industries for One Minute." *Naked Security by Sophos.*

YF. 2017. "Pool's Closed." Know Your Meme, Last Modified October 6, 2017. Retrieved May 20, 2019 (http://knowyourmeme.com/memes/pools-closed).

DISCUSSION QUESTIONS

Chapter 1: Social Movements as Politics

What are the advantages of differentiating between social movements and other types of protest activity? What are the disadvantages of making these distinctions?

Do oppressed people always revolt?

What do we mean by contentious repertories and performances?

Chapter 2: Inventions of the Social Movement

How are social movements different from revolutions?

Do you think that ordinary people benefitted from the social movement as a way of doing politics? What categories of people achieved the most? The least?

Chapter 3: Nineteenth-Century Adventures

How did local and regional culture and political systems affect the development and practices of social movements in your country? How are civil and political rights tied to the expansion of the social movement?

Where do rights come from?

Chapter 4: Twentieth-Century Expansion and Transformation

Are social movements always progressive?

Do you think that right-wing social movements are more likely in democratizing regimes?

What are the implications of developing regularized interactions between police and protesters?

How does TV coverage affect how citizens understand movement goals?

Chapter 5: Social Movements Enter the Twenty-First Century

How have new communication technologies influenced social movements?

How have global categorical inequalities affected the development of social movements?

What would a truly global movement look like? Is a truly global movement possible?

The authors issue the "tedious but essential warning that social movements by no means reduce to social movement organizations." Is it possible to have a social movement without a social movement organization? What about the reverse?

The chapter closes with a reflection on the impact of contemporary social movements on democracy. Do you agree that such a split exists? What do you think would, or will, be the effect of that split on democracy?

Chapter 6: Democratization and Social Movements

What is the relationship between trust and democracy? What are the implications of this relationship for social movements?

How do social movements further democratization?

Chapter 7: Futures of Social Movements

To what extent do you agree with the authors' predictions about the future of social movements?

What might help to overcome the bifurcation of social movements? Do you agree with these predictions? Why or why not?

What are some new ways in which mobile phones and social media may affect mobilization in the near future?

Overall Research Questions for Part II

Would you call the cases studies in the second part of the book social movements or not? Explain.

Is it possible to know from the beginning whether a social justice campaign or a large protest will grow into a full-fledged social movement as defined in this book?

If a social movement must satisfy a number of criteria to be called so, why are the media so fast to call some faddish activism a movement, while they are quick to dismiss organized and coordinated campaigns about certain social issues?

Analyze a street demonstration that you personally witnessed or participated in. To what degree does it contain aspects that relate to the model the authors propose? Do you think anything was left out of this analysis?

How would you construct more detailed event catalogues for contemporary social movements?

Can you predict what the next social movement will be? What do you base your prediction on?

Do social movement campaigns have to achieve their stated goals to be called social movements?

REFERENCES FOR PART I

350.org. 2011. "Moving Planet Was Amazing!" *Moving Planet*. Retrieved October 29, 2011 (www.moving-planet.org/).

Abramovich, Paulina. 2011. "Una líder estudiantil chilena aspira a un movimiento social más amplio." *Agence France-Presse*. September 23, 2011.

Ackerman, Peter, and Jack DuVall. 2000. *A Force More Powerful: A Century of Nonviolent Conflict*. New York: Palgrave.

Agence Press France. 2008. "Egypt Police Stripped and Beat Facebook Activist: HRW." May 11, 2008.

Alapuro, Risto. 1988. *State and Revolution in Finland*. Berkeley, CA: University of California Press.

Albrow, Martin, and Marlies Glasius. 2008. "Democracy and the Possibility of a Global Public Sphere," in *Global Civil Society 2007/2008*, edited by Mary Kaldor, Marlies Glasius, Helmut Anheier, Martin Albrow, and Monroe E. Price. London: Sage.

Alexander, John K. 2002. *Samuel Adams: America's Revolutionary Politician*. Lanham, MD: Rowman & Littlefield.

Al Jazeera. *People and Power*. "Egypt: Seeds of Change." February 9, 2011.

——. 2011. *Empire*. "Egypt: Revolution in Progress." July 14, 2011.

Al Masrya al Youm. 2011. "Ain Shams University Students Demand Dismissal of University Leaders." September 13 2011.

Amar, Paul. 2011a. "Why Mubarak is Out." *Jadaliyya*. February 1, 2011.

——. 2011b. "Why Egypt's Progressives Win." February 11, 2011. *Jadaliyya*. Retrieved March 21, 2012 (www.opendemocracy.net/paul-amar/why-egypt%E2%80%99s-progressives-win).

Amnesty International. 2007/2008/2009/2010. *Egypt Report: Human Rights in Arab Republic of Egypt*. Retrieved June 20, 2012 (www.amnesty.org/en/region/egypt).

——. 2011. "Egypt: Stop Forced Evictions and Consult Slum-Dwellers to Resolve Housing Crisis." August 23, 2011. Retrieved February 6, 2011 (www.amnestyusa.org/research/reports/egypt-stop-forced-evictions-and-consult-slum-dwellers-to-resolve-housing-crisis).

Aminzade, Ronald. 1993. *Ballots and Barricades: Class Formation and Republican Politics in France, 1830–1871*. Princeton, NJ: Princeton University Press.

Anderson, Eugene N., and Pauline R. Anderson. 1967. *Political Institutions and Social Change in Continental Europe in the Nineteenth Century*. Berkeley, CA: University of California Press.

Andrey, Georges. 1986. "La Quête d'un état national," in *Nouvelle Histoire de la Suisse et des Suisses*, edited by Jean-Claude Fayez. Lausanne: Payot.

Anheier, Helmut K., Friedhelm Neidhardt, and Wolfgang Vortkamp. 1998. "Movement Cycles and the Nazi Party: Activation of the Munich NSDAP, 1925–1930." *American Behavioral Scientist* 41: 1262–81.

Anheier, Helmut, and Thomas Ohlemacher. 1996. "Aktivisten, Netzwerke und Bewegungservolg: Die 'Einzelmitglieder' der NSDAP, 1925–1930." *Kölner Zeitschrift für Soziologie und Sozialpsychologie* 48: 677–703.

Anheier, Helmut, and Nuno Themudo. 2002. "Organisational Forms of Global Civil Society: Implications of Going Global," in *Global Civil Society 2002*, edited by Marlies Glasius, Mary Kaldor, and Helmut Anheier. Oxford: Oxford University Press.

Annual Register. 1758–2010. Retrieved June 26, 2012 (http://annualregister.chadwyck.co.uk/info/home.htm).

d'Anjou, Leo. 1996. *Social Movements and Cultural Change: The First Abolition Campaign Revisited.* New York: Aldine de Gruyter.

Arakan Rohingya Union. 2011. Rohingya held "The Rohingya Global Day for Action." *Kaladan News.* September 16, 2011. Retrieved October 29, 2011 (www.arunion.org/index.php/news/62-rohingya-held-the-rohingya-global-day-for-action).

Archer, John E. 1990. *By a Flash and a Scare: Incendiarism, Animal Maiming, and Poaching in East Anglia 1815–1870.* Oxford: Clarendon Press.

Armstrong, W. W. 1989. "Labour I: Rural Population Growth, Systems of Employment, and Incomes," in *The Agrarian History of England and Wales. Vol. 6, 1750–1850*, edited by Joan Thirsk. Cambridge, UK: Cambridge University Press.

Ash, Roberta. 1972. *Social Movements in America.* Chicago, IL: Markham.

Asia News. 2011. China: Hubei: thousands take to the streets to protest the suspicious death of a popular official. June 11, 2011. Retrieved October 9, 2011 (www.speroforum.com/a/55371/China-Hubei-thousands-take-to-the-streets-to-protest-the-suspicious-death-of-a -popular-official).

Awad, Marwa. 2010a. "Egyptians Protest Over Minimum Wage of $6 a Month." *Reuters.* May 2, 2010.

——. 2010b. "Egyptians protest detention law, hardline comments." *Reuters.* April 20, 2010.

AZ Central.com 2010. "Who Is Boycotting Arizona?" August 27, 2010. Retrieved October 24, 2011 (www.azcentral.com/business/articles/2010/05/13/20100513im migration-boycotts-list.html).

Bagla, Pallava. 2003. "Ayodhya Ruins Yield More Fuel for Ongoing Religious Fight." *Science* 301 (September 5): 1305.

Balbus, Isaac. 1973. *The Dialectics of Legal Repression: Black Rebels before the American Criminal Courts.* New York: Russell Sage Foundation.

Ballbé, Manuel. 1983. *Orden público y militarismo en la España constitucional (1812–1983).* Madrid: Alianza.

Barrington, Lowell. 1995. "The Domestic and International Consequences of Citizenship in the Soviet Successor States." *Europe-Asia Studies* 47: 731–63.

BBC. 2005. "Timeline: Ayodhya Crisis." Retrieved April 21, 2008 (http://news.bbc.co.uk/2/hi/south_asia/1844930.stm).

Becker, Elizabeth. 2003. "Hark! Voices from the Street Are Heard in the Trade Talks." *New York Times*, September 13, A6.

Beissinger, Mark. 1993. "Demise of an Empire-State: Identity, Legitimacy, and the Deconstruction of Soviet Politics," in *The Rising Tide of Cultural Pluralism*, edited by Crawford Young. Madison, WI: University of Wisconsin Press.

——. 1998a. "Nationalist Violence and the State: Political Authority and Contentious Repertoires in the Former USSR." *Comparative Politics* 30: 401–33.

——. 1998b. "Event Analysis in Transitional Societies: Protest Mobilization in the Former Soviet Union," in *Acts of Dissent: New Developments in the Study of Protest*, edited by Dieter Rucht, Ruud Koopmans, and Friedhelm Neidhardt. Berlin: Sigma.

——. 2002. *Nationalist Mobilization and the Collapse of the Soviet State*. Cambridge, UK: Cambridge University Press.

Belchem, John. 1990. *Industrialization and the Working Class: The English Experience, 1750–1900*. Aldershot, UK: Scolar.

Bennett, W. Lance. 2003. "Communicating Global Activism." *Information, Communication and Society* 6: 143–68.

Bernstein, Thomas P., and Xiaobo Lü. 2002. *Taxation without Representation in Contemporary Rural China*. Cambridge, UK: Cambridge University Press.

Binder, Amy J. 2002. *Contentious Curricula: Afrocentrism and Creationism in American Public Schools*. Princeton, NJ: Princeton University Press.

Birmingham, David. 1993. *A Concise History of Portugal*. Cambridge, UK: Cambridge University Press.

Birnbaum, Pierre. 1993. *"La France aux Français": Histoire des haines nationalistes*. Paris: Seuil.

Black, Eugene C., Ed. 1969. *British Politics in the Nineteenth Century*. New York: Walker.

Blackstock, Allan. 2000. "'The Invincible Mass': Loyal Crowds in Mid-Ulster, 1795–96," in *Crowds in Ireland c. 1720–1920*, edited by Peter Jupp and Eoin Magennis. London: Macmillan.

Bob, Clifford. 2005. *The Marketing of Rebellion: Insurgents, Media, and International Activism*. Cambridge Studies in Contentious Politics. Cambridge, UK: Cambridge University Press.

Bogolyubov, N. D., V. P. R'izhkova, B. C. Popov, and A. M. Dubinskii, Eds. 1962. *Istoria myezhdunarodnovo rabochevo I natsional'no-osvoboditel'novo dvizheniya*. 2 vols. Moscow: V'ishaya Partiinaya Shkola.

Boli, John, and George Thomas. 1997. "World Culture in the World Polity: A Century of International Non-Governmental Organization." *American Sociological Review* 62: 171–90.

Böning, Holger. 1998. *Der Traum von Freiheit und Gleichheit: Helvetische Revolution und Republik (1798–1803)—Die Schweiz auf dem Weg zur bürgerlichen Demokratie*. Zurich: Orell Füssli.

Bonjour, Edgar. 1948. *Die Gründung des schweizerischen Bundesstaates*. Basel: Benno Schwabe.

Bonjour, Edgar, H. S. Offler, and G. R. Potter. 1952. *A Short History of Switzerland*. Oxford: Clarendon.

Bose, Sugata, and Ayesha Jalal. 1998. *Modern South Asia: History, Culture, Political Economy*. London: Routledge.

Botz, Gerhard. 1976. *Gewalt in der Politik: Attentäte, Zusammenstösse, Putschversuche, Unruhen in Osterreich 1918 bis 1934*. Munich: Wilhelm Fink.

——. 1987. *Krisenzonen einer Demokratie: Gewalt, Streik und Konfliktunderdrückung in Österreich seit 1918*. Frankfurt: Campus Verlag.

Bourges, Hervé, Ed. 1968. *La Révolte étudiante: Les Animateurs parlent*. Paris: Seuil.

Bradsher, Keith. 2011. "China Moves Swiftly to Close Chemical Plant After Protests." *New York Times*, August 14, 2011.

te Brake, Wayne. 1989. *Regents and Rebels: The Revolutionary World of the Eighteenth Century Dutch City*. Oxford: Blackwell.
——. 1990. "How Much Is How Little? Dutch Revolution in Comparative Perspective." *Tijdschrift voor Sociale Geschiedenis* 16: 349–63.
——. 1998. *Shaping History: Ordinary People in European Politics 1500–1700*. Berkeley, CA: University of California Press.
Brass, Paul R. 1994. *The Politics of India since Independence*. The New Cambridge History of India, IV-1, rev. ed. Cambridge, UK: Cambridge University Press.
Brewer, John. 1976. *Party Ideology and Popular Politics at the Accession of George III*. Cambridge, UK: Cambridge University Press.
Bright, Charles, and Susan Harding, Eds. 1984. *Statemaking and Social Movements*. Ann Arbor, MI: University of Michigan Press.
Brinkley, Alan. 1983. *Voices of Protest: Huey Long, Father Coughlin, and the Great Depression*. New York: Vintage.
Broeker, Galen. 1970. *Rural Disorder and Police Reform in Ireland, 1812–36*. London: Routledge & Kegan Paul.
Brown, Richard Maxwell. 1975. *Strain of Violence: Historical Studies of American Violence and Vigilantism*. New York: Oxford University Press.
Bruneteaux, Patrick. 1993. "Le Désordre de la répression en France 1871–1921: Des conscrits aux gendarmes mobiles." *Genèses* 12: 30–46.
Brustein, William, Ed. 1998. "Nazism as a Social Phenomenon." Special issue of *American Behavioral Scientist* 41: 1189–1362.
Bryan, Dominic. 2000. *Orange Parades: The Politics of Ritual, Tradition and Control*. London: Pluto Press.
Buchan, Nancy R., Rachel T. A. Croson, and Robyn M. Dawes. 2002. "Swift Neighbors and Persistent Strangers: A Cross-Cultural Investigation of Trust and Reciprocity in Social Exchange." *American Journal of Sociology* 108: 168–206.
Bucher, Erwin. 1966. *Die Geschichte des Sonderbundskrieges*. Zurich: Berichthaus.
Buechler, Steven M. 1990. *Women's Movements in the United States: Woman Suffrage, Equal Rights, and Beyond*. New Brunswick, NJ: Rutgers University Press.
——. 2000. *Social Movements in Advanced Capitalism: The Political Economy and Cultural Construction of Social Activism*. New York: Oxford University Press.
Burke, Edmund, III, Ed. 1988. *Global Crises and Social Movements: Artisans, Peasants, Populists, and the World Economy*. Boulder, CO: Westview.
Calhoun, Craig. 1995. "'New Social Movements' of the Early Nineteenth Century," in *Repertoires and Cycles of Collective Action*, edited by Mark Traugott. Durham, NC: Duke University Press.
Capitani, François de. 1986. "Vie et mort de l'Ancien Régime," in *Nouvelle histoire de la Suisse et des Suisses*, edited by Jean-Claude Fayez. Lausanne: Payot.
Caramani, Daniele. 2003. *The Formation of National Electorates and Party Systems in Europe*. Cambridge, UK: Cambridge University Press.
Carey, Sabine C. 2009. *Protest, repression and political regimes: an empirical analysis of Latin America and Sub-Saharan Africa*. ADD City: Routledge.
Carr, Sarah. 2011. "With Latest Protest, Doctors Continue Fight for Better Conditions." *Al Masrya al Youm* (English Edition). September 22, 2011.
Cassidy, Megan. 2017. "Former Maricopa County Sheriff Joe Arpaio Guilty of Criminal Contempt," in *The Republic*. Phoenix, AZ.
Carter, Neal Allan. 2003. "Political Identity, Territory, and Institutional Change: The Case of Belgium." *Mobilization* 8: 205–20.

Castañeda, Ernesto. 2006. "Los Minutemen En La Universidad: El Debate Migratorio Actual Y Los Debates Ideológicos Pasados." *Estudios de Política y Sociedad* 2(3): 29–40.

——. 2013. "Living in Limbo: Transnational Households, Remittances and Development." *International Migration* 51: e13–e35.

——. Editor. 2018. *Immigration and Categorical Inequality: Migration to the City and the Birth of Race and Ethnicity*. New York: Routledge.

——. 2019. *Building Walls: Excluding Latin People in the United States*. Lanham, MD: Lexington.

Castañeda, Ernesto and Cathy Schneider, Eds. 2017. *Collective Violence, Contentious Politics, and Social Change: A Charles Tilly Reader*. New York: Routledge.

Castells, Manuel. 1983. *The City and the Grassroots: A Cross-Cultural Theory of Urban Social Movements*. Berkeley, CA: University of California Press.

Chabot, Sean. 2000. "Transnational Diffusion and the African-American Reinvention of the Gandhian Repertoire." *Mobilization* 5: 201–16.

Chabot, Sean, and Jan Willem Duyvendak. 2002. "Globalization and Transnational Diffusion between Social Movements: Reconceptualizing the Dissemination of the Gandhian Repertoire and the 'Coming Out' Routine." *Theory and Society* 31: 697–740.

Chandhoke, Neera. 2002. "The Limits of Global Civil Society," in *Global Civil Society 2002*, edited by Marlies Glasius, Mary Kaldor, and Helmut Anheier. Oxford: Oxford University Press.

Chaturvedi, Jayati, and Gyaneshwar Chaturvedi. 1996. "*Dharma Yudh*: Communal Violence, Riots, and Public Space in Ayodhya and Agra City: 1990 and 1992," in *Riots and Pogroms*, edited by Paul R. Brass. New York: New York University Press.

China Worker. 2011. Kazakhstan: "Kurmanov to be jailed?" September 17, 2011. (www.chinaworker.info/en/content/news/1577/).

Church, Roy A. 1966. *Economic and Social Change in a Midland Town: Victorian Nottingham 1815–1900*. New York: Augustus Kelley.

Clark, S. D. 1959. *Movements of Social Protest in Canada, 1640–1840*. Toronto: University of Toronto Press.

Clark, Samuel D., J. Paul Grayson, and Linda M. Grayson, Eds. 1975. *Prophecy and Protest: Social Movements in Twentieth-Century Canada*. Toronto: Gage.

Clemens, Elisabeth S. 1997. *The People's Lobby: Organizational Innovation and the Rise of Interest Group Politics in the United States, 1890–1925*. Chicago, LA: University of Chicago Press.

Cody, Edward. 2008. "Protest over Factory Spreads in China." *Washington Post*, March, 4, A14 (www.washingtonpost.com/wp-dyn/content/article/2008/03/03/AR2008030301072.html).

Cohen, Jean. 1985. "Strategy or Identity: New Theoretical Paradigms and Contemporary Social Movements." *Social Research* 52: 663–716.

Cohen, Jean L., and Andrew Arato. 1992. *Civil Society and Political Theory*. Cambridge, MA: MIT Press.

Collier, David, and Steven Levitsky. 1997. "Democracy with Adjectives: Conceptual Innovation in Comparative Research." *World Politics* 49: 430–51.

Collier, Ruth Berins. 1999. *Paths toward Democracy: The Working Class and Elites in Western Europe and South America*. New York: Cambridge University Press.

Cone Sexton, Connie. 2011. "SB 1070 Opponents March on Law's Anniversary." *AZCentral.com*, April 23, 2011.

Cooper, Jonathan J. 2010. "Tea Party Activists Rally Along Arizona-Mexico Border to Protest Illegal Immigration." *Huffington Post*, August 15, 2010.

Cronin, James E., and Jonathan Schneer, Eds. 1982. *Social Conflict and the Political Order in Modern Britain*. London: Croom Helm.

Council for Foreign Relations. 2011. "Interview with Ragui Assaad. Demographics of Arab Protests." February 14, 2011 (www.cfr.org/egypt/demographics-arab -protests/p24096).

Cunningham, David. 2005. *There's Something Happening Here: The New Left, the Klan, and FBI Counterintelligence*. Berkeley, CA: University of California Press.

Daily Mail. 2011. "How the Internet Refused to Abandon Egypt: Authorities Take Entire Country Offline . . . But Hackers Rally to Get the Message out." January 30, 2011.

Daily Sun. 2011. "Call to Forge Social Movement Against Corruption." April 1, 2011.

Daly, Kyle. 2010. "Demonstrators Face Off Over Immigration Measure." *State Press*, April 25, 2010.

Davis, David Brion. 1987. "Capitalism, Abolitionism, and Hegemony," in *British Capitalism and Caribbean Slavery: The Legacy of Eric Williams*, edited by Barbara Solow and Stanley Engerman. Cambridge, UK: Cambridge University Press.

Davis, Gerald F., Doug McAdam, W. Richard Scott, and Mayer Zald, Eds. 2005. *Social Movements and Organizational Theory*. Cambridge, UK: Cambridge University Press.

Davis, Gerald F., and Tracy A. Thompson. 1994. "A Social Movement Perspective on Corporate Control." *Administrative Science Quarterly* 39: 141–73.

Deibert, Ronald J. 2000. "International Plug 'n' Play? Citizen Activism, the Internet, and Global Public Policy." *International Studies Perspectives* 1: 255–72.

Dekker, Rudolf. 1982. *Holland in beroering: Oproeren in de 17de en 18de eeuw*. Baarn: Amboeken.

——. 1987. "Women in Revolt: Popular Protest and Its Social Basis in Holland in the Seventeenth and Eighteenth Centuries." *Theory and Society* 16: 337–62.

della Porta, Donatella. 1995. *Social Movements, Political Violence, and the State: A Comparative Analysis of Italy and Germany*. Cambridge, UK: Cambridge University Press.

della Porta, Donatella, Massimiliano Andretta, Lorenzo Mosca, and Herbert Reiter. 2006. *Globalization from Below: Transnational Activists and Protest Networks*. Minneapolis, MN: University of Minnesota Press.

della Porta, Donatella, and Manuela Caiani. 2007. "Europeanization from Below? Social Movements and Europe." *Mobilization: An International Quarterly* 12(1): 1–20.

della Porta, Donatella, Abby Peterson, and Herbert Reiter, Eds. 2006. *The Policing of Transnational Protest*. Burlington, VT: Ashgate.

della Porta, Donatella, and Herbert Reiter, Eds. 1998. *Policing Protest: The Control of Mass Demonstrations in Western Democracies*. Minneapolis, MN: University of Minnesota Press.

della Porta, Donatella, and Sidney Tarrow. 2004. *Transnational Protest and Global Activism*. Boulder, CO: Rowman & Littlefield.

Deneckere, Gita. 1997. *Sire, het volk mort: Sociaal protest in België (1831–1918)*. Antwerp: Amsab.

Deutsch, Karl. 1976. *Die Schweiz als ein paradigmatischer Fall politischer Integration*. Bern: Haupt.

Diani, Mario. 2001. "Social Movement Networks: Virtual and Real," in *Culture and Politics in the Information Age: A New Politics*, edited by F. Webster, 117–28. London: Routledge.

——. 2003. "Introduction: Social Movements, Contentious Actions, and Social Networks: 'From Metaphor to Substance'?" in *Social Movements and Networks:*

Relational Approaches to Collective Action, edited by Mario Diani and Doug McAdam. Oxford: Oxford University Press.

Díaz Cepeda, Luis Rubén, and Ernesto Castañeda. 2019. "Motivations and Activist Typologies: Core Activists in Ciudad Juarez." Working paper.

DiMaggio, Paul, Eszter Hargittai, W. Russell Neuman, and John P. Robinson. 2001. "Social Implications of the Internet." *Annual Review of Sociology* 27: 307–36.

Dolléans, Édouard, and Michel Crozier. 1950. *Mouvements ouvrier et socialiste: Chronologie et bibliographie: Angleterre, France, Allemagne, États-Unis (1750–1918)*. Paris: Éditions Ouvrières.

Dowe, Dieter. 1970. *Aktion und Organisation: Arbeiterbewegung, sozialistische und kommunistische Bewegung in der preussischen Rheinprovinz 1820–1852*. Hannover: Verlag für Literatur und Zeitgeschehen.

Drescher, Seymour. 1982. "Public Opinion and the Destruction of British Colonial Slavery," in *Slavery and British Society, 1776–1946*, edited by James Walvin,. Baton Rouge, LA: Louisiana State University Press.

——. 1986. *Capitalism and Antislavery: British Mobilization in Comparative Perspective*. London: Macmillan.

——. 1994. "Whose Abolition? Popular Pressure and the Ending of the British Slave Trade." *Past and Present* 143: 136–66.

——. 2009. *Abolition: A History of Slavery and Anti-Slavery*. Cambridge, UK: Cambridge University Press.

Drobizheva, Leokadia, Rose Gottemoeller, Catherine McArdle Kelleher, and Lee Walker, Eds. 1996. *Ethnic Conflict in the Post-Soviet World: Case Studies and Analysis*. Armonk, NY: M. E. Sharpe.

Dumont, Georges-Henri. 2002. *Le Miracle belge de 1848*. Brussels: Le Cri.

Duyvendak, Jan Willem. 1994. *Le Poids du politique: Nouveaux mouvements sociaux en France*. Paris: L'Harmattan.

Duyvendak, Jan Willem, Hein-Anton van der Heijden, Ruud Koopmans, and Luuk Wijmans, Eds. 1992. *Tussen Verbeelding en Macht: 25 jaar nieuwe social bewegingen in Nederland*. Amsterdam: Sua.

Earl, Jennifer, and Katrina Kimport. 2011. *Digitally Enabled Social Change: Activism in the Internet Age*. Boston, MA: MIT Press.

Earl, Jennifer, Sarah A. Soule, and John D. McCarthy. 2003. "Protest under Fire? Explaining the Policing of Protest." *American Sociological Review* 68: 581–606.

Economist. 2003. "The Perils of Recycling: Excise Hate from One Place, and It Pops up in Another." August 30: 22.

——. 2011. "China Politics: Rising Unrest." June 23, 2011.

Economy Watch. 2011. "Egypt Economy." Report. (www.economywatch.com/world_economy/egypt/).

Edelman, Marc. 2001. "Social Movements: Changing Paradigms and Forms of Politics." *Annual Review of Anthropology* 30: 285–317.

Edwards, Bob, Michael W. Foley, and Mario Diani, Eds. 2001. *Beyond Tocqueville: Civil Society and the Social Capital Debate in Comparative Perspective*. Hanover, NH: University Press of New England.

Ekiert, Grzegorz, and Jan Kubik. 1999. *Rebellious Civil Society: Popular Protest and -Democratic Consolidation in Poland, 1989–1993*. Ann Arbor, MI: University of Michigan Press.

Elinson, Zusha, and Walter, Shoshana. 2011. "Latest BART Shooting Prompts New Discussion of Reforms," *The New York Times*, July 16.

Ellis, Stephen, and Ineke van Kessel, Eds. 2009. *Movers and Shakers: Social Movements in Africa*. Leiden/Boston, MA: Brill.

Eltis, David. 1993. "Europeans and the Rise and Fall of African Slavery in the Americas: An Interpretation." *American Historical Review* 98: 1399–1423.

Emsley, Clive. 1983. *Policing and Its Context, 1750–1870*. London: Macmillan.

Emsley, Clive, and Barbara Weinberger, Eds. 1991. *Policing in Western Europe: Politics, Professionalism, and Public Order, 1850–1940*. New York: Greenwood.

Epstein, James A. 1994. *Radical Expression: Political Language, Ritual, and Symbol in England, 1790–1850*. New York: Oxford University Press.

Eriksen, Mette, 2011. "Al Enough cars! Get ready for Friday's Moving Planet event in Cairo," *Al Masrya al Youm* (English Edition), September 21, 2011.

EuroAnarkismo. 2011. A motion passed by the conference which met in London (UK) in February 2011. "Against the Crisis in Europe, towards a European Social Movement." Retrieved August 2011 (www.anarkismo.net/article/19165).

Fallon, Kathleen M. 2008. *Democracy and the Rise of Women's Movements in Sub-Saharan Africa*. ADD City: JHU Press.

Farrell, Sean. 2000. *Rituals and Riots: Sectarian Violence and Political Culture in Ulster, 1784–1886*. Lexington, KY: University Press of Kentucky.

Favre, Pierre, Ed. 1990. *La Manifestation*. Paris: Presses de la Fondation Nationale des Sciences Politiques.

Fendrich, James Max. 2003. "The Forgotten Movement: The Vietnam Antiwar Movement." *Sociological Inquiry* 73: 338–58.

Fillieule, Olivier. 1997a. *Stratégies de la rue: Les Manifestations en France*. Paris: Presses de la Fondation Nationale des Sciences Politiques.

——. 1997b. "Maintien de l'ordre." Special issue of *Cahiers de la Sécurité Intérieure*.

Flaherty, Jordan. 2010. "A Movement Rises in Arizona." *Huffington Post*, July 29, 2010.

Florida, Richard. 2009. "How the Crash Will Reshape America." *The Atlantic Online*. March 2009.

Fredrickson, George M. 1997. *The Comparative Imagination: On the History of Racism, Nationalism, and Social Movements*. Berkeley, CA: University of California Press.

Freedom House. 2011. *Freedom in the World Report: India*. Retrieved March 2012 (www.freedomhouse.org/report/freedom-world/2011/india).

Freedom's Wings. 2010. "Buycott for Arizona." (http://freedomswingspolitics.com/2010/04/buycott-for-arizona/).

Frey, Bruno, and Alois Stutzer. 2002. *Happiness and Economics: How the Economy and Institutions Affect Well-Being*. Princeton, NJ: Princeton University Press.

Fu, Diana. 2017. *Mobilizing without the Masses: Control and Contention in China*. New York: Cambridge University Press.

Gaillard, Jeanne. 1971. *Communes de Province, Commune de Paris 1870–1871*. Paris: Flammarion.

Gamson, William A. 1990. *The Strategy of Social Protest*, 2nd ed. Belmont, CA: Wads-worth.

Gans, Herbert J. 2003. *Democracy and the News*. Oxford: Oxford University Press.

García de Cortázar, Fernando. 2007. *Los Perdedores de la Historia de España, Booket*. Barcelona: Editorial Planeta.

Garrett, R. Kelly, and Paul N. Edwards. 2007. "Revolutionary Secrets: Technology's Role in the South African Anti-Apartheid Movement." *Social Science Computer Review* 25(1): 13–26.

Geddes, Barbara. 1999. "What Do We Know about Democratization after Twenty Years?" *Annual Review of Political Science* 2: 115–44.

Gerbaudo, Paulo 2012. *Tweets and the Streets*. London: Pluto Press.
Gildea, Robert. 2002. *Marianne in Chains: In Search of the German Occupation 1940–45*. London: Macmillan.
Gilje, Paul A. 1987. *The Road to Mobocracy: Popular Disorder in New York City, 1763–1834*. Chapel Hill, NC: University of North Carolina Press.
——. 1996. *Rioting in America*. Bloomington, IN: Indiana University Press.
Gilliard, Charles. 1955. *A History of Switzerland*. London: George Allen & Unwin.
Gitlin, Todd. 1980. *The Whole World Is Watching: Mass Media in the Making and Unmaking of the New Left*. Berkeley, CA: University of California Press.
Giugni, Marco G., Doug McAdam, and Charles Tilly, Eds. 1998. *From Contention to Democracy*. Lanham, MD: Rowman &Littlefield.
Glen, Robert. 1984. *Urban Workers in the Early Industrial Revolution*. London: Croom Helm.
Glenn, John K., III. 2001. *Framing Democracy: Civil Society and Civic Movements in Eastern Europe*. Stanford, CA: Stanford University Press.
GlobalVoicesOnline. 2011. "Egypt: A List of Demands from Tahrir Square, 10 February 2011." (http://globalvoicesonline.org/2011/02/10/egypt-a-list-of-demands-from-tahrir-square/).
Goldstein, Robert J. 1983. *Political Repression in Nineteenth-Century Europe*. London: Croom Helm.
——. 2001. *Political Repression in Modern America from 1870 to 1976*. Urbana, IL: University of Illinois Press.
Goldstein, Robert J., Ed. 2000. *The War for the Public Mind: Political Censorship in Nineteenth-Century Europe*. Westport, CT: Praeger.
Goldstone, Jack A. 2003. "Introduction: Bridging Institutionalized and Noninstitutionalized Politics," in *States, Parties, and Social Movements*, edited by Jack A. Goldstone. Cambridge, UK: Cambridge University Press.
González Calleja, Eduardo. 1998. *La Razón de la Fuerza: Orden público, subversion y violencia política en la España de la Restauración (1875–1917)*. Madrid: Consejo Superior de Investigaciones Científicas.
——. 1999. *El Máuser y el Sufragio: Ordén público, subversión y violencia política en la crisis de la Restauración*. Madrid: Consejo Superior de Investigaciones Científicas.
Goodway, David. 1982. *London Chartism 1838–1848*. Cambridge, UK: Cambridge University Press.
Gossman, Lionel. 2000. *Basel in the Age of Burkhardt: A Study in Unseasonable Ideas*. Chicago, IL: University of Chicago Press.
Greenberg, Louis. 1971. *Sisters of Liberty: Paris, Marseille, Lyon and the Reaction to the Centralized State*. Cambridge, MA: Harvard University Press.
Griffith, Robert. 2017. "Behind the Headline: Why is Catalonia Vying for Independence?" *Cat Flag*, November 23. https://catflag.wordpress.com/2017/10/22/behind-the-headline-why-is-catalonia-vying-for-independence/
Grimsted, David. 1998. *American Mobbing, 1828–1861: Toward Civil War*. New York: Oxford University Press.
Gurr, Ted Robert. 2000. *Peoples versus States: Minorities at Risk in the New Century*. Washington, DC: United States Institute of Peace Press.
Gusfield, Joseph R. 1966. *Symbolic Crusade: Status Politics and the American Temperance Movement*. Urbana, IL: University of Illinois Press.
Gwertzman, Bernard, and Michael T. Kaufman, Eds. 1991. *The Collapse of Communism*, rev. ed. New York: Times Books.

Hanagan, Michael. 1998. "Irish Transnational Social Movements, Deterritorialized Migrants, and the State System: The Last One Hundred and Forty Years." *Mobilization* 13: 107–26.

——. 2002. "Irish Transnational Social Movements, Migrants, and the State System," in *Globalization and Resistance: Transnational Dimensions of Social Movements*, edited by Jackie Smith and Hank Johnston. Lanham, MD: Rowman & Littlefield.

Hardin, Russell. 2006. *Trust*. Cambridge, UK: Polity Press.

Haythornthwaite, Caroline, and Barry Wellman. 2002. "The Internet in Everyday Life: An Introduction," in *The Internet in Everyday Life*, edited by Caroline Haythornthwaite and Barry Wellman. Malden, MA: Blackwell.

Heberle, Rudolf. 1951. *Social Movements: An Introduction to Political Sociology*. New York: Appleton-Century-Crofts.

Hinde, Wendy. 1992. *Catholic Emancipation: A Shake to Men's Minds*. Oxford: Blackwell.

Hirschfeld Davis, Julie, and Maggie Haberman. 2017. "Trump Pardons Joe Arpaio." in *The New York Times*. New York.

Hisham, Omar, and Abdel Halim. 2011. Salafis demand release of Sheikh Abu Yehya. *Al Masrya al Youm* (English Edition). September 23, 2011.

Hobsbawm, E. J. 1975. *The Age of Capital, 1848–1875*. London: Weidenfeld & Nicolson.

——. 1988. *The Age of Imperialism*. New York: Pantheon.

——. 1994. *The Age of Extremes: A History of the World, 1914–1991*. New York: Pantheon.

Hocke, Peter. 2002. *Massenmedien und lokaler Protest: Eine empirische Fallstudie zur Medienselektivität in einer westdeutschen Begwegungshochberg*. Wiesbaden: Westdeutscher Verlag.

Hoerder, Dirk. 1977. *Crowd Action in Revolutionary Massachusetts, 1765–1780*. New York: Academic Press.

Hoffmann, Stefan-Ludwig. 2003. "Democracy and Associations in the Long Nineteenth Century: Toward a Transnational Perspective." *Journal of Modern History* 75: 269–99.

Honacker, Karin van. 1994. *Lokaal Verzet en Oproer in de 17de en 18de Eeuw: Collectieve Acties tegen het centraal gezag in Brussel, Antwerpen en Leuven*. Heule: UGA.

——. 2000. "Résistance locale et émeutes dans les chef-villes brabançonnes aux XVIIe et XVIIIe siècles." *Revue d'Histoire Moderne et Contemporaine* 47: 37–68.

Huggins, Martha Knisely. 1985. *From Slavery to Vagrancy in Brazil*. New Brunswick, NJ: Rutgers University Press.

——. 1998. *Policing: The United States and Latin America*. Durham, NC: Duke University Press.

Human Rights Watch. 2000. *World Report 2000*. New York: Human Rights Watch.

——. 2011. *World Report 2011: Kazakhstan* (www.hrw.org/world-report-2011/kazakh stan).

——. 2017. EU Needs to Press for Kazakhstan Reforms Now. https://www.hrw.org/news/2017/11/30/eu-needs-press-kazakhstan-reforms-now

Hunt, Lynn. 1978. *Revolution and Urban Politics in Provincial France: Troyes and Reims, 1786–1790*. Stanford, Calif.: Stanford University Press.

——. 1984. *Politics, Culture, and Class in the French Revolution*. Berkeley, CA: University of California Press.

Husung, Hans-Gerhard. 1983. *Protest und Repression im Vormärz: Norddeutschland zwischen Restauration und Revolution*. Göttingen: Vandenhoeck & Ruprecht.

Ibarra, Pedro, Ed. 2003. *Social Movements and Democracy.* New York: Palgrave Macmillan.

Ibarra, Pedro, and Benjamín Tejerina, Eds. 1998. *Los movimientos sociales: Transformaciones políticas y cambio cultural.* Madrid: Trotta.

Imig, Doug, and Sidney Tarrow. 2001. "Mapping the Europeanization of Contention: Evidence from a Quantitative Data Analysis," in *Contentious Europeans: Protest and Politics in an Emerging Polity,* edited by Doug Imig and Sidney Tarrow. Lanham, MD: Rowman & Littlefield.

Infoshop. 2011. "In Global Day of Action, Kosher Consumers Join with Workers." September 26, 2011. (http://news.infoshop.org/article.php?story=20110926232104981).

Inkeles, Alex, ed. 1991. *On Measuring Democracy, Its Consequences and Concomitants.* New Brunswick, NJ: Transaction.

International Telecommunications Union. 2010. *Market Information and Statistics.* Retrieved October 5, 2011 (www.itu.int/ITU-D/ict/statistics/).

International Telecommunications Union. 2011. *Introduction—Evolution of the Mobile Market.* Retrieved October 29, 2011 (www.itu.int/osg/spu/ni/3G/technology/index.html).

International Telecommunications Union. 2017. "ICT Facts and Figures 2017." International Telecommunications Union. Geneva, Switzerland.

International Telecommunications Union 2017. ITU Yearbook of Statistics 2017. https://www.itu.int/en/ITU-D/Statistics/Pages/publications/yb2017.aspx.International Telecommunications Union. 2019. "5G - Fifth generation of mobile technologies" https://www.itu.int/en/mediacentre/backgrounders/Pages/5G-fifth-generation-of-mobile-technologies.aspx.

Ivanova, Evgenia. 2017. "The Protest of Belarus' 'Social Parasites.'" *Al Jazeera,* March 30 (www.aljazeera.com/indepth/opinion/2017/03/protest-belarus-social-parasites-170329125858783.html).

Jackson, Julian. 2001. *France: The Dark Years, 1940–1944.* Oxford: Oxford University Press.

Jamal, Amaney A. 2007. *Barriers to Democracy: The Other Side of Social Capital in Palestine and the Arab World.* Princeton, NJ: Princeton University Press.

Jameson, J. Franklin. 1956. *The American Revolution Considered as a Social Movement.* Boston, MA: Beacon. First published in 1926.

Jarman, Neil. 1997. *Material Conflicts: Parades and Visual Displays in Northern Ireland.* Oxford: Berg.

Jessen, Ralph. 1994. "Polizei, Wohlfahrt und die Anfänge des modernen Sozialstaats in Preussen während des Kaiserreichs." *Geschichte und Gesellschaft* 20: 157–80.

Johnson, Gordon. 1996. *Cultural Atlas of India.* New York: Facts on File.

Johnston, Hank, and Paul Almeida. 2006. *Latin American Social Movements: Globalization, Democratization, and Transnational Networks.* Rowman & Littlefield.

Jones, Peter. 2003. *Liberty and Locality in Revolutionary France: Six Villages Compared, 1760–1820.* Cambridge, UK: Cambridge University Press.

Juris, Jeffrey. 2008. *Networking Futures: The Movements against Corporate Globalization.* Durham, NC: Duke University Press.

Kaiser, Robert J. 1994. *The Geography of Nationalism in Russia and the USSR.* Princeton, NJ: Princeton University Press.

Kakar, Sudhir. 1996. *The Colors of Violence: Cultural Identities, Religion, and Conflict. Chicago*: University of Chicago Press.

Kaplan, Temma. 1992. *Red City, Blue Period: Social Movements in Picasso's Barcelona.* Berkeley, CA: University of California Press.

Karatnycky, Adrian, Ed. 2000. *Freedom in the World: The Annual Survey of Political Rights and Civil Liberties.* Piscataway, NJ: Transaction.

Katsiaficas, George. 1988. *The Imagination of the New Left: A Global Analysis of 1968.* Boston, MA: South End.

Kaufman, Jason. 2002. *For the Common Good? American Civic Life and the Golden Age of Fraternity.* New York: Oxford University Press.

Keck, Margaret, and Kathryn Sikkink. 2000. "Historical Precursors to Modern Transnational Social Movements and Networks," in *Globalizations and Social Movements: Culture, Power, and the Transnational Public Sphere*, edited by John A. Guidry, Michael D. Kennedy, and Mayer N. Zald. Ann Arbor, MI: University of Michigan Press.

Kennedy, Jamie. 2007. "China: Liveblogging from Ground Zero." *Global Voices Online*, 1 June. Retrieved May 8, 2008 (www.globalvoicesonline.org/2007/06/01/china-liveblogging-from-ground-zero). Accessed 8 May 2008).

Kerby, Troy. 2010. "Suns to Wear 'Los Suns' Uniforms to Honor Phoenix's Latino Community," *Ball Don't Lie: A Yahoo Sports Blog.* May 4, 2010.

Khazanov, Anatoly M. 1995. *After the USSR: Ethnicity, Nationalism, and Politics in the Commonwealth of Independent States.* Madison, WI: University of Wisconsin Press.

Kinealy, Christine. 2003. "Les Marches orangistes en Irlande du Nord: Histoire d'un droit." *Le Mouvement Social* 202: 165–82.

Kish Sklar, Kathryn, and James Brewer Stewart, eds. 2007. *Women's Rights and Trans-Atlantic Antislavery in the Era of Emancipation.* New Haven, CT: Yale University Press.

Klausen, Kurt Klaudi, and Flemming Mikkelsen. 1988. *Konflikter, kollektive aktioner og protestbevaegelser i Danmark.* Copenhagen: Samfunds Fagsnyt.

Kohn, Hans. 1956. *Nationalism and Liberty: The Swiss Example.* London: George Allen & Unwin.

Koopmans, Ruud. 2004. "Movements and Media: Selection Processes and Evolutionary Dynamics in the Public Sphere." *Theory and Society* 33, no. 3–4 (June): 367–91.

Koshar, Rudy. 1986. *Social Life, Local Politics, and Nazism: Marburg, 1880–1935.* Chapel Hill, NC: University of North Carolina Press.

Kriesi, Hanspeter, Ruud Koopmans, Jan Willem Duyvendak, and Marco Giugni. 1995. *New Social Movements in Western Europe: A Comparative Analysis.* Minneapolis, MN: University of Minnesota Press.

Kriesi, Hanspeter, René Levy, Gilbert Ganguillet, and Heinz Zwicky. 1981. *Politische Aktivierung in der Schweiz, 1945–1978.* Diessenhofen: Verlag Rüegger.

Kuczynski, Jürgen. 1967a. *Darstellung der Lage der Arbeiter in Frankreich von 1789 bis 1848.* Berlin: Akademie Verlag.

——. 1967b. *Darstellung der Lage der Arbeiter in Frankreich seit 1848.* Berlin: Aka-demie Verlag.

Kwan Lee, Ching, and Mark Selden. 2007. "China's Durable Inequality: Legacies of Revolution and Pitfalls of Reform." *ZNet Japan Focus*, January 24. Retrieved July 15, 2008 (www.zmag.org/content/showarticle.cfm?ItemID=11949).

Laitin, David. 1998. *Identity in Formation: The Russian-Speaking Populations in the Near Abroad.* Ithaca, NY: Cornell University Press.

——. 1999. "The Cultural Elements of Ethnically Mixed States: Nationality Reformation in the Soviet Successor States," in *State/Culture: State Formation after the Cultural Turn*, edited by George Steinmetz. Ithaca, NY: Cornell University Press.

Landa, Janet Tai. 1994. *Trust, Ethnicity, and Identity: Beyond the New Institutional Economics of Ethnic Trading Networks, Contract Law, and Gift-Exchange*. Ann Arbor, MI: University of Michigan Press.

Leever, Randy. 2010. "Tea Party Rally Draws Hundreds at Ariz. Border." *Chron.com*. (http://blog.chron.com/immigration/2010/08/tea-party-rally-draws-hundreds-at-ariz-border/).

Lemons, Stephen. 2010. "Activists Chain Themselves to Arizona Capitol to Protest Russell Pearce's SB 1070," in "Feathered Bastard," *Phoenix New Times Blogs*. April 20, 2010.

Lepetit, Bernard. 1982. "Fonction administrative et armature urbaine: Remarques sur la distribution des chefs-lieux de subdélégation en France à l'Ancien Régime." In Institut d'Histoire Economique et Sociale de l'Université de Paris I, *Recherches et Travaux* 2: 19–34.

——. 1988. *Les Villes dans la France moderne (1740–1840)*. Paris: Albin Michel.

Levi, Margaret, and Laura Stoker. 2000. "Political Trust and Trustworthiness." *Annual Review of Political Science* 3: 475–508.

Liang, Hsi-Huey. 1992. *The Rise of Modern Police and the European State System from Metternich to the Second World War*. Cambridge, UK: Cambridge University Press.

Lida, Clara E. 1972. *Anarquismo y revolución en la España del XIX*. Madrid: Siglo XXI.

Lijphart, Arend. 1999. *Patterns of Democracy: Government Forms and Performance in Thirty-Six Countries*. New Haven, CT: Yale University Press.

Lindenberger, Thomas. 1995. *Strassenpolitik: Zur Sozialgeschichte der öffentlichen Ordnung in Berlin 1900 bis 1914*. Bonn: Dietz.

López-Alves, Fernando. 2000. *State Formation and Democracy in Latin America, 1810–1900*. Durham, NC: Duke University Press.

Lüdtke, Alf. 1989. *Police and State in Prussia, 1815–1850*. Cambridge, UK: Cambridge University Press.

——. 1992. *"Sicherheit" und "Wohlfahrt": Polizei, Gesellschaft und Herrschaft im 19. und 20. Jahrhundert*. Frankfurt: Suhrkamp.

Lundqvist, Sven. 1977. *Folkrörelserna i det svenska samhället, 1850–1920*. Stockholm: Almqvist & Wiksell.

McAdam, Doug, Sidney Tarrow, and Charles Tilly. 2001. *Dynamics of Contention*. Cambridge, UK: Cambridge University Press.

McCammon, Holly J., and Karen E. Campbell. 2002. "Allies on the Road to Victory: Coalition Formation between the Suffragists and the Women's Christian Temperance Union." *Mobilization* 7: 231–52.

McCarthy, John D., Clark McPhail, and Jackie Smith. 1996. "Images of Protest: Estimating Selection Bias in Media Coverage of Washington Demonstrations 1982 and 1991." *American Sociological Review* 61: 478–99.

McCormick, Ty. 2011. "The Road to Tahrir." *Foreign Policy*, August 18, 2011.

McFaul, Michael. 1997. "Russia's Rough Ride," in *Consolidating the Third Wave Democracies: Regional Challenges*, edited by Larry Diamond, Marc F. Plattner, Yun-han Chu, and Hung-mao Tien. Baltimore, MD: Johns Hopkins University Press.

McKivigan, John R., and Stanley Harrold, Eds. 1999. *Antislavery Violence: Sectional, Racial, and Cultural Conflict in Antebellum America*. Knoxville, TN: University of Tennessee Press.

McPhee, Peter. 1988. "Les Formes d'intervention populaire en Roussillon: L'Exemple de Collioure, 1789–1815," in *Centre d'Histoire Contemporaine du Languedoc Méditerranéen et du Roussillon: Les Pratiques politiques en province à l'époque de la*

Révolution française. Montpellier: Publications de la Recherche, Université de Montpellier.
Madan, T. N. 1997. "Religion, Ethnicity, and Nationalism in India," in *Religion, Ethnicity, and Self-Identity: Nations in Turmoil*, edited by Martin E. Marty and R. Scott Appleby. Hanover, NH: University Press of New England/Salzburg Seminar.
Maier, Pauline. 1972. *From Resistance to Revolution: Colonial Radicals and the Development of American Opposition to Britain, 1765–1776*. New York: Vintage.
Mamdani, Mahmood, and Ernest Wamba-dia-Wamba, Eds. 1995. *African Studies in Social Movements and Democracy*. Dakar: CODESRIA.
Margadant, Ted. 1992. *Urban Rivalries in the French Revolution*. Princeton, NJ: Princeton University Press.
Markoff, John. 1996a. *The Abolition of Feudalism: Peasants, Lords, and Legislators in the French Revolution*. University Park, PA: Pennsylvania State University Press.
——. 1996b. *Waves of Democracy: Social Movements and Political Change*. Thousand Oaks, CA: Pine Grove Press.
Marx, Karl, and Friedrich Engels. 1958. *Selected Works*. 2 vols. Moscow: Foreign Languages Publishing House.
Marx, Karl. 1847. "Wage Labour and Capital," (www.marxists.org/archive/marx/works/1847/wage-labour/ch06.htm).
Mendle, Michael, Ed. 2001. *The Putney Debates of 1647: The Army, the Levellers, and the English State*. Cambridge, UK: Cambridge University Press.
Meyer, David S., and Sidney Tarrow, Eds. 1998. *The Social Movement Society: Contentious Politics for a New Century*. Lanham, MD: Rowman & Littlefield.
Mihalisko, Kathleen J. 1997. "Belarus: Retreat to Authoritarianism," in *Democratic Changes and Authoritarian Reactions in Russia, Ukraine, Belarus, and Moldova*, edited by Karen Dawisha and Bruce Parrott. Cambridge, UK: Cambridge University Press.
Mikkelsen, Flemming, Ed. 1986. *Protest og Oprør*. Aarhus: Modtryk.
Mirala, Petri. 2000. "'A Large Mob, Calling Themselves Freemasons': Masonic Parades in Ulster," in *Crowds in Ireland, c. 1720–1920*, edited by Peter Jupp and Eoin Magennis. London: Macmillan.
Monjardet, Dominique. 1996. *Ce que fait la police: Sociologie de la force publique*. Paris: La Découverte.
Montgomery, David. 1993. *Citizen Worker: The Experience of Workers in the United States with Democracy and the Free Market during the Nineteenth Century*. Cambridge, UK: Cambridge University Press.
Morgan, Edmund S. 1988. *Inventing the People: The Rise of Popular Sovereignty in England and America*. New York: W. W. Norton.
Munger, Frank. 1979. "Measuring Repression of Popular Protest by English Justices of the Peace in the Industrial Revolution." *Historical Methods* 12: 76–83.
——. 1981. "Suppression of Popular Gatherings in England, 1800–1830." *American Journal of Legal History* 25: 111–40.
Nabholz, Hans, Leonhard von Muralt, Richard Feller, and Edgar Bonjour. 1938. *Geschichte der Schweiz*. 2 vols. Zurich: Schultheiss.
Nahaylo, Bohdan, and Victor Swoboda. 1990. *Soviet Disunion: A History of the Nationalities Problem in the USSR*. New York: Free Press.
Nazarbayev, Nursultan. 2011. "Kazakhstan's Steady Progress Toward Democracy." *Washington Post*. March 31, 2011.

Nelson, Joan M., Charles Tilly, and Lee Walker, Eds. 1998. *Transforming Post-Communist Political Economies.* Washington, DC: National Academy Press.

Newman, Richard, and James Mueller. 2011. *Antislavery and Abolition in Philadelphia: Emancipation and the Long Struggle for Racial Justice in the City of Brotherly Love.* Baton Rouge, LA: LSU Press.

Newsweek. 2011. "The Facebook Freedom Fighter." February 13, 2011.

New York Times. "Egypt to Get an I.M.F. Loan." May 18, 1991.

Ngoma Leslie, Agnes. 2006. *Social Movements and Democracy in Africa: The Impact of Women's Struggle for Equal Rights in Botswana.* New York: Routledge.

Nicolas, Jean, ed. 1985. *Mouvements populaires et conscience sociale, XVIe–XIXe siècles.* Paris: Maloine.

Norton, Quinn. 2011. "BART's Cell-Service Cuts: Not Egypt, But Not Quite America Either." *The Atlantic.* August 26, 2011.

O'Brian, Kevin J. 2008. *Popular Protest in China.* Cambridge, MA: Harvard University Press.

O'Ferrall, Fergus. 1985. *Catholic Emancipation: Daniel O'Connell and the Birth of Irish Democracy 1820–30.* Dublin: Gill & Macmillan.

Öhngren, Bo. 1974. *Folk i rörelse: Samhällsutveckling, flyttningsmonster och folkrörelser i Eskilstuna 1870–1900.* Uppsala: Almqvist & Wicksell.

Oliver, Pamela E., and Gregory M. Maney. 2000. "Political Processes and Local Newspaper Coverage of Protest Events: From Selection Bias to Triadic Interactions." *American Journal of Sociology* 106: 463–505.

Oliver, Pamela E., and Daniel J. Myers. 1999. "How Events Enter the Public Sphere: Conflict, Location, and Sponsorship in Local Newspaper Coverage of Public Events." *American Journal of Sociology* 105: 38–87.

Olzak, Susan. 2006. *The Global Dynamics of Racial and Ethnic Mobilization.* Stanford, CA: Stanford University Press.

Ozouf-Marignier, Marie-Vic. 1986. "De l'universalisme constituant aux intérêts locaux: Le Débat sur la formation des départements en France (1789–1790)." *Annales: Economies, Sociétés, Civilisations* 41: 1193–1214.

Paige, Jeffery M. 1997. *Coffee and Power: Revolution and the Rise of Democracy in Central America.* Cambridge, MA: Harvard University Press.

Palmer, Stanley H. 1988. *Police and Protest in England and Ireland 1780–1850.* Cambridge: Cambridge University Press.

Paxton, Robert O. 1995. "Leçon sur les fascismes." *Vingtième Siècle* 45: 3–13.

Pérez-Stable, Marifeli. 1993. *The Cuban Revolution: Origins, Course, and Legacy.* New York: Oxford University Press.

Perry, Elizabeth J. 2002. *Challenging the Mandate of Heaven: Social Protest and State Power in China.* Armonk, NY: M. E. Sharpe.

Petrova, Tsveta, and Sidney Tarrow. 2007. "Transactional and Participatory Activism in the Emerging European Polity: The Puzzle of East Central Europe." *Comparative Political Studies* 40(1): 74–94.

Pigenet, Michel, and Danielle Tartakowsky. 2003. "Les marches en France aux XIXe siècle et XXe siècle: récurrence et métamorphose d'une démonstration collective." *Le mouvement social* 202: 69–94.

Plus News Pakistan. 2010. "Pakistan: Thousands in Phoenix Protest Arizona's Immigration Law." May 30, 2010.

Poulson, Stephen C. 2006. *Social Movements in Twentieth-Century Iran: Culture, Ideology, and Mobilizing Frameworks.* Lanham, MD: Lexington.

Price, Richard. 1986. *Labour in British Society: An Interpretive History*. London: Croom Helm.

Prothero, Iowerth. 1979. *Artisans and Politics in Early Nineteenth-Century London: John Gast and His Times*. Folkestone, UK: Dawson.

——. 1997. *Radical Artisans in England and France, 1830–1970*. Cambridge, UK: Cambridge University Press.

Przeworski, Adam, Michael Alvarez, José Antonio Cheibub, and Fernando Limongi. 2000. *Democracy and Development: Political Institutions and Well-Being in the World, 1950–1990*. Cambridge, UK: Cambridge University Press.

Ray, Raka, and Mary Fainsod Katzenstein. 2005. *Social Movements in India: Poverty, Power, and Politics*. Lanham, MD: Rowman & Littlefield.

Ray, Raka, and A. C. Korteweg. 1999. "Women's Movements in the Third World: Identity, Mobilization, and Autonomy." *Annual Review of Sociology* 25: 47–71.

Reitan, Ruth. 2007. *Global Activism*. London: Routledge.

Remak, Joachim. 1993. *A Very Civil War: The Swiss Sonderbund War of 1847*. Boulder, CO: Westview.

Reporters without Borders. 2011. "Enemies of the Internet."

Reuters. 2010. "Protesters, Police Clash over Egypt Flood Aid." January 20, 2010.

Reuters. 2010. "Copts Protest Christmas Killings at Cairo Cathedral." January 13, 2010.

Rheingold, Howard. 2003. *Smart Mobs: The Next Social Revolution*. New York: Perseus.

Riles, Annelise. 2000. *The Network Inside Out*. Ann Arbor, MI: University of Michigan Press.

Robert, Vincent. 1996. *Les Chemins de la manifestation, 1848–1914*. Lyon: Presses Universitaires de Lyon.

Rock, David. 1987. *Argentina 1516–1987*. Berkeley, CA: University of California Press.

Rude, Fernand. 1969. *L'Insurrection lyonnaise de novembre 1831: Le Mouvement ouvrier à Lyon de 1827–1832*. Paris: Anthropos.

Rudé, George. 1962. *Wilkes and Liberty*. Oxford: Clarendon Press.

——. 1971. *Hanoverian London, 1714–1808*. London: Secker & Warburg.

Ryan, Mary P. 1997. *Civic Wars: Democracy and Public Life in the American City during the Nineteenth Century*. Berkeley, CA: University of California Press.

Sabato, Hilda. 2001. *The Many and the Few: Political Participation in Republican Buenos Aires*. Stanford, CA: Stanford University Press.

Sahlins, Peter. 1989. *Boundaries: The making of France and Spain in the Pyrenees*. Berkeley, CA: University of California Press.

Saleh, Yasmine, and Mohamed Abdellah. 2010. "Protesters Seek Change in Egypt, Scuffle with Police." *Reuters*, April 6, 2010.

Samuel, Elias. 2011. "Egypt is Online without Internet Service, Cell Phones or Social Networking." *International Business Times*, January 30, 2011. Retrieved June 20, 2012 (www.ibtimes.com/articles/106660/20110130/egypt-is-online-without-internet-service-cell-phones- or-social-networking.htm).

Sanders, Elizabeth. 1999. *Roots of Reform: Farmers, Workers, and the American State 1877–1917*. Chicago, IL: University of Chicago Press.

Sassen, Saskia. 2002. "Toward a Sociology of Information Technology." *Current Sociology* 50: 29–52.

Scalmer, Sean. 2002a. *Dissent Events: Protest, the Media and the Political Gimmick in Australia*. Sydney: University of New South Wales Press.

——. 2002b. "The Labor of Diffusion: The Peace Pledge Union and the Adaptation of the Gandhian Repertoire." *Mobilization* 7: 269–85.

Schama, Simon. 1977. *Patriots and Liberators: Revolution in the Netherlands 1780–1813*. London: Collins.
Schultz, Patrick. 1982. *La Décentralisation administrative dans le Département du Nord (1790–1793)*. Lille: Presses Universitaires de Lille.
Scott, James C. 1985. *Weapons of the Weak*. New Haven, CO: Yale University Press.
Seip, Jens Arup. 1974, 1981. *Utsikt over Norges Historie*. 2 vols. Oslo: Gylendal Norsk Forlag.
Seligman, Adam. 1997. *The Problem of Trust*. Princeton, NJ: Princeton University Press.
Service, Robert F. 2003. "'Combat Biology' on the Klamath." *Science* 300 (4 April): 36–39.
Sexton, Connie, Ofelia Madrid, and Dustin Gardiner. 2010. "The Arizona Republic. Arizona Immigration Law Supporters Gather for Rally." June 5, 2010. (www.azcentral.com/community/phoenix/articles/2010/06/05/20100605arizona-immigration-law-supporters-protest-ON.html).
Shapira, Harel. 2013. *Waiting for José: The Minutemen's Pursuit of America*. Princeton, NJ: Princeton University Press.
SIPRI (Stockholm International Peace Research Institute). 2001. *SIPRI Yearbook 2001: Armaments, Disarmament and International Security*. Oxford: Oxford University Press.
Skidmore, Thomas E., and Peter H. Smith. 1984. *Modern Latin America*. New York: Oxford University Press.
Skocpol, Theda. 1992. *Protecting Soldiers and Mothers: The Political Origins of Social Policy in the United States*. Cambridge, MA: Harvard University Press.
——. 1999. "How Americans Became Civic," in *Civic Engagement in American Democracy*, edited by Theda Skocpol and Morris P. Fiorina. Washington, DC: Brookings Institution Press, and New York: Russell Sage Foundation.
Smith, Adam. 1910. *The Wealth of Nations*. 2 vols. London: Dent. Originally published in 1776.
Smith, Graham, Vivien Law, Andrew Wilson, Annette Bohr, and Edward Allworth. 1998. *Nation-Building in the Post-Soviet Borderlands: The Politics of National Identity*. Cambridge, MA: Cambridge University Press.
Smith, Jackie. 2002. "Globalizing Resistance: The Battle of Seattle and the Future of Social Movements," in *Globalization and Resistance: Transnational Dimensions of Social Movements*, edited by Jackie Smith and Hank Johnston. Lanham, MD: Rowman & Littlefield.
——. 2004. "Exploring Connections between Global Integration and Political Mobilization." *Journal of World Systems Research* 1 (Winter): 255–85.
——. 2007. *Social Movements for Global Democracy*. Baltimore, MD: Johns Hopkins University Press.
——. 2008. *Social Movements for Global Democracy*. Baltimore, MD: Johns Hopkins University Press.
——. 2018. Transnational Social Movement Organizations and Counter-hegemonic Struggles Today. *Journal of World-Systems Research* 24(2): 372–403.
Sorbello, Paulo. 2017. "Miners Strike in Central Kazakhstan, Protesting Bad Work Conditions and Pay." *The Diplomat*. December 15, 2017. (https://thediplomat.com/2017/12/miners-strike-in-central-kazakhstan-protesting-bad-work-conditions-and-pay/).
Sorensen, Georg. 2007. *Democracy and Democratization: Process and Prospects in a Changing World*. Boulder, CO: Westview Press.
Southern Poverty Law Project. 2011. "Active 'Patriot' Groups in the United States in 2010." (www.splcenter.org/get-informed/intelligence-report/browse-all-issues/2011/spring/active-patriot-groups-in-the-us).

Southern Poverty Law Center. 2018. Antigovernment Movement. (www.splcenter.org/fighting-hate/extremist-files/ideology/antigovernment).

Stein, Lorenz von. 1959. *Geschichte der sozialen Bewegung in Frankreich von 1789 bis auf unsere Tage*. Hildesheim: Georg Olms.

Steinberg, Jonathan. 1996. *Why Switzerland?* 2nd ed. Cambridge, UK: Cambridge University Press.

Stelter, Brian. 2010. "Progressive Radio Hosts Say Air America Closing Won't Affect Them." *New York Times*, January 22, 2010.

Stenius, Henrik. 1987. *Frivilligt, Jämlikt, Samfällt: Föreningsväsendets utveckling I Finland fram till 1900–talets början med speciell hänsyn till massorganisationsprincipens genombrott*. Helsinki: Svenska Litteratursällskapet I Finland.

Storch, Robert D. 1976. "The Policeman as Domestic Missionary: Urban Discipline and Popular Culture in Northern England, 1850–1880." *Journal of Social History* 9: 481–509.

Stutzer, Alois, and Bruno Frey. 2002. "What Can Economists Learn from Happiness Research?" *Journal of Economic Literature* 40: 402–35.

Suny, Ronald Grigor. 1993. *The Revenge of the Past: Nationalism, Revolution, and the Collapse of the Soviet Union*. Stanford, CA: Stanford University Press.

——. 1995. "Ambiguous Categories: States, Empires, and Nations." *Post-Soviet Affairs* 11: 185–96.

Suri, Jeremy. 2003. *Power and Protest: Global Revolution and the Rise of Détente*. Cambridge, MA: Harvard University Press.

Take the Square.net. 2011. "#Syntagma Call for global action day against the markets dictatorship #Antibanks #Sept17 #OccupyWallStreet." *Take the Square*. Retrieved October 29, 2011 (http://takethesquare.net/2011/09/14/syntagma-call-for-global-action-day-against-the-markets-dictatorship-antibanks-sept17-occupywallstreet/).

Tambiah, Stanley J. 1996. *Leveling Crowds: Ethnonationalist Conflicts and Collective Violence in South Asia*. Berkeley, CA: University of California Press.

Tarrow, Sidney. 1989. *Democracy and Disorder: Protest and Politics in Italy 1965–1975*. Oxford: Clarendon Press.

——. 1996. "Movimenti politici e sociali." *Enciclopedia delle Scienze Sociali* 6: 97–114.

——. 1998. *Power in Movement*, 2nd ed. Cambridge, UK: Cambridge University Press.

——. 2002. "From Lumping to Splitting: Specifying Globalization and Resistance," in *Globalization and Resistance: Transnational Dimensions of Social Movements*, edited by Jackie Smith and Hank Johnston. Lanham, MD: Rowman & Littlefield.

——. 2005. *The New Transnational Activism*. Cambridge, UK: Cambridge University Press.

Tarrow, Sidney, and Doug McAdam. 2005. "Scale Shift in Transnational Contention," in *Transnational Protest and Global Activism*, edited by Donatella della Porta and Sidney Tarrow. Lanham, MD: Rowman & Littlefield.

Tartakowsky, Danielle. 1997. *Les Manifestations de rue en France, 1918–1968*. Paris: Publications de la Sorbonne.

——. 1999. *Nous irons chanter sur vos tombes: Le Père-Lachaise, XIXe–XXe siècle*. Paris: Aubier.

Temperley, Howard. 1981. "The Ideology of Antislavery," in *The Abolition of the Atlantic Slave Trade: Origins and Effects in Europe, Africa, and the Americas*, edited by David Eltis and James Walvin. Madison, WI: University of Wisconsin Press.

Thompson, Dorothy. 1984. *The Chartists: Popular Politics in the Industrial Revolution*. New York: Pantheon.

Thompson, E. P. 1972. "Rough Music: Le Charivari anglais." *Annales; Economies Sociétés, Civilisations* 27: 285–312.

——. 1991. *Customs in Common*. London: Merlin Press.

Thompson, Ginger. 2003. "Protesters Swarm the Streets at W.T.O. Forum in Cancún." *New York Times*, online edition, September 14.

Tilly, Charles. 1962. "Rivalités de bourgs et conflits de partis dans les Mauges." *Revue du Bas-Poitou et des Provinces de l'Ouest* 4 (July–August): 3–15.

——. 1983. "Speaking Your Mind without Elections, Surveys, or Social Movements." *Public Opinion Quarterly* 47: 461–78.

——. 1984. "Demographic Origins of the European Proletariat," in *Proletarianization and Family Life*, edited by David Levine. Orlando, FL: Academic Press.

——. 1986. *The Contentious French*. Cambridge, MA: Harvard University Press.

——. 1992. *Coercion, Capital and European States: AD 990–1992*. Studies in Social Discontinuity. Hoboken, NJ: Wiley-Blackwell. Revised edition.

——. 1995. *Popular Contention in Great Britain, 1758–1834*. Cambridge, MA: Harvard University Press.

——. 1997. "Parliamentarization of Popular Contention in Great Britain, 1758–1834." *Theory and Society* 26: 245–73.

——. 1998. *Durable Inequality*. Berkeley, CA: University of California Press.

——. 1999. "Conclusion: Why Worry about Citizenship?" In Michael Hanagan and Charles Tilly, eds., *Extending Citizenship, Reconfiguring States*. Lanham, MD: Rowman & Littlefield.

——. 2001a. "Mechanisms in Political Processes." *Annual Review of Political Science* 4: 21–41.

——. 2001b. "Historical Analysis of Political Processes," in *Handbook of Sociological Theory*, edited by Jonathan H. Turner. New York: Kluwer/Plenum.

——. 2002a. *Stories, Identities, and Political Change*. Lanham, MD: Rowman & Littlefield.

——. 2002b. "Event Catalogs as Theories." *Sociological Theory* 20: 248–54.

——. 2003. *The Politics of Collective Violence*. Cambridge, UK: Cambridge University Press.

——. 2004. *Contention and Democracy in Europe, 1650–2000*. Cambridge, UK: Cambridge University Press.

——. 2005. *Trust and Rule*. Cambridge, UK: Cambridge University Press.

——. 2006. *Regimes and Repertoires*. Chicago, IL: University of Chicago Press.

——. 2007. *Democracy*. Cambridge, UK: Cambridge University Press.

——. 2007b. "Trust Networks in Transnational Migration." *Sociological Forum* 22: 3–24.

——. 2008a. *Contentious Performances*. Cambridge, UK: Cambridge University Press.

——. 2008b. *Credit and Blame*. Princeton, NJ: Princeton University Press.

——. 2008c. *Why?* Princeton, NJ: Princeton University Press.

Tilly, Charles, and Sidney Tarrow. 2006. *Contentious Politics*. Boulder, CO: Paradigm Publishers.

Tilly, Charles, and Sidney Tarrow. 2015. *Contentious Politics*. New York: Oxford University Press.

Tilly, Charles, Louise Tilly, and Richard Tilly. 1975. *The Rebellious Century, 1830–1930*. Cambridge, MA: Harvard University Press.

Tilly, Charles, and Lesley Wood. 2003. "Contentious Connections in Great Britain, 1828–1834," in *Social Movements and Networks: Relational Approaches to Collective Action*, edited by Mario Diani and Doug McAdam. New York: Oxford University Press.

Tilly, Richard. 1980. *Kapital, Staat und sozialer Protest in der deutschen Industrialisierung.* Göttingen: Vandenhoeck & Ruprecht.

Titarenko, Larissa, John D. McCarthy, Clark McPhail, and Boguslaw Augustyn. 2001. "The Interaction of State Repression, Protest Form and Protest Sponsor Strength during the Transition from Communism in Minsk, Belarus, 1990–1995." *Mobilization* 6: 129–50.

Tocqueville, Alexis de. 1983. *Correspondance d'Alexis de Tocqueville et de Francisque de Corcelle.* Oeuvres Complètes, t. XV. Paris: Gallimard.

Torpey, John. 2000. *The Invention of the Passport: Surveillance, Citizenship and the State.* Cambridge, UK: Cambridge University Press.

Touraine, Alain. 1968. *Le Mouvement de Mai ou le communisme utopique.* Paris: Seuil.

Touraine, Alain, François Dubet, Michel Wieviorka, and Jan Strzelecki. 1982. *Solidarité: Analyse d'un mouvement social, Pologne 1980–1981.* Paris: Fayard.

Trechsel, Alexander. 2000. *Feuerwerk Volksrechte: Die Volksabstimmungen in den scheizerischen Kantonen 1970–1996.* Basel: Helbing & Lichtenhahn.

Tufekci, Zeynep 2017. *Twitter and Tear Gas: The Power and Fragility of Networked Protest.* New Haven, CT: Yale University Press.

UNDP (United Nations Development Program). 2001. *Human Development Report 2001: Making New Technologies Work for Human Development.* Oxford: Oxford University Press.

United Press International (UPI). 2010. "Tea Party protesters rally in Arizona." *UPI News.* Retrieved October 29, 2011 (www.upi.com/Top_News/US/2010/08/16/Tea-Party-protesters-rally-in-Arizona/UPI-43641281968994/).

Uslaner, Eric M. 2002. *The Moral Foundations of Trust.* Cambridge, UK: Cambridge University Press.

van der Veer, Peter. 1996. "Riots and Rituals: The Construction of Violence and Public Space in Hindu Nationalism," in *Riots and Pogroms*, edited by Paul R. Brass. New York: New York University Press.

US State Department. 2016. Kazakhstan 2016 Human Rights Report (www.state.gov/documents/organization/265750.pdf).

Vanhanen, Tatu. 2000. "A New Dataset for Measuring Democracy, 1810–1998." *Journal of Peace Research* 37: 251–65.

Vernon, James. 1993. *Politics and the People: A Study in English Political Culture c. 1815–1867.* Cambridge, UK: Cambridge University Press.

Via Campesina. 2019. "17 April, Day of Peasant's Struggle." Retrieved June 20, 2019 (http://viacampesina.org/en/index.php?option=com_content&view=section&layout=blog&id=4&Itemid=26).

Vogel, Kenneth P., and Lucy McCalmont. 2011. "Rush Limbaugh, Sean Hannity, Glenn Beck sell endorsements to conservative groups." *Politico*, June 5, 2011. (www.politico.com/news/stories/0611/56997.html).

Voss, Kim, and Irene Bloemraad. 2011. *Rallying for Immigrant Rights: The Fight for Inclusion in 21st Century America.* Berkeley, CA: University of California Press.

Wåhlin, Vagn. 1986. "Opposition og statsmagt," in *Protest og Oprør: Kollektive aktioner i Danmark 1700–1985*, edited by Flemming Mikkelsen. Aarhus: Modtryk.

Walsh-Russo, Cecelia. 2017. "Mutual Brokerage and Women's Participation in Nineteenth-Century Anglo-American Abolitionist Movements." *Social Movement Studies* 16(6): 633–46.

Walsh-Russo, Cecelia, and Ernesto Castañeda. 2018. "Charles Tilly." in *Oxford Bibliographies in Sociology*, edited by L. Spillman. New York: Oxford University Press.

Walton, John, and David Seddon. 1994. *Free Markets and Food Riots: The Politics of Global Adjustment.* Oxford: Blackwell.

Walvin, James. 1980. "The Rise of British Popular Sentiment for Abolition, 1787–1832," in *Anti-Slavery, Religion, and Reform: Essays in Memory of Roger Anstey*, Christine Bolt and Seymour Drescher. Folkestone: Dawson/Archon.

——. 1981. "The Public Campaign in England against Slavery, 1787–1834," in *The Abolition of Atlantic Slave Trade: Origins and Effects in Europe, Africa, and the Americas*, edited by David Eltis and James Walvin. Madison, WI: University of Wisconsin Press.

Ward, J. T. 1973. *Chartism.* London: B. T. Batsford.

Warren, Mark E., Ed. 1999. *Democracy and Trust.* Cambridge, UK: Cambridge University Press.

Wellman, Barry. 2000. "Changing Connectivity: A Future History of Y2.03K." *Sociological Research Online* 4(4).

——. 2001a. "Physical Place and CyberPlace: The Rise of Personalized Networking." *International Journal of Urban and Regional Research* 25: 227–52.

——. 2001b. "Does the Internet Increase, Decrease, or Supplement Social Capital? Social Networks, Participation, and Community Commitment." *American Behavioral Scientist* 45: 437–56.

Westhues, Kenneth. 1975. "Inter-Generational Conflict in the Sixties," in *Prophecy and Protest: Social Movements in Twentieth-Century Canada*, edited by Samuel D. Clark, J. Paul Grayson, and Linda M. Grayson. Toronto: Gage.

Wignaraja, Ponna, Ed. 1993. *New Social Movements in the South: Empowering the People.* Atlantic Highlands, NJ: Zed Books.

Williams, Robin M., Jr. 2003. *The Wars Within: Peoples and States in Conflict.* Ithaca, NY: Cornell University Press.

Wilson, Frederick T. 1969. *Federal Aid in Domestic Disturbances 1787–1903.* New York: Arno Press and *New York Times.*

Wimmer, Andreas. 2002. *Nationalist Exclusion and Ethnic Conflict: Shadows of Modernity.* Cambridge, UK: Cambridge University Press.

Wirtz, Rainer. 1981. *"Widersetzlichkeiten, Excesse, Crawalle, Tumulte und Skandale": Soziale Bewegung und gewalthafter sozialer Protest in Baden 1815–1848.* Frankfurt: Ullstein.

Woloch, Isser. 1970. *Jacobin Legacy: The Democratic Movement under the Directory.* Princeton, NJ: Princeton University Press.

——. 1994. *The New Regime: Transformations of the French Civic Order, 1789–1820s.* New York: W. W. Norton.

Wood, Lesley J. 2004. "Breaking the Bank and Taking to the Streets: How Protesters Target Neoliberalism." *Journal of World Systems Research* 10(1) (Winter): 69–89.

——. 2012. *Direct Action, Deliberation and Diffusion: Collective Action after the WTO Protests in Seattle.* New York: Cambridge University Press.

——. 2014. *Crisis and Control: The Militarization of Protest Policing.* London: Pluto.

Wyrsch, Paul. 1983. *Der Kanton Schwyz äusseres Land 1831–1833.* Schwyzer Hefte, Band 28. Lachen: Gutenberg.

Young, Michael P. 2006. *Bearing Witness against Sin: The Evangelical Birth of the American Social Movement.* Chicago, IL: University of Chicago Press.

Zaleski, Eugène. 1956. *Mouvements ouvriers et socialistes (Chronologie et bibliographie. La Russie, t. I: 1725–1907).* Paris: Éditions Ouvrières.

Zelizer, Viviana A. 1999. "Multiple Markets: Multiple Cultures," in *Diversity and Its Discontents: Cultural Conflict and Common Ground in Contemporary American Society*, edited by Neil J. Smelser and Jeffrey C. Alexander. Princeton, NJ: Princeton University Press.

——. 2004. "Circuits within Capitalism," in *The Economic Sociology of Capitalism*, edited by Victor Nee and Richard Swedberg. Princeton, NJ: Princeton University Press.

Zepeda-Millán, Chris. 2017. *Latino Mass Mobilization: Immigration, Racialization, and Activism*. Cambridge, UK: Cambridge University Press.

Zhao, Dingxin. 2001. *The Power of Tiananmen: State–Society Relations and the 1989 Beijing Student Movement*. Chicago, IL: University of Chicago Press.

Zolberg, Aristide. 1978. "Belgium," in *Crises of Political Development in Europe and the United States*, edited by Raymond Grew. Princeton, NJ: Princeton University Press.

PUBLICATIONS ON SOCIAL MOVEMENTS BY CHARLES TILLY, 1977-2010

1977 "Getting It Together in Burgundy, 1675–1975." *Theory and Society* 4: 479–504.
"Collective Action in England and America, 1765–1775." In Richard Maxwell Brown and Don Fehrenbacher, eds., *Tradition, Conflict, and Modernization: Perspectives on the American Revolution.* New York: Academic Press.

1978 *From Mobilization to Revolution.* Reading, MA: Addison-Wesley.

1979 "Repertoires of Contention in America and Britain." In Mayer N. Zald and John D. McCarthy, eds., *The Dynamics of Social Movements.* Cambridge, MA: Winthrop.

1981 "The Web of Contention in Eighteenth-Century Cities." In Louise A. Tilly and Charles Tilly, eds., *Class Conflict and Collective Action.* Beverly Hills, CA: Sage.

1982 "Britain Creates the Social Movement." In James Cronin and Jonathan Schneer, eds., *Social Conflict and the Political Order in Modern Britain.* London: Croom Helm.
"Charivaris, Repertoires, and Urban Politics." In John Merriman, ed., *French Cities in the Nineteenth Century.* London: Hutchinson.

1983 "Speaking Your Mind without Elections, Surveys, or Social Movements." *Public Opinion Quarterly* 47: 461–78.

1984 "Social Movements and National Politics." In Charles Bright and Susan Harding, eds., *Statemaking and Social Movements: Essays in History and Theory.* Ann Arbor, MI: University of Michigan Press.
"Les Origines du répertoire de l'action collective contemporaine en France et en Grande Bretagne." *Vingtième Siècle* 4: 89–108.

1985 "De Londres (1768) à Paris (1788)." In Jean Nicolas, ed., *Mouvements populaires et conscience sociale: XVIe–XIXe siècles.* Paris: Maloine.
The Contentious French. Cambridge, MA: Belknap Press of Harvard University Press.

1988 "Social Movements, Old and New." In Louis Kriesberg, Bronislaw Misztal, and Janusz Mucha, eds., *Social Movements as a Factor of Change in the Contemporary World.* Research in Social Movements, Conflicts and Change, vol. 10. Greenwich, CT: JAI Press.

1992 "Réclamer Viva Voce." *Cultures et Conflits* 5: 109–26.

1993 "Contentious Repertoires in Great Britain, 1758–1834." *Social Science History* 17: 253–80. Also in Mark Traugott, ed., *Repertoires and Cycles of Collective Action.* Durham, NC: Duke University Press, 1995.

1994 "Social Movements as Historically Specific Clusters of Political Performances." *Berkeley Journal of Sociology* 38: 1–30.

1995 *Popular Contention in Great Britain, 1758–1834.* Cambridge, MA: Harvard University Press.

1997 "Parliamentarization of Popular Contention in Great Britain, 1758–1834." *Theory and Society* 26: 245–73.

1998 "Social Movements and (All Sorts of) Other Political Interactions—Local, National, and International—Including Identities: Several Divagations from a Common Path, Beginning with British Struggles over Catholic Emancipation, 1780–1829, and Ending with Contemporary Nationalism." *Theory and Society* 27: 453–80.

1999 "From Interactions to Outcomes in Social Movements." In Marco Giugni, Doug McAdam, and Charles Tilly, eds., *How Social Movements Matter.* Minneapolis: University of Minnesota Press.

2001 (with Doug McAdam and Sidney Tarrow) *Dynamics of Contention.* Cambridge, UK: Cambridge University Press.

2002 *Stories, Identities, and Political Change.* Lanham, MD: Rowman & Littlefield.

2003 "When Do (and Don't) Social Movements Promote Democratization?" In Pedro Ibarra, ed., *Social Movements and Democracy.* New York: Palgrave.

(with Lesley Wood) "Contentious Connections in Great Britain, 1828–1834." In Mario Diani and Doug McAdam, eds., *Social Movements and Networks: Relational Approaches to Collective Action.* New York: Oxford University Press.

"Agendas for Students of Social Movements." In Jack A. Goldstone, ed., *States, Parties, and Social Movements.* Cambridge, UK: Cambridge University Press.

The Politics of Collective Violence. Cambridge, UK: Cambridge University Press.

"Political Identities in Changing Polities." *Social Research* 70: 1301–15.

2004 "WUNC." In Jeffrey T. Schnapp and Matthew Tiews, eds., *Crowds.* Stanford, CA: Stanford University Press.

Contention and Democracy in Europe, 1650–2000. Cambridge, UK: Cambridge University Press.

"Terror, Terrorism, Terrorists." *Sociological Theory* 22: 5–13.

"Social Movements and Democratisation." In Anna-Maija Castrén, Markku Lonkila, and Matti Peltonen, eds., *Between Sociology and History: Essays on Microhistory, Collective Action, and Nation-Building.* Helsinki: SKS/Finnish Literature Society.

"Social Movements Enter the Twenty-First Century." *Il Dubbio* 5: 31–54.

"Regimes and Contention." In Fredrik Engelstad and Øyvind Østerud, eds., *Power and Democracy: Critical Interventions.* Aldershot, UK: Ashgate.

2005 (with Maria Kousis) *Economic and Political Contention in Comparative Perspective.* Boulder, CO: Paradigm Publishers.

(with Sidney Tarrow) "Social Movements, Contentious Politics, and Institutions." In Carles Boix and Susan Stokes, eds., *Oxford Handbook of Comparative Politics.* New York: Oxford University Press.

"Repression, Mobilization, and Explanation." In Christian Davenport, Hank Johnston, and Carol Mueller, eds., *Repression and Mobilization.* Minneapolis, MN: University of Minnesota Press.

"Regimes and Contention." In Thomas Janoski, Robert R. Alford, Alexander M. Hicks, and Mildred Schwartz, eds., *The Handbook of Political Sociology: States, Civil Societies, and Globalization.* Cambridge, UK: Cambridge University Press.

"Terror as Strategy and Relational Process." *International Journal of Comparative Sociology* 46: 11–32.

2006 *Regimes and Repertoires*. Chicago IL: University of Chicago Press.

(with Sidney Tarrow) *Contentious Politics*. Boulder, CO: Paradigm Publishers.

2007 *Democracy*. Cambridge, UK: Cambridge University Press.

2008 *Contentious Performances*. Cambridge, UK: Cambridge University Press.

2010 "The Rise of the Public Meeting in Great Britain, 1758–1834", *Social Science History* 34: 291–299, as part of the Special Section on "History and the Social Sciences: Taking Stock and Moving Ahead. The Public Sphere and Comparative Historical Research."

INDEX

ABOUT THE AUTHORS

Charles Tilly was Joseph L. Buttenwieser Professor of Social Science at Columbia University. Tilly was one of the premier sociologists of our time. He is the author of more than fifty influential books including *The Vendée: A Sociological Analysis of the Counter-Revolution of 1793* (Harvard University Press 1964); *Durable Inequality* (University of California Press 1999); *Contentious Performances* (Cambridge University Press 2008); and coauthored with Sidney Tarrow *Contentious Politics* (2nd Edition, Oxford University Press 2015).

Ernesto Castañeda is the author of *A Place to Call Home: Immigrant Exclusion and Urban Belonging in New York, Paris, and Barcelona* (Stanford University Press 2018), *Building Walls* (Lexington 2019), coeditor with Cathy L. Schneider of *Collective Violence, Contentious Politics, and Social Change: A Charles Tilly Reader* (Routledge 2017), and editor of *Immigration and Categorical Inequality: Migration to the City and the Birth of Race and Ethnicity* (Routledge 2018).

Lesley J. Wood is Associate Professor and Chair of Sociology at York University in Toronto. She is the author of *Crisis and Control: The Militarization of Protest Policing* (Pluto Press 2014); and *Direct Action, Deliberation and Diffusion: Collective Action after the WTO Protests in Seattle* (Cambridge University Press 2014).